D0593138

WHAT PEOPLE ARE SAYING ABOUT

Community
Building

Renewing Spirit & Learning in Business

Community Building: Renewing Spirit & Learning in Business may just be the best book yet to come from New Leaders Press. It is a truly wonderful book, a spectacular collection, a compendium of clearly the best thinking and writing I've ever seen on community. And its critical strength is that it does not stop at theory and philosophy but presents straightforward, experience-based practical insights and advice. I could give no more enthusiastic recommendation for a book than for this one. It will serve anyone in any kind of organizational setting.

—James A. Autry, author
Love & Profit and *Life & Work*

Community Building is a highly important book because it pioneers in addressing a major change taking place in American life: the emergence of the workplace as the new community for a growing number of people. As the decade ends, where one works will take the place for many of the neighborhood, the church, the union hall and other places which have been the traditional communities for many people.

—Lawrence Perlman, chairman & CEO
Ceridian Corporation

I have lived in the life-giving community of Arthur Andersen & Co. for thirty-two years and from that experience I can heartily endorse the values woven throughout this anthology. As my firm embraces the opportunities of the knowledge economy, we are incorporating many of the innovative—even transformative—concepts of collaboration and interconnectedness presented by these authors. Building community is more than just concept and more than just staying comfortable—it will take courage for each of you to turn the vision of this book into reality.

—Robert L. Elmore, senior partner
Creating Our Future Team, Arthur Andersen & Co.

This is a masterful text. It challenges assumptions. Its themes are learning, experimentation, development, and evolution within a dynamic universe. The authors share both vision and experience and present useful concepts to build relationships with ourselves, with each other, within organizations and throughout society.

—Linda E. Morris, director
Ernst & Young

Whatever our society tries to diminish, it is the community that keeps pushing up like flowers in the cracks of pavements. This wonderful collection of essays brings that message home loud and clear.

—Anita Roddick, founder
The Body Shop

"Ninety-five percent of American managers today say the right thing, five percent actually do it." (*Fortune*, February, 1994) Genuine community provides a fertile and safe practice-field in which to perceive and close the gap between what one espouses and actually does. Kaz Gozdz' anthology offers a variety of multifaceted lenses to approach and enable community building. A gem.

—Sarita Chawla, partner, MetaLens
co-editor, *Learning Organizations:*
Developing Cultures for Tomorrow's Workplace

To withstand today's hurricane of change, communities will be our anchor, our island of stability, and our wall against the storm. This book is a community itself, rich in the diverse views of its authors, and strong in the common understanding that unites them.

—William E. Halal, author, *Internal Markets*
professor of management
The George Washington University

Beyond teams there is community. Community, these authors contend, can exist despite, or perhaps because of, the uncertainty, tumult, and pressure to produce or perish in today's marketplace. [This collection is] a primer on the coming of global tribalism and community without geography.

—Ron Zemke, senior editor
Training Magazine

The quaint notion of organizations as hierarchies has proven to be hollow in these final years of the twentieth century. Enlightened managers know that serving and supporting unleashes much more energy, talent, and commitment than commanding and controlling. The metaphor for the twenty-first century is "community." This dazzling collection of essays is sure to become *the* essential reference for finding the common ground upon which we can build productive work communities where people constantly learn, grow, and contribute. Hurry up and read it if you want to be on the leading edge of organizational change.

—Jim Kouzes, co-author
The Leadership Challenge and *Credibility*
chairman & CEO, Tom Peters Group/Learning Systems

I began reading as one who loves his colleagues but who always worked alone. I finished thinking of collaboration with everyone I meet. My outlook has changed forever.

—Michael W. Munn
Lockheed Corporation

Community Building

Renewing Spirit & Learning in Business

FEATURING ESSAYS BY:

John Gardner • Peter Senge • Michael Ray • Amitai Etzioni
Beth Jarman & George Land • Marvin Weisbord • John Nirenberg • M. Scott Peck
Terry Mollner • Juanita Brown & David Isaacs • Stephanie Ryan • Barbara Shipka
Joel & Michelle Levey • Bill Veltrop • Glenna Gerard & Linda Teurfs • Jim Rough
Elemer Magaziner • Darla Chadima & Geoffrey Hulin • Susan Campbell
Rondalyn Varney Whitney • Jordan Paul • Craig Fleck • Jim Ewing
Peter & Trudy Johnson-Lenz • Jerry Michalski • George Por • Robert Mang
David Goff • Terry Anderson & Edward Klinge • Ann Roulac • Hope Greenfield
William Clarkson & Lyman Randall • Jeanne Borei & John Pehrson
Dinesh Chandra & Buddy Johnson

Editor: Kazimierz Gozdz

NewLeadersPress

STERLING &
STONE, INC.

San Francisco

Copyright © 1995 by Sterling & Stone, Inc.
All rights reserved. No part of this publication may be reproduced, distributed, or trans-mitted in any form or by any means, including photocopying, recording, or other elec-tronic or mechanical methods, without the prior written permission of the publisher, except in the case of brief quotations embodied in critical reviews and certain other non-commercial uses permitted by copyright law. For permission requests, write to the pub-lisher, addressed "Attention: Permissions Coordinator," at the address below.

New Leaders Press
Sterling & Stone, Inc.
1668 Lombard St.
San Francisco, CA 94123
415/928-1473

To purchase additional copies or inquire about bulk discounts for multiple orders of this Executive Edition, contact any of the distributors listed in the rear of this book.

PERMISSIONS AND CREDITS

The editor and publisher wish to acknowledge the following sources:

"Creating Quality Communities" by Peter Senge was first published in *Executive Excellence* (June 1994), published by Executive Excellence Publishing, and is published with permission of the author and publisher.
"The New Leadership Agenda" by John Gardner was published in a similar form as "Community Building" in a pamphlet for Independent Sector and is pub-lished with permission of the author.
"Back to We: The Communitarian Nexus" by Amitai Etzioni was first pub-lished as "Back to We," a chapter in his book *The Spirit of Community: Rights, Responsibilities and the Communtarian Agenda* (Crown Books, 1993) and is published with permission.
The table titled "The Organization of Nature" contained in Michael Ray's essay, "A Metaphor for a Worldwide Paradigm Shift," is published with permission of the author, August T. Jaccaci.
The two diagrams contained in Kazimierz Gozdz essay, titled "Creating Learning Organizations Through Core Competence," are published with permission of *The Systems Thinker* newsletter.

Photo credits: Peter and Trudy Johnson-Lenz by Fredric Lehrman, Will Clarkson by Alison Clarkson, M. Scott Peck by John Kane, Jim Ewing by Paul Boyer, and Bill Veltrop by Sarah G. Gist of Elizabeth's.

♻ Printed in the United States of America on recycled paper.

Community Building: Renewing Spirit and Learning in Business. Editor: Kazimierz Gozdz

ISBN 0-9630390-5-9

First Edition
Executive Edition

Table of Contents

This compilation of essays represents a wide variety of perspectives of what it will take to renew one of our most depleted resources—a sense of community with each other. In our modern quest for the "perfect part" we have lost touch with the "interconnectedness of the whole"—a byproduct of our fixation with the Industrial Age and its requisite mechanistic thinking.

Nearly every problem facing our modern societies seems to stem from this loss of "being in communion" with our fellow human beings. The "haves" versus the "have nots," the abuse of our natural environment, and the dehumanization of the workplace are all resolvable if we rekindle the flame of community. A relatively small group of scholars, business practitioners, and consultants has been studying this topic for the past decade. Its members have become catalysts for a movement that began in local settings and various organizations and is now catching hold in corporations.

The world of commerce and private enterprise is engaged in a tremendous storm of change these days. Many organizations are reaching for one "flavor of the month" technology after another in the hope of becoming more productive, maintaining market share in a highly competitive environment, or merely winning the fight for survival.

Some of the more visionary organizations—or certain people within them—are beginning to see the value of having a "community of stakeholders," whereby employees, vendors and customers feel part of something important. A movement is underway, not toward something new and intriguing but back to basic human values such as mutual caring and trust, dependability on each other, sharing a common dream, and feeling valued in the undertaking. In his book *Love and Profit*, James Autry, former president of the Meredith Corporation's Magazine Group, writes:

> By invoking the metaphor of community, we imply that we in business are bound by a fellowship of endeavor in which we commit to mutual goals, in which we contribute to the best of our abilities, in which each contribution is recognized and credited, in which there is a forum for all voices to be heard, in which our success contributes to the success of the common enterprise and to the success of others, in which we can disagree and hold differing viewpoints without withdrawing from the community, in which we are free to express what we feel as well as what we think, in which our value to society is directly related to the quality of our commitment and effort, and in which we take care of one another.

This anthology contains many viewpoints—sometimes in opposition—offered by the best scholars of this renaissance, this return to wholeness. M. Scott Peck's writings over the past decade have generated significant acceleration for this movement.

The response to Peck's books and the yearning for a "return to civility," as he expressed it, gave rise to his starting the Foundation for Community Encouragement (FCE). Trainers certified by FCE offer community-building workshops that explore Peck's Four Stages of Community. Several of our authors refer to these stages, which are as follows:

1. Pseudo-Community
2. Chaos
3. Emptying
4. Community

Kazimierz Gozdz, known to his friends and colleagues as "Kaz," was trained by Peck. As editor of this book, he has invited an impressive array of experts, representing various areas within the discipline of community building, to participate in this collection.

Starting with the global context, the book quickly shifts to "corporate community," since this book is being published principally for organizations and people in them. Skills and practices for developing community are visited as well as the interpersonal dimensions. Modern technology and its usefulness are explored along with the structural aspects that support this renaissance. Finally, we examine case histories where applications have been made and benefits realized.

Following the book's Introduction, written by Dr. Peck especially for this collection, we embark on a journey of learning about community and what potential it holds for our future. We've organized the book into seven parts, each containing a number of essays contributed by our co-authors. Starting with the global context, we proceed to corporate application, practices, interpersonal applications, technology, structure, and case studies.

This book has taken more than a year to complete. Nearly all of these essays are original, specially written for this collection. We are proud to offer it to all those who aspire to a world—in society as well as in business—in which civility, caring, and sustainability are restored.

—the publishers
New Leaders Press
July, 1995

Acknowledgments

This book would not exist without the talent, experience, and participation of each contributing author. This collection has been a collaborative partnership in a very real sense, whereby the authors, editors, and publisher have worked together in creating this rich potpourri of wisdom. We salute and thank every one of them for their contribution.

Some of the authors wish to thank certain people for their past help or inspiration.

Terry Mollner would like to acknowledge two groups for helping him learn what he has so he could write his essay. The first is the Austrian-Hungarian community around Saint Joseph's Church in Omaha, Nebraska. They held onto the remnants of the old village system so he could experience them while he was growing up. The second is the friends who have joined with him to create the new village system called Friends and Lovers Community. For twelve years it has allowed him to discover the reasons village life has been so important throughout history.

Juanita Brown and David Isaacs owe a debt of gratitude to John Gardner for his lifelong commitment and work regarding institutional renewal and the characteristics of healthy communities, and to Sherrin Bennett of Interactive Learning Systems for her collaboration in developing the core processes of community at work. They also thank Bryan Smith for his input on their essay concerning practical tips for developing community at work. A special acknowledgment is due to Mike Szymanczyk, Mike Pfeil, Martin Paley, and other corporate executives with whom they have partnered in applying community development principles to organizational strategy and large-system change.

Stephanie Ryan's deepest appreciation extends to Kellie Wardman and Colleen Lannon-Kim for editing and publishing the first edition of her article in The Systems Thinker. She thanks Sheryl Erickson and Rita Cleary for extending its readership to many others across the country by including it as handouts for learning organization related events. She is grateful to Scott Peck and the work of FCE for educating her in the stages of community. Special thanks go to the work of Sue Miller Hurst for challenging her assumptions about being a writer and to JoAnne Segotta for being a wonderful client and friend and for appearing like an angel at just the right times. Lastly, her love and appreciation go to Michael Goodman and Jenny Kemeny for teaching her the discipline of systems thinking.

Barbard Shipka wishes to acknowledge all of the teams she has worked with over the years—from whom she has learned so much—and especially those at Cray Research, Green Giant, Honeywell, IDS Financial Services, and Medtronic. She also gratefully acknowledges Kaz Gozdz for his friendship and for all he has offered her through his presence and his understandings of life, relationships, and community.

Joel and Michelle Levey offer their heartfelt thanks to the members of the teams at Hewlett-Packard, Weyerhauser, Group Health HMO, AT&T, Travelers Insurance, NASA, US Army, Petro Canada, and International Center for

Organization Design for their contributions to evolving and validating the methods outlined in this essay. They also thank their colleagues Bill Veltrop, George Pór, Geoffrey Hulin, Darla Chadima, Ruth and Chris Thorsen, Richard Moon, Peter and Trudy Johnson-Lenz, Kaz Gozdz, Suzanne Mamet, Tom Hurley, and Mario Narduzzi for their inspiration in this work.

Bill Veltrop acknowledges and honors Geoffrey Hulin and Kristin Anundsen for their deft use of scalpel and forceps in the preparation of his essay. He also thanks Marilyn Sammons for "her wondrous capacity to both inspire and ground my work."

Marvin Weisbord acknowledges Ronald Lippitt, Eva Schindler-Rainman, and Eric Trist, who supported him most in his future search explorations. Nor would this design exist but for Fred and Merrelyn Emery in Australia. However, the present evolution owes most to Sandra Janoff, his workshop partner and co-director of SearchNet, and to hundreds of SearchNet members working in their own communities. Without their bedrock experience, future search would be "vaporware."

Glenna Gerard and Linda Teurfs are deeply grateful to the late David Bohm, whose inspiration led to their work with dialogue. They also would like to acknowledge the support, encouragement, and excellent editorial comments given to them by Kaz Gozdz and offer a special thanks to Stephanie Ryan for her suggestions from a systems perspective.

Jim Rough acknowledges J. Paul Everett who, as manager at Simpson Timber Company, created a living laboratory for him and his colleagues to become their best. Paul heroically supported experiments in group process, creative thinking, and community building. Ned Crosby, founder of the Jefferson Center for New Democratic Processes, laid the foundations for the Wisdom Council with his Citizen Jury process. For twenty years, Ned has spearheaded the formation of Citizen Juries in the public arena, proving many times over that random citizens will seriously and intelligently address vital issues in our society. Bill Idol, consultant and trainer extraordinaire, once brought Jim to his seventeen-day workshop, at his expense, to be sure he "got it." Bill's influence on him is greatly appreciated.

Elemer Magaziner gratefully acknowledges his sponsor, The Foundation of Global Wellness. He also expresses deep gratitude to John Sich, who gifted him with the opportunity to apply community concepts in real life in highly significant corporate settings.

Darla Chadima and Geoffrey Hulin are deeply grateful to their teachers, WindEagle and RainbowHawk, for their help in clarifying their thinking about The Wheel of Community Building. Their dedication to the teachings of Mother Earth and Medicine Ways for living in balance in today's world continues to inspire and nourish them. They are also grateful to their dear friend George Pór for his help in getting them started on this project, for his feedback as it evolved, and for his scouting party into collective intelligence on behalf of the whole "tribe." They also thank Bill Veltrop for his coaching, appreciation, and wise council.

Rondayln Varney Whitney thanks the following people who were her inspirations, her sources, and her caring community as she wrote her chapter: Jan Nickerson, who faxed her cross-continent encouragement to speak from the heart; Cathyann Swindlehurst, who graced her with the linguistic wizardry only known from Starry Beings; Claire for her warm-fuzzy edits; her husband Whit—her hero, partner, and friend; her son Zachary, a constant reminder that there is nothing more sacred, more angelic than unsuppressed power hugs; Barbara Helfgott Hyett, Carolyn Baum, and Michael Ray, her role models of loving, polychotomous thinking; Kaz Gozdz, who melts her heart when she thinks of his devoted caring; John and Gaia, Wings and Cougar for all their angelic influence and secrets. And to the practitioners of occupational therapy, with whom she feels honored to share the profession known to patients everywhere as "those who love us back to wellness."

Craig Fleck would like to thank Stephanie Ryan for many deep and insightful conversations which refined the ideas contained in his essay. Tom Starrs and Kristen Anundsen provided much needed editorial expertise. A host of other colleagues offered their time and insight to improve his fledgling attempts to articulate ideas, particularly Ron Kertzner, Greg Zlevor, Steven Milden, Charles Parry, and David Banner. Ted Castle and Marlene Dailey of Rhino Foods made time in their schedules for conversation which led to the example used. He applauds their efforts to create community at Rhino. Fleck considers this the start of his personal work to express the importance and necessity of building community in our organizations as a foundation to return our society to creative function. He welcomes any comments, suggestions, or expansion of the thoughts expressed in his essay and the book.

Jim Ewing thanks Pat Heneghan, Jane Steven, Alex Tregellas, Dennis DeWilde, and John Morgan, who were among the many more at BP who provided real challenges and the space to experiment and learn about group behavior together. He has long believed that good work with groups comes out of potent and open work with individuals. Stan Herman and Mike Korniche were profound teachers in that department many years ago at TRW. Treva Sudhalter was always there for him in his beginning attempts to be some kind of genuine human being. She opened the doors of distinction between the many voices in the person. In a three-year partnership, Roger Gould generously opened Ewing's eyes to the nuts and bolts of transition. Stanley Keleman's ideas about living and dying were foundations for the three-voice idea. Tim Galway shared his efforts to get a new brand of coaching across to managers at Apple. Work with Hal Stone at the Center for the Healing Arts, Los Angeles, broadened the meaning of 'transformation.' Peter and Trudy Johnson-Lenz provided encouragement and trust in many silent and not so silent ways. Barbara, his wife and partner; Heather, his acquired grown-up daughter; and Jennifer, his real-time, here and now six-year-old have been more than patient and forgiving with dad's general madness.

Peter and Trudy Johnson-Lenz gratefully acknowledge the work, thinking, and support of Angeles Arrien, Michael Begeman, Lansing Bicknell, Juanita Brown, Susan Campbell, Marie Case, Jeff Conklin, Duane Elgin, Jim Ewing, Kazimierz

Gozdz, Joe Griffith, Willis Harman, David Isaacs, Charles Johnston, Gary Lapid, Joel and Michelle Levey, Susanna Opper, Jordan Paul, George Pór, Howard Rheingold, Peter Russell, Craig Schindler, Michael Schrage, Peter Senge, Ron Short, and Robert Theobald.

George Pór is deeply grateful to his friend Rita Risser for the many ways she has been supporting his quest for "collective intelligence." Her insightful editing, heartfelt encouragement, and generosity of her time all contributed to awaken his passion for writing.

John Nirenberg would like to acknowledge Allyson Villars for reviewing an earlier draft of his essay and for her many useful suggestions.

Robert Mang is grateful to Bruce Busching, Charles Krone, and Larry Orman for numerous stimulating conversations that included various seminal concepts from which "Sustainable Principles" evolved, and to his wife Pamela for her wise counsel and editing.

David Goff recognizes that to glimpse, and come to know, the magnificent and commonplace unity that is our natural inheritance is an exquisite gift. He gained access to this ambiguous and paradoxical reality through the work of the late Victor Turner, Scott Peck, The Foundation for Community Encouragement, and Joanna R. Macy. He also relied upon the struggles, insight, and encouragement of those in the community movement. Their efforts to face themselves, each other, and the mysteries of this existence blazed the trail, and their willingness to share and endure the rigors of the way with him made his journey possible. He is grateful for his dialogues with friends and colleagues such as Kazimierz Gozdz, Jeffrey Scannell, Carl Culberson, Maurice Friedman, and Cynthia McReynolds, who clarified his thoughts and understanding. His essay is an attempt to describe and affirm his shared struggle for peace, community, and attunement with the larger processes of life.

Terry Anderson and Ed Klinge thank Carol Sanford, who talked them into describing some of their work, and Amy Kahn, who helped translate their thinking into a chapter. They offer special thanks to their families: to Jo for not letting them off the hook, and to Kellie and Steve for their energizing push over the last big hill. Finally, they credit the people of the community within whom lives the wisdom to create a future with potential.

Ann Roulac acknowledges her father, Phil, for providing her with inspiration for her chapter; her mother, Libby Roulac, from whom she developed a sense of spatial and visual clarity and focus, and her brother Stephen, a master wordsmith, whose ease at putting words to paper encouraged her to write her chapter; John Renesch, for making this book possible; and Kazimierz Gozdz, for his adept coaching.

Hope Greenfield gratefully acknowledges Claudia Mueller, who provided impetus, inspiration, and immeasurable help in writing her chapter.

As editor of this book, Kazimierz Gozdz wishes to thank John Renesch for challenging him to participate in this project, understanding his love for community, and mentoring him through his first book project. He further acknowledges John for the style and copyediting, for which he took primary responsibility. He thanks all the authors who dedicated themselves to translating their passion into gifts to be shared by a world in need of community. Special thanks to Marvin Weisbord, Terry Mollner, George Land, Beth Jarman, Jordan Paul, and Peter and Trudy Johnson-Lenz. Had they not contributed effort at special moments, the project would not have come to pass. Special thanks also to Kristin Anundsen, who translated three drafts of ideas into the body of his own manuscript and nurtured five other essays to fruition. Thanks to Amy Kahn for her efforts in coordinating and communicating with authors and for her efficiency with countless administrative details.

He is grateful to M. Scott Peck for acting as a mentor and friend who has always encouraged and challenged his thinking on community with a respectful and loving kindness. Deepest appreciation to Michael Ray, who acts continually with faith and cheerfulness in our collaboration. Appreciation to Peter Senge, who has created a format for his next steps in learning, and Mary Ann Schmidt for having always acted as a guiding hand. Thanks to the Foundation for Community Encouragement, Inc., the FCE Leader Core, and the thousands of people that have participated in community-building experiences, for providing a platform for exploring the edges of learning in community. As always, great appreciation to the Wolf Pack: Rusty Myers and Robert Reusing for healing the world and watching his back as he has sought his own healing through this anthology.

Gozdz offers special thanks to Barbara Morrill, his intellectual, spiritual, and soul partner with whom he practices community as a spiritual discipline, for creating a sacred space in their relationship to support not only this project but also his calling to community. Special thanks to her for mentoring his understanding of racism and issues of diversity. Appreciation to Sandi McCall who has suffered most at the hands of his theories as they have placed them into practice. Her support has been without reservation. He also thanks Wanda Gozdz, who let go of their business partnership so he could follow this path, and David Goff, who has acted as a sounding board and editor for various formulations of a developmental process of community. Thank you to Ann Hoeing and the LEP team who gave him the space to test and perfect task/process integration.

Finally, he would like to thank Barbara Shipka, Phil Mirvis, Bob Frager, Sarita Chawla, Brenda Ringwald, Rita Risser, Dennis Rathnaw, Dan Kim, Claudia Mueller, Pat Bartley, Dominick Volini, Carol Sanford, Cynthia McReynolds, Laura Melvin, Collin Harrison, Ann Monger, The Group of Twelve, The Pier Group, Ben Mancini, Tom Hardenberg, Justin Streurer, John Brozovich, Jeffrey Mishlove, Bill Isaacs, Claire Brown, and Paul and May Ann Strenger for special roles they have played in bringing this project to fruition.

New Leaders Press, the anthology's publisher, wishes to acknowledge Kazimierz Gozdz for his dedication and persistence in assembling this remarkable collection of essays. Since nearly all of these writings are original pieces, his tireless efforts in supporting the authors through the process of generating final manuscripts and his insistence upon quality essays are to be applauded with gusto.

It is with particular gratitude that we thank M. Scott Peck, a leader in the field of community building, for contributing the book's Introduction. His passion clearly lies in this work and we are grateful for his role in completing the anthology.

Members of the book's production team are to be praised for their contributions: John Renesch, New Leaders Press' founder and publisher, for his collaboration with Gozdz on the creation of this collection and ongoing oversight throughout the process; production editors Kristin Anundsen and Dennis Rathnaw for their work with certain individual authors in the closing weeks; jacket designer Sue Malikowsky of Autographix; the composition and production team of Jennifer Barclay and Alis Valencia and Claudia Gioseffi of Blue Sky Studio; New Leaders Press staff members Amy Kahn, Gretchen Andrews, Cathleen Moore, and Laura Kothavala for their continuous support; our printer for this book, Publishers Press, and the personal attention and caring of Lyle Mumford.

John Renesch wishes to thank the advisory board of New Leaders Press/Sterling & Stone, Inc. for their invaluable support. These people are Pat Barrentine, David Berenson, William Halal, Willis Harman, Paul Hwoschinsky, Jim Liebig, William Miller, Shirley Nelson, Christine Oster, Steven Piersanti, Catherine Pyke, James O'Toole, Michael Ray, Stephen Roulac, Jeremy Tarcher, Peggy Umanzio, and Dennis White.

For those who took the time to review early drafts of this collection and provide their feedback and comments, verbal and written, everyone involved with this book thanks you all. Our appreciation goes to Jim Autry, Sarita Chawla, Bob Elmore, Bill Halal, Jim Kouzes, Linda Morris, Michael Munn, Larry Perhlman, Anita Roddick, and Ron Zemke.

We believe that all people somehow possess a divine potentiality; that ways may be worked out—specific, systematic ways—to help, not the few, but the many towards a vastly expanded capacity to learn, to love, to feel deeply and to create. We reject the tired dualism that seeks the divine and human potentialities by denying the joys of the senses, the immediacy of unpostponed life. We believe that most people can best find the divine and themselves through heightened awareness of the world, increased commitment to the eternal in time.

We believe, too, that if the divine is present in the individual soul, it must be sought and found in human institutions as well; for people will not readily achieve individual salvation without a saving society. We envisage no mass movement, for we do not see people in the mass; we look instead to revolution through constant interplay between individual and group, each changing the other.

The revolution has begun. Human life will be transformed. How it will be transformed is up to us.

—George Leonard
from *A Proclamation for Human Potential*
given at Grace Cathedral, San Francisco,
January 6, 1966

M. Scott Peck, M.D., is the author of The *Different Drum: Community Making and Peace, The Road Less Traveled*, and *A World Waiting to be Born*. In 1984, he and his wife met with nine others to establish The Foundation for Community Encouragement, a tax-exempt, non-profit educational foundation, whose mission is to promote and teach the principles of community building. Working with the Foundation has been the cutting edge of his life since it was started. More than sixty workshops a year are conducted by the Foundation with a faculty of seventy trained facilitators.

Peck served in the U.S. Army from 1962 to 1973 as a psychiatrist and consultant to the Surgeon General, departing as a Lieutenant Colonel. His books have sold millions of copies in the United States and have been translated into more than twenty languages.

Introduction:
The Frontier of Group Space

M. Scott Peck

My consistent all-time favorite TV show has been Star Trek. Each episode begins with the visual splendor of the Starship Enterprise streaking past stars and through galaxies as the off-screen voice of the captain dramatically announces, "Space: the final frontier." By space he means, of course, outer space.

Back when I was still engaged in the practice of psychotherapy, I would occasionally suggest to patients that they were hiring me as a guide through "inner space." It was an exciting role for me to play for two reasons: One was that each patient's inner space was unique, so it was a different journey each time; the other was that I believed at the time that inner space—not outer space—was the final frontier. It seemed to me that our survival as a species probably depended far more upon our willingness and capacity to explore our own minds than it did in our minds focusing more or less exclusively upon things "out there."

Over the past dozen years my primary focus has switched to the exploration of yet another kind of space: group space. It now seems to me that this is truly the final frontier. Unless we can quite rapidly learn how to better live and work *together*, there is every reason to believe that humanity will go down the tubes despite all of its sophistication about quasars and lasers, nebulae and black holes.

I don't want to downplay learning about anything. All three types of space are important—and utterly interrelated. Indeed, *Star Trek* is such an effective program precisely because its focus is every bit as much on inner space and group space as on the galaxies. The voyages of the Starship Enterprise are also inner psychospiritual journeys of its individual crew members and their various adventures as teams.

So we need outer space and its scholars just as we need the sun and pho-tosynthesis, the oceans and the rain forests, fishing and agriculture, computers and computer scientists, and stockbrokers. But as all the authors of this book have agreed, the conquest of the external world has gotten out of hand. It has become unbalanced, and more than anything else the imbalance is because of our rela-tively gross neglect of inner space and group space.

I don't want to downplay the exploration of inner space just to promote that of group space. Despite the admonition of the wise throughout the ages, "Know thyself," all but a tiny percentage of human beings remain woefully self-ignorant. Nothing contributes more to the dysfunctionality of our groups than the lack of insight the individual members have into themselves. This is one of the reasons for the ancient monastic dictum that, "You're not ready to live in com-munity until you can live by yourself."

Nonetheless, while I am fortunate to have a great deal of contact with the small segment of humanity that is rich in self-consciousness and knowledge, I have been astonished by the poverty of their knowledge about groups. Conscious though they may be of their individual journeys, the vast majority of them are amazingly unconscious of the organizations to which they belong. Moreover, they demonstrate relatively little motivation to become more socially conscious. The phenomenon is so striking I have labeled it "the hole in the mind." Our knowledge of psychodynamics lags far behind that of the dynamics of molecular bonding, and our knowledge of group dynamics lags far behind our understand-ing of psychodynamics. The exploration of group space is not the only frontier, but I believe it is the *final* frontier.

I know of no person who has more brilliantly or courageously set out to explore this final frontier than Kaz Gozdz, the editor of this collection. After being selected and trained as a member of the Leader Corps of the Foundation for Community Encouragement (FCE) he forsook a successful career in commerce to earn a master's degree in transpersonal psychology. He did not do this because of a mid-life crisis or transition; he did it because he desired to learn all that acade-mia had to teach that might bear upon the subject of group space and communi-ty. Meanwhile, he continued not only to lead community-building workshops but, largely for free and with extraordinary creative genius, designed three innovative new programs to improve the teaching of community and community principles. Now he has somehow managed to gather together forty-four fellow explorers—no mean feat—to produce a groundbreaking book about the final frontier.

Why? What makes Kaz tick? I don't know. I've accused him of being dri-ven by some strange kind of personal yet holy ambition. Mostly what drives him, I suspect, is love. He has a deep love for humanity. He does not want to see us go down the tubes. He yearns for us to save ourselves, and his extraordinary dedica-tion is born of the knowledge that community is the missing piece needed for our salvation.

This is not a book of traditional "hard" science. It contains no statistics, no controlled studies. One of the book's authors, David Goff, has included a summary of his own research in his chapter. Otherwise, what evidence is presented herein would cause many traditional scientists to sneer at as "merely anecdotal." As someone whose primary identity is that of a scientist, a small part of me wishes that it could be otherwise. But the larger part knows it cannot be for three different and compelling reasons.

One is that there do not currently exist enough properly scientific studies of the subject to even begin to comprise a book. To some extent this is because it is a difficult subject to study scientifically. Primarily it is because this area is such a frontier that society has not yet chosen to devote the considerable resources necessary to study it with scientific rigor. A hope I have for this work is that it will help inspire society to mobilize such resources. Although the applications of the scientific method alone will never be sufficient to bring about the social transformation required for survival, there are ways to study community scientifically, and the resultant hard data can only help.

The second reason is that this work is transformational or "reformational." Traditionally, science defines itself as "value free" and hence examines what is, not what ought to be. Healthy communities do exist, but they are not the norm. For a long time to come the scientific study of them will be a study of exceptions. Indeed, even the word "healthy" on this frontier smacks of a value judgment, and it is doubtful that the motivation to study the exceptions can be entirely value free.

A story may help to illustrate this. Six years ago the director of R&D for a Fortune 100 company was at a point of mid-life transition and came to see me because he was considering the bizarre possibility of taking an 85 percent salary cut in order to conduct scientific research of FCE's work. As a physicist and well-trained hard scientist (who ultimately chose a more lucrative career change), he wanted to zero in on the most basic assumptions. He was also a man accustomed to the competitiveness of academia and the corporate world of industrial secrets. After three hours of querying me about the underlying assumptions of our work, he suddenly looked at me with an expression of amazement as he exclaimed, "You guys at FCE really do want people—I mean everyone—to succeed!"

The third—and, I believe, most compelling—reason that this is not a traditionally scientific book is that its subject is too large. Science is primarily analytical, breaking a subject down into bite-sized pieces that can submit themselves to digestion by the scientific methods. As I've indicated, I believe this can and should be done with community, even though the subject will never be entirely manageable by virtue of its size. At this point in time, however, when the frontier of group space remains entirely open, the editor and contributors have chosen by necessity a holistic rather than traditional analytic approach. Indeed, one of the themes of the book is that community is inherently holistic. Is it an accident, do you suppose, that not one of the forty-four authors of the thirty-four chapters of this work on community and business has chosen to offer a serious definition of either business or community? Are they too ignorant or are they too smart? I suspect it is the latter.

There are many things too large to submit to any single adequate definition, of which business is perhaps the smallest. We can only define those things that are less than us. For instance, in my office I have a little electrical space heater. Were I an electrical engineer, I could take it apart into its different components and explain to you exactly how it works. I could define it—save for the fact that it is connected by a plug to something called electricity. There are factors about electricity, power, energy, or light that even the most advanced nuclear physicists cannot explain or tie up in a nice, neat, definable intellectual package. This is because as soon as you get to talking about energy you have gotten into something larger than us.

There are many such things, each of which I believe have something to do with God, the largest and most indefinable of all. It is proper that the Muslims should have a prohibition against the depiction of images of God because any such image will inevitably represent just a tiny piece of the whole and will hence be a distortion—a desecration of sorts—of the larger reality. We have the same kind of difficulty when we attempt to define love or consciousness or prayer. People have been praying for millennia, for instance, and one would think that by now theologians at least would have arrived at an adequate definition of prayer. But they haven't.

And so it is with community. A federal judge at an FCE workshop, echoing a Supreme Court justice, once jokingly commented, "Community is like pornography. I don't know how to define it but I sure know it when I see it." And we know it when we don't see it, when we see human beings unnecessarily isolated or adversarial, fragmented and frightened.

I will say this much: When we talk about community at FCE we are not referring to any aggregate of people but to the quality of communication among them. For us community has to do with communication, and one way of expressing FCE's mission as an educational foundation is that it is to teach the principles of healthy communication within and between groups.

While not one of the thirty-four chapters that follow will offer a precise definition of community, you will find through them certain recurring themes. This need not be boring. To the contrary, you can make it into an exciting and important game if you choose. I suggest you consider writing each theme down when you first encounter it. Then make a mark whenever you re-encounter it. Finally, select out those themes that three or more chapters have in common, and I suspect you will have a very broad and deep understanding of what community is all about. It will not exactly be a definition; it will be more like a marvelous collection of a thousand names or faces of God. It will provide a vision of what humanity can be.

One such recurring theme is the extraordinary potential that resides in business for restoring community to our increasingly fragmented society. I won't belabor this because it is eloquently elaborated in the chapters to come—except to note that it is a historical phenomenon. History is the account of change, and it has dramatically speeded up over the past 200 years. The church, which once did much to create community, has changed. Our dwelling patterns, once predominantly stable and rural, have changed us into a predominantly mobile and urban society. These changes have been major causes for the breakdown of community, and they are irreversible. It would be no more realistic to look to the church or the neighborhood (as many are still inclined to do) for the significant restoration of community than to argue for a complete reversal of history and some magical return to a theocracy or predominantly agricultural life.

Over the same years business—originally never expected to provide community—has also changed from a relatively small and simple family affair to a predominantly large, complex institutional one where community in the workplace is not only possible but rapidly becoming essential. By essential we do not mean that corporations have some sort of social obligation to heal all of society's ills; we mean that they are going to have to become learning communities in order to remain creative and profitable enterprises in this rapidly changing world. I think all the authors of this book could be called idealists, but that is not because we are looking to business to be nobly self-sacrificial. To the contrary, we are not at all talking about some corporate giving program. We do not envision community in the workplace as a gift that business might altruistically offer to humanity. Rather we see it as a gift that business will give itself.

It is not an easy gift. All of us working on the frontier of group space are profoundly aware of not only the difficulty of building community in our modern culture but the even greater difficulty of sustaining it. This is because certain fundamental processes and procedures of community require us to change—change that often seems to go against the grain of our current human nature.

Quite a few have referred to me over the years as an idealist—not infrequently, a "fuzzy-headed idealist." They are right. Not about the fuzzy-headed part, but about being an idealist, for I would define an idealist as someone who believes in the potential for transformation of human nature. Those who think me fuzzy-headed invariably refer to themselves as "realists," by which they mean that they don't believe that we humans have the capacity to transform our nature. They say such things as "We humans are naturally competitive. We've always had war and we always will have. It's human nature. That's reality and we'd best accept it and stay armed to the teeth for eternity. Human beings change? Ha!"

But the realists seem to have forgotten a great deal. They who wouldn't dream of defecating on the floor or not brushing their teeth in the morning apparently don't recall that it was once very much their nature to go to the bathroom in their pants and to resist brushing their teeth. They do not remember that what we call war crimes today were obligatory military rituals 3,000 years ago. Or that a mere 200 years ago slavery was generally considered to be the natural order of things. In fact, everything we know about psychology suggests that the most salient feature of our human nature is its capacity for transformation. What distinguishes most humans from other creatures is our extraordinary adaptability and variability, our flexibility to do the different and often seemingly unnatural thing. Birds go south in the winter. Some of us do too, but others of us turn around and go north to slide down icy hills on little slats of wood or fiberglass.

We are the creatures who can do it differently.

So it is we idealists who are in accord with the central reality of human nature. It is the so-called "realists" who are off base—as well as being cynical and unhelpful. I do not mean to tout romanticism. I define a romantic as "someone who not only believes in the transformation of human nature but also believes it ought to be easy." It isn't easy. There are profound reasons why it isn't easy. Our tendency to resist new ways is just as much a part of our nature as our capacity to change.

What this dichotomy means should be obvious, although it often isn't due to our distaste for paradox. It means that we have free will. We have a choice. Community in the workplace is not some airy-fairy, impossible ideal. It does require considerably more sustained psychospiritual exertion from the top management on down than does "business as usual." On the other hand, it will also make most work, from top management on down, ultimately more satisfying and fulfilling, more creative and productive, more profitable and cost effective.

Business as usual, or shall we do it differently? Shall we do it differently now and wholeheartedly or only halfheartedly—even hypocritically—at the last moment when change is being forced upon us and maybe it's too late? We have the choice.

Still it is not an easy choice. Remember that community building and maintenance—requiring as it does the *personal* exploration of group space—is the final frontier. The authors of this book offer a wide array of hints and guidelines, but they have wisely refrained from offering precise definitions or clear formulas. This is because they have been on the frontier long enough to know that it will always be a frontier.

No matter how much more we gain in knowledge, building and sustaining community will always demand from those involved initiative and courage, self-knowledge and wisdom, commitment and enormous integrity. Each person is unique, each group is unique, each business and corporate culture is unique. By all means make use of consultants, but don't expect them to give you a certified, foolproof detailed map for community in your unique business. It is in the nature of businesspeople to usually ask us community builders what the guaranteed outcomes will be. But it is in the nature of frontiers that there are no such formulas that can relieve you of all anxiety and risk. This particular frontier carefully preserves—insists upon—its "empty" spaces and wilderness areas. However, it is enormously exciting to be on a frontier, and especially meaningful to be on this one because you won't be there alone. You'll be working in a group, transcending isolation.

How is the global context of a re-emergence of community
relevant to this situation?

Part One: A Global Context for the Re-emergence of Community

Is the yearning for community a worldwide phenomenon? In this age of rapid communication and ease of travel, can we develop true community in one part of the world and exclude other countries or cultures? What will a shift in global perspective require of each of us as individuals?

The larger context of community—from the global perspective—is explored by four "global thinkers" in this opening segment. Stanford Business School professor Michael Ray links community building with the paradigm shift he sees going on worldwide.

George Land and Beth Jarman, co-authors of *Breakpoint and Beyond,* examine what they see as a natural evolutionary flow toward community. Terry Mollner probes for solutions of the science-spirituality riddle that is affecting life everywhere in the industrialized world.

Each of these authors sees the re-emergence of community from their unique worldview perspective, setting the tone or resonance for the segments that follow.

Michael Ray, Ph.D., is the first John G. McCoy-Banc One Corporation Professor of Creativity and Innovation and of Marketing at Stanford University's Graduate School of Business. A social psychologist, Ray is a Fellow of the World Business Academy and received that organization's Willis Harman Award in 1991. He has served on ten public and nonprofit boards.

Among his more than 100 publications are *Creativity in Business* (with Rochelle Myers) and *The Path of the Everyday Hero* (with Lorna Catford), based on his Stanford creativity course. This course also inspired the PBS series "The Creative Spirit" and a companion book with the same title that he co-authored. Ray is co-editor (with Alan Rinzler) of *The New Paradigm in Business* and (with John Renesch) of *The New Entrepreneurs.*

He has served as a member of the National Committee of the Foundation for Community Encouragement, and has brought community-building work into his courses at Stanford and to other organizations.

1

A Metaphor for a Worldwide Paradigm Shift

Michael Ray

I have had a personal experience that makes me believe that it is essential that we engage in the process of building community at this time in world history. It started with a colleague who did a study of natural and human-caused disasters over the most recent historical period in which recording was reliable and in which there hadn't been significant changes in measurement procedures. His conclusion was that there had been a significant increase in disasters over the last fifty years and that the increase was increasing.

As he presented his results, he asked us why we thought this was happening. The human-caused disasters could be explained by population increases and technology changes. But the natural disasters were the major part of the increase, and they had no explanation other than divine intervention. But being a scientific group, we offered plausible rival hypotheses for his basic conclusion and thereby ignored the possible implications.

Then in July 1991 a freight train was rolling through Northern California when it derailed. Coincidentally, part of the train was going over the Sacramento River. The derailment caused a car containing highly toxic pesticide concentrate to fall down the bank, split open and pour its contents into the river, killing all life on, in and around the river for miles, including a part of Shasta Lake to the south. The contingency of so many coincidences that led to that disaster made me think again about my colleague's trend study. Was there some message we were supposed to be getting?

Later I saw evidence that the hole in the ozone layer over the Southern Hemisphere was growing at twice the expected rate and was at that time (1992) about the size of North American continent. Already at the southern end of Argentina, for instance, babies and animals were being blinded, skin cancer was increasing at an alarming rate, and crops were not growing properly.

Of course I attributed this to human-generated pollution. But then I read about another hole in the ozone layer that occurred over New England. The scientific evidence on this one was that it had been caused, not by manmade pollutants, but by a huge volcanic eruption. Again, I began to think of some sort of intervention that was coming from nature herself.

All this was churning in me when I attended the first World Business Academy San Francisco chapter dialogue group on sustainability. We were asked to go into silence and see what question came up for us about sustainability. The question that came to me was "What does God want us to do?" It seemed to be a culmination of all this history about disasters and the possibility of divine messages:

I didn't have long to wait for the answer. One of the participants in the dialogue, Al Smith, told about his being on Kauai during and after Hurricane Iniki. People had pulled together and helped each other without reservation. After a few days the outpouring of help and caring was so profound that people started putting little handmade thank you signs along the highway and on buildings. You'd drive along the highway, said Al, and you'd see repeated over and over again the Hawaiian word for thank you: mahalo.

That was my answer. I remembered recent disasters, some of which I had been through, and the comparable stories that came out of every one. People pulled together and treated each other with love and respect in these situations. People became more important than anything. Could it be, I thought, that God wants us to behave this way toward each other *all the time?*

How could this happen? Wouldn't it be a miracle? But community building offers hope. Consider this children's play poem:

> One for the money,
> Two for the show,
> Three to get ready,
> Four to go.

Just as the poem says, "one for the money," the first community building stage of *pseudo-community* happens because people are relating for and on the basis of something as artificial as money might seem to be in the new world we are moving into. When we are in the second community-building stage of *chaos,* we are acting "for the show" as we try to fix other people, show others that we are right, really know something, and that we can help without even having to truly listen to them. When we "get ready" in the third or *emptiness* stage of community building we are dropping all the pretension and mind chatter to go into a deeper place where the core of true human relationship exists. Then we can glide into *community,* the fourth stage, where we can "go" not only in terms of our relationships themselves but also in terms of what those relationships can become— a co-creative state of self conscious consensus that is generative for both the individual and the whole and that represents the best of what a new paradigm for the world might be.

When the play poem is recited, each line is said in order. And so too for the process of community building—each stage has value and meaning and must happen in some way in order to move on to the next. Everything can be grist for the mill. It is dysfunctional to attack ourselves or others on the basis of the stage we happen to be in. We can't move immediately to community any more than we can move immediately to, say, new paradigm business just because we have a concept of it. We have to move through the intervening stages. And we are never at a "destination" of a stage for very long. The achievement is in the process of relationship itself and the creativity that comes from that.

Paradigm Shift

This process happens in the world as a whole, just as it has occurred and must occur in individuals and in groups. In this chapter I explore these phenomena by taking Thomas Kuhn's approach in the realm of history and philosophy of science (as represented, for instance, in his *The Structure of Scientific Revolutions*) and applying it to examine the overarching mind set that people of all walks of life have in each historical period, whether they are in science or not. Just as Kuhn says that a particular paradigm or set of fundamental assumptions are what make a science, so too we live in this world with a set of fundamental beliefs that are so ingrained in our society that we hardly know they exist, much less examine them.

Kuhn claims that science moves in infrequent paradigm shifts or scientific revolutions with long intervening periods of normal science done within a particular paradigm. Some argue that this structure for science can't really be applied to the world as a whole. Of course the world isn't really as unified in thought as are those who practice within a science. On the other hand, when you read about the Copernican Revolution in Kuhn's book itself, it is hard not to leap immediately to a consideration of the effect these changes had on the whole world, not just in science.

We regularly recognize periods in the history of the known world in which these kinds of changes occur. For instance Richard Tarnas organizes his overview of Western thought, *The Passion of the Western Mind*, into four stages: classical (dominated by the Greek philosophers), medieval (dominated by Christianity), modern (dominated by scientific thought, largely the paradigm we are living under today), and the postmodern (the transformation of the modern mind that is the discontinuity happening at the end of the twentieth century in ourselves, our organizations and our world).

In the shifts or revolutions moving the world from one of these eras to the next, there is a mind shift across the world of the time. This occurred, for instance, in what the philosopher and historian Huston Smith calls "the triumph of Christianity" in the fourth century A.D., as the world moved from the classical to the medieval periods. Although Christianity initially borrowed much from Hellenic thought, the shift at that time centered life and all of its activity in a completely different way from the Roman times. The dominating paradigm of Christianity, for instance, considered much of the previous paradigm to be pagan in nature and even punishable by death. This is not to say that in the Western world there weren't those that still practiced the "pagan" beliefs or that there weren't other parts of the world that weren't affected by this new Western paradigm. But in the known world of the time there was one paradigm that dominated.

Similarly, as the futurist Willis Harman puts it in his book *Global Mind Change*, the scientific revolution that followed Copernicus was so profound that if you could speak to a reasonably well-informed citizen in 1601 and then to the same sort of person in 1701, the fundamental basis of the conversations would be completely different. Today we are still speaking basically with the assumptions of 1701, the scientific mind-set that says that all knowing comes objectively from the senses, from perceiving the outer world and from believing only what we can see. Since this last change in mind set into the current dominant paradigm, even those not involved directly in science see the world in this way.

Of course those early revolutions in the change in mind set or societal paradigm were confined to what is now known as the Western world. They were not as unified within the whole world as a paradigm shift is unified within a science. But that is the most telling aspect of what is going on now. Both the scientific paradigm that is dominant and the mind shift that is happening now truly do seem to be global because of global industrialization and information technology. These forces can link virtually everyone in the world in a mind set that is controlling the way we try to deal with world problems. And the problems are getting so enormous that they are drawing us together to see if there is a better way, a new paradigm that will be more functional.

Perhaps the most succinct statement of the spread of the dominant, scientific paradigm, the difficulties it has spawned and need to examine it or make a change on a worldwide basis was made by African educator Motumbe Mpana when he said, "The American Dream is the World's Nightmare." Just as the scientific paradigm has produced technologies and societies that have advanced the world in many ways, it is obvious from even a cursory examination that there have also been significant negative consequences. We are so caught up in that paradigm that even those who are suffering most from it want to emulate those such as the Americans who are benefiting, economically in the short term, from it. When we are willing to look at them at all, we attempt to solve problems such as environmental degradation, military conflict and human suffering with the same technology that is causing them. As Einstein once implied, you cannot simultaneously be the cause and the solution of the problem.

The Process

In science, Kuhn tells us, paradigm shifts happen when there are anomalies—disparate, odd scientific results that cannot be explained away by inadequate method. When sufficient anomalies occur, those in any science must begin to consider that the paradigm under which they are doing their work is no longer of use or is actually dysfunctional. Today we are faced with the same kind of situation in the world overall, where our paradigm is dysfunctional and a large minority is saying that we have to move to different fundamental assumptions.

When a paradigm shift occurs in science, according to Kuhn, it has the violence of a revolution. The leaders of the dominating paradigm seem to want to kill off those who are proposing the emerging paradigm. And they do kill people, if not physically, then in terms of career, recognition and psychological well-being. Past paradigm shifts in the world have produced actual violence as in the persecution of the Christians by the Romans during the shift from the classical to the medieval mind or in the inquisitions that sometimes involved scientists during the seventeenth century that marked the shift from the medieval to the modern or scientific mind.

We see some forms of violence today as we begin to move into a new paradigm. This is particularly true in institutions like government, education, health care, law, and religion where the restrictions against fundamental change are strong indeed. Such restrictions from the dominant paradigm can be found in business also. However business is seen by many as the lead institution in this paradigm shift, not only because it is the dominant institution on the planet but also because it is an institution that, relatively speaking, seems to thrive on change.

It seems that those of us who work in business organizations have some advantage in getting through the process of change we are going through. There is a survival instinct in business that pushes us toward accepting new ideas and new approaches that can help us to deal with crisis once we recognize it.

Whereas the shift from the classical to the medieval world took some three to four hundred years and the shift from the medieval to the modern scientific paradigm took nearly two hundred years, the shift we are going through now seems to be happening somewhat faster. Of course the groundwork for the current worldwide mind change started around the turn of the century in science with quantum mechanics in physics, in psychology with the recognition of the unconscious, in chemistry with polymers, in biology with hybrids, and in ecology with whole systems.

But the acceleration of change really began in the last third of the century as these ideas began to filter into and intermingle with changes in society. Now there is a vision of what the emerging paradigm might be (even though such speculation must necessarily be tentative and evolving). It seems to include the assumption of consciousness as being causal, a basis of wholeness and system thinking, and a dependence on inner wisdom and authority rather than on the senses and outer proof as in the current dominant paradigm. Rather than believing it only when we see it, the emerging viewpoint seems to be that we will see it only when we believe it—shifting the locus of control from the outside to the inside.

For business this seems to indicate an over-arching purpose of enlightenment for all those in a business and the corresponding service to the surrounding environment and peoples. In other words many now have the hope that the institution of business offers the most fertile ground for application and development of the emerging paradigm. Then business, through the developing individuals in it, can begin to take responsibility for the whole rather than just operating in a competitive market system with its attendant negative externalities.

The Community Metaphor

The key question, then, is how do we get there from here? How can we move from the current idea of business based on the scientific paradigm to something more humane and functional? How we can we start living our deepest held values and beliefs?

Historically, there is not much hope for a smooth transition to a new worldwide paradigm. Not only is there the violence noted earlier, but there haven't existed technologies for making this change. Kuhn seems to offer only one: The leaders of the old paradigm will die off. This is clearly not a viable alternative today since the pace of events is so accelerated and life expectancies are at such a high level and increasing around the world.

The process itself, however, does offer some hope. And this is where community building and related technologies come into play. Over and over we see that the four stages of community building—pseudo-community, chaos, emptiness, and community—are represented in models of the general change process. This implies that the process that we do at the group level is supported by and supports change at other levels.

Land's S-Curves.

One of the most general depiction's of the change process in nature and organizations is George Land's growth curve application (see Jarman and Land's essay on page 21). Like the product life cycle, Land's is an S-shaped curve with four stages. In life cycle analysis these are called introduction, growth, maturity, and decline. Land and Jarman make a critical contribution, however, when they point out that the decline part of the process is accompanied by the starting of a new process, a new S-curve, which, when it happens in a worldwide sense, constitutes the start of a new paradigm.

This breakpoint or bifurcation, where the curve of the S for the old paradigm begins to go down and the new paradigm begins the introduction phase of the a new S-curve, is a period of great turmoil, as we seem to be in today. We must live with unpredictability because the new ways may work for awhile and then be thrown back, due to such factors as our not living by our principles, imperfect implementation, and reaction from those holding on to the old, dominant paradigm.

This is what can happen when a group finds itself in the state of community, comparable to the new S-curve that starts at the point of bifurcation in the Land and Jarman model. The experience in a group that has moved into community can be one of uncertainty, especially when they have to get back to work and they forget the discipline it takes to get to and maintain community.

In fact, whenever something new—such as a new golf grip or dance step—is tried, there is a difficult period (the dip in the first part of the S-curve) when only its potential keeps us toward the second stage of growth in this new state. We face that kind of down and up almost every day as we try to live with what is now only a vague indication of what the new paradigm might be. And if these difficulties with implementation get exacerbated by our lack of resolve and attacks from the dominant paradigm, it is not surprising that the process moves in fits and starts and seems to fold back on itself because of negative feedback.

We can suffer depression, confusion, and frustration if we don't understand that what is going on is the normal process of the universe. Ancient spiritual teachings tell us that the Universe or God is constantly creating, maintaining, destroying, concealing, and revealing. And this truth is now supported largely by scientific theories and findings: from the dance of elemental particles to the movement of chemical solutions to the synergy of our mental processes to the joys and sorrows of our interactions with others to the rise and fall of organizations and nations to the evolution of galaxies.

Creative Dynamic	Gather	Repeat	Share	Transform	
Level	Unit	Pair	Group or field	Compound or new unit	
MICROPHYSICAL REALM (Strong, electric, and weak forces. Four quantum numbers in three dimensions)					
Particles	Photons	Particle/antiparticle	Three families of four particles; Three forces in four dimensions	Baryons; confinement by gluons	
Atomic	Baryons	Electron-proton pairs Lepton pairs Quark pairs	Four quantum numbers x electrons, protons, and neutrons	Atoms; electron	GATHER
Molecular	Atoms	Electron shell bonding; Inorangic molecules	Carbon: three Alphas of four nucleons; four valence electrons in third shell	Organic molecules and crystals	
DNA	Organic molecules	Double helix; Base paring	Four bases of three chemical groups	DNA	
BIOPHYSICAL REALM (Life force; four nucleotides code in triplets)					
Cell	DNA	Replication	Genetic code; four bases code in triplets	Cell; membrane	
Organism	Cell	Cell division	Three functions x four tissues	Organism; skin	REPEAT
Species	Organism	Sexual reproduction	Population structure x evolutionary fitness	Species; reproductive isolation	
Gaia	Species	Speciation; hybrids and polyploids	Ecosystem homeostasis; four seasons of three months	Gaia; Earth life Atmosphere	
ASTROPHYSICAL REALM (Gravitation; four third-order equations)					
Star	Earth; Gaia	Earth-moon; gravitational orbits	Four x three gravitational field	Star; fusion	
Galaxy	Star	Binary stars Earth-sun	Four spiral arms x three supernova generations	Galaxy: heavy elements	SHARE
Universe	Galaxy	Andromeda Milky Way	Four dimensions x leptons, hadrons, and bosons	Universe; evolutionary time and space	
First cause	Universe	Universe/anti-universe	Natural and divine law; four elements x three qualities	First cause; energy, conservation, information	

Figure 1: Reprinted with permission from the artist, August Jacacci, ©1989.

Jacacci's Metamatrix

The four step process of the Land and Jarman curve is echoed in a number of other conceptual models of the change process. August Jacacci and John Gowan offer the most general and expanding of these. With their "Metamatrix" they have achieved a dynamic amalgamation of the models that have been used by futurists and others looking at growth and change processes. Their four stages are gather, repeat, share, and transform—similar in many ways to the stages of the growth process and of community building but having special meaning in the way that they evolve. These four stages can be used for both the columns and the rows of a sixteen-cell table to create the Metamatrix itself (see Figure 1).

The Metamatrix throws light on any process, historically and into the future. Jacacci has called it the "periodic table for everything." It allows speculation as to where any process might go. When it is combined with the model of community building, it indicates the generative nature of the process if we can stay in it, despite the disruptions and negative feedback situations that can occur as we proceed.

Maynard and Mehrtens' Four Waves.

In Herman Maynard and Susan Mehrtens' book, *The Fourth Wave: Business in the 21st Century*, recent history and the future are put into four stages, roughly equivalent to the ages of agriculture, industrialization, information, and the emerging new paradigm.

These stages are not the equivalent of the stages of community building but rather call for the use of community building as we move from where we are now (the information age) into the new paradigm, particularly in business. Figure 2 is taken from Maynard and Mehrtens' book and shows how the change that has happened and will happen affects business and society in general.

The message, once again, is that we have to be aware of where we've been and where we're going. We have to move through these experiences to get to the ideal of our visions. Just as in community building, we can't jump immediately into the fourth wave, or the new paradigm, without going through the interim experiences.

Grof's Perinatal Sequence

We see this in dramatic fashion in the psychotherapist Stanislav Grof's work putting people through an experience of their birth process by use first of psychotropic substances and, later, nondrug therapeutic methods to catalyze unconscious memories.

In *The Passion of the Western Mind*, author Richard Tarnas calls Grof's contribution "the most epistemologically significant development in the recent history of depth psychology and indeed the most important advance in the field as a whole since Freud and Jung themselves." He goes on to point out that Grof "has not only revolutionized psychodynamic theory but also brought forth major implications for many other fields, including philosophy."

Parameter	Second Wave	Third Wave	Fourth Wave
Philosophy	Rooted in materialism and the supremacy of man	Manifests growing concern for balance and sustainability	Central foci are integration of life and responsibility for whole
Environmental Emphasis	Self preservation, consumption	Sanctity of life, conservation	Recognition of all living systems, preservation
Relationships	We are separate and must compete	We are connected and must cooperate	We are one and choose to co-create
Stakeholders	Owners of stock in business	Owners of stock in business and direct internal and external relationships	All people and all systems that interface directly or indirectly with business including planet
Wealth	Mostly tangible with little incentive to consider social accounting	Tangible and intangible with increasing use of social accounting	Mostly intangible reflecting quality of life: social accounting is convention
Business Model	Hierarchical matrix and business unit: the "army" model with military values	"Team value:" democratic processes focused on creating value	Community focused on co-creation, equality, and flexibility
Business Values	Control, profit, survival	Learning, creation of value, understanding broader picture	Stewardship for whole, serving, and creating value for all stakeholders
Management Role	Appointed to serve higher levels of management, seen as decision makers	Elected to serve teams; decision making shifts to person at interface	No managers; leadership rotates with need; decision making throughout consistent with shared vision, principles, values
Technology	Invent and exploit sophisticated technology	Become aware of concept of "appropriate technology" and begin to implement its theories	Evaluate and act in accordance with principles of "appropriate technology"
Politics	Politics and ecology seen as separate: politics viewed with suspicion	Ethical dilemmas begin to be faced blurring public and private spheres	Biopolitical context where all decisions are recognized as having environmental and human consequences
Copyright © 1992, Herman Bryant Maynard, Jr. and Susan E. Mehrtens			

Figure 2: Reprinted with permission from the authors, ©1992

There are also implications for community building and for our struggle in organizations through the paradigm shift. Once again, a consistent four step process emerged, although the experiences from the thousands of Grof's subjects in Europe and America occurred in a highly variable order. The experience of the perinatal (surrounding birth) sequence itself constitutes a highly effective therapy tool which changes peoples' lives in dramatic ways, not only dropping away psychological problems but also giving them a view of the world that is transpersonal in nature. People see their birth experience and themselves as representative of the whole of human culture, its evolution and possibilities. This is similar to the community stage of the community-building process as well as the paradigm shift revolution of Kuhn's conceptualization, the break-point or bifurcation of Land and Jarman, Jacacci's transformation stage, and movement into Maynard and Mehrten's Fourth Wave.

Like community building, the Grof sequence is painful and causes much discomfort along the way but it ends in the sort of exultation that can give people a way to move forward with greater humanity.

The first stage of the perinatal sequence is a state of undifferentiated unity. Then in the second stage, just as in the chaos period of community building, there is constriction, conflict, and contradiction with an accompanying sense of separation, duality, and alienation. The third stage, somewhat comparable to emptiness, is like a death. Subjects talk about it as complete annihilation. And then there is a final stage, like community, that Tarnas describes as "an unexpected redemptive liberation that both overcame and fulfilled the intervening alienated state—restoring the initial unity but on a new level that preserved the achievement of the whole trajectory."

Danger and Opportunity

The world is in crisis—filled with danger and opportunity. And we have to get into the flow of the process of the world as it is transformed. Community building is the best way that I know for doing this work, whether it is mandated by God or not. The charge we have now was expressed by Albert Schweitzer in this way:

> A man is ethical only when life, as such, is sacred to him, that of plants and animals as well as that of his fellowman, and when he devotes himself helpfully to all life that is in need of help.

Even earlier this charge was given by Marcus Aurelius:

> Constantly regard the universe as one living being, having one substance and one soul; and observe how all things have reference to one perception, the perception of this one living being; and how all things act with one movement; and how all things are the cooperating causes of all things which exist.

George Land

is the chairman and a founding partner of Leadership 2000. He served as chief executive of an international television network and founded Innotek Corporation, a research and consulting institute devoted to the search for further knowledge about the enhancement of creative performance. He is the author of *Grow or Die: The Unifying Principle of Transformation* and co-author of *Breakpoint and Beyond.* Land appears in Who's Who in America and Who's Who in the World and is a Fellow of the New York Academy of Sciences and a Colleague and Fellow of the Creative Education Foundation.

Beth Jarman

is a founding partner of Leadership 2000, Inc., an international leadership development corporation. Her first book, *You Can Change Your Life by Changing Your Mind,* emphasized the importance of individuals taking personal responsibility for their lives by maximizing their creative potential. She is the coauthor of *Breakpoint and Beyond: Mastering the Future Today.* Jarman has been at the forefront of change, holding major leadership positions as a cabinet secretary to two governors, a state legislator, and a social entrepreneur.

2

Beyond Breakpoint: Possibilities for New Community

Beth Jarman and George Land

Within our cities, corporate superstructures, small businesses, classrooms, and even within the walls of single family homes, there seems to be a yearning for a new definition of community. In point of fact, the idea of community, one we have lived with for thousands of years, has become a dangerous anachronism. What is emerging is a totally new perspective of what community really means. We are following a natural flow of evolutionary forces leading us to cross the threshold into a new possibility of what community can become. Unless we understand these forces, we will be unable to avoid the crises that accompany an unwillingness to embrace a new possibility of community.

The last few decades have heralded in a period of both breakdown and breakthrough in the American community. Since the sixties, when the very social fabric of our nation was intensely challenged, all of our major institutions have been faced with tremendous upheaval. Whether it be in education, business, politics, or the shattering of the "typical" American family, the solid foundations upon which we once stood are turning to quicksand. Newspapers and television reports bring us pictures and stories of violence, race riots, economic distress and crises in health care and education. Our response to such problems has been an attempt to "fix" them and return everything back to "normal." We tend to isolate and analyze issues, treating crime, for example, as a separate issue to wage war against rather than as a symptom of a breakdown in the community as a whole. From a broader perspective, it becomes evident that the central challenge is to understand the interrelationship of all of these "problems" and get underneath what community truly means. We must uncover what people are searching for individually in their attempt to create a broader sense of community in their lives.

As we have posed the question of what the ideal community would be like to friends and business associates, similar themes emerged. Many people yearn to live among people without fear, where trust is given and received freely, a place of belonging, where a sense of connectedness and unity provides the foundation for life sustaining and enhancing interactions. Others expressed a desire to live in communities where many races, socio-economic levels and age groups interact and build meaningful relationships. The underlying ideal is that everyone in the community is accepted and treated as a valuable, integral member.

These desires are substantially different from the beliefs we have inherited about community. The very root notion of community means having something in common, whether it be ideology, values, religion, or race. We often join a community because we share the same basic beliefs, perceptions, and biases. Most communities are very good at identifying and welcoming those who are like them, but fall woefully short in embracing diversity. The idea of questioning age-old assumptions and disagreeing with long held traditions shatters the very essence of community agreements. Yet by questioning these deeply rooted beliefs, perhaps we can move to a broader perspective about what our new communities might become. Women, by their very presence in the world of work, have upset the traditional notion of community.

The Bridge to the Future

As large numbers of women began to enter the world of business, they learned the rules of success from the men who had mastered them. This was a natural way to move into a realm of work largely unfamiliar to them. However, in the process of learning the rules of a new game, many women subordinated their natural impulses in order to appear strong, in control, and to be accepted by the members of this new and somewhat foreign community. The result has been the development of a whole generation of women who have been playing a role that was largely defined by men. For some women, this role was natural, but for many the role negated parts of them and didn't allow them to express unique perspectives and ideas. In more recent years, many women have brought unique leadership styles focused on building organizations based on cooperation, kindness, honesty, compassion, and a more nurturing environment. As a result of these changes, a new consciousness is emerging, one that acknowledges that the needs of both women and men should be discussed and integrated in healthy work environments.

Other areas of national concern reveal a similar theme. In education, where success has been based on linear reasoning, stressing the fundamentals taught through lecture and the written word, artistic, kinesthetic and visual learners have struggled for achievement. These students, unrecognized for their unique talents, often have been branded as challenged and given the message that they are less able than their peers. From the dropout rate in public schools, it is obvious that such a limited picture of learning is destructive, not just to individual students, but to the future of our society. Pioneering teaching methods which integrate art, music, and experiential learning are beginning to demonstrate the power of inclusion rather than exclusion. The philosophical base of these newer approaches encourages varied methods of teaching and learning, giving students the resources to learn in ways most natural to them, thus creating a new and enriched community of learners. For too long, the education system has had an underlying goal of training students in social compliance, rather than encouraging individual creativity both in learning and expression. Breakdown in education has been largely a result of an unwillingness and inability to celebrate and resource individual differences.

As we look at the undercurrent in other problem areas of our society, the same theme appears. On the social scene, as African-Americans, Native Americans, gays, and other groups fight their independent battles, one theme rises above the rest. All of these groups are calling for greater understanding and inclusion in the larger community. In the process of their struggle, the whole society has begun to be educated. It is no longer acceptable to ask people to deny parts of their beliefs, history, or selves in order to fit into a framework which was built to exclude them. Far too often in the present, as in the past, people feel compelled to lie about who they really are or otherwise adapt themselves to be included within a tightly defined structure.

Out of the Box

Today, more and more people are challenging the belief structures and systems already in place. Our institutions now face the tremendous challenge of integrating the vast differences that make up the populace of our nation and world. These new communities are not only being created by human pioneers, but by technological breakthroughs as well. Electronic connections cross time zones, smash national boundaries, keep identities invisible, and shatter long-held assumptions about how the world works. Whether it be electronic communities, ecological, ecumenical, or new corporate communities, something different is emerging.

Our friend David, a forty-eight year old college professor, knew very little about computers, just enough to get on a network and ask for help. Fortunately, a more experienced user came to his aid, never failing to give just the right advice. One morning, when a vexing problem was plaguing him, his expert adviser who had been on-line with him for over an hour, said. "I'm sorry, I've got to go." David pleaded with him, "You can't leave me, we've almost found the solution." Across the electron world shot the next sentence: "You don't understand, my school bus won't wait for me." David thought for a moment, his curiosity mounting, "How old are you?" he asked. "I'm twelve," was the response on his screen, "and I'll talk to you tonight."

Through the invisible network of an electronic community, old barriers crumbled and a new community emerged. Where once close proximity and common identifiers brought people together, today a twelve year old offers advice to a college professor. We are living in a new world indeed. Surface identifiers that once formed the very heart of community are being shattered.

The Evolution of Community

We have indeed come to a unique point in the evolution of community, where the long held assumptions of how community works and where individuals fit into respective groups are coming into question. We call this unique juncture a "breakpoint" because it demands that people shift belief structures, methods of relating, and day-to-day living in drastic and often very challenging ways. This period of transition requires us to break from how we once looked at the world—to see with new insight, new vision, and new values. As we look at the creation of community from this vantage point, it is important to expand our scope to see our collective growth from a holistic perspective, building a new foundation from both the breakdowns and breakthroughs of the last few decades.

How the definition and experience of community can evolve beyond where it is today is a complex question. Whole systems thinking invites us to approach the understanding of community in terms of all the potentials that exist within the environment—how all the varying parts, elements, and divisions relate and connect with one another. A corporation, for example, is composed not only of employees working in separate divisions but also customers, suppliers, stockholders, families of employees, and the communities the company affects. In essence, all the stakeholders that have any relationship to the company are part of the corporate community.

The vital insight we can gain about our emerging future comes from the acknowledgment that communities, like all systems in nature, follow a dynamic and creative process of growth and change. We learn from fifteen billion years of evolution that over time natural breakpoints occur, breakpoints that shift the most fundamental rules that govern successful life. Three distinctly different

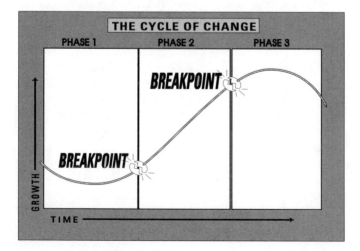

Figure 1. The Cycle of Change

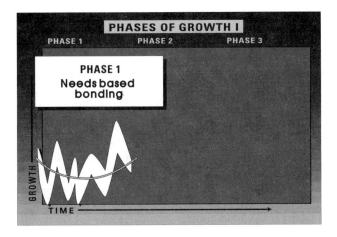

Figure 2. Needs-Based Bonding

phases of growth are required to reach the full potential of any system—including human communities. Each phase follows certain fundamental patterns that lead to the next stage of growth (a phase describes an interval within the cycle of change between breakpoints). After a breakpoint, the rules governing what works and what doesn't work change dramatically. Successful methods in one phase actually become counterproductive in another.

These phases can be thought of by drawing an S curve that shows change across time. The horizontal movement shows the passage of time, the vertical motion indicates growth.

In order to understand the process of change as communities evolve, an understanding of each phase is essential. Fortunately we have vital information from all of the living systems that preceded human communities. Drawing from the experience of primordial cellular life, from the evolution of ecological systems, and from animal evolution, we can grasp the deep and powerful forces driving natural systems. We learn that all natural systems reach points where past successes lead to failure and require the adoption of totally new growth processes. With earlier systems, these natural breakpoints have usually lead to devastation before the system learned to adopt new ways of living. In the case of human communities, it is possible to reflect on that great learning to find fresh and less painful solutions to the giant challenge of breakpoint change.

The most important thing we can learn is that the three phases are each distinct with unique qualities and characteristics that assure success.

Phase One—Needs-Based Bonds

The first phase of growth in all of nature is to find a pattern of life that insures survival. Cells, for example, explore their environment and discover how to use the available resources for nourishment. They naturally bond together in colonies that provide mutual support. Community bonding for human beings also revolves around how ones basic needs are satisfied. The most important community is the family because families provide the foundation of one's psychological and physical development. In societies around the world, the family, clan, or tribe has always served this vital function, providing love, a sense of belonging, safety, food, and shelter. The kind of bonds established around fulfilling basic needs is crucial—not only to the individual—but to the larger community as well.

One of our most vexing problems in modern society is dealing with large populations who are not having their basic needs met. Without a feeling of security and love, a sense of belonging, and a deep sense of safety, some individuals come to a point of acting out their unbonded aggression. Even a lone cell will attack its neighbors if denied food. In humans, a feeling of deep resentment and hostility plays itself out in rage, anger, and revenge undermining the entire social fabric. If one's basic needs are not met, it is often impossible for a person to begin to experience the fullness of what it means to be human.

Phase Two—Commonality Based Bonds

How basic needs are met determines the character and quality of the next stage of community building. It is out of our relationships with family that we are introduced to the larger groupings of people with whom we share common bonds. Cells gather together in clusters that are similar—fending off threats and food competition from neighboring organisms. Likewise in humans, one's extended family where similarities are shared—a common religion, corresponding cultural patterns, and expectations—all form around an individual providing messages of who one is and equally important, who one is not, who to approach, and who to avoid. Acceptable behavior is clearly rewarded and unacceptable

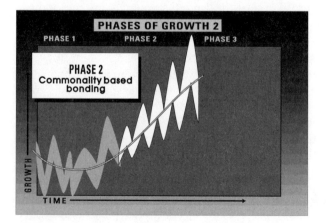

Figure 3. Commonality Based Bonding

behavior is suppressed and discouraged. This second phase of community is built around conforming to the mores, values, and norms of the sub-culture into which one is born.

The journey through youth and young adulthood is usually a march across time, perfecting the critical second phase "likeness bonds" of community building. Children from kindergarten through college quite naturally develop ways of identifying those who are most like them and learn to discriminate against those outside their peer group. Teenagers take this natural tendency to cluster around those who have common interests and similar beliefs even more seriously. They are dedicated to being "in" with their crowd even if it risks the alienation of their parents. The peer group is vital. It is a rare individual in adolescence who has a sense of self that allows the questioning of these powerful second phase bonds based on commonality.

The power of commonality based bonds extend far past adolescence. They form the very foundation of most successful organizations. Corporations large and small build their internal cultures by identifying those who are most like them and excluding those who are different. To be recruited by IBM one dresses a particular way, has a certain level of educational attainment, and behaves within the accepted IBM value system. Arthur Andersen recruits young college graduates based on a profile of what makes a successful partner. Organizations like Microsoft and Apple have a much different corporate culture. Those who prefer a more casual, non-conformist environment seek a home with them. Nonetheless, they recruit those who are most like them. Even today, it is a rare exception to see a woman or minority person sitting in the executive suite of a Fortune 500 company. Corporate boards are dominated by white men. Opening up the tight second phase commonality bonds to bring in those who are different requires a dramatic shift in thinking.

Corporate America is not the only institution facing the challenge of loosening its tight second phase commonality bonds to include those who are different. Today, the U.S. Congress, professional schools (whether law, medical, or engineering) are all experiencing the difficulty of moving beyond the breakpoint of commonality based bonds to understanding, welcoming and including those who are different.

However, it is from opening up to that which is new and different that the potential for unexpressed creativity manifests itself. Our daughter in third grade waged a one-person campaign to protect a young Australian who moved to her school. Her classmates terrorized him after school, laughed at his accent, made fun of him for not being a cub scout, and taunted him because he wasn't in their church. She sobbed at the treatment he received, and determined to become his friend. Even though many of her friends didn't understand, she was enriched by the friendship, and received a wonderful lesson about the power of unconditional acceptance. Sometimes it is the young ones who haven't yet conformed to our cultural rules who can teach all of us important lessons of humanity.

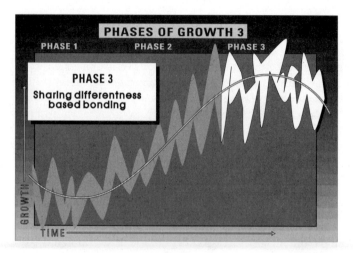

Figure 4. Sharing Differentness-Based Bonding

Phase Three—Bonds Based on the Reciprocal Sharing of Differences

First phase community is built around basic needs. Second phase community is about bonding with those who are like us. Third phase community bonds are only achieved when we open ourselves to the full potential that exists within any environment. It requires a maturity based on accepting and celebrating the richness of diversity. Cellular life made this discovery almost nine hundred million years ago. Once the oceans were heavily populated with distinct colonies of separate kinds of cells when a dramatic and unprecedented shift occurred. Cells that were quite different began to get together and share their DNA; genetic recombination was invented. Suddenly new forms emerged that combined the distinctive properties of two different kind of cells. Hybrid vitality surged upon the scene. The new cells were stronger, lived longer, grew faster and soon became the dominant form of life. They set the stage for the emergence of plants and animals. If those early cells had not made the shift to sharing differences, we would not be here to face our own challenge of breakpoint change!

In human communities this third phase of growth is when we integrate the vast diversity that lies within the broader society. It is only through the deep appreciation of differences and the willingness to share our uniqueness that the third phase of community building can be reached. It is at this stage that we remove the barriers that only allowed us to mingle with people who were like us. The challenge is to become expansive enough in our hearts and minds to include the incredible variety that exists within our places of work, our nation, and the world. This is where a virtual cornucopia of undeveloped potential lies ready to be developed and expressed.

The Creativity of Chaos

Some view all these changes as evidence of chaos and decline. From our vantage point, what we're experiencing is absolutely natural. From an evolutionary standpoint, the changes going on in the American community as a whole are happening at lightning speed with comparable intensity. It is essential, in this time of dramatic change, to remember that without the chaos of creativity, a restructuring would never be possible. This chaos has a larger purpose of creating an opening for something new to be born; its center is a new form of relationship and the foundation of new possibilities for communities to realize their full potential.

The shift to the third phase—where large groups of people accept and celebrate their differences—takes firm intention and can be tremendously difficult. It requires going through a breakpoint. One must be able to shift from a viewpoint focused exclusively on what is good for "me and mine" to what would be good for "we and ours." Moving from "me" to "we" is a place where one must change his or her mind and heart in order to experience the profound bonding that comes with opening to the creative possibilities of diversity and difference.

For instance, in South Central Los Angeles many diverse cultures live together, yet, like most communities across the country, they have been living in a second phase worldview which stresses exclusivity—bonding with people who are similar, not those who are different. The whole of American society watched as that polarization erupted in violence and rage. The riots in Los Angeles were a natural result of such a belief structure; little else is possible when differences among people are seen as marks of separation and danger. However, if we were to change our perspective to one of embracing and celebrating differences among individuals and cultures, the community of South Central Los Angeles becomes one of immense possibilities, not of problems. If the community members would begin to look at what they can offer to each other, rather than what they can take, a completely new focus would be born. With the wisdom, art, dance, history and culture of such diverse peoples as Koreans, Mexicans, African-Americans, and whites, creative multi-cultural events could become commonplace. When the focus is shifted from how we are different and therefore separate to how we are different and thus enriched, miracles of creation become possible.

Making Miracles

As heirs to a powerful tradition of rational, logical second phase thinking, we aren't in the habit of creating or even accepting the idea of miracles. Yet, if we turn our lens to how nature evolves and changes, we gain a different perspective. In plant biology, for example, miracles have become mundane. Appreciating differences is the foundation of nature's third phase creative process. In plant hybridization, when two types of corn that were never before combined were brought together, the crop yield per acre went from 20 to 120 bushels—an impossible improvement under the limited notion of a rational second phase perspective. Creativity and hybrid vigor draw upon the same basic assumption—that great inventions come from unusual, even paradoxical combinations. The results can only be labeled miraculous. The real miracle in human communities is connected to opening the heart to what is new, unknown and different. Only then can creating what never before existed become a reality.

Transforming the limitations of the second phase worldview demands a conscious commitment and willingness to change beliefs and behaviors that have become second nature. It is the individual who chooses to offer his or her creative gifts or to withdraw them. As noted psychologist Erich Neumann states: "It is the little creature that is the bearer of the divine miracle, for this little creature is nothing less than the creative individual, and it is under his guidance that the human race makes progress on its journey through history."

The Heart of Community

The cornerstone of the third phase of community resides within the individual. As we have repeatedly said to corporate clients, "Organizations don't change, people do." True and lasting change in any environment, whether it be academic, corporate, social, political, or familial, must begin at the personal level. Change in structure and form can be imposed externally, but if people don't experience these changes as their own, any new momentum will be impossible to sustain.

Edicts from above are expected in second phase environments. Change is not discussed, felt, or chosen; change is ordered and carried out by subordinates. Beyond breakpoint, however, something new must emerge. The third phase maintains a dynamic climate through a form of hybrid vitality which requires individuals and ideas to connect in new ways. Environments that support such creative expansion are built not only around new ideas but around new values and practices as well. Our experience is that these values come from a partnership of the heart and mind of the individual. Moving out of a second phase "mindset," where rationality, logic, and reason reign supreme, to the possibility that the mind can be even more effective when taking directives from the heart requires a shift not only in thinking but in feeling as well.

The business world has been inundated with programs of "Total Quality Management," yet their effectiveness is limited by a top-down approach. The Institute of HeartMath, a research center devoted to discovering the role the heart plays in emotional and physical health and the overall quality of life, has shifted the focus of this approach by naming their corporate programs "Inner Quality Management." Seeing the individual as the center of change turns the focus from organizational change to personal self-management and balance, which will inevitably affect corporate culture. We have found the Institute's research to be profound; it reinforces the values we have seen as guideposts to the future: nonjudgment, learning to listen and act on one's inner knowing, compassion, appreciation, and unconditional acceptance.

At the Institute of HeartMath, they have been able to measure the power of emotions, such as care and appreciation in comparison to anger and frustration. The results show that care and appreciation are at least three times more powerful. In partnership with them, we provide simple, commonsense tools to begin the process of stress reduction and emotional and mental balance, which we see as a powerful foundation for building a healthy environment in any community.

As communities of all kinds face the challenge of accepting and celebrating differences, more inclusive values must inevitably be born. One of the major obstacles to this transformation is the need many people have for a new form to replace the old. It is natural to want to have the new structure in place before discarding the old, but it is actually the willingness to let go of basic assumptions of the past that clears a path for a new form to be brought into being. Within the unknown and seeming chaos of letting go, an anchor can be found in the heart, providing stability in the midst of transformation. From the balance point in the heart, new values emerge organically, setting the stage for communities of wholeness.

It's important to note that movement forward doesn't depend on everyone changing. When just one person takes on the challenges of becoming more accepting, allowing, and strong, a ripple effect is created. Everyone in that person's sphere is now touched by a new possibility. Even if the reasons are unclear, anyone who plays by new rules will be noticed by others. Individuals functioning from this level of transformation are the pioneers of the new community, planting seeds of the future.

Creating Holistic Community

Openness and inclusion will come when we approach others with non-judgment, valuing and celebrating their differences. In order to have this happen, people must be willing to speak the truth, manage negative thoughts and emotions, and face conflicts in healthy ways. The new community is built around self-responsibility, where building strength in the individual is seen as valuable. Self-responsibility does not imply a me-only perspective but requires a commitment to personal development and to the good of the whole. In our personal work, we have discovered that as we have grown better at appreciating, allowing, and not judging, there is a natural consideration of all the people and other variables when we make decisions. Trusting the heart has actually proven to be a benefit for the mind as well, allowing for better decisions, less time spent oscillating between choices, and less negative thoughts to drain energy. Imagine whole teams made of individuals in personal balance, putting all of their creative energy into projects in service of the whole.

In corporations, "cross-functional teams" are emerging. These teams are oriented to bringing together all of the previously separate functions. Instead of marketing, sales, manufacturing, and administration operating as distinct and adversarial divisions, the new orientation is to create teams that work together creatively and cooperatively, sharing their differences to serve customers at a much higher level. Whenever a system evolves into maturity, all parts work together for the benefit of the whole. The adult human body is a mature system. No one would survive if the blood supply refused to serve all of the organs of the body. The consequences would be fatal if the kidney, heart, liver, or pancreas refused to cooperate.

Nature surrounds us with astounding examples of third phase cooperation and mutual support. The carbon atom forms the basis of all life because it can bond in all directions with different atoms and molecules. Without the carbon atom, we simply wouldn't have life. The technological revolution depends on the third phase behavior of silicon, which is similar to carbon in its ability to bond with a host of different kinds of materials. When a silicon crystal is doped with so called "impurities," only then is it able to perform its startling capabilities. In a few short years, our world has been linked more intricately because of the scientific application of nature's third phase rules.

Compelling Vision

One of the most vital components in developing a new kind of community is that the group write around a compelling vision of what is possible. The original definition of community was "to serve together." Having a purpose of service sets the foundation around which the form will grow. Fulfilling the vision pulls members of a community out of purely individual concerns into something far greater than themselves. Vision is the basic building block of new communities, from couples joining in partnership, schools creating learning environments, neighbors caring for one another, to businesses seeing themselves in service of the larger society.

Having a vision is different from having a plan. A vision inspires creativity while a plan simply dictates actions. A vision of landing a man on the moon within one decade galvanized a nation in the 1960s. A vision catches the spirit of a people. It never identifies how something will happen.

One of the assumptions that must be made in building new communities is that everyone is creative and that each person has a unique contribution to make to the whole. The rigid structure of the second phase assumes that people must be controlled and managed. In the third phase, the role of leadership is to hold the vision and purpose, calling forth the latent capabilities of every individual. The greatest asset of every community is its human potential. Organizations who realize this are experiencing incredible success.

The British-based The Body Shop has turned business upside down. Anita Roddick built one of the most successful line of body care products on values and principles connected to saving the rain forests, protecting animals from cruel testing, and recyclable packaging in support of the environment. The Body Shop's values are the bottom line, and many consumers buy their products primarily in support of their values. Roddick has become a pioneer into the new world of possibility in business, based on being connected to the environment of which her company is a part, treating people with fairness, and trusting them to make a difference in their own communities.

The Community-Building Process

The new kind of community building is not an event; it is a process. During moments when the breakdown seems much more prevalent than breakthrough, we must remember that the chaos has a purpose; that what appears to be a crisis is, in a natural evolutionary sense, the door opening to move us beyond breakpoint. Each of us has the power to decide where to focus our strength. At this juncture, we can either continue to empower a defunct structure, or shift into a new awareness, with purpose, open minds and hearts, and begin to lay the bricks to build the communities we have long yearned to have.

We are sure that within the hearts of a vast number of people rests a deep yearning for communities that celebrate the magnificence of our diversity. The natural pull we are experiencing is to evolve past where we presently are. It requires courage, boldness, and deep commitment. Guillaume Apollinaire put into words what we think could happen if we dared build new communities:

> "Come to the edge, he said.
> They said: We are afraid.
> Come to the edge, he said,
> They came. He pushed them
> and they flew."

Terry Mollner, Ed.D., is founder and chair of Massachusetts-based Trusteeship Institute, Inc. (TI), which consults with corporations converting to the Relationship Age (or post-Science-Spirituality Riddle) worldview. TI assists firms at any stage in the process, especially, when appropriate, in the conversion to employee ownership. Mollner is a founding board member of the Calvert Social Investment Fund, the Calvert World Values Global Fund, and the Calvert Social Investment Foundation High Impact Fund. He is a Fellow of the World Business Academy and a founder of the Connecticut River Valley Network of Business for Social Responsibility. He is currently writing a new book with the working title *It Takes a Village to Raise a Child: The Story of My Discovery of the First Seven Stages of Wisdom.*

3

Getting Beyond the Riddle

Terry Mollner

If there is one thing we humans hate it is living as if two opposing statements are true.

One of the great fundamental contradictions in history was the knowledge that the Earth was both flat and curved—flat and level when we are building a house but curved when a ship disappears "from the bottom up" when it goes out to sea. The more we became aware that we were living as if a contradiction were true, the more frustrated and angry we became. Life based on contradictions has no meaning, and without meaning we have no basis for doing one thing rather than another. Eventually, we demand that our minds find a new point of view which eliminates the contradiction. When someone finally convinced us that the Earth was round, the contradiction evaporated. This is the painful process through which evolution pushes us into greater wisdom.

As I am writing this, both Eastern and Western cultures, each in its own way, are living a contradiction of which many have become aware. The frustration with this riddle has reached a high level because it is at the center of our self-definition. It is not difficult to predict that soon we will find a new point of view which will allow this contradiction to evaporate as well.

I call this contradiction the Science-Spirituality Riddle. You will not find it discussed on the evening news programs. However, in all the private places throughout the world—in the board rooms and lunch rooms on Wall Street, Main Street, Industrial Park Road, Rodeo Drive, Madison Avenue, Pennsylvania Avenue, University Circle, etc. people are now openly and very seriously searching for the solution to this riddle. Unraveling it has become crucial because we will not be able to go to the next level in personal fulfillment, organizational productivity, community cohesion, and new ideas until we as a culture and business community get beyond being stumped by this riddle.

THE SCIENCE-SPIRITUALITY RIDDLE

How many of us have a religious or spiritual life which assumes that we are all part of God's family cooperating for the common good? How many of us also believe that, by nature, all things compete with one another for their own self-interests? These are opposite assumptions about reality; yet how many of us live as if they are both true? This is the Science-Spirituality Riddle.

To solve the riddle we must find the relationship between cooperation and competition which eliminates contradiction.

Ideological Coatrack

Usually when confronted with two opposing points of view, we choose between them, determining that one is true and the other false. This is an ideological approach. The "coatrack" in our minds upon which we are hanging our thoughts like jackets has only two hooks: right or wrong, true or false, good or bad, etc. This is the easiest way to think and we love setting up worlds, like wars and competitive sports, which allow us to think in pure win-lose terms.

Developmental Coatrack

There is another possible coatrack our minds could use: the developmental coatrack. It allows for change, including cycles and evolution, over time. It has two dimensions: right or wrong is one polarity and change (time and space) is the polarity perpendicular to it. When looking at the world with a developmental coatrack as the structure of the mind, something can be "right" this moment but "wrong" the next. There will be no experience of contradiction. Things are not static but constantly changing, evolving, or going through cycles.

When a tree is a seed it does not have leaves. When it is fully grown, it does. So, does a tree have leaves? Ideological thinking would have us respond "yes" because we usually think of a tree fully grown. Ideological answers are nearly always partial answers which perpetuate conflict rather than agreement.

Comprehensive Coatrack

However, there is one more possible coatrack our minds could use: the comprehensive coatrack. It also defines who we are in relationship to everything else, something the other two do not do. It has three dimensions: right or wrong, change, and all things as parts of one thing. This polarity is perpendicular and running threw the other two which creates a three dimensional picture. However, since the third dimension stands for all time and all space and not a particular part of them as the other two dimensions do, it is represented not just by a line but also by a ball within which the other three lines exist and sometimes only by the ball. Could this be the "six directions" in Native American thinking and "the

Holy Trinity" of the Father, Son, and Holy Spirit in Christian thinking?

When we are using the comprehensive coatrack, we are bringing every-thing else into our awareness, making it important as well, and defining our body as a part of everything. When we realize that the universe continues but our bodies are here for only a small piece of time, we give priority to the good of all instead of just the good of our bodies. In so doing, we redefine ourselves not only as our bodies but as everything else as well. The good of all rather than the good of our bodies—or anything else—has become our highest priority.

If we use the three-dimensional, comprehensive coatrack when trying to solve the Science-Spirituality Riddle, we discover that there is a relationship between cooperation (the good of all) and competition (self-interest) which eliminates the contradiction that is present when using the ideological or devel-opmental coatracks. If this is true, we will no longer have to choose between them, or settle for a compromise position often called "enlightened self-interest." Instead, they will become two parts in a meaningful and understandable rela-tionship within one whole. More importantly, it will be possible for us to agree to a solution to the riddle.

The answer is not determined by the words but by the coatrack upon which they hang in our minds.

THE NATURAL STAGES OF HUMAN MATURATION

I now believe the human mind naturally evolves through seven stages, which I call "baby," "toddler," "child," "teenager," "adult," "wise elder," and "mature elder." These stages, I believe, will reveal the relationship between competition and cooperation in nature. They provide a three-dimensional way of answering the question.

Baby

Think back to the last time you held a six month old baby in your hands. If you are like most people, you probably put its face right across from yours, looked the baby directly in the eyeballs, and said something like, "Hi! Aren't you a beautiful baby! Yes, you arrrrrrrrre beautiful." If you didn't scare him or her, the baby would look right back at your eyeballs, maybe look away a little, and then look right back at you. All other things being equal, based on how at ease you were at being in his or her world, the baby would comfortably look directly into your eyes for longer or shorter periods of time, but directly into your eyeballs without inhibition.

A baby does not yet have the abilities we call language and self-conscious-ness. That means that he or she is not able to define "self" and "not self." Therefore, by default, his or her unconscious self-definition is, "I am all that is." The baby is in the unconscious state of oneness. Practically, this means that there is nothing which is not experienced by the baby as part of himself or herself.

This is why we love babies! They are love in motion. Because they do not have the ability to distinguish "self" as separate from anything else, they are giving priority to the "good of all" (their "self") at all times. They have no choice in this. It is the nature of this pre-self-conscious stage in human development. The other side of this is that they are totally interdependent with us. If we are loving, they are loving back. If we are scary, they cry. They do not have the self-conscious skill of being able to smile in the face of anger.

Toddler

As the baby grows older, he or she learns language and, with it, the skill we call "self-consciousness"—the ability to choose and know when and what he or she is choosing. The toddler becomes the "watcher" as well as the "doer."

First, the toddler learns differences in polarity—mommy-not mommy, up-down, black-white, yes-no, and so on. What is interesting about this phase is that the polarities learned are abstract—that is, not in the context of time and space. For instance, a child at this stage will want milk. If you try to explain that there are six people and only a pint of milk left to be shared, the child will not understand. The child only knows "milk" or "no milk." You have to either give the child milk or let him or her cry. The toddler only knows how to use the ideological coatrack for thoughts.

Child

Once the toddler has learned enough polarities and continuums, you can begin to teach him or her that one is more important than the others. All toddlers are taught that the time-space continuum is more important than all other continuums, polarities, or differences. This is usually done using the word "share." As the toddler becomes able to understand that the time-space continuum is more important than all the others, we are able to ask the toddler to share the milk that is left, and he or she will accept the compromise. The developmental coatrack becomes available.

This is the first experience of one of the most important concepts the child will ever learn: prioritizing. The child has learned that the time-space polarity is more important than all the others.

Teenager

The next major stage of development occurs during or just prior to what we call "the teenage years." During this period the child becomes what I call "self-consciously self-conscious." Let me explain.

In any human interaction, there are three broad aspects to the conversation: content, process, and context. Content is the "stuff" that is being communicated, for example, "I would like you to go to dinner with me tonight." The process is the "way" it is being communicated, for example, in English rather than French, in a consensus rather than hierarchical format, and so on. Context is "who I am"—the one who is having the conversation; that is, I decide what worldview I am living by and what our roles are in it. For example, I am a free person in a free society where my freedom to do whatever I like is my highest value at all times.

Up to the teenage years, the adults around children have been able to determine the context because the child hasn't fully comprehended that he or she could choose the context as well as the process and content. For instance, children go to school because they understand that is what they are supposed to do. They believe in Santa Claus because we say he is real.

The teenager has become self-consciously self-conscious—he or she learns to also choose the context within which the secondary choices of content and process are made. Once this phase of growth sets in, the teenager is very concerned about choosing his or her own self-identity and perpetuating it in other people's minds, e.g. "I love Guns and Roses and I hate REM," or "I think Michael Jordan is the best basketball player ever and Larry Bird wasn't even close." Usually, they choose haircuts and clothes which are very different from the norm as part of making this statement. It is as if they are shouting, "No longer do I let you decide what world I live in. From now on, just like you, I will make up my own worldview in each situation and live in it as I choose."

Adult

From this point on, the maturation of the human being is not as much biologically determined as culturally and intellectually determined. Some people never develop beyond the teenage phase. Some do not move to the adult stage until very late in life. However, most people move into the adult stage by their twenties.

The adult stage begins at the point a person realizes that there are contradictions in all the particular choices he or she has made and it is recognized that the only way to get rid of them is to choose one fundamental worldview and to align all his or her secondary choices with it.

Of course, this fundamental worldview is based on what the adult believes is true. Seldom does a person begin to build an entire metaphysics of his or her own. Rather, the person chooses from among the world views which are available, e.g. joining a religion, identifying with a scientific worldview, becoming an acceptable member of the corporate culture, and so on.

Probably the current most popular fundamental worldview in American society is that "evolution is the survival of the fittest through competition." It is logical that a person in the adult phase would choose this worldview because it is an extension of the process of learning language and becoming self-conscious. In this process, everything is separated from everything else in our mind so it can be identified with a word and talked about. The natural extension of this process is to view one's self as only one's body. The natural extension of this choice is to make the rest of one's choices from an ideological perspective—"this or that"—or from a developmental perspective—"this now, that later"—rather than from a comprehensive perspective—"this now, that later, and the good of all and each is what is most important."

Wise Elder

The wise elder is the adult who, in an effort to escape the remaining layers of pain, has figured out that the baby had it right in the first place.

The difference is that the wise elder can now choose to have the natural, unconscious worldview of the baby be his or her *chosen worldview*. He or she can become the watcher of the watcher—the universe watching the body watching what it does.

The wise elder is the adult who has realized that an ideological approach to choosing a fundamental worldview is not adequate because there is change. Not only are there cycles like the seasons but there is also evolution into previously unimagined new forms. The developmental approach also isn't adequate. The wise elder has noticed that his or her body came into existence and will go out of existence, but the universe will continue on. Obviously, the body is only a part of the bigger whole. It follows that a person is at least as much the larger whole as he or she is the transient part. By nature, all things give priority to the good of the one big whole, the universe, over the parts that come and go. Realizing this, the wise elder freely chooses to do so as well. In so doing, he or she expands the primary definition of "self" from only the body or family (the Western idea), or even the religion, nationality, or state (the Eastern idea), to be "all that is." Now the comprehensive coatrack is preferred.

Mature Elder

The seventh stage is reached when the wise elder realizes, "Yeah, I am all that is, but I primarily interact in the world of self-consciousness with other humans, and in that layer of evolution *I only have decision power over my body*." Up to this point the wise elder may be wide-eyed, purely open and accepting, and, in the perception of others, "not fully in his or her body." This is often the case. The wise elder has redefined self as "I am all that is" and is focused on this redefinition of self. The mature elder, however, has become so secure in this new definition that he or she has moved on to making the next key distinction in the maturation process: the difference between who I am and where I have decision power.

The mature elder has learned that in the mutually created game of self-consciousness (choice), the natural laws are that I only have decision power over my choices, not those of others. More importantly, I am the only person able to make my choices and I have total decision power over how I think and feel inside my body. Even if another holds a gun to my head, how I think and feel is still solely my choice. In other words, if I have the wisdom to enjoy inner peace regardless of what else is occurring, I can enjoy it by choice.

The wise elder may have headed for the monastery (or the equivalent) to have uninterrupted time with the beautiful, newly discovered, self-conscious feeling of oneness with all things. The mature elder, on the other hand, like Mahatma Gandhi, Martin Luther King, and others, leaves the monastery to attend to what the or she sees as the most important task: the eldering of others to higher stages of maturation. This is because the mature elder's primary focus is now on his or her choices—the same thing everyone but the wise elder focuses on. It is not on who he or she is. The mature elder is back in his or her body. The significant difference is that the mature elder, unlike the toddler, child, teenager, and adult, is now making his or her choices from a different definition of self.

There are three main exceptions to the rule "I only have decision power over my body": (1) one has full decision power (or responsibility) over one's children, a power gradually reduced as they grow toward the adult stage; (2) one has degrees of decision power over other children when they are in one's sphere of influence, up to the adult stage of their maturation; and (3) one has limited decision power for others when serving as their representative, whether under circumstances of dictatorship, democracy, or consensus. In nearly all other situations, joint decisions are naturally made by consensus. This is easily confirmed by watching people walk pass one another on a busy sidewalk or by observing how a group of friends decides where to go for dinner.

These first seven stages of human maturation are illustrated in Figure 1 below.

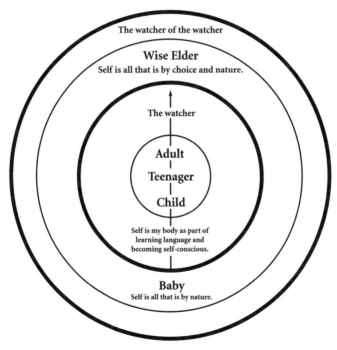

Figure 1: The Natural Stages of Human Maturation

The mature elder realizes that it is not possible to become a mature elder without first being a baby, toddler, child, teenager, adult, and wise elder. Therefore, the mature elder has total compassion toward others who still think in those ways. After all, they are now viewed as parts of one's self. From the perspective of the mature elder, the obvious highest priority in all things becomes assisting people to become mature elders. Only mature elders can act like mature elders. Wise elders, adults, teenagers, children, and babies cannot. The solution to our chronic social problems of violence, loneliness, and greed lies in creating communities of mature elders who joyfully accept the responsibility of eldering youth into full membership in the community of elders. There is an African saying, "It takes a village to raise a child."

We need to bring up the children within mature elder communities so they do not need to acquire wisdom at the expense of more suffering and harm—to themselves, others, and society—and so they not only increase but sustain increases in productivity and creativity in our corporate communities.

The mature elders are those who no longer are concerned about the legal restrictions placed on their behavior and have their entire hearts and souls in all they do. These are the kinds of partners and employees we all want in our companies. If they are not behaving as mature elders, it is probably because they are not being led by mature elders.

If employees do not feel that they are working for mature elders, they see themselves as slaves. Slaves have only two goals: escape slavery and only do what is necessary to get by until then.

Throughout history, tribes and communities have seen the importance of bringing children out of the ignorance of childhood and into the wisdom of the mature elders by creating special rites of passage. These rites are now absent or hollow exercises in our culture. Companies whose leadership is beyond the Science-Spirituality Riddle will stage defining events and alter procedures that will serve as the equivalent of a rite of passage for everyone in the company. The leadership will then accept responsibility for sustaining the company as a community of mature elders. If this is genuine, the "secondary" rewards of increased profitability and creativity will surely follow.

CORPORATIONS: THE MATURE ELDER COMMUNITIES OF THE FUTURE

Sadly, our culture is trapped in the adult stage of the maturation process. We champion competition ("We're number one!") more than cooperation ("We're all in this together."). Thus, there is little to no coming together of the community of mature elders to initiate our teenagers (the earliest age at which this can be fully comprehended) into the greater wisdom. Parenting is often seen as complete when the child has reached the teenage years.

Parents who have achieved the wisdom of the mature elders create communities with friends who share this worldview so their children will have intimate contact with mature elders as they are growing up. Then, when the children are teenagers, they will be part of a community of mature elders whom they respect and who exercise responsibility in partnership with their parents to guide them to wisdom and full, equal membership in the community.

Why will corporations be so different that they will primarily be communities or villages that are growing people to full membership in the community of mature elders? Because the tribes, communities, or villages defined by blood and biology have been destroyed by our industrial age. Most new communities will be communities by choice. The second criteria will be that they must be self-sufficient because that which determines one's livelihood has the greatest power over a person. There will be communities of friends and church communities as well. However, once the Riddle is considered solved and the worldview of the mature elder is embraced, the corporate and workplace *communities* that will emerge will, in most cases, be the most significant for people.

Of course, nearly everything about corporations will change except the continuation of the production of products and services. When the openly pro-fessed highest priority of the corporation is the good of each and all rather than profits for shareholders, profits will become secondary yet far greater on average. People will be able to commit their entire life and soul to the company because it will be in alignment with nature and their deepest beliefs. The company will be honest and expand its activities into every area of life that is of interest to the peo-ple working in it. It will become more like a healthy tribe than what we now call a "corporation." For instance, there will be an entrepreneurial department focused on assisting each person in the company to move on to the next thing he or she wants to do in his or her life. If it is not a job inside the company, this department may create a new division of the company to go into this business, even if it is something as different from the main services of the company as a blues band. Corporations will feel more like healthy villages or tribes and less like armies.

COMPETITION VS. COOPERATION

As you have surely noticed, the wise and mature elders assume that nature is fundamentally cooperative. If this is so, where does competition fit in? How does it fit in so that the Science-Spirituality contradiction is eliminated?

If nature is fundamentally cooperative, then competition cannot be what is fundamental in nature. It can only be a form of cooperation, that is, a certain kind of cooperation. When we take a closer look, we can see that this is so. It is much like the Earth. It was finally determined that the Earth was curved (round) and flat was seen as a part of the curve but not what was fundamental.

If, like most animals and insects, you are a being who does not have the skill of language and self-consciousness, then you cannot communicate in a direct, cooperative fashion through conversation. Therefore, by default, you are left with only an indirect means of reaching agreement with another. That is what competition is. It is an indirect means of reaching agreement. This is a less mature form of cooperation than direct cooperation through conversation, but it is a more mature form of cooperation than not reaching agreement at all.

In the wild, when two male elks bang their antlers together in a fight to determine which is the strongest, it is an indirect means of reaching an agreement on who will mate with the doe. The strongest male will mate because that is best for the good of all. This "competitive process" is fundamentally a cooperative process. The two male elks are using indirect "elk language" to determine which will mate with the doe for the good of all. If they had the ability we call language, they could have reached an agreement through conversation. Lacking language, they made the decision through an indirect means we call "competition." What is most important is that they reached an agreement, not that they did it indirectly or directly—through conversation or competition. Cooperation for the good of all is what is fundamental.

So what is the relationship between competition and cooperation? Just as flat can only exist within a curved context, competition can only exist within a cooperative context. Because nature is in a constant state of cooperation with itself for the good of itself, competition, like conversation, is a form of cooperation, not something fundamental in nature. It is also a lower form of cooperation; yet it is the highest form of cooperation possible for plants and animals as we see them at this time. Human beings, however, can cooperate directly through the use of our skills of language and self-consciousness. This is a more mature form of cooperation. This is why we prefer agreement over struggle, love over conflict.

SOLVING THE RIDDLE

Does this solve the Science-Spirituality Riddle? I think it does. What does it mean to us in the 1990s? I think it means we have to stop championing competition as the most fundamental principle in nature, the marketplace, society, and any of our relationships with anything or anyone else. We must move out of the adult stage of development and into the wise and mature elder stages as individuals, companies, and societies. We need to consistently use the comprehensive coatrack.

Stop and think about it for a minute. If everyone in a company is giving priority to their own self-interests, being productive will always be a secondary concern. Anything else will also always be a secondary concern at best. This is what is so frustrating to managers. They would prefer to be working with people where being productive was their top priority. A switch to the above worldview, which I refer to as the Relationship Age worldview to distinguish it from the Material Age worldview of the toddler-child-teenager-adult stages in development—will allow this to happen.

If my highest priority is the good of all and I admit this publicly and proudly and everyone in the company sincerely does the same, *we will all have the exact same top priority*. We will be united at the core of our being in all we do. Being productive is then seen not only as a service for the common good but the very best way to serve the good of each including my own bodily self-interests because I no longer see myself as separate from what is around me.

We become much wiser players in the marketplace as well. We no longer operate on the naive myth that the marketplace is fundamentally competitive. If it was, we would all be killing each other. If we are not killing each other, obviously we are operating on some cooperative agreements—like not killing each other—within which competition is occurring as a limited activity. Competition is not fundamental in the marketplace—cooperation is. All the state laws and social agreements are the cooperative rules within which the competition occurs. It is just like a basketball game. The focus may be on the competition, but the rules of the game are what is fundamental and allow for the limited competition to occur. Without agreements, competition without death could not exist. If the two elks did not agree that who mated with the doe was important, there would not have been a basis for competition to reach agreement. And if the good of all was not more important, they would have fought until one died rather than the winner allowing the loser to live and the loser choosing to move on while still in good shape.

Smart businesspeople understand this. They establish cooperative relationships with anyone with whom they may need to do business. When needs arise, they know it is much easier to reach agreements with friends rather than strangers or enemies. If one is able to set up one's shops, get approvals from the state, good terms from the banks and suppliers, etc., it is easier to be successful and to get the time and money to regroup if the competition comes out with a better product or service. If people think the marketplace is fundamentally competitive, they will not as easily see the importance of maintaining quality relationships with people throughout the community, as well as within the company.

What is the best way to do this? Deep inside, we all know at some level that we give priority to the good of all—and that we have no choice in the matter (it is nature). We give priority to our own self-interests only because we think we have to in order to survive. If we have the courage to publicly proclaim that we will give priority to the good of all in all we do, people in this adult society will see us as naive. However, if we have the above understanding of the relationship between competition and cooperation, we ought to be able to be more successful in the marketplace as a mature elder community company.

THE FUTURE IS HERE

Try to imagine a day when all the great spiritual and scientific leaders appear together on global television and say with one voice:

> We hold these truths to be self-evident. The universe is one indivisible whole. Cooperation, not competition, is fundamental in evolution, nature, and spirit. Science and spirituality are now united into one force, and we will from this day forward cooperate for the good of us all. The Science-Spirituality Riddle is solved.
>
> This means that we are all primarily in the business of building wise elder communities within which to raise our children, do business, and deepen our freely cooperative—and friendly competitive—relations with one another for the good of us all and the good of each.

You may think this day is in the distant future. If you know what you are looking for, you will discover that it is already emerging in pockets all over the landscape. The most advanced and substantial mature elder phase group of which I am aware is the Mondragon Enterprises in the Basque region of northern Spain—more than 200 employee-owned enterprises, encompassing 100 industrial enterprises, with 25,000 employees, a bank, 40 schools, a university, health clubs, farms, grocery and retail stores, and so on. This association of for-profit and non-profit organizations is a new kind of nation defined by agreement rather than geography. Their entrepreneurial division has nearly a 100 percent success rate at creating new industrial enterprises using a policy incomprehensible in the adult phase: the riskier the loan the lower the interest rate. Things are very different in the mature elder phase.

The Grameen Bank in Bangladesh is at the other end of the continuum. Whereas Mondragon is high-tech and capital intensive, the Grameen Bank makes loans to the rural poor to begin and sustain small businesses. It currently has over two million borrowers (94 percent women), is growing by 8,000 new borrowers a month, has an average loan size of $100, loans out more than $20 million each month in 34,000 of Bangladesh's 64,000 villages, and has a 98 percent repayment rate over its first eighteen years—better than most major banks. Even more remarkable, people all over the world (Accion and Finca in Central and South America, Freedom From Hunger in Asian and Africa, Opportunity International in South Africa, Russia, and Eastern Europe) and in the USA as well (Working Capital in New England, Lakota Fund in South Dakota, Women's Self-Employment Project for welfare mothers in Chicago) have used the same methods with similar success. Their secret? Five friends co-sign each other's loans so their bonds of friendship, rather than their material possessions, are their collateral. This also bonds them together into mutual help friendship groups.

Ben and Jerry's Homemade, Inc., Timberland Company, Herman Miller, Inc., Lotus Development Corporation, Stride Rite Corporation, and the Calvert Group of mutual funds are some well known, mainstream companies attempting to move into the realm of mature elder community companies. There are many more not so well known.

Just as the mature elder phase is a wiser way to be a human being, it is a wiser way to be a company or a society of any kind. In words of their own choosing, people everywhere have moved beyond the Science-Spirituality Riddle into the wisdom of the mature elder. It is not an ideological or developmental choice. When you use your three dimensional comprehensive coatrack, you realize that it is the next phase of the evolutionary process. It contains less pain and more joy in all directions. Once this is understood, it will be impossible to resist seeking to be a part of it.

Given my organization's dynamics and culture,
how can I best understand key leverage points for change?

Part Two: The Corporate Community

Since this edited collection is a business book, this section begins an exploration into the creation of communities in the workplace. One of the paths to organizational community is by developing learning organizations, cultures of continuous inquiry and dialogue, as described by MIT's Peter Senge in his book *The Fifth Discipline.*

Senge opens this segment with an essay on quality communities of learning. Editor Gozdz examines core competencies in developing learning communities. Juanita Brown and David Isaacs identify specific processes, offering action guidelines for building community in organizations. Stephanie Ryan focuses on learning in community with others, building on Peck's *Four Stages Model.*

Barbara Shipka looks at structures and assumptions behind the development of work teams, particularly in technical organizations. Joel and Michelle Levey explain how to build the dynamic synergy of quality relationships, teamwork, personal mastery, and organizational support necessary for creating community in the workplace. Bill Veltrop calls for alliances of change agents and visionaries in reinventing the game of organizational change.

Each of these nine authors brings their own "flavor" of wisdom to this section, offering promise for the workplace for tomorrow.

Peter M. Senge
is director of the Center for Organizational Learning at MIT's Sloan School of Management. He is the author of the widely acclaimed book, *The Fifth Discipline: The Art and Practice of the Learning Organization*, and a co-author of *The Fifth Discipline Fieldbook*. He is also a founding partner of the management consulting and training firm, Innovation Associates.

Senge received a B.S. in engineering from Stanford University, an M.S. in social systems modeling, and a Ph.D. in management from MIT. He lives with his wife and two children in central Massachusetts.

This essay is reprinted with permission of *Executive Excellence* newsletter; telephone (801) 375-4060.

4

Creating Quality Communities

Peter M. Senge

Along with total quality management and process reengineering, "organizational learning" has become a buzzword. But there is no such thing as a "learning organization." Like every linguistic creation, this phrase is a double-edged sword that can be empowering or tranquilizing.

When I speak of a learning organization, I'm articulating a view that involves us—the observers—as much as the observed in a common system. We are taking a stand for a vision, for creating an organization we would like to work within and which can thrive in a world of increasing interdependency and change. It is not what the vision is, but what the vision does that matters.

FIVE PRINCIPLES

Five operating principles are emerging. These principles are neither rigid nor all-encompassing.

1. The learning organization embodies new capabilities. A learning organization must be grounded in a culture based on transcendent human values of love, wonder, humility, and compassion; a set of practices for generative conversation and coordinated action; and a capacity to see and work with the flow of life as a system.

In learning organizations, cultural norms defy our business tradition. Acceptance of others as legitimate beings (love) replaces the traditional will toward homogeneity. The ever-surprising manifestations of the world show up as opportunities to grow, as opposed to frustrating breakdowns for which somebody must take the blame (wonder). People understand that life is not condensable, that any model is an operational simplification always ready for improvement (humility). And when they encounter behaviors that they neither understand nor condone, people appreciate that such actions arise from viewpoints and forces that are, in some sense, as valid as the viewpoints and forces that influence their own behaviors (compassion).

Learning organizations are spaces for generative conversations and concerted action. In them, language functions as a device for connection, invention, and coordination. People can talk from their hearts and connect with one another in the spirit of dialogue. Their dialogue weaves a common fabric and connects them at a deep level of being. When people talk and listen to each other this way, they create a field of alignment that produces tremendous power to invent new realities in conversation, and to bring about these new realities in action.

One reason the myth of the great leader is so appealing is that it absolves us of responsibility for developing leadership capabilities more broadly. In learning organizations, the burden is shifted: a perceived need for leadership (symptom) can be met by developing leadership capacities throughout the organization (fundamental solution), not just by relying on a hero leader (symptomatic solution). Success in finding a hero leader reinforces a belief in the group's powerlessness, thus making the fundamental solution more difficult.

In learning organizations, people are always inquiring into the systemic consequences of their actions, rather than just focusing on local consequences. They understand the interdependencies underlying complex issues and act with perceptiveness and leverage. They are patient in seeking deeper understanding rather than striking out to "fix" problem symptoms—because they know that most fixes are temporary at best, and often result in more severe problems later.

Learning organizations are both more generative and more adaptive than traditional organizations. Because of their commitment, openness, and ability to deal with complexity, people find security not in stability but in the dynamic equilibrium between holding on and letting go of beliefs, assumptions, and certainties. What they know takes a second place to what they can learn, and simplistic answers are always less important than penetrating questions.

2. Learning organizations are built by communities of servant leaders. Leadership takes on new meanings in learning organizations. The leaders are those building the new organization and its capabilities. They walk ahead, regardless of their position or hierarchical authority. Such leadership is inevitably collective.

Our conventional notions of leadership are embedded in myths of heros—great individuals severed from their communities who make their way through individual will, determination, and cleverness. While there may be much to admire in such persons, our attachment to individualistic notions of leadership may block the emergence of the leadership of teams, and, ultimately, organizations and societies that can lead themselves. While we wait for the great leader who will save the day, we surrender the confidence and power needed to make progress toward learning organizations.

As the myth of the hero leader fades, a new myth of teams and communities that can lead themselves is emerging. But the emergence of collective leadership does not mean that there are no "leadership positions" like CEO or president in learning organizations. Management hierarchies are often functional.

The clash of collective leadership and hierarchical leadership poses a core dilemma for learning organizations. This dilemma can't be reconciled given traditional notions of hierarchal leaders as the people "in control" or "in charge." For this implies that those "below" are not in control. A hierarchical value system then arises that, as Analog Devices CEO Ray Stata puts it, "holds the person higher up the hierarchy as somehow a more important being."

Alternatively, the dilemma can become a source of energy and imagination through the idea of "servant leadership," people who lead because the choose to serve, both to serve one another and to serve a higher purpose. Servant leadership offers a unique mix of idealism and pragmatism. At one level, the concept is an ideal, appealing to deeply held beliefs in the dignity and self-worth of all people and the democratic principle that a leader's power flows from those led. But it is also highly practical. It has been proven in military campaigns that the only leader whom soldiers will reliably follow when their lives are on the line is the leader who is both competent and whose soldiers believe is committed to their well-being.

3. Learning arises through performance and practice. It was common in native American cultures to set aside sacred spaces for learning. So too today, learning is too important to leave to chance. It will not be adequate to offer training and hope that people will apply new insights and methods. Nor will help from consultants be sufficient to bring about the fundamental shifts in thinking and interacting and the new capabilities needed to sustain those shifts. It will be necessary to redesign work if progressive ideas are to find their way into the mainstream of management practice.

A guiding idea for redesigning work will be virtual learning spaces or "managerial practice fields." The learning that occurs in sports teams and the performing arts is embedded in continuous movement between a practice field and a performance field. It is impossible to imagine a chamber music ensemble or a theater troupe learning without rehearsal, just as it is impossible to imagine a championship basketball team that never practices. Yet, that is exactly what happens in most organizations. People only perform. They rarely get to practice, especially together.

Several design principles come together in creating effective practice fields: (1) the learner learns what the learner wants to learn; (2) the people who need to learn are the people who have the power to take action; (3) learning often occurs best through "play," through interactions in a practice field where it is safe to experiment and reflect; (4) learning often requires altering the flow of time— slowing down the action to enable reflection on tacit assumptions and counterproductive ways of interacting, or speeding up time to reveal how current decisions can create unanticipated problems in the long term; (5) learning often requires compressing space so that the learner can see the effects of his or her actions in other parts of a larger system (computer simulations may be needed);

(6) this practice field must look like the action domain of the learners; and (7) the learning space must be shamelessly integrated into the work space for an ongoing cycle of reflection, experimentation, and action.

4. Process and content are inseparable. Because our culture is so caught up in separation, we have been led, according to David Bohm, "to seek some fantasy of action that would end the fragmentation in the content (of our thought) while leaving the fragmentation in the actual process of thinking untouched." So, for example, executives seek to improve fragmented policies and strategies without addressing the fragmented and competitive relationship among the managers who formulated the strategies and policies. Consultants propose new process-oriented designs without addressing the mode of thinking and interacting that cause us to focus on things rather than processes in the first place. Management educators treat either "technical" issues like operations, marketing or finance, or behavioral issues like culture, decision making, or change.

The separation between the issues we are interested in and the processes we might use to learn about them may be the primary obstacle to potential breakthroughs. For example, in one field project, the team addressed the company culture of punishment for bad news. But, rather than blaming the "culture" or "management," the members of the group explored their own reactions to hearing about problems, especially from subordinates. They began to surface their fears about mistakes and their automatic reactions and defensive responses, like heightened competitiveness or a tendency to cover up the problems. Gradually, they reached some deep insight into their "culture of punishment" and their own role in sustaining it.

5. Learning is dangerous. Learning occurs between a fear and a need. On the one hand, we feel the need to change if we are to accomplish our goals. On the other hand, we feel the anxiety of facing the unknown and unfamiliar. To learn significant things, we must suspend some basic notions about our worlds and ourselves. That is a frightening proposition for the ego.

Conventional learning is transactional. There is a learner who has a certain way of operating and a certain knowledge. If this knowledge proves to be incomplete or ineffective, the learner may drop part of it, changing some of it, or add some new ideas to it. This may be an accurate description of how we learn to find better bargains or make better investments, but it fails to get to the heart of the learning involved when we question deep beliefs and mental models.

The problem with this view is that the self is not separate from the ideas and assumptions that form it. Our mental models are not like pieces of clothing that we can put on or take off. Our mental models are not like pieces of clothing that we can put on or take off. They are basic constitutive structures of our personality. Most of the time, we are our mental methods.

The learning required in becoming a learning organization is "transformational learning." Static notions of who we are must be checked at the door. In transformational learning, there are no problems "out there" to be solved independent of how we think and act in articulating these problems. Such learning is not ultimately about tools and techniques. It is about who we are. We often prefer to fail again and again rather than let go of some core belief or master assessment.

This explains the paradox of learning. Even when we claim we want to learn, we normally mean that we to want acquire some new tool or understanding. When we see that to learn, we must be willing to look foolish, to let another teach us, learning doesn't always look so good anymore. It is little coincidence that virtually all spiritual disciplines, regardless of culture or religious setting, are practiced in communities. Only with the support, insight, and fellowship of a community can we face the dangers of learning meaningful things.

DEVELOPING LEADERSHIP COMMUNITIES

Once we realize that building learning organizations is grounded in developing leadership communities, a core question remains: "How do such communities form, grow, and become influential?" Ford's Vic Leo suggests a three-stage architecture of engagement: (1) finding those predisposed to this work, (2) core community-building activities, and (3) practical experimentation and testing.

1. Predisposition. It's easy to waste time trying to make changes with people who do not want, or are not ready for, such changes. For example, when people reflect on how they become involved in systemic thinking and organization learning, they discover that they are drawn to "systems perspective" by academic training or life experiences. They are skeptical of conventional strategies for improvement—reorganizations, training management programs, speeches from "on high." Predisposition is important, especially in the early stages of building momentum when there are few practical results to point to. Those not predisposed to systems thinking should not be excluded, but they may play less importance at the outset. If they are not included, because they raise difficult questions or disagree with certain ideas, what starts as a learning community can degenerate into a cult.

2. Community-building activities. How those predisposed begin to know each other and to work together involves a cycle of community-building activities and practical experimentation. The former must be intense enough and open-ended enough to foster trusting personal relationships and to lay a foundation of knowledge and skills. The latter must offer realistic starting steps in applying new knowledge and skills to important issues.

For example, at the Learning Center, we explore the tools, methods, and personal dimensions of systems thinking, often resulting in a "piercing experience," where the systems perspective begins to take on a deeper meaning and the nature of the journey ahead becomes clearer. On this journey, there are no "teachers" with correct answers, only guides with different areas of expertise and experience that may help along the way. Each of us gives up our own certainty and recognizes our interdependency within the larger community of practitioners. The honest, humble, and purposeful "I don't know" grounds our vision for learning organizations.

3. Practical experimentation and testing. What nurtures the unfolding community is active experimentation where people wrestle with crucial strategic and operational issues. In our work, we undertake learning projects that focus on key issues, because of the motivation for learning and because of the potential for significant improvement in business results.

Currently, two "practice field" projects are underway: dialogue projects and learning laboratory projects. Dialogue projects focus directly on the deeper patterns of communication that underlie whatever issues are being confronted by a management team. Learning laboratory projects focus on areas such as new product development, management accounting and control systems, and services management.

For example, a team at Ford, responsible for creating the next generation Lincoln Continental, is also creating a New Car Development Learning Laboratory. The project has two objectives: to improve the effectiveness of the team in its current project and to develop better theory and tools that will lead to broader systemic thinking in product development at Ford. Early returns show unprecedented levels of internal coordination.

The learning laboratories and dialogue projects all follow the operating principles. What started as a "practice field" has led to penetrating insights into critical business issues. The practice fields are becoming integrated into everyday company activities. When we started the pilot projects, we had a vision of transforming organizations through learning processes focused on significant business problems. We saw practice fields as a place where teams could meet to reflect on structures, identify counterproductive behaviors, experiment with alternative strategies, and design solutions for actual work settings. The core of the projects were "management flight simulators," computer simulations based on systems thinking. The simulators would enable managers to "compress time and space" to better understand the long-term consequences of their decisions and to reflect on their assumptions.

We find that when people have a practice field where they can relate to each other safely and playfully, where they can openly explore difficult issues, they begin to see their learning community as a new way of managing.

NEW ALTERNATIVES

Building learning organizations is not an individual task. It demands a shift that goes all the way to the core of our culture. We have drifted into a culture that fragments our thoughts, that detaches the word from the self and self from a community. We have gained control of our environment, but we have lost our artistic edge. We are so focused on our security that we don't see the price we pay: living in bureaucratic organization where the wonder and joy of learning have no place. Thus we are losing the spaces to dance with the ever-changing patterns of life. We need to invent a new learning model for business, education, health care, government, and family. This invention will come from the patient, concerted efforts of communities of people invoking aspiration and wonder. As these communities manage to produce fundamental changes, we will regain our memory—the memory of the community nature of the self and the poetic nature of language and the world—the memory of the whole.

Kazimierz "Kaz" Gozdz is a specialist in creating sustainable community in organizations. He is the founder and principal of Gozdz & Associates, an organization development firm which supports groups and organizations in incorporating new paradigm business perspectives.

Since 1986 he has worked with M. Scott Peck and The Foundation for Community Encouragement, Inc. to extend Peck's original model of community building, creating a technology for community making applicable within organizations. He has collaborated with Michael Ray of Stanford's Graduate School of Business to co-create The New Paradigm Business Course. He is working with Peter Senge at MIT's Organizational Learning Center to elaborate the link between learning organizations and creating sustainable learning communities.

Gozdz has managed a manufacturing facility, worked in the automotive industry, and owned a specialty services company. He has an undergraduate degree in chemistry and business administration as well as an M.A. in transpersonal psychology.

5

Creating Learning Organizations Through Core Competence in Community Building

Kazimierz Gozdz

Because businesses vary in complexity, maturity, size, vision, and culture, there are many paths to creating a learning organization—an enterprise defined by Peter Senge as one "that is continually expanding its capacity to create its future." One of these many paths is through developing a strategic core competence in community building.

Through my work facilitating Community Building Workshops for The Foundation for Community Encouragement, collaborating with M. Scott Peck to expand his original theories on community, and teaching businesses to embody community, I became convinced that living communities need learning organizations in which to grow. As I pursued the development of organizational forms that can sustain an experience of community, I found that Senge and others seeking to create learning organizations are having a parallel experience, but in reverse: they are seeking forms of community that are compatible with learning and business.

Intrigued by this confluence of ideas, I began to formulate a model for business that incorporates and extends both Peck's and Senge's visions. Imagine this developmental process as a map. It focuses on developing an organizational core competence that sustains both learning and community over time. Such a core competence requires the mastery of specific aspects of community that, taken together, comprise a system of skills for sustaining learning.

Sustaining community, however, also requires that the organization prepare itself for, and nurture itself through, stages of growth, each with its own set of developmental challenges. With our map, we can anticipate new challenges that arise as a natural result of a community's growth process. We can prepare organizational responses that optimize growth while minimizing chaos.

Of course, as with all maps, this one can only attempt to describe the territory. Individual cases will almost never match the map, as pioneers in the days of the early West can attest. Organizational leaders will need to pay close attention to the reality of their organization's actual growth process.

How Learning, Community and Spirituality Are Related

To grasp the essence of a core competence in community building, we need a systems perspective. Though composed of numerous parts, a community is something larger their sum. Some of the elements that characterize a mature, living community are: inclusiveness of diverse people and information, semi-permeable boundaries, collective intelligence, flexibility, discipline, and a systems-oriented paradigm. The benefits of corporate community include a profound sense of trust and collaboration, leading to a coherent organizational vision; there is an openness to creativity and innovation. Authentic community makes love in the workplace possible by creating a group of all leaders who embody a profound sense of mutual respect and have the ability to fight gracefully while transcending differences.

When I say a learning organization has a core competence in community building, I mean that it has a central commitment and capacity to learn and grow, throughout its life cycle. It is a living community that learns Senge states that for a learning organization "it is not enough merely to survive. 'Survival learning' or what is often termed 'adaptive learning' is important—indeed it is necessary. But for a learning organization, 'adaptive learning' must be joined by 'generative learning,' learning that enhances our capacity to create." The model described in this essay is my approach to actualizing this vision.

Peck, a theologian and psychiatrist, has articulated the foundation of a psychology which includes several dimensions of personal and social development. I have sought to integrate these dimensions into a system of growth and development for learning organizations. The core competence model for business, based in part on Peck's perspectives, is first and foremost transpersonal. That is, it includes aspects of life that are spiritual, psychological, and physical. The business that is unwilling to embrace the transpersonal or spiritual aspects of community will disable itself—becoming unable to nurture that spirit over time.

When a group seeks to learn as a community, it simultaneously seeks psychological and spiritual growth for the organization. Community building is a process of learning and spiritual growth. Senge points out that learning has varying qualities. When a community probes its deepest assumptions, exploration invariably challenges the spiritual foundations around which it is organized. Having these qualities, learning is not only generative, it becomes synonymous with spiritual growth. Such learning is a lifelong task beginning with the organization's birth and continuing throughout its life cycle.

ASPECTS OF CORE COMPETENCE IN COMMUNITY BUILDING

Sustainability of a living sense of community—and of learning—depends on a balanced approach to the growth of three essential, interrelated aspects: the experience of interconnectedness, sustainable collective intelligence (mind), and learning architecture (body).

The Experience of Interconnectedness

I recently interviewed a group at a high-tech computer company that once had a very alive sense of community. Everyone experienced it. Productivity and learning were phenomenal. Results were so good, in fact, that management gave the group a million dollars to build a new facility and to add more resources. A year later, the group no longer felt like a community and everyone was afraid to say so. Management was pretending that all was as it had been, and evidence to the contrary was shunned as traitorous.

In examining the history of their process, it was easy to see that no effort had been expended to keep alive the resource that had made the group so successful: its spirit of community. It was just assumed that the sense of community would automatically transfer to new conditions as long as management financed an expansion of the project. A collective spirit of community is highly prized in organizations. Yet, more often than not, actions to preserve this spirit actually drive it out instead. In this case it was largely "ignored to death."

The opposite can also be true—where managers "control" for a sense of community. Not knowing that the experience of community transcends control, some managers apply traditional management methods to the community's detriment. They ask: How is community defined? How can it be measured? What results it will produce? Often, this kind of leadership leaves organizations starving for an authentic connection.

Because of its associations with religion, the idea that there is a "spirit" in community can become controversial. But the spirit referred to here is non-religious.

Almost anyone who has survived a significant crisis in a group knows this spirit of community. Starting a new organization, enduring a tragedy like the death of a close colleague, a natural disaster such as a hurricane, flood, or earthquake—all can lead to a spirit of interconnectedness. Most often, community arises as the result of a group's need for survival.

In business, this spirit emerges primarily during crisis. It can be translated into a culture which deliberately seeks to foster community . Rather than depending on haphazard events such as crises, a team can nurture its capability to create experiences of interconnectedness through authentic communication. Paradoxically, the team does this by acknowledging differences.

The typical organization is actually what Peck called a "pseudo-community," an organization unwilling or unable to acknowledge its differences. Steps in creating the experience of interconnectedness can begin with authentic and vulnerable communication, the use of "I" statements, avoidance of generalizations,

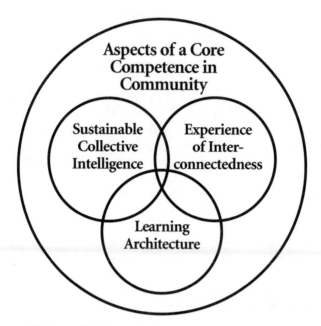

Figure 1: Source: *The Systems Thinker*

and a willingness to hear multiple viewpoints. A group can be taught this discipline—learning to acknowledge and transcend these differences. If members are willing to learn to face reality together, they can develop true connectedness. Through such a process the organization can become aware of its barriers to true community.

In my work with business organizations, I have observed a recurring phenomenon: When teams and organizations manage to experience interconnectedness, complete with its benefits of authentic communication, safety, and intimacy, they are so enthusiastic about these benefits that they try to stay in this state continually. But after a while, they notice that their attempts actually create less community. The spirit of community, which manifests as a sense of interconnectedness, is not a permanent state. It ebbs and flows with the community's life cycle.

Sustainable Collective Intelligence

The second aspect of core competence, sustainable collective intelligence, is the organization's ability to translate the experience of interconnectedness into organizational learning. It is an integration between the process of creating collective intelligence and accomplishing the tasks on a group's agenda.

Although the experience or spirit of community is essential to core competence, it is not sufficient unto itself. If the group cannot convert collective intelligence into organizational action it can easily become a bonded support group rather than a high performing learning community. Sustainable collective intelligence represents the organization's ability to sustain itself as a learning community while simultaneously acting and making decisions with the group intelligence, surpassing the sum of the IQ of individual members.

A currently popular method for developing collective intelligence in learning organizations is the dialogue process introduced by physicist David Bohm. This process focuses on creating shared meaning through both surfacing and examining assumptions within a group. It emphasizes the importance of rational and largely cognitive group learning. As described by Bohm, the Greek words "dia" and "logos" create a new picture for what collective intelligence in a group can be. He says: "The picture or image that this derivation suggests is of a stream of meaning flowing among and through us and between us. This will make possible a flow of meaning in the whole group, out of which will come some new understanding."

Bohm's approach to collective intelligence is effective yet limited in two important ways. First, it produces temporary rather than sustainable intelligence. Second, it limits the range of emotion within a group, its focus being on cognition. An alternative process which addresses both these weaknesses is to use a community-building process that incorporates both Bohm's cognitive emphasis and Peck's focus on authentic feeling states and the four stages of community building.

Making collective intelligence part of everyday work life requires a skill that neither technology has developed; shifting back and forth on demand from generating collective intelligence to attending to the organization's everyday work agenda. By emphasizing this skill neither the intense feeling states of a community-building process nor the disciplined demands of creating shared meaning in dialogue stand at odds with the accomplishment of work. In short, rapidly shifting between the group's "head" and "heart" allows for a collective intelligence which can be put into action.

Chris Argyris and others have described organizational "defense routines" that are obstacles to collective intelligence in organizations. These defenses tend to prevent groups from dealing with the actual issues at hand and can be highly charged emotionally. Group defenses (like personal defenses) tend to have deep roots. Neither emotionally processing the issues at hand nor identifying actual causes suffices because overcoming obstacles to learning entails dealing with both competently. By disciplining themselves to move rapidly and easily from working on interpersonal awareness to organizational tasks, the group intelligence can more thoroughly uncover its collective barrier to learning.

The experience of interconnectedness and collective intelligence are cornerstones on which the systems and structures of a learning organization are built. Collective thought and action is a requirement for groups to change the complex architecture which either supports or discourages community.

Learning Architecture

The learning architecture of community consists primarily of the systems and structures that sustain memory and learning in the organization over time.

Examples include the compensation system, the career development process, style of leadership, methods for distribution of power and governance, what George Por has called "learning system architecture," and even the physical structure of the site. Both visible and invisible structures, systems, and forces affect a group's ability to experience itself as an authentic community.

Unless these forces are acknowledged and examined, the organization will stay trapped in the pseudo-community stage. Structures will prohibit its maturation. No amount of attention to interconnectedness, collective intelligence, team spirit, or learning will be productive if insight into unjust or unethical structures are not translated into action.

This is why Peck has suggested that the only obstacle to true community in organizations is politics. Without commitment to true growth, a community-building process leads to disempowerment and the loss of hope. Community routinely dies in organizations where the politics of the organization cannot or will not allow real change. Peck's insight must be backed by the an acknowledgment that complex systems are not readily changed. Even with commitment from an organization to change, it must do so as a system. It is here that Senge's tools for mapping systems dynamics and focusing on system leverage change are most critical to sustaining community.

But how will an organization know if its systems are growing toward maturity and health? Based on Peck's attributes of true community, I often use this list as a diagnostic framework in organizations:

- Is the organization moving toward greater inclusivity of information, people, and ideas?
- Is the organization sharing power effectively, becoming more consensual and democratic?
- At the organizational level, is the community becoming more capable of contemplative learning?
- Is the organization a safe place, a practice field for exploring each person's full potential?
- Can the group fight gracefully?
- Is the group moving toward or away from becoming a group of all leaders?
- Is there a spirit of interconnectedness present?

All the above indicators are related to functions and processes that systems and structures create and support. While each question points toward an element for creating authentic community, their power is significantly enhanced when these elements are seen as a system.

Senge points out that invisible structures generate patterns of behavior. According to systems thinkers, these invisible structures are more permanent than the events they shape. It is for this reason that intervention at the learning architecture level can be more powerful than simply creating a feeling of community. More often than not, an organization that is having difficulty sustaining a sense of community is operating with systems that create fragmentation or disempowerment. The reason for this will become more clear when we discuss the nature of paradigms.

The learning architecture aspect of a core competence in community building has, as a basic tool, the capability to map and change system-level forces. Such competency would involve, for example, identifying, reinforcing, and balancing feedback loops, system delays, and exponential growth patterns. Even when the organization's leadership politically backs the enhancement of community, if the enterprise cannot gain the competence to create change, it can inadvertently destroy hope. Understanding how the organization's learning architecture enhances or blocks community is critical to realizing the trust, joy and flexibility of community.

With the actualizing of these three aspects of core competence—interconnectedness, sustainable collective intelligence, and learning architecture—the organization takes its first steps in becoming a community. Unlike other organizations facing challenges to survive and thrive, the organization operating as a community can do so more competently. These first steps lead to an extensive growth process beginning with questioning the current business paradigm, adopting a commitment to discipline and mastery, and finally leading to embracing a call to social responsibility.

THREE DEVELOPMENTAL CHALLENGES TO SUSTAINING COMMUNITY

A core competence of community in the workplace must be nurtured through three significant stages of growth. By definition, growth necessitates a certain amount of pain. When we grow as individuals, we have to give up the innocence of childhood in order to meet the challenges of adulthood, and later face the loss of physical agility and health to embrace our dying process. We cannot avoid these transitions as we mature—and neither can a community.

If the organizational community avoids the pain of growth, it stops the learning process. But if it consciously embraces the three learning challenges, it finds opportunities to grow spiritually, psychologically, and competitively.

Paradigm Shift—Embracing Wholeness

Businesses cannot sustain themselves as communities or as learning organizations unless they become capable of embracing a paradigm of wholeness, a paradigm compatible with a living systems perspective. The skills of the learning organization and of community building can be temporarily grafted onto an old worldview, which rejects a spiritual sense of life, seeks answers in linear causality, and fragments system problems into symptoms for easier comprehension. But such a transplant will not "take" permanently. Community is a living system, and the organization will see that it dies if it is treated like a machine or factor of production—behavior the current mechanistic worldview reinforces.

The first developmental stage in sustaining a core competence in community is to wrestle with the assumptions of its prevailing mechanistic paradigm. Larger than individual and organizational mental models, a paradigm determines what an individual, organization and an individual can or cannot learn and remain part of a community. A paradigm contains the operating assumptions of the corporation's prevailing world view, translated into rules by which issues and solutions are experienced and evaluated.

In his ground-breaking work on paradigms, *The Structure of Scientific Revolutions*, Thomas Kuhn revealed how a scientific discipline (in his case, a group of practitioners in the hard sciences) creates a picture of how the world works and defends it via an invisible process that pre-selects what is perceived as valid, significant enough to merit attention, and meaningful enough to command resources. He showed that, more often than not, a group holding onto old ideas and values will die conserving these rather than risking the learning required for change. The only technology Kuhn offered to remedy this situation was to wait for people to die off over time. Unlike these ill fated groups, businesses can use the technology of community building to transition between paradigms consciously.

Michael Ray, co-editor of *The New Paradigm in Business*, has been at the forefront of articulating an alternative view that is just beginning to emerge. He states:

> ...doing business from our most profound inner awareness and in connection with the consciousness of others and the earth. Simply put, this means that we each acknowledge that we have inner wisdom and authority and that others have it too. And as...virtually all scientists operating from the new paradigm tell us, there is a wholeness and connectedness between all living things. Everything and everyone is connected in some way to everything else.

Senge suggests that systems thinking must become integral to a learning organization's culture and, further, that "direct experience" of the "indivisible wholeness" of systems is critical for individuals becoming systems thinkers. Developing core competence in community building calls for organizations to model community as a living system rather than a mechanically controllable program, to experience chaos as a process that is creative rather than destructive, and to embrace diversity as a pathway to an underlying wholeness.

There is a clash between the assumptions operating within almost every company in the West and the assumptions within those few that Ray feels are moving toward a new business paradigm. Our traditional organizations create and legitimize paradigms. Since this happens in groups, acts of individual leadership are ineffective for changing a paradigm. It is a community-building process that must challenge and transform a collective worldview. Senge uses the term "metanoia" to describe a "fundamental shift in mind," a generative learning that radically affects an individual's worldview.

Ray and I have been exploring community-based teaching methodologies whereby individuals could "try on" new paradigm assumptions in a practice field created in the safety of a learning community. In community, a paradigm becomes more apparent, in fact, it becomes open to challenge. Learning in community solves the puzzle for business on how to avoid a premature organizational death brought about by holding onto an expiring worldview. This learning process offers a technology for shifting paradigms effectively.

Few communities can do this quickly, or through just one effort. The change is more likely to occur over years or even decades; therefore, the community's task is to engage in a process of discipline and mastery to facilitate this change over time.

Discipline and Mastery—The Journey Few Travel

"Life is difficult," says Peck. "This is a great truth, one of the greatest truths. It is a great truth because once we truly see this truth, we transcend it. Once we truly know that life is difficult—once we truly understand and accept it—then life is no longer difficult. Because once it is accepted, the fact that life is difficult no longer matters."

And so it is with sustaining community. A learning organization that embraces community as a core competence requires day-in and day-out practice of discipline and mastery, so that the community and the individuals within it cannot help but move toward optimum professional competency, joy, and aligned organizational purpose.

No learning organization is fully mature, fully in community at its birth. Life in our organizations is significantly more ordinary than a constant state of generative learning or communal bliss will allow. No organization can constantly create a positive learning environment or always feel like a "family." The evolution of a living community will include turbulent times as we encounter one another's and the organization's shadow sides. The learning organization will constantly cycle through the stages of pseudo-community, chaos, emptiness, and glimpses of community as it grows toward wholeness.

The primary task during the paradigm-shift stage was to develop a sense of connectedness that emerges from shared vision and purpose. At this stage, the group must move beyond the excitement of bonding and interconnectedness in community (akin to what Peck called the myth of romantic love in individual relationships.) Signs of health in community rest not in how interconnected and bonded the group feels, but how flexibly and responsively it moves from its existing reality toward the one it desires.

Like Peck, Senge sees learning as a lifelong program of study—what he calls "discipline." He explains, "By 'discipline,' I do not mean 'enforced order' or 'means of punishment,' but a body of theory and technique that must be put into practice. A discipline is a developmental path for acquiring certain skills or competencies. As with any discipline...anyone can develop proficiency through practice." Senge has elaborated five central disciplines for the learning organization: systems thinking, team learning, team vision, personal mastery, and mental models. These disciplines, like sustainable community, are developmental. A core competence in community can be added as a sixth discipline.

In order to help individuals master lifelong learning, Peck developed a four-part system of techniques—an algorithm for problem solving, which I have applied as a process for organizations or groups to become masterful at any discipline. When applied as an algorithm for problem solving, these four steps become a tool for gaining mastery of discipline itself:

• *Delay gratification*: In any situation, foster the ability to hold tension, seeing the actual reality of a situation without jumping to problem solving. Embrace larger and more complex system truths, avoiding the simplicity of linear causes and fixing the obvious.

• *Dedicate to the truth*: Boldly acknowledge what learning the organization needs to pursue. Seek to embrace unpleasant truths. Acknowledge the gap between intend and actual outcomes, so as to make possible the removal of barriers to learning.

• *Assume responsibility*: Practice a fearless willingness to act as a learner, move beyond blame or judgment of self and others for the purpose of creating improvement. Take responsibility for change.

• *Balance learning*: Modulate or bracket an attachment to learning, real growth occurs in cycles which must be respected. Foster the practice of embracing the wholeness of what is unfolding. Empty of attachment to individual actions and nurture well-being over accomplishment.

Any organization or individual willing to master a discipline, in the way Senge uses the term, can apply this four-step learning system. For a community, it can be applied to the mastery of all three aspects of core competence: interconnectedness, sustainable collective intelligence and learning architecture.

Social Responsibility

Once a learning organization has embraced a paradigm of wholeness and established itself as a sustainable learning community, it will find itself called to the responsibilities of the larger society. This final developmental stage is really just a starting place for another level of growth.

Community, which is comprised of multiple levels of systems, always acts interdependently. Each level, while a whole system in itself, is also a part of a more comprehensive whole. For example, the individual self is a whole, and simultaneously part of the learning organization. The self and the organization are part of a larger whole: society.

The developmental challenge for individuals, organizations, and societies is to understand the interdependence of these levels and act to develop each appropriately while keeping the whole in mind. With experiences of interconnectedness to inform its view, a community will undoubtedly discover that its survival is linked to that of the larger society. If the organization has achieved a level of maturity and has integrated the prior two stages, it can take systems-oriented actions. Otherwise, it will again be treating symptoms rather than root causes of problems.

An organization at this level of development will discover that its impediments to community tend to be drawn from the larger social system. For example, the interlocking systems of oppression—racism, classism, sexism, and

Three Systems Levels of Community

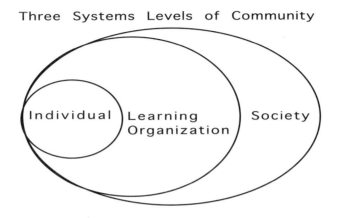

Figure 2: Source: *The Systems Thinker*

homophobia—will emerge as obstacles. Many organizations are surprised by the level of tension and struggle intrinsic to reaching mature community. Community is paradoxical; the more spiritually mature it becomes, the deeper the questions and concerns.

The fully mature community will once again encounter turbulent times, because this level of development is just the beginning. Once individuals reach this level of social awareness, the organization will need to re-clarify its fundamental vision, values, and purpose. It will require this new clarity to balance its fundamental vision against its need to act on awareness of social issues.

CONCLUSION

Learning, community building, and spiritual growth are interdependent, like systems in a body or an organization. A business seeking to become a learning organization can choose to take the path of developing a core competence in community. If it does, however, it will be embarking on a complex journey. The reward is to become involved in the larger world's problems.

This map for sustaining community outlines critical aspects of core competence needed to create and sustain community. It also describes the developmental challenges to growth that the community will face as it matures.

Embracing this journey can and does provide a means whereby a pseudo-community, or old paradigm business, can transform itself into a more authentic community. Learning can become a central competitive advantage and also lead to personal and organizational satisfaction far beyond what is possible in the absence of a spirit of community.

Juanita Brown
is president of Whole Systems
Associates, an international consulting consortium dedicated to strategic
change management. She has
worked with corporate clients
throughout the United States, Europe,
and Latin America, including Kraft
General Foods, Procter & Gamble,
Scandinavian Airlines System, Exxon,
Hewlett-Packard, and the National
Bank of Mexico.

David Isaacs
is president of Clearing Comm-unica-
tions, a business and organizational
strategy consulting firm. He uses his
broad and varied experience as a
line executive and personal coach to
assist leadership teams in managing
crisis and transition, developing a
clear sense of longer range purpose
and vision, creating effective strategy,
and fostering communications that
support the organization's primary
goals and objectives.

Juanita and David served jointly as Senior Associates of the Norwegian
Center for Leadership Development and as Senior Affiliates of the MIT
Organizational Learning Center. This article is adapted from a chapter appear-
ing in *The Fifth Discipline Fieldbook* by Peter Senge, Art Kleiner, Charlotte
Roberts, Richard Ross, and Bryan Smith. New York: Doubleday/Currency, 1994.

6

Building Corporations as Communities: The Best of Both Worlds

Juanita Brown & David Isaacs

Let's begin with a simple experiment. Take a moment to think of the word "corporation." What images, words, and feelings, come to mind? Now, take another moment to allow the word "community" to appear on your mental screen. What images, thoughts or associations does that word suggest?

We have invited senior executives, middle managers, and line personnel from major corporations, as well as members of the private, public, and non-profit sectors throughout the United States, Europe, and Latin America to join in the same experiment. No matter what part of the organizational world enters the dialogue, the responses are surprisingly consistent. "Corporation" brings up images of authority, bureaucracy, competition, power and profit. It evokes pictures of well-oiled machines where order prevails and the chain of command is reinforced by superiors directing subordinates. People are reminded of battle strategy and gamesmanship.

By comparison, people describe very different images of "community." Some talk of worthwhile projects where people contribute mutual help and volunteer support. Others think of town meetings, democracy, and personal responsibility for the common good. Still others talk about commitment, team spirit, and fun. They speak of caring about future generations as well as maintaining a healthy environment. People refer to learning and education, quality of life, and cooperation. Whatever the specifics may be, "community" images evoke a richer, more involved sense of ourselves in relationship to a larger whole.

We may want to ask ourselves if the images, associations, and feelings that are implicit in many contemporary views of the corporation are the ones we want to guide and motivate our business behavior in today's changing world. Gareth Morgan, in his landmark book *Images of Organization,* explores how the future of an enterprise is often determined by the images or dominant metaphors that guide the organization:

> Organizations enact metaphors. To manage an organization as if you were operating a mechanism, steering a ship, or wielding a weapon is to embody that metaphor in action. Managers may unwittingly construct a reality they dread through an incapacity to reflect upon the metaphor in use.

In the growing knowledge economy, processes for self-management, collaboration, and localized decision making, as well as relationships based on partnership and trust with key stakeholders are becoming essential to success in a global marketplace. These requirements are more in line with our images of community than our images of the traditional corporation. Current research suggests that the power of guiding images is not just an illusion or wish but is arguably a key factor in promoting effective action. Adopting the guiding image of "corporation as community" may become a key factor in revitalizing corporate life and achieving outstanding business results.

HONORING THE PAST TO CREATE THE FUTURE

For millennia, communities have been the most powerful mechanisms for creating human cooperation and reliable interdependence. By contrast, corporations and large-scale organizations have been a powerful force only for the past hundred years or so. By fulfilling their economic mission, industrial enterprises improved living standards for many millions of people. But they also separated us from our traditional ties to the land, to our families, and to our communities of place—without filling the vacuum left by a diminished sense of common purpose and social values. In the process, millions of us have been cut off from our yearning to be part of a larger community of endeavor that is worthy of our best effort. The consequences we see in the workplace—personal stress, family crises, drug abuse, and other chronic health issues—cause as many problems for the organization as they do for society and for the affected individuals.

People have always found their sources of meaning and larger purpose where they spend the majority of their time. Many of us today spend the majority of our time in the workplace. But the term "workplace" hearkens back to an era before industrialization, when people used to live and work in one locale. As Daniel Kemmis points out in his pathbreaking reflections in *Community and the Politics of Place,* local communities were the place where people learned, through personal discipline and practice, the skills of local participation and the meaning of the common good. Organizations can best serve their own interest by becoming "practice fields" for the skills that will lead to more democratic and collaborative behavior than that which has characterized corporate life in the past. These practices, which link the individual to larger communities of interest, help sustain the web of shared meaning and larger purpose that is essential for both business and society to thrive.

This is not primarily a humanitarian question or a moral issue; it represents a corporation's real opportunity to contribute simultaneously to its own renewal and strength and, at the same time, fortify the foundations for a democratic society. In his book *The Living Organization*, John Nirenberg emphasizes that it is a practical requirement for increasing commitment and productivity among employees and other constituencies who interact directly with the organization throughout its life. It is no coincidence that the call today for empowerment and self-management as keys to competitiveness is linked to the need to develop higher levels of informed participation and collaborative action.

There is a growing body of evidence that, in the years to come, a consciously combined "corporation as community" form can produce better performance than any of the traditional forms of organization. However, it will be critical to design organizations of the future to support not only the personal experience of community, but also to assure the long term *sustainability* of community. This means that any designer of organizations as communities will immediately be challenged to explore questions of infrastructure and how people in these new workplace communities will manage and govern themselves.

We don't think organizations should ever replace "communities of place" or "communities of interest." In fact, most people will probably continue to belong to several communities at once, including the community of work. Nor should the old "company town" concept be revived. Company towns and all other forms of benevolent paternalism discourage the active personal responsibility and self-management required to sustain the vitality of true workplace communities. Finally, the reconception of organizations as communities does not mean throwing out the entrepreneurial spirit of the business world. Instead, it provides the opportunity to merge the best of community development traditions with the best of the free-enterprise system.

DISCOVERING THE COMMUNITY DEVELOPMENT TRADITION

The concept of community development is rooted solidly in our democratic traditions. The United States and Canada have a history of voluntary associations in which people regularly helped each other and collaborated as responsible citizens. The Quakers and New Englanders in their town meetings and the frontier communities of the West were focused on people living up to their commitments to themselves and to each other in practical ways. These communities governed themselves through local, informed, democratic participation. The tradition continues today in Neighborhood Crime Watch groups, Town Councils, Little Leagues, the Cancer Society, the Heart Association, the United Way, and a myriad of other community efforts. These remain a living legacy of our capacity as a people to support and serve the common good as well as our individual interests.

Action techniques emerged from the community development movement and from voluntary organizations. Myles Horton and the Highlander Institute in the southern United States were early innovators. Paulo Freire's pioneering work with dialogue and social change in Brazil has made an impact. Leonard Oliver is the first to reveal to us the tradition of the Scandinavian "study circles." The community activism of local democratic participation encouraged by Saul Alinsky's Industrial Areas Foundation form another thread in the tapestry. More recently, M. Scott Peck and the Foundation for Community Encouragement have added to the range of approaches (see page 2). Marvin Weisbord's work in developing future search techniques is an extension of community development traditions (see page 131).

There is also no doubt that leaders of large scale social change efforts like Ghandi, Martin Luther King, Jr. and Cesar Chavez were gifted innovators in designing creative approaches for engaging large numbers of community members in working together toward a shared vision of a better future. Business leaders can benefit from their learnings as well.

In business circles in the past, the idea of gathering and encouraging high involvement by hundreds or thousands of people using community development principles as part of a large system change process made corporate leaders apprehensive. But times are changing. Today, to capitalize on shifting markets and customer needs, it is important to mobilize fast responses by large numbers of employees who operate from common values and a shared vision. Community development approaches can involve multiple stakeholders in large group settings that can be augmented through teleconferencing and other communications technology. Community development methods help break down the "corporate arthritis" and "hardening of the categories" which slow down effective action These methods can also be utilized as an integral part of business process redesign. Creative approaches to large-scale interactive planning help the organization to engage the energy, commitment, and critical mass required for effective change.

In addition to large group involvement, the architecture of engagement in community development involves thinking about creative ways of tapping into the deep traditions of service, informed participation, and individual contribution that have formed part of our national heritage. Luckily, we are beginning to see businesses experiment with community-building practices. For example:

- Motorola has made a huge investment in capability and learning, not only with its own employees, but with the local school districts that provide the continuity of future talent for the company. Retirees, the "elders" in the corporate community, are serving as adjunct faculty at learning sites, thus bridging between the past and the future of the Motorola community.
- Steelcase has created physical "neighborhoods" where product and business teams work together in close proximity. They have designed a type of community "commons" adjacent to these office neighborhoods to encourage the kind of informal conversation and collaboration that we associate with small towns.
- Herman Miller has focused on the nature of the organization's "convenant"

with employees—both the rights and responsibilities of membership in the corporate community as well as the idea of leadership as community service.

Our fundamental traditions of community and the value of connection to that which is beyond self and wealth still have strong roots—roots that the contemporary corporation can now help nourish in the soil of modern life in ways that also fulfill its economic potential.

THE CORE PROCESSES OF COMMUNITY

Over the last several years, together with key people at a number of organizations, we have identified several core processes which are fundamental to creating and sustaining organizations as communities. We call them the seven C's of community building. These key elements represent core processes, similar to business processes for enhancing commitment, competence, contribution, collaboration, continuity, and conscience. A final core process, conversation, serves as an essential catalyst that enables the others to increase their capacity for strengthening the organizational community. The exploration and examples offered here are designed to stimulate your own thinking about creative ways of developing organizational communities.

Commitment

Fred Kofman and Peter Senge (see page 49) have pointed to the importance of developing the communities of commitment that lie at the heart of learning organizations capable of leading the way toward a sustainable future. Commitment emerges when people work together to create something they value. As we experience intensive mutual learning experiences, work toward shared ideals, collaborate on needed tasks, or jointly face adversity and life's difficulties, we discover in others—and in ourselves—the resources, spirit, and energy that "move" us to stay engaged.

Common language, symbols, and metaphors help us find shared meaning which is one foundation for committed action. That's why using the language of community is valuable. It calls forth the intuitive image which most people have about real life actions of mutual commitment and contribution—in contrast to formal training programs that teach people how they "should behave" in a high commitment work system.

Many of today's organizations are facing adversity. Under the stress of unrelenting change, serious attention must be paid to *mutual* commitment. What commitments will the organization ask of its employees, and what commitments will the organization make and keep in return? While commitment can only come from inside the heart and mind of each individual, it is nurtured by reliable interdependence *in community*.

Many employees are willing to commit themselves to a truly engaging purpose larger than simply personal self interest. They are willing to give of themselves to help create the collective enterprise. Living in a free enterprise system, the employees also seek concrete evidence that the enterprise is committed to them. They want to see tangible results from the investment of their efforts. For example, it's hard to build strong commitment to a total quality effort involving re-engineering when thousands of members fear losing their jobs and being cast out of the community.

It's especially tough to sustain commitment when few employees own stock in the company, or when they feel that the social contract to which they pledged their loyalty is endangered. If the analogy of communities is appropriate, then talk of "owning your part of the business" is most effective in building commitment when accompanied by some *actual* ownership and participation in the financial and social benefits of contributing to success. Otherwise, the commitment leaders seek may be seen as simply lip service. If people are given the hard economic truths, they will be willing to share the pain during hard times. But as key stakeholders, members of the organizational community reasonably want to share in the tangible rewards from helping to save the day.

Recently, faced with a budget crunch, a division of Intel instituted a graduated pay cut. The highest-paid employees, including executives, reduced their pay by 10 percent while the lowest paid employees lost nothing and there were no layoffs. Volkswagen Europe, in similar circumstances, moved to a shortened, four-day, 29 hour work week to save 30,000 jobs among its 100,000 person workforce. In other companies, employees have volunteered for early retirement or temporary leave without pay, or have bought the company (as at Avis) and saved it from bankruptcy. These are all examples of community development principles at work.

It is critical that executives be honest with everyone about the realities of life in the business so that people can actively join together at all levels to determine what are broadly perceived as *fair* ways to solve common problems in a manner that enhances human dignity and mutual respect. Without this foundation, building and sustaining true communities of commitment will remain a distant dream.

Competence

Vital communities are capable—they have the skills, knowledge, and personal qualities to renew themselves and reinvent their future. They do this by encouraging learning and improvement among their citizens as both an individual and a collective undertaking. Peter Senge focused on the three areas of deeper skills and capabilities that enable true learning communities to develop—aspiration, reflective conversation, and conceptualization.

The capacity for *aspiration* requires developing the skills and capacities to focus on what we as members of the organizational community truly care about in order to create the future we *want* rather than being left to react to the future we get. Developing the capability to create from aspiration rather than from fear or crisis is a critical shift of mind that requires discipline and practice. It is important to develop collective aspiration, especially under conditions of unrelenting change. As individuals, we always exist in relation to a larger community. The challenge for organizational leaders is to create an architecture of engagement which enables people to discover and build a common "field of dreams," thus creating a new story of business based on shared purpose, true partnerships, and integrated processes.

Building the capability for *reflective conversation* becomes critical to understanding the deeper patterns of beliefs and assumptions that guide decision making. Paolo Freire, in his work in Brazilian community education and Bjorn Gustavsen, a pioneer in participative work-life activities in Scandinavia, point to the critical interplay of action and reflection through democratic dialogues in which community members can see new possibilities for coordinated action. In healthy work communities, there are "replays" where members gather in the twilight of a common undertaking—anything from a meeting, to a major strategic initiative, to a new product introduction. Teams reflect together, as if surveying the field of play, to understand more deeply the related dimensions of their work, possibilities for breakthrough insights, and strategic opportunities.

Developing the capacity for *conceptualization* enables members to think more systemically and holistically about the deeper structures and dynamic interdependencies that are required to support coherent and coordinated action. Simply introducing members to the concept of community begins to encourage more holistic thinking. Members are able to intuitively grasp the many dimensions of ordinary life that must be integrated for vital, healthy communities to be sustained. Using the concept of community as a springboard for deeper work in systems thinking also helps members consider the importance of interdependence among many diverse elements in sustaining healthy community life.

Over the last several years, Ford has been collaborating with MIT's Organizational Learning Center in developing these core learning capabilities as part of a pilot project developing the new Lincoln Continental. The dramatic improvements in cycle time and other key measures stemming from building a learning community which integrates the core competencies of aspiration, reflection, and conceptualization are unprecedented. For example, in a recent assessment, the "parts-on-time" ratio achieved by the Ford team was at least twice the former average—more than doubling their previous performance!

These core learning competencies lead to deeper awareness and sensibilities, which, in the long run, tend to evolve into a more nurturing and life-sustaining set of beliefs and assumptions. They can guide future business practice as they replace the assumptions underlying the "command and control" paradigm. When combined with elements of organizational architecture that allow these evolving capabilities to be channeled into effective action, powerful synergies for desired results are generated.

Contribution

Contribution is the lifeblood for building strong communities. Essentially, people want to give, especially if it's to something they think is needed and worthwhile. That's why it's important to develop ways for people to see clearly how their daily work makes a real contribution to the organization's success. Business process improvement incorporates this concept. However, unless process re-design is seen as one key to building the caring and reliable interdependence that is the heart of community, people feel like *they've* been re-engineered out of making their unique contribution to the business and that their very presence may be threatened with extinction.

Healthy communities provide opportunities to utilize the full diversity of members' talents and contributions to the community's sustenance. These opportunities are not just in narrowly defined roles; each person's gifts are unique and considered a vital community resource. Each enables the community to continue developing and serving the common good.

For example, at a large, technologically advanced plant, we involved all the employees in a large scale strategic planning initiative. One of the maintenance workers became a lead member of a plant-wide singing group which began to write and perform songs about the strategic planning and visioning effort. His music helped engage everyone in a common image of the future—and was a lot of fun. No one would have ever known his talents if we hadn't had a Volunteer Sign-Up process where people could offer whatever they thought would help out the overall effort.

Another line employee had a talent for video and communications. The strategy team put him on special assignment as the "reporter on the beat" in a program modeled after NBC-TV's *Today Show*, to keep up to date on progress. His teammates helped fill in for him during this project since they knew he was making a special contribution to the overall effort.

In a community model of contribution, a company's hiring and interviewing systems track the multiple talents of employees. Today, these are rarely shared on the job because no one ever asks. In a community model, people are encouraged to bring their whole person to the workplace. Reward systems recognize members for volunteerism—for what they undertake on their own initiative outside of their ordinary scope of work in an effort to contribute to the success of the larger enterprise.

The difference between average and excellent performance in a corporation often lies with its members' willingness to volunteer their discretionary effort—that which is available beyond what is required to simply retain one's job. That contribution cannot be forced, especially from today's knowledge workers. It can only be evoked in a community of purpose in which people choose to contribute their best.

Collaboration

Developing *reliable interdependence* is the essence of effective collaboration in a community. Corporate community developers are interested in building collaboration across large populations by creating a web of multiple constituencies and stakeholders—engaging, involving, and mobilizing members until there is a critical mass of hundreds or thousands of people who can move together on a common path. They may move autonomously in many different locations, but they move with a clear shared vision, values and overall strategy in common. Organization development and team building, by contrast, have often focused on building collaboration in much smaller groups.

Collaboration does not live in the abstract. It depends, for example, on the web of information that, in thriving communities, flows freely in all directions. When members know what's going on in the community and why, they can act autonomously to achieve common goals without being supervised or monitored. Town criers served the public information function in medieval communities. Local newspapers, television, and radio play that role in towns and cities today. In organizations, this function is often served by computer networks and electronic mail, as well as by organization-wide interactive planning processes.

Collaboration is also strengthened through weaving the web of personal relationships. Even in the most technologically advanced organizations, people need face-to-face meetings and communication. Community-builders recognize that, as human beings, we need the opportunity to *respond personally* to each other and, as importantly, to feel known and "seen" as valued community contributors. Ultimately, a focus on personal relationships allows people to develop a web of mutual trust in which the members of the workplace community know they can count on one another and on their leaders for honesty and support. All of these factors—stakeholder involvement, continuous information, and personal relationships—can be delicately woven together in a way that nurtures and sustains the process of collaboration for results.

Continuity

Communities can't survive without some measure of continuity. If we want to gain the benefits of healthy communities in the workplace, we need to become more creative about how to "build in" continuity. Otherwise, the knowledge of mature citizens literally gets lost in the constant churn of career moves, downsizing, and reorganization.

For example, in many companies, there is a tacit mental model that managers who stay in their jobs longer than two years are considered "dead wood" or "unmotivated." Workplace communities would foster a different view of career paths, allowing people to develop continuity and longer-term accountability for results without sacrificing their professional development opportunities. In many workplaces, employees can be compensated at higher levels without having to change job roles by gaining a broader range of skills or taking on more tasks. In the future, as people change roles, part of their compensation could be based on how well they serve as bridges of continuity for sharing knowledge and strengthening the corporate memory.

An institutional memory is one of the most critical factors for continuity. In pre-industrial times, the community's memory was transmitted by word of mouth. Elders kept and shared knowledge of "best practices"—how we planted, harvested, and distributed the fruits of our labor. Today, the organizational counterpart to that knowledge—that is, "How we developed and marketed a new product"—can be captured and shared through computer networks and data banks. Technology supports a common knowledge base that the community can draw on for years.

Other aspects of institutional memory must be carried person-to-person. For example, organizations have difficulty maintaining continuity unless they create ways to help new members understand the rights, responsibilities, and practices of the community. To provide continuity in self-managing teams, it is also valuable for organizations to encourage rotating team leadership, even at very senior levels, through innovations in personnel practices, performance standards and pay systems. If one person moves on, others retain the history, vision, and values. A team doesn't have to start all over because a new leader comes in who wants to "make his own mark."

Conscience

All healthy communities incorporate processes which could be described as conscience mechanisms. The organization finds ways to embody, or invoke, guiding principles, ethics, and values like service, trust, and mutual respect. These, in turn, translate into daily actions and concrete decisions. But most organizational conscience mechanisms are tacit. Even when there is a value or mission statement, the question "To what or whom are we responsible?" is rarely raised explicitly today. Community building brings that question to the surface.

We often associate conscience with guilt. We speak of having a guilty conscience. But it's more useful to think of people and organizations having a positive conscience stemming from the choices they have made to be responsible individual and organizational citizens. This is the basis of maintaining a democratic society. Eleanor Roosevelt put it this way:

One's philosophy is not best expressed in words.
It is expressed in the choices one makes....
The process never ends until we die.
And the choices we make are ultimately our responsibility.

We are beginning to accumulate evidence that having a conscience also pays off in the bottom line. In their work on corporate culture and performance, Kotter and Haskett explored research that showed that over an 11-year period net profits grew 756% in companies which had an ethic of "multiple stakeholder satisfaction and involvement," compared to 1% increase in a comparable set of companies that kept to traditional management practices.

Organizational conscience may ultimately take its shape as a Bill of Rights and Responsibilities for organizational citizens. Workplace Constitutions, Credos of Conscience and "Green" policies have also been formed. The famous Johnson & Johnson Tylenol case is an example where a credo helped provide guidelines for practical decision making. When tainted Tylenol was discovered, J&J's leaders could quickly make the decision to immediately remove all Tylenol from the nation's shelves because they were following the organization's credo which said that J&J's first responsibility was to provide quality products to doctors, nurses, and patients. This dramatic action helped ensure a reinstatement of both public trust and employee pride in the integrity of the company, and led to higher long-term sales.

Exploring the question of conscience is a first step toward repositioning the organization both with its own members and within its larger community. When corporations start to see themselves as active members of a larger interconnected web of concern for a positive future for all key stakeholders, then the community orientation begins to yield benefits in increasingly larger systems.

Conversation

Conversation is the medium through which collective action emerges. It is the primary vehicle through which we as individuals conceive our world and embrace relationships with others. It is how we make and share the meanings that form the foundation of community life.

We think in language. Today, our heads and not our hands have become the means for adding value in the new economy. The quality of our thinking counts as never before. A spirit of inquiry fueled by great conversation about strategic questions and operational issues provide the sustenance for the life and health of the workplace community.

In fact, as Alan Webber points out in *Harvard Business Review*, conversations in which trust and team learning are the currency of exchange may become the primary source of competitive advantage in the knowledge era. It is through conversation that we create the relationships and partnerships with employees, customers, and suppliers that define long-term value in the corporation. Both personal and electronic conversations enable members of the corporation to share learnings, to create innovative products and services, and to collaborate for continuous improvement.

In our work over the last twenty years applying community development approaches to organizational strategy and large system change, we have affirmed the importance of great conversations as the glue that enables other community building processes to succeed. A key function of leadership is to create a climate where candid conversation can flourish and where differences in perspective can be utilized for the common good.

William Isaacs, our colleague, has pointed out in his research that the exploration of core beliefs and assumptions that dialogue encourages has the potential to create a radically different type of self-directed and coordinated action which normal problem solving and action planning rarely achieves. Workplace communities which enhance their skills in self-management through democratic dialogue and real conversation will develop "the collaborative advantage" in ways not easily copied by others.

Practical Tips for Developing Community at Work

Here are some of the techniques that can help bring people together and enable them to mobilize collective efforts. Many of these practices were developed with volunteers, who can't be commanded through authority. As authority rests more and more with employees, and empowerment is seen as a key to business success, these sorts of approaches, rooted in our traditions of participatory democracy, will become increasingly important, whether you define your organization as a "community" or not.

We don't see these techniques as solely useful for formal "change agents." They're more for anyone—individual or group—who feels, "I wish I worked in a place that was more like a community." Positive change can begin anywhere with anyone who cares enough to get started.

Focus on the Real Work

Successful community development work starts with the challenges people face in real life. There are gangs afoot, so we begin a neighborhood crime watch. There is garbage in the streets, so we get together for a cleanup campaign. Similarly, in a business, avoid a narrow focus on "building community" in the abstract. Focus on the immediate things people care about. "We're drowning in piles of paper; our workload is overwhelming; the communication system is wacky; we need better training to do a good job with the company." Later, the group can broaden its interest.

Keep It Simple

What one specific thing could you and others do that will have multiple business and personal payoffs? Generally, the simplest, most effective things you can begin with are the things that touch people's concrete business issues, but with approaches that touch their hearts and spirits as well—like informal gatherings and celebrations. Sometimes the most powerful leverage points for change are the most simple, especially if they are chosen with an understanding of underlying structures and dynamics of the system in which you are operating.

See the Glass as Half Full

Community developers say: "Build from good, expect better, make great." Even in organizations with lots of problems, focus on the best, most life-giving forces which are already present. Involve the people associated with them. Look for the wellness and wholeness which exists even in the sickest organization, and start there. For example, in a large organization, some people may already be doing a great job with customer service or improved paperwork flow. What can you learn from that and how can you capitalize on these positive examples?

Aim High and Act

It's not enough to build from good. You must expect better and make it great. For example, if you correct a painful situation through a community effort, you don't want to stop with simple relief. You want to ask, "Where do we go from here?" and advance toward a better future. Act. Take a step. Learn by doing, and see where it takes you. Community-building is an organic process. One thing leads to the next and the learning, excitement and self-confidence build.

Seek What Unifies

As you talk with people, try to find not only what pulls you apart, but what brings you together. Sniff out the people who care, and bring them together using dialogue, pot-luck suppers, or house meetings. Start a small group talking about what the issues are, what they've tried, and what worked well or less well. Your best power might be providing them with lunch. The important thing is to start great conversations about things that matter. Reflecting together is a foundation for discovering common ground and for building community.

Do It When People Are Ready

Timing is everything in community development. It's often better to wait until you sense that people are ready to move forward. For example, some managers wonder why they hear so much complaining and groaning and so little positive suggestion. They are tempted to say to their subordinates, "Don't you have any vision?" But when there is a sense of injury, comments like that will squelch the needed collective healing process. It's more effective to be subtle. Do what you can to help alleviate the immediate pain, while encouraging people to focus on their best hopes. When the pain is acknowledged, ideas about larger vision will start to emerge on their own.

Design Spaces Where Community Can Happen

How would organizations be designed physically to support community? Maybe you would create the equivalent of a central plaza or common square where people came to have coffee and conversation. The water cooler would not be a forbidden place. In one factory, the teams developed the Blue Room—a living room right in the middle of the plant floor where there had been a storeroom before. When people needed to think and reflect together, they would go there.

Find and Cultivate the "Zoysia Plugs"

Zoysia is a grass, originally indigenous to Asia, which people sometimes use to start lawns. You water and fertilize plugs of grass scattered far apart. Eventually they find each other and meld into a beautiful carpet covering the whole lawn. In organizations, "zoysia plugs" are people who share your passion. They are also the informal leaders who know how to make things happen. Find them, wherever they might be, and support them however you can. Eventually, when you reach a level of critical mass, you may feel the atmosphere of the entire enterprise shift.

Be Willing to Change Plans

In any community there are unintended consequences, even with the best of intentions. When situations change, or new perceptions emerge, you've got to be willing to be flexible and shift course. Something better than you ever thought of may come up in the course of your efforts. Go with it!

Learn How to Host Good Gatherings

Any community builder should know certain fundamental skills of hosting great conversations and designing gatherings. These may be different than the traditional skills of good organizational meeting management, particularly when dialogue for deeper understanding is the goal. Look for meeting sites that feel relaxing. Avoid formal conference rooms because of the stultified associations people have with them. Sit at round tables—or better yet, choose a living-room atmosphere, with informal comfortable seating. Try to have food available as often as possible, and stop periodically for "fun" breaks.

When you can, have a scribe capture people's ideas and points of focus on flipcharts so they can "see" what they're talking about. Encourage the group to take responsibility for deciding what should be the next steps in their conversation right there on the spot. Find out what people can contribute. Get volunteer "sign ups." Finally, take time for sharing "learnings" and "yearnings." What have we learned? What do we want to do to improve our next get-together?

Acknowledge People's Contributions

One of the most fundamental tools in community building is honoring individual and team contribution. Everyone who contributes should be thanked and acknowledged for what they have done. One organization concluded its visioning effort with a mock Academy Awards ceremony in which every member present was nominated for at least one award. Some awards were hilarious: for example, a "foot in mouth award"—to acknowledge the biggest gaffes that people could remember. Others were quite serious: a "beyond-the-call-of-duty" award. Each person left the ceremony knowing that others appreciated what they had contributed.

Involve the Whole Person

Use music, art, symbols and drama to tap deeper sources of knowing and intuition. In one mass visioning and strategy effort, a large hot air balloon floated outside the plant to symbolize the importance of a larger perspective. Strategic conversations, called Balloon Meetings, were held with groups of employees, customers, suppliers, and other corporate stakeholders. For the first time in the organization's history, members brought food to their meetings. Muralists sketched what people envisioned the plant might become. Employees drew possible logos for the plant. Eventually the strategy teams, made up of both managers and line workers, made creative presentations about the plant's future direction. These presentations included skits, murals, and music. The managers contributed an understanding of the business focus, so that all the visioning and strategy work was tied directly into the improvement of the business. That plant became the highest-producing plant of its type in the world. Eight years later, results continue to be sustained.

Celebrate

What's the point of building community if you can't have fun? Community development work engages people's hearts, minds, spirits, and bodies. A key vehicle for this is celebration. In one company, we began the community-building effort with a kick-off extravaganza for all employees and their families in the local high school. The international singing group Up With People was invited to perform. The members of the group, mostly high school students from all over the world, lived in the homes of managers and hourly employees for several days before the event. The kids from the singing group talked to everyone about what it was like to work with people from different cultures. This happened to be a locale with severe racial issues, and the celebration gave people an opportunity to see how things could be different. Celebrate and recognize success, even if it's small. Fan the sparks into flames of hope and faith that it can really work. Celebrations don't have to cost lots of money. The only real requirement is imagination.

LEADING THE WORK COMMUNITY

The role of leadership is critically important in facilitating the merger between the traditional world of the corporation and developing the corporation as a community. Leaders interested in exploring this "merger possibility" have found it necessary to confront their own deeply held assumptions and beliefs about the ways outstanding performance is achieved. What if we thought of ourselves as leaders of a corporate community? How would this affect our overall strategy? What are the operating principles which would inform our decision making? What kinds of guiding ideas, governance, and other dimensions of organizational infrastructure support the corporate community model? Most importantly, what is required of us as leaders to truly embody this innovative way of thinking and action?

These are not easy questions. But leaders are being challenged to ask the hard questions. The time has come to examine the fundamental beliefs that have guided past success but are yielding unintended economic, social, and environmental consequences. Leaders are being called on to share personal responsibility for creating a corporate legacy which enables business to fulfill its economic potential while also serving as a positive force for creating organizations as communities that can help assure a sustainable future. The vitality of business, the strength of democratic society, and the healing of our planet may depend on it.

Stephanie Ryan
is a facilitator of organizational learning and founder of In Care, a
Massachusetts-based consulting com-
pany. She helps clients to see, understand, and improve the systems they are
a part of by exploring the assumptions that influence their ability to produce
results. Her primary focus is on creating learning communities, particularly
exploring the kinds of relationships across traditional boundaries that are the
fertile ground for collaboration. Her preferred clients recognize the emerging
need to serve their communities and are willing to experiment with new ways
of thinking and operating. She regularly delivers speeches and workshops on
the disciplines of systems thinking, team learning, and mental models.

Prior to founding In Care, Ryan worked for a management consulting
firm, Innovation Associates, Inc. for six years, where her work involved the
design and delivery of management training programs focused on the disciplines of organizational learning discussed in *The Fifth Discipline: The Art and
Practice of Learning Organizations* by Peter Senge, co-founder of Innovation
Associates.

7

Emergence of Learning Communities

Stephanie Ryan

The union of Curiosity and Commitment
is barren without Experimentation.
They may dream of taking action,
but ideas are simply that, ideas.
Ideas are no substitute
for the life blood of exploration
found in Experimentation.

Meeting the challenges that face our society today will require going beyond traditional, organizational, gender, and ethnic boundaries. Our tendency to think and operate within the limited scope these artificial boundaries create prevents us from accurately defining the issues, undermines our ability to perceive root causes and blinds us to the impact of our actions in other parts of organizational systems. It is sadly true that yesterday's solutions are often the cause of today's problems.

This essay offers learning in community as one way to connect the fragmented thinking and acting that perpetuates continued suboptimization in our organizations and society as a whole. The inherent challenge of learning communities is in sustaining cooperative and collaborative practices across a diverse range of thought. A structure for collaborative learning is described both in how it ideally unfolds and what can prevent it from occurring. Lastly, a closer look is taken at the quality of relationship which is required of self and others if learning is to occur in community.

Perceiving Wholeness

The sense of wholeness inherent in a learning community is captured by the African expression "It takes a whole village to educate a child." This recognition of the invisible fabric of relationships that contributes to achieving more visible results is why communities can be a fertile ground for learning.

In the United States, parent-teacher conferences are held quarterly to monitor the students' performance. Few schools have altered this traditional format to directly include the students themselves in the conversation. How can such an obvious omission in representing the whole persist? How often is your customer present in conversations of customer service? Why do we consider these invitations inappropriate? Can we afford to keep excluding diversity of thought, excluding the very stakeholders we aim to serve?

The antithesis of a learning community is exclusivity. Exclusivity can take two forms. The most obvious is to exclude the participation of another. More subtly, individuals can exclude themselves from full participation by not giving voice to their true thoughts or feelings. This self-censorship might occur when speaking one's heart or mind risks being seen as impolite, foolish, wrong, incompetent or risks inviting conflict. Stifling thoughts and feelings robs a community from perceiving the whole system of which they are a part.

Harvesting the Potential for Learning Communities

Learning communities are more likely to arise when certain critical conditions are present within a group, including—but not limited to—curiosity, commitment, and a desire to act collaboratively with a spirit of experimentation.

The ongoing presence of choice is critical to sustain a learning community. Yet, choice in organizations tends to fade in the routine of going to the office and receiving a paycheck. Members of a learning community are rarely paid to show up; they are there because of curiosity and a commitment to create something they care about. Learning community members are connected by matters of the heart as well as the mind; they share a desire for learning, not an obligation.

When people come together, curious about something they "don't know," and can adequately represent the whole system they are curious about, the seeds of a learning community are being planted. Harvesting the product of these seeds takes time, calling for patience and trust because the new life is invisible, underground so to speak.

One way to cultivate the soil for learning communities is to practice new patterns of thinking, communicating, and interacting. Creating a structure that can support this interaction is the first step in sustaining learning within the community. Figure 1 shows a reinforcing structure that can promote such learning. Briefly, shared curiosity, which motivates collaborative designs, can seed joint experimentation and lead to reflection that generates shared insight to improve collaborative designs for future experimentation.

Figure 1. Collaborative Learning

A stunning example of cooperation across traditional boundaries is the Association of Mondragon Cooperatives in Spain. Terry Mollner writes about these unique communities in his *World Business Academy Perspectives* article, "Mondragon: Archetype of Future Business?" The Mondragon Cooperative was founded in 1956 with funds raised from local townspeople to open a small paraffin stove factory with 24 people. Today, they have over 160 cooperative enterprises, employing more than 23,000 members. Their actions are based on a single guiding principle: "How can we do this in a way that serves equally both those in the enterprise *and* those in the community, rather than serving one at the expense of the other?"

GETTING STARTED

Individual learning takes place, in part, through curiosity followed by experimentation. For collaborative learning to occur, shared curiosity must be present and translated into the choice of what people want to collectively explore. Members of the community need to make thoughtful and heartfelt choices about the journey of shared exploration they commit to embark on together.

Once the path has been chosen, designers who can represent the whole system are selected. These designers—a diverse body of stakeholders with the potential for seeing things differently—typically cross many boundaries and represent the whole process in question. Their diversity is welcomed and seen as essential to the design of a robust experiment.

MOVING TO JOINT EXPERIMENTATION

The designers selected are also the experimenters, exploring the edges of learning that their questions reveal. As experimenters, they are clear about their role and expectations, and they are genuinely curious about the results. Too often a group of people design an experiment and then ask another group to accomplish it. This typically results in asking later why the "implementation" failed, why the experimenters had no ownership in completing the "task," and why the momentum was lost.

SETTING THE STAGE FOR PUBLIC REFLECTION

This continuity of designers and experimenters creates the possibility for a common experience that can be publicly reflected on afterward. The possibility of open reflection is only realized if there is an ability and willingness to share and suspend one's thoughts. An interim step of journaling or silence is helpful for setting the stage for dialogue to begin.

REAPING THE REWARDS

Success depends on the extent to which people can openly share their experiences, assumptions, and beliefs. Ideally, the discrepancy between what they thought would happen (what the design was intended to produce) and what actually happened (the results of joint experimentation) can be perceived and understood. The conversation is often rich with diverse views because we all filter information differently. New understanding can emerge if people can suspend their views of what is "right" or what "actually" occurred long enough to be influenced by another's perception. Frequent questions and slower pacing often yield shared insight into the nature of the issue. Recording these insights in some form of group memory can inform future collaborative designs.

HONORING THE PROCESS

Capturing a systemic "picture" of collaborative learning in a casual loop diagram illustrates the importance of the process of interaction rather than focusing attention on a single player or an illusive end-state. Areas of highest leverage, where a small intervention can significantly affect the health of the system, can be made more visible, comprehensible, and practical. The beauty of the spiral is threefold: you can start anywhere, it is never over, and there is no focus on individual blame.

Learning communities involve an ongoing commitment to the collaborative journey of thinking, communicating, and acting together in service of the whole. It is never over, you are never *there*, there is always something more to learn in service of the community. The Mondragon Cooperative has drawn the circle defining "we" as the owner-employees, consumers, bank depositors, and the community. Hence it has not limited its activities to business and banking, rather it has participated in nearly every realm of community development, building more than forty cooperative housing complexes, creating private day care, grade school, high school, and higher education facilities.

LIMITS TO LEARNING

An understanding of systems reveals nothing grows forever. Consequently the question arises, "What are the limits to learning as a community?" Brakes to learning come in several forms: fear of failure, denial or perception of failure, and the inability to deal with diverse viewpoints gracefully. What all of these forms have in common is the net effect of increasing defensive behaviors (fight or flight) in the community at the expense of open reflection. Here are a few loops and stories that elaborate on these themes:

Figure 2. Limits to Learning

One of the consequences as we begin to learn together is that our expectations start to grow (spiral B2 in Figure 2). If expectations are growing, however, it becomes harder and harder for us to meet them. Fear of failure tends to emerge quickly. Although the group is successfully overcoming impasses in its collective understanding, each new gap can seem farther apart than the last one, and uncertainty grows.

When insecurity increases, the need to be defended also grows. People behave defensively to avoid threat, embarrassment, conflict, and anything associated with being "wrong." Since "the best defense is a strong offense," people may even begin finger pointing or blaming others as a means of escaping personal blame.

Defensive routines often appear in the form of denial, which quickly escalates from the personal to the collective (from illusion to delusion to collusion). At some level, I start telling myself "Everything's fine, I hope." I begin to buy into this illusion and the need to believe everything is okay. If a community member and I collectively say that everything is okay (because we do not want to acknowledge any problems), we begin to delude ourselves about what is true. Consciously or unconsciously, we have collectively agreed not to question it. We collude not to inquire into the nature of our actions, and performance becomes undiscussable. Unfortunately, our ability to reflect or collectively generate insights about the systems of which we are a part also deteriorates. The gap between our desired end state and the immediate reality has become undiscussable. With no shared understanding of the gap, the capacity for aligned action to address the gap is undermined and the gap persists or worsens.

Another potential limit sprouts from the fertile ground of diverse stakeholders participating in the design phase. The greater the diversity of viewpoint, the higher the likelihood people will interpret these views as conflicting and shy away from exploring ideas and suspending assumptions. If conflict avoidance arises, open and honest public reflection is undermined and the possibility of creating shared insight or learning dissipates (B3).

A further limit to learning results when an experiment is interpreted as a failure, rather than another opportunity for learning. Once again, the need to avoid blame or justify money spent causes defensiveness to dominate over reflectiveness. Soon the collective learning breaks down as people begin to "posture" (sometimes politically) to look good. Information is no longer freely shared; in fact the willingness to look at the data is often undermined in the form of denial (B4).

The nature of the reinforcing loop (R1) is reflective and collective. "We're in this together" captures the underlying assumption. The balancing loops, however, represent distinctly protective, individualistic behavior, which is more about looking good even if at the expense of others (suboptimization). This is the land of the "hero," "lone ranger," or "rugged individualist" who prides him or herself on their ability to "make it work." This is the one person who can be counted on to pull it out in the end without needing help from anyone. Yet today's world of rapid change and complexity is making it harder and harder for any one hero to save the day. The need for collaboration is painfully apparent.

What these limits to learning in community all have in common is the deterioration of relationships, whether it is the relationship with oneself or others. When defensive behaviors predominate, they not only defend against perceived threat, they also preclude the sharing and vulnerable exploration of the unknown. The need to be defended runs counter to the vulnerability felt when one acknowledges privately or publicly—"I don't know" or "I'm not sure." The tendency then is to lie, to pretend one does know, to be certain and advocate this view rather than inquire with others in the spirit of curiosity.

EMPTINESS: AN ALTERNATIVE TO DEFENSE

In M. Scott Peck's book *The Different Drum*, the model of "community making" includes a stage that is not found in traditional team development models. He characterizes it as "emptiness." Emptiness can be either the barrier or gateway to community, depending on how the fear is dealt with. If fear of the unknown, fear of failure, and fear of conflict can be acknowledged, engaged with curiosity and reflection, this openness can lead to genuine listening and the capacity to generate shared meaning within the community. If the fear is met with a need to control, fix, pretend, lie, or avoid, the tendency to generate answers rather than questions, the need to advocate rather than inquire, typically wins. If the latter is true a group moves back to one of the previous stages, chaos or pseudo-community.

At the individual level, emptiness is about letting go of whatever is in the way of one's relationship to oneself or others because this is a barrier to communication. It may involve suspending assumptions, attributions, judgment, or expectations. However, in order for this to occur, we must first realize that we have and hold these mental models.

Appreciating and understanding emptiness is crucial for managers who want to facilitate collaborative learning processes in their organizations. A common dilemma managers face is "How can I facilitate collaborative learning if I can't do it myself—if I'm not even sure it's possible?" The temptation is to supply a ready-made solution. However, the real power lies in simply acknowledging that the dilemma is part of the journey; one of many that will be encountered along the path. Learning requires living in the space of the unknown, hanging out in the fertile ground of "I don't know." Learning with others requires going public with "I don't know" and acknowledging "we don't know" sometimes.

To the extent these kinds of dilemmas can be voiced rather than hidden, that voice serves the community's learning. The moment it is denied, groups retreat into chaos (believing they know what is right and attempting to convince or fix everyone else) or pseudo community (speaking in generalities, pretending everything is fine, and never voicing a strong personal opinion).

LIVING IN EMPTINESS

To reach community in Peck's model, the only pathway is "into and through" emptiness. Emptiness can be a gateway to community if the capacity to communicate undefended is present. The kind of conversation that supports connection, discovery and collaborative learning is found more in the interaction of dialogue than discussion. The roots of the word "dialogue" are *dia* and *logos*. *Dia* is defined as *through*, not two and *logos* is defined as *meaning*. Hence dialogue is the ability to have a conversation where the meaning flows through people. In a dialogue, people are open to being influenced, literally willing to be changed by the meaning of the words of others. The root of the word "discussion" is similar to the root of the words "concussion" and "percussion," where people heave their views of right and wrong at one another, much like the stage characterized as chaos. If people are willing to let go of their tightly held and defended views, the ability to dialogue can offer a bridge from chaos through emptiness and over to community. When groups learn to dialogue together, learning occurs because individuals have emptied themselves of their "knowing" long enough to create room for perceiving and acting anew.

> The real voyage of discovery lies not in seeking new landscapes
> but in having new eyes.
>
> —Marcel Proust

LEADERSHIP IN LEARNING COMMUNITIES

Leadership in learning communities is shared; it moves freely as needed among the group members. This shared sense of responsibility is different from traditional teams where the leader is often held accountable, especially if something isn't working as intended. In a learning community each person feels equally responsible for the "success" of the community's learning. Individuals are willing to look inward at what they are consciously or unconsciously doing to support or hinder that goal. The commitment toward open and honest reflection is internally fueled and renewed by the choice to be an ongoing member of the learning community.

I prefer to position the "leaders" of learning communities as facilitators or guides. Guides may make occasional comments on the journey, pointing out what is happening along the way. Guides know they can't lead a group into community, any more than they can try and learn for another—each individual must choose to go there for her or himself. The commitment to remain on the learning journey is directly sourced from the care an individual has for learning.

What guides can do is facilitate the emptying process by continually emptying themselves and requesting the same of the group. Emptying in this case includes discarding "old baggage" which may prevent members from truly listening or speaking with each other. For example, the most powerful thoughts and feelings I often need to empty have to do with "fixing" myself or others to make everything okay. Learning communities are thus born out of total acceptance for self and others. They are born out of trust.

POWER RESIDES WITHIN

The ability to communicate meaning comes from being willing and able to see, hear, and feel oneself. The quality of that relationship determines the capacity to hear and speak one's voice with few words and great clarity. Solitude can offer the space to let the soul speak and reveal itself. The silence found in solitude is invaluable; quiet is needed to hear the soul speak through us. Moments of quiet reflection offer the time to connect to self and the opportunity to communicate from that space.

Sharing meaningful conversations requires leaving the quiet and solitude while still honoring the openness it has created within. Becoming masterful at the art of conversation means communicating with others in a way that leads to greater connection so that the need to defend can fall away. In learning communities people can be defenseless; they can share their vulnerability and their humanness. When I am open to listening to what is meaningful for others, feeling their life experiences, letting them into my heart and not just my mind, I can tap into this sacred space which captures the essence of community.

VULNERABILITY

Peck states "there can be no vulnerability without risk; there can be no community without vulnerability; there can be no peace—and ultimately no life—

without community." Nor can there be learning without vulnerability, admitting I don't know, we don't have the answer. If communities are a safe container for risk and vulnerability, then perhaps they will also be fertile ground for learning.

In many organizations I witness an oscillation between pseudo-community and chaos, either superficial conversation or unyielding attempts to fix everything and everyone in sight. These groups appear caught in self-sealing vicious spirals because the undiscussable by its nature is undiscussable, which precludes authentic communication or relationships. If groups find themselves in emptiness, typically somebody (often a traditional leader) steps in to fix it, to try to make it better. Although the move is well intended, it is counterproductive. Yet this isn't apparent unless an appreciation for emptiness is present.

Emptiness is a healthy sign of development. Unfortunately, because it is not yet part of a popular model of development, it is rarely recognized by facilitators. Typically, people panic when they sense it. Too often the traditional facilitator leads the retreat back to pseudo-community, (pretending things are better than they are) or chaos (fixing people and converting to a "right" point of view) because it is too difficult to be in the place of "not knowing."

Developing the capacity to live with emptiness means developing the capacity to be in relationship with oneself and others in learning communities. Cultivating emptiness offers a reflective, non-defensive field for the undiscussable to become more discussable and the invisible web of interrelationships to become more visible. Community is a place where I am and others are willing to see and be seen, hear and be heard, feel and be felt. The experience of giving voice to what needs to be said, and seeing what has always been there, is the experience of learning in community.

Learning communities are a place of truth seeking and speaking without fear of reprisal or judgment. They are a place where curiosity reigns over knowing and a place where experimentation is welcome. Developing the capacity to live with "not knowing" when it naturally arises, to be in relationship with oneself, and to be reflective more often than defensive provides the leverage for learning.

Barbara Shipka serves on the Board of Directors of the World Business Academy and initiated the Minnesota Chapter. In addition to the corporate sector, she has worked with the United Nations, government, the non-profit sector, and education. She has lived and worked in Lebanon, the Dominican Republic, Somalia, Ethiopia, the Sudan, Czechoslovakia, and Switzerland.

Her consulting practice focuses primarily in the arenas of creating a global orientation, anticipating increasing interdependence, leveraging growth and transitions, working with differences and diversity, and developing resilient work roles. Among her corporate clients are American Express, Cargill, Cray Research, Honeywell, Levi Strauss, Medtronic, The Pillsbury Company, and Wilson Learning.

Shipka is a contributing author to several anthologies, including *When the Canary Stops Singing, Leadership in a New Era, Learning Organizations,* and *Rediscovering the Soul in Business.* She is profiled in *Merchants of Vision* by Jim Liebig and *Who We Could Be at Work* by Margaret Lulic.

8

Softstuff Application: Developing Work Teams in Technical Organizations

Barbara Shipka

Imagine yourself at a mountain overlook. You are gazing out over a panoramic view of incredibly beautiful, varied, rich landscape—valley and mountain, forest and village, river and grassland. The range of the view is so vast, so global, that you find it hard to take it all in. Yet, there it all is.

Now imagine you are able to zoom in on one tiny portion of this view. It's an area small and focused enough that you are able to see the individual blades of grass and the individual pebbles at the river's edge. Even though you know other regions of the panoramic vista are different in many ways from this small piece of land, you also know that, at its elemental level, this land has many properties in common with all land as far as you can see—and far beyond; that, at some basic level, we can learn the nature of all land by deeply exploring one piece.

You also notice that, given passing seasons, the people on that land have a relationship to it that is cyclical; that they have more than one chance to learn how best to support the land and have it support them. The soil isn't right for some particular crop? Fine, next season they can try another. It's an iterative process.

Then, when a few people learn how best to have a mutually satisfying relationship between human and land, they can move to other small pieces and use the same iterative discovery process to figure out what's best for the new land. Further, given that these people now know more about the elemental nature of land in general than they did when they began to explore the first piece they can potentially assist others in also consciously exploring and learning more.

By focusing on one small area of a much larger landscape, it's possible to learn much about land in general, learn much about the specific and varied assets throughout the landscape, and build specific, local relationships that can have a global impact over time.

This is an analogy. Community is the expanded landscape. Developing work teams is an elemental aspect of community, an initial and fundamental aspect of the learning process, and can be likened to the small focused piece of land.

This chapter on building teams within technical organizations is intended as a discrete and concrete way to look at the very deep, complex, and fundamental human endeavor of building community. Building work teams and networks of work teams is a means, a form for getting work done, for achieving goals. Exploring team processes initiates an opportunity for people to move into deeper and richer levels of relationship. The development of teams and networks of teams at work provides a platform for accessing assumptions, acquiring skills, and engaging in experiences that can continuously be built upon and further articulated into the fuller process of building community—anytime, anywhere.

Many people in technical organizations find building work teams to be a baffling, bewildering, often intimidating ordeal. It is not apparent to them that there are frameworks and tools to draw on, predictable patterns that occur, and ways of thinking and being that expedite and inform the process. It is also not clear that building a network of work teams is an ongoing, iterative process rather than an event in time. For many technically-trained people, building work teams is akin to looking at a painting where a tree is suspended in space and the ground has been left out, forgotten. Until the ground is added, the painting appears surreal.

Thus members of technical groups must *ground* their experiences of being together and working together creatively and productively. Once the ground is firm, people can design and build *appropriate structures* to "house" themselves and their work. Finally, people can make the house into a place of safety, caring, and intimacy—*a home.*

THE GROUND

If the ground is missing, the experience is surreal. In addition, if the ground is not firm, stable, and sturdy, anything atop it lives a precarious—and frequently short—life. Let us explore three critical grounding or foundational aspects of building community through developing team processes in the workplace.

Learning to Tap into the Potential

Often, in my experience, little initial preparation or training is provided to assist people in developing high performance work teams. In addition, those individuals newly entering organizations have to fend for themselves; have to pick "it" up as fast as they can, however they are able.

I am reminded of when I first bought my computer. I was given a few ad hoc lessons—how to turn it on, open a word processing program, save, back-up, print, shut it down. It didn't seem much different from the fancy electric type-writer I'd been using. Now and then I'd learn something new either because I had to call for technical assistance or because I accidently bumped a key that then offered me big surprises—some helpful, others disastrous. I was learning acci-dentally rather than by design. I was using perhaps 5 percent of the potential of the machine—and I didn't have a clue as to what the other 95 percent offered. Many technical people in organizations are accessing the potential of communi-ty about as much as I initially accessed the potential of my computer.

Tapping into the potential of community begins with learning some basic principles, such as:

- Processes can be accelerated when learning occurs by design.
- A "just do it" attitude is inefficient.
- It's difficult to assess what it is that you don't know.
- An entire body of knowledge and skill is waiting to be accessed.
- Like technology, teamwork is here to stay.
- It's essential to become "team literate" for tomorrow's workplace.

When I question people about what "team" means, I find they have an expansive range of definitions—almost entirely based on each individual's past experiences. What logically follows is that those who have had good experiences like the idea of working in teams and those who have not had good experiences do not. To access more of the available potential, deliberate, and common defin-itions and understandings must be developed.

Providing Context

To maintain enthusiasm and motivation during the difficult times—and all communities, whether work teams or otherwise, have them—people need to develop a better grasp of "Why teams?" and "Why networks of teams?" Following are four levels of context that are essential to comprehend in order to develop the staying power and commitment required for the evolution and success of team and community processes.

The interconnected, systemic nature of technical work is making it less and less possible for an individual to achieve his or her objectives alone. As technology and goals become more and more part of a whole and as they become more complex and interrelated, each person's work tends to be only part of a much larger service, product, or system. Thus, it makes sense to organize in ways that model and aid the work to be achieved and allow the greatest possibilities for collaboration.

Technology has increased the activity level and accelerated the pace of work. As the depth and complexity of tasks and requirements intensify, no one person can be the expert. People need to focus on different pieces of the pie, rely on each other for expertise on other pieces of the pie, and support each other in integrat-ing it all into a whole pie. In order to accomplish this, teams of people must for-mally and informally communicate well, turn on a dime together, and trust each others' expertise and motives.

Expectations of performance are also changing dramatically. The single act of distributing responsibility—to lessen delays resulting from decision-making processes that go up the chain and then back down again for implementation—has changed everything. Additionally, over the last decade many people's expectations of the workplace have changed. More and more they want work to be meaningful—beyond a paycheck and promotions. To accommodate these polar changes, groups of people need to be able to draw deeply on their collective whole—for creative new solutions, for weathering changes, and for developing the best work possible with the least resource in the smallest amount of time.

Organizational environments provide us with interesting times of flux as giants fall, babes in the woods grow, and businesses of all shapes and sizes work to "reinvent" or "reengineer" themselves in the quest to stay viable. Rules are changing at some very basic level. Once power is distributed, organizational life becomes a whole new experience. Learning to work in teams and to get work done through teams is great career enrichment.

Working Toward Congruence

Creating a congruent work environment includes continuously searching for and challenging assumptions, consciously aiming for resonance between beliefs and behaviors, naming the truth, and listening carefully to the truth being named by others. Congruent situations feel honest, natural, and balanced.

Building a network of work teams does not easily occur—if it occurs at all—where those in power operate on the principle of "Do as I say, not as I do." For example, it is difficult to believe that teams are the most valued principle for organizing where rewards are almost entirely based on individual performance. This does not mean organizations must solely reward teams. However, in this case congruence can best be demonstrated by rewarding both individual and team excellence—if that is what is truly desired and valued.

Myths develop in attempts to quiet the dissonance of incongruent messages within work environments. One I frequently hear is that "teams only work well where everyone is equal". In this case "equal" means people have similar backgrounds, are at the same grade level, and do similar work. On the contrary, it is possible and useful for highly diversified groups of individuals to be very effective teams. In fact, many teams must draw on differences in order to achieve their objectives. Think, for example, of a hospital emergency room team.

Having to appear equal is a tyranny that can lead to mediocrity. Highly talented people with personal authority and natural leadership fear being overbearing and so deprive themselves, their colleagues, and the organization of their best contribution. On the other hand, people who choose to be more low key or who have few aspirations for "getting ahead" hide what they really want out of work—or apologize for it. Those who have less experience hide their lack of competence rather than being able to vulnerably learn from the more experienced.

In truth, no one is equal to any one else in terms of experience and talent. Yet, everyone is equal in that each person deserves to be able to make his/her fullest contribution and to be respected for it. Equality is often confused with "sameness." Fairness and respect—allowing for a multitude of differences—need to be the goals.

Another myth that attempts to quiet incongruence revolves around the roles and expectations of managers. Because of rank, goes the myth, managers are supposed to know more about being in teams and networks of teams than anyone else does, to be perfect models, and to have the answers. Often, however, they have no more experience or understanding of teams and community than do the people who report to them. Everyone is learning together at the same time. On the other hand, many managers believe that if they distribute power they abdicate rights to have an opinion or to veto a group's recommendations. Teams have been known to bully managers with statements like "But you told us we were empowered! You can't have it both ways!" In truth, it *is* both ways. Sharing power is not abdication of responsibility or accountability. Leading in a network of work teams is a case of both distributing power to others and keeping it for oneself.

DESIGNING APPROPRIATE STRUCTURES

As with designing a house, everything from personal preference and available materials to cost considerations must be factored in when deciding what structure is most appropriate for any given organization. It is critical to approach team and community development with basic questions such as "What's the most sensible and efficient way to get our work done with the people and other resources available?" Far more success results from a simple, straightforward approach than from attempting to fit into a template or, in other words, from seeking to "do it right". Having to follow someone else's formula establishes artificial boundaries and can stifle natural growth and creative potential. When it comes to human interaction, frameworks are more useful for purposes of informing us than for purposes of conforming us.

Structure is a veneer, simply superficial. Form, or structure, must follow function to be useful and meaningful. Function can be defined as a reason for being. In other words, the most effective structures somehow manage to mirror the work to be done and blend it with the skills, talents, and needs of the individuals present. When there is a myth that the form, the outline, of an organization is of primary importance, it's possible to conclude that "if we can get everything very clearly defined and literal then we'll be able to erase the ambiguities" that are inherent in today's workplace. It's not likely. In most cases, work and roles are dynamic not static. Together, any group of people embodies a living, growing, and changing system. Thus, about the time things seem to get "pinned down," something else changes, affecting everything.

Let us consider some critical success factors for developing appropriate designs for teams and networks of teams.

Architectural Style

Each team and manager needs to decide together what the most appropriate relationship is between them—based on what makes the most sense for getting the work done, given where they are in the construction process. For team processes to fully function at early stages of development, managers need to more fully integrate themselves with the teams than would be true of being in a traditional, hierarchical structure. Further developed teams can create relationships where the managers attend team meetings as contributing members without being expected to lead, without being deferred to, and without the team missing a beat in its usual, ongoing processes and everyday personality. Or, conversely, in yet more fully developed teams managers can be absent for significant periods of time.

Alignment of Language and Expectations

A recent, high profile template emerging in business organizations is called "self-directed teams." In truth, it is not possible for a group of people to function within a larger system and be self-directed. Each team is a component of a larger system. If I have a self-directed eye or leg, it's a problem for my entire body. The eye and the leg may each have independent tasks and different functions but they serve a larger whole. In fact, that's all they do. No matter what, they are part of the hierarchical system of my body. The term "self-directed" leaves many people new to working with team processes with dashed expectations. They tend to identify "self-directed" with "unmanaged" or "autonomous." While it may appear to an outside observer that a team is operating autonomously, to be truly effective, team structures—no matter what they are called—actually require more interdependence and integration than do top-down organizations.

The Blend of Circle and Triangle

As team processes are introduced in technical organizations there can be a tendency to conclude that forming teams means eliminating the hierarchy. Rather than either hierarchy or teams, the focus needs to be on creating the most productive interactions between dynamics of the two forms. The merging of and interplay between the triangle and circle is an evolutionary leap for western culture. The triangle, or hierarchy, has been the primary organizing principle for getting work done at least since the Roman Army. The circle, the team, has been present throughout human history but primarily outside the western workplace. Given the magnitude of the changes occurring in the hierarchical form, how can we expect to "get it" in a couple of years or a couple of tries? This is a deep and powerful change.

A HOME IS MORE THAN A HOUSE

Even if the ground is firm and the building design wins awards for having superb architecture, success toward developing work community is not assured. These additional ingredients are also important to consider.

The Nature of Human Relationships

First, in establishing team processes or in deepening them, the most essential ingredient is the energy already present. It is essential to attend to and develop the existing passions and interests and/or dissatisfactions and desires for change. In human systems, no matter where we begin, we will touch all aspects. Relationships are an intricate web where everything is connected to everything else.

Second, for a collection of individuals to become a team, it takes everyone to say "Yes." The range of positive contribution can be from cheerleader to devil's advocate. However, the person who does not find positive ways to serve the whole can have tremendous negative power. Even though building teams and community may not be easy, it can be fulfilling and enjoyable when everyone is sincerely invested in working together. In groups where people have interdependent goals and one or two don't buy in, the entire group flounders.

Viewing Human Processes Along a Continuum

One can see a profound relationship between what's changing in the world and what's changing in our minds. Western science is leading the way in helping us see that things are not always as they seem; that there are myriad shades of gray between black and white. Developing a field of view in addition to a point of view becomes paramount when focusing on human relationships. This can be hard work and is truly a growing edge for technical people whose life work supports binary systems based on 0 and 1.

But, technical or otherwise, developing the ability to perceive shades of gray takes both time and practice for anyone. Here are three suggestions on how to do this:

Hybrid. Create new solutions and further develop current methods, mechanisms, and structures so that they become stronger, more resilient, flexible, fluid, and effective in meeting the honest needs of the environment; be open to continuous change as needed in order to move from the current state toward the vision of an ideal state.

Approximation. Recognize and then continuously remember that all teams are a complex web of human relationships; that in human relationships progress is made by moving through a series of iterations. We are in a continuous state of learning about ourselves, each other, and what makes our relationships work best. Thus, safety to make mistakes—created in measure by both humility and forgiveness—supports this form of learning enormously.

Process. Establish constant reminders that it is the journey itself and the inns along the way that are primary and that offer learning and meaning. In human relationships perfect or final destinations are elusive illusions. Each of us is headed toward a unique individual destination and, for particular periods of time, we travel a road together. Building teams and networks of teams is a dynamic, ever-changing, ever-evolving expression of human interaction. Attempts to "achieve" or solidify community in time, space, membership, or other physical attributes cause its tender, vulnerable, ever-shifting nature to crumble or shatter.

Ensuring Conditions for Success

For teams to flourish and for the possibility of deeper community to evolve, certain conditions must exist. Some of these conditions are:

- a clear, shared vision and purpose.
- ongoing support and commitment.
- a value for everyone as a learner.
- encouragement of risk-taking and experimentation.
- the discipline of inquiry, of living in unanswered questions.
- an aspiration for collaboration toward synergy.

A FINAL NOTE

In climbing Everest an expedition team may spend eleven months or more preparing to best insure that the one month climb goes as successfully as is humanly possible. By the time the climb occurs, the team members have built up significant trust in one another. They know each other so well that they can anticipate each others' moves and operate with speed, precision, efficiency, and compassion. These same principles apply to teamwork and the interdependent relationships within communities of people climbing the mountains in today's marketplace.

Once the ridge of the Marketplace Mountains is reached, however, another much higher mountain range still exists and must be crossed. It is the incredibly high and seemingly endless mountain range of our global predicament. The magnitude of what faces us is overwhelming. It appears there are no conventional planning or climbing techniques to help us surmount these mountains. We cannot "fix" the symptoms of social disintegration and violence, of environmental degradation and overpopulation by staying within the confines of the problem solving frameworks of our past.

Community can provide the sanctified space for us to explore our minds and discover deeply held assumptions that contribute to our current predicament. Then, that same blessed space can be used to draw out the unlimited creative potential of our collective consciousness. Community offers us possibility that is simultaneously ancient in its origin and futuristic in our life's experience.

Business, being the most functional, powerful, and dynamic infrastructure that currently exists, provides both the stage and the purpose for learning how to work together creatively. Birthing teams and networks of teams and further developing them into communities that are safe, compassionate, and resilient allows us to achieve business success on a specific, small plot of land. It also offers us the possibility of evolving together in new ways; of trailblazing toward unprecedented breakthrough learning and creativity that may offer new hope for regenerating the entire vista of our ailing and only home.

Michelle & Joel Levey

are synergy builders who specialize in personal mastery, team and community building, and transformational leadership skills. The Leveys' pioneering work has inspired leaders and teams in more than 150 major organizations including AT&T Bell Labs, Du Pont, Hewlett-Packard, Travelers Insurance, Group Health Cooperative, and NASA. As core faculty for the International Center for Organization Design, the International Institute for Innovation, and The Performance Edge, their work with change strategy teams from large organizations focuses on building synergy between personal, professional and organizational change and development.

The Leveys are co-authors of *Quality of Mind* and the best-selling business audio program *The Focused Mindstate*. They are based in Seattle and are co-founders of InnerWorkTechnologies, Inc., a firm that works with leaders in business to build high performing, change resilient individuals, teams, leaders, and organizational cultures.

9

From Chaos to Community at Work

Joel and Michelle Levey

The most exciting breakthrough of the 21st century will occur not because of technology, but because of an expanding concept of what it means to be human."
—John Naisbitt, *Megatrends 2000*

For millions of years we primates have faced the chaos of our world by taking refuge in community. Just as our ancestors huddled together for warmth, banded together for protection, teaching the young, gathering provisions, we gather today to seek out warmth, nourish ourselves, and find safe passage and clear direction in the company of others. From recent research in the natural sciences it is clear that cooperation is a more cogent force for survival and sustainability than competition. Feeling ourselves as members of a community seems essential to our well-being and our health. As former health care providers and medical researchers—and corporate consultants for fifteen years—we can assure you that the "dis-ease" of loneliness is one of the most common and devastating illnesses of our time and our culture.

People are starving for meaningful, nourishing, supportive relationships. In a culture where more than 75 percent of the population do not know their neighbors, people are starving for connectedness, belonging, and for the assurance and fulfillment that comes from being in the midst of a circle of deeply committed friends. The malaise seems largely due to a lack of knowing people more deeply and failing to discover a common sense of purpose, meaning, vision, and values that are vital to community life.

COMMUNITY AT WORK

In response to this time of radical, unrelenting change, more and more business leaders are searching for effective strategies to build more high performing organizations. Challenged to learn and adapt to increasingly complex pressures and to use material and human resources more efficiently, many organizations are demonstrating a commitment to building organizations where people and teams are equipped to learn and develop themselves in the midst of change. What these leaders are looking for are ways to improve productivity, job effectiveness, communications, teamwork, creativity, and innovation. Regardless of the inclinations of management, or the brand of management philosophies they ascribe to, it seems that all of our clients are attempting to improve the quality of their business by helping their people build a better quality of relationships and work life. As this aspiration is fulfilled, a noticeable sense or spirit of community begins to emerge within an organization, accompanied by a greater potential for synergy, innovation, and transformation.

In our work, community building isn't necessarily an explicit goal at the outset. However, a spirit of community will often emerge as we create a context for people to remember, discover, and share their personal values and priorities.

The most efficient, productive, fulfilling, healthy and sustainable forms of human relationships take place within community. If we are committed, communicative, and creative enough we can foster conditions that nurture the potentials of both individual and organization excellence by building quality working relationships. Since most people spend the bulk of their life at work, it makes good sense—both socially and businesswise—to foster the development of community in the workplace. As the rate of change continues to escalate, it is clear that ways of working based solely on competition, individualism, and leadership must give way to wiser ways of working more cooperatively and supportively in teams and adaptable workplace communities.

SYNERGY: THE STRENGTH OF COMMUNITY

The strength of a relationship or community can be measured by the magnitude of challenge it can sustain. When faced with challenges, relationships and communities either come together or fall apart. Each community is comprised of complex and multidimensional individuals. Each individual is also, in a very real sense, a community composed of a multitude of dynamic forces. The learning necessary for an individual human being to efficiently manage the interplay of his or her own physiological, emotional, and mental processes is mind boggling. As social and business concerns bring us together, this mind-boggling complexity quotient goes up exponentially with each person added to the intricate web of relationships that weave us into community.

As social beings living amidst a myriad of complex personal and professional relationships, we are continually challenged to effectively communicate and harmonize our inner feelings, values, intelligence, and experience with others. To the degree that we are successful at this we are able to respond to enormous amounts of information and to effectively carry out patterns of behavior that are synergistically more complex and far reaching than any individual could ever accomplish.

CONSCIOUSNESS AND COMMUNITY

In the early days of research on complex systems, mechanistic theories posited that consciousness was merely an artifact of the number of elements within a system. With the evolution of science, more contemporary views now regard consciousness as a property that emerges within a system when a certain level of organization (that is, relationship, connectivity, and communication) is reached.

According to many respected systems thinkers, any system capable of self-organization or self-management is endowed with some level of consciousness. The quality of consciousness within a system is defined not by how many neurons, or members, it has but rather by the quality of relationships, interactions and communication among its members. As the quality of relationship is developed, the system grows in its ability to receive, process and generate appropriate information, and the level of consciousness within the system is raised. From this point of view individuals, teams, and organizations are all endowed with some level of consciousness. Each has the ability to absorb, assimilate, and generate meaningful information that is vital to self-management, learning and adaptation.

THE EMERGENCE OF COMMUNITY AT WORK

Community, like consciousness, is a property that will emerge in complex, living systems under conducive conditions. When a certain threshold of complexity is reached in a biological system, consciousness emerges. When the quality of relationship (that is, the quality of information flow among members of a social system), reaches a certain threshold, the consciousness of community emerges. The presence and power of a community at work are measurably indicated by significantly higher levels of adaptability, change resilience, productivity, efficiency and lower levels of distress, wasted resources, time, effort, and people.

SPECTRUM OF COMMUNITY DEVELOPMENT

As the spirit of community emerges there is the potential for development along multiple dimensions. Based on mutual concerns and values, "de facto communities" are linked by proximity or affiliation. Such communities may be comprised of employees of the same company, residents of the same neighborhood, members of an ethnic group or religion, or survivors of a disaster who are all drawn together out of a common set of circumstances. If members of a "de facto community" increase their communication and develop and align around a shared set of purpose, vision, values, and codes of conduct, they may make the evolutionary step to become an "intentional community."

A further leap on this continuum of community development leads to resilient "generative learning communities" where there is a high priority on

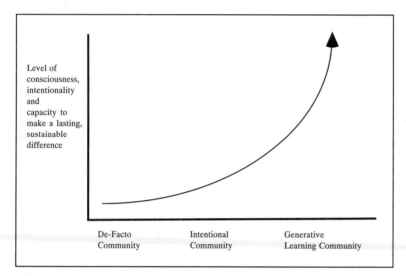

Figure 1

continuous learning and sustainable improvement of the quality of work and of work life.

THE EXPERIENCE OF COMMUNITY

Pause for a few moments to reflect on what you have experienced when you've been part of a community. In your mind's eye recall and replay those moments and scenes when you felt a sense of belonging to a larger social network of interests and concerns, a time when communications flowed easily between the people with whom you were working.

When you remember these times, what qualities of relationship leap out for you? What factors were present or absent in the physical or social environment that allowed this sense of community to emerge? What inner qualities of mind and heart were most alive within you? What challenges were met and what strategies did you share to meet these challenges?

Now, looking forward, what would "building a sense of community" look like at work? What indicators would tell you and your co-workers that you had been successful in building a community at work?

We have found that effective working communities are created through building the dynamic synergy and interplay of three primary and interrelated dimensions: individual, interpersonal or team, and organizational. Looking more deeply into each of these three domains will provide an outline of the skill-sets and qualities necessary for individuals, teams and organizations to build a strong spirit of community at work and keep it going and growing.

On the individual level, this triple matrix is founded in the enhancement of personal awareness and skills. It is cultured in the seedbed of interpersonal or team factors such as the quality of communications, trust, alignment on purpose, values, vision, care, appreciation and shared learning. Organizational factors such as the role, quality and motivation of leadership, organization design and infra-structure, social architecture and knowledge architecture provide the ongoing

PERSONAL MASTERY *Building Synergy of* *ORGANIZATIONAL EXCELLENCE*

Creative Intelligence

Wisdom & Love at Work

Organization Design

Reward & Recognition Systems

QUALITY RELATIONSHIPS *At the Heart of Community*

Mastery of Attention

Knowledge Architecture

Mastering Stress

Leadership

Trust

Quality Communications

Commitment to Common Purpose, Vision, Values and Strategies

HIGH PERFORMANCE TEAM WORK

© Joel Levey,
InnerWork Technologies, Inc., 1992.

Figure 2

vital nourishment necessary to sustain and nurture the community's generative potential. The common ground for all of these factors is the quality of working relationships. (See Figure 2)

QUALITY RELATIONSHIPS

Quality relationships are at the heart of community. To understand how essential they are, pause to consider first how the quality of relationships affects you personally: For example, when you have breakdowns in relationships with people at work or at home, how does that affect the level of your distress? How does that affect the quality of your attention? The quality of your work? The quality of your safety?

An example comes to mind of a man who through his intensity had pushed to the top of his sales force. He was considered very successful by his peers but admitted that he was usually distracted and plagued by feelings of guilt at giving such poor attention and care to his two small children. He realized that if he didn't give his family priority, his professional success, his health, and his family were all in jeopardy. He would be well advised to build greater balance in his whole life.

On the other side of the spectrum, can you remember times when you have felt respected, supported and cared for by the people with whom you lived or worked? How has the support, and appreciation of your co-workers affected how you showed up at home? How has the love and care you experience with your loved ones and family influenced what you were able to contribute and bring to work?

Consider how important the quality of relationships is to the success of your business? Can you imagine how much time, energy, effort, and precious human resources are wasted each day and each year because of breakdowns in relationship? Most costly problems in business are the result of breakdowns in relationship.

High Performance Teamwork

Over the years, we've asked the individuals and teams that we work with, "What qualities of relationships are vital to the spirit of community emerging on your team at work?" The responses we receive generally cluster into four main categories, which are intrinsically interwoven.

Build Trust

The sense or spirit of community can only fully blossom in an environment of trust. To build, nurture and sustain an environment of trust in a working community, requires frequent, open, honest, heartfelt communication. Such an ongoing gesture of caring for the community will assure that breakdowns in trust are addressed when they are whispers and are not allowed to grow into screams and schisms of distrust and separation.

Improve Communication

The flow of information between people is the lifeblood of communities. For communications to be effective, we must learn and practice skills for communicating with ever increasing clarity and caring. These skills are especially important for working with conflict and for transforming breakdowns into breakthroughs.

Shared Purpose, Vision, and Values

Clarity and alignment around purpose, vision and values create the necessary organizational context for community to emerge. They guide the work processes and strategies that we use to transform our vision into a living, working reality. When members of a team or organization have clarity, coherence and commitment regarding their purpose, values and vision virtually anything can be accomplished. Purpose guides our vision. Vision informs our values.

Commitment

When the members of a community/team/ organization are truly committed to realizing a goal, they will muster the energy, creativity and resources necessary to accomplish it. Being committed to a vision or goal doesn't necessarily imply that the strategy or means of fulfilling that vision are known with complete certainty. But when we share a commitment to work together in a certain way and toward a certain goal, we will find a way to realize our goal.

PERSONAL MASTERY

Our ability to be effective and to do a quality job of managing our working relationships is directly related to our level of personal awareness and skills. The quality of our relationships is certain to reflect many of the strengths and weaknesses of our work with ourselves. The attitudes and actions of a single individual can have an enormous impact on leading a community toward breakdown or breakthrough.

Again and again, we have seen that the most effective "change champions" and community leaders are those who understand and embody the synergy between personal and organizational change and transformation. With these ideas in mind, let's look at five primary areas of personal inner work that determine our effectiveness in moving from chaos to community.

Mastering Stress

Learning to master stress is a gesture of personal conflict resolution and non-violence. Unchecked distress accumulates gradually, almost imperceptibly over time. It is essential that we learn to check in with ourselves frequently throughout the day. If we do this, we will hear many whispers but few screams. Our energy will be channeled productively and efficiently with little wasted time and effort. If stress is not allowed to accumulate, people will not experience stress-related illness. In working teams and relationships the same principle holds true: If we recognize and respond to the early warning signs of distress, we will seldom encounter major breakdowns.

> Since wars begin in the minds of men, it is in the minds of men
> that we have to erect the ramparts of peace.
> —UNESCO Charter

Mindfulness and the Mastery of Attention

The quality of your attention is a key to the quality of your personal health and performance as well as a major factor in determining the quality of presence that you bring to your community. *Mindfulness*, the fundamental attentional skill, provides a powerful alternative to the all too common practice of *mindlessness* that leads to so many problems and missed opportunities in our lives. Mindfulness enables you to focus wholeheartedly and be present with whatever you are doing or experiencing moment to moment. Mindfulness is the key to quality relationships, quality communications, intuition, creativity, and wisdom.

Wisdom at Work

As we learn to recognize and reduce our internal turbulence and to build the power of our mindfulness, the natural clarity, stability and peace of mind reveals itself. This is the ground of all true insight. With greater sensitivity to the flow of information from both our inner and outer environments, we are better equipped to respond with deeper insight, wiser decisions and more efficient actions. As our personal energy management skills grow, the clarity and power of the mind emerges. We live more "in the flow", accomplishing more with less and less effort. Managing our energy more effectively, we accomplish the minor miracle of being more present with whomever we are with and whatever we are doing.

Love and Compassion at Work

Just as prejudice, hatred, and violence spring naturally from a turbulent and undisciplined mind, love and compassion spring naturally from a mind that has been tamed and is able to be really present with others. Through living with the calm intensity of mindfulness, you'll be more likely to experience a quality of connectedness to others that gives rise to a genuine and heartfelt sense of empathy, care, concern and compassion. You find yourself living in a world to which you feel you belong and are deeply connected to. And as your concentration and mindfulness deepen, so does your sense of connection and caring for everyone you meet. Understanding this you discover that the experience of community is to be found in the quality of heart-mind with which you regard your world. As Einstein so poignantly reminded us:

> A human being is part of the whole called by us 'universe', a part limited in time and space. We experience ourselves, our thoughts and feelings as something separate from the rest. A kind of optical delusion of consciousness. This delusion is a kind of prison for us, restricting us to our personal desires and to affection for a few persons nearest to us. Our task must be to free ourselves from the prison by widening our circle of compassion to embrace all living creatures and the whole of nature in its beauty....We shall require a substantially new manner of thinking if humankind is to survive.

Creative Intelligence at Work

Living and working with less distress, greater wisdom, compassion and creativity helps you to build better working relationships. With better quality relationships, you will be less likely to be burdened by excess tension and anxiety. This will leave your mind undisturbed and better equipped to focus your attention in order to see more deeply, clearly and sensitively into whatever is going on—within you and around you. With greater insight and peace of mind you will experience a deeper quality of regard and compassion for others, and you will become more sensitive to the interplay of the myriad systems and fields of influences that weave the complex fabric of our lives together. This enhanced ability to analyze and think clearly in terms of complex interrelated systems will open new dimensions of reasoning, intuition, power and innovative potential. Greater wisdom and insight coupled with the generative power of empathy and compassion will give you the strength of will and the fierce commitment needed to live and work with the kind of integrity that can build the synergy of wisdom, love, and creativity so vital to community.

As Vaclav Havel, former President of Czechoslovakia, reminded us as he spoke to the U.S. Congress,

> ...the salvation of this human world lies nowhere else than in the human heart, in the human power to reflect, in human meekness and in human responsibility. Without a global revolution in the sphere of human consciousness, nothing will change for the better in the sphere of our being as humans, and the catastrophe towards which this world is headed—be it ecological, social, demographic or a general breakdown of civilization—will be unavoidable.

Organizational Excellence

It makes good business sense for a business or organization to foster a spirit of community at work because it is simply more energy efficient, productive and motivating for its members to make their maximum contribution. Every business and organization is made of people who, regardless of their cultural and psychological backgrounds, share similar human values and concerns. Rolf Österberg, former President of Svensk Filmindustri, has said it well:

> The key to our inner resources is self-knowledge. Self-knowledge is gained by personal development—that is by collecting experiences out of which new insight and wisdom are born. In fact, this comes close to being the meaning of life. Consequently, the raison-d'etre for a company is to supply an environment in which personal development of the human beings involved in the company can best take place... What a precious gift to humankind and to our planet it would be if the remarkable knowledge we have achieved should be united with wisdom. Then our planet would be the paradise it is meant to be. Business life has the opportunity to bring that gift forward.

When personal priorities are aligned with the values and aims of an organization, people are willing to generously participate in their work. At an organizational level, numerous factors may encourage or discourage the emergence of a sense of community at work. Let's look at some of the important factors that emerge when we ask, "How do we design an organization that is conducive to building a sense of community at work?"

Quality of Leadership

For communities to emerge at work, inspiring and intelligent leadership is essential. Keep in mind that the leaders in organizations are not necessarily the people who hold the highest positions in the business hierarchy. Leaders are key players in helping a community to discover, define, and pursue its sense of purpose, vision, values and direction. In ideal circumstances, leaders will serve as inspiring role models and mentors for others by how they embody and communicate the personal qualities necessary to be a good team player and member of the community.

Organization Design and Infrastructure

The design of an organization plays a significant role in helping or hindering the emergence of community at work. There are many models and examples of ways to organize the work in an organization. When in doubt of what would work best within your organization, involve the people who do the work in a process to define and design your organization. Matching responsibility with ownership and authority is an important way to build a sense of community and involvement at work.

Reward and Recognition Systems

These play an important part in determining the quality of working relationships and either encouraging or discouraging the emergence of a sense of community. In most organizations that we have worked in existing rating and recognition systems are a major inhibition to building community. If your organization is committed to building a spirit of community at work, the reward and recognition systems can be used to help the process when:

- The community is entrusted with the task of revising these systems to work for them.
- A system of rewards and recognition is put in place that is fair and conducive to recognizing both individual and collaborative contributions.

Knowledge Architecture

An organization's "knowledge architecture" determines the community effectiveness in every activity of communication, planning, and learning. All human systems are nourished by information, and a community's ability to access, assimilate, learn, remember, tap collective experience, and wisely respond depends on the integration and orchestration of many hard and soft information technologies at work.

THE LEADER'S CHALLENGE

Never doubt that a small group of thoughtful, committed citizens can change the world. Indeed, it's the only thing that ever has.
—Margaret Mead

Communities and businesses are composed of individuals who, each in their own way, are engaged in a personal experiment of self-discovery and understanding. If we take this inquiry to heart we will gain valuable insight into human nature and the forces that drive us all. By learning about our values, thought processes, emotions, and physiological processes we can gain a tremendous appreciation for how these powerful forces are at work in our co-workers and loved ones. Your hunger teaches you about the hunger of others. Your feelings of anger or joy, accomplishment or frustration, are similar to my own. Learning about ourselves provides valuable insights about working effectively with others. The better we are able to understand and support each other, the better prepared we are to build the qualities of relationship necessary for a spirit of community to emerge at work.

In the years to come the complexity, pressure, uncertainty, and change that people in business will be challenged to adapt to will intensify and accelerate beyond our imaginations. With this in mind we often invite the business leaders and change champions we work with to engage in the following inquiry:

- What would happen if you were to turn up the intensity of your own commitment to personal inquiry?
- Can you imagine what would happen in your organization if you were to take these principles to heart and build a business or organization in which these qualities of personal and interpersonal relationships could synergize to allow the emergence of a spirit of community at work?
- What would happen if you were to invite and encourage others in your organization to join you in this work and actively share their insights?
- Can you afford not to support the people in your organization as they do the inner and outer work necessary to accept this challenge?

Bill Veltrop

is a leading "evolutionary agent" in the fields of organization design, learning, and change. He is convinced we are in the early stages of a quantum shift in the life-giving potential of our organizing forms. He is the founder of The International Center For Organization Design, a network of leading-edge change champions passionately committed to supporting this shift.

A consultant with more than twenty years of innovative organization design and large-scale change implementation experience in the United States, Canada, Europe, and the Far East, Veltrop has discovered that magic is possible when spirit and heart are evoked.

A hands-on futurist, he is particularly adept in serving as architect to alliances, designs, change strategies and events that help unfold generative new futures for all involved. As visionary author and speaker, he challenges leaders and providers of change services to weave creative new alliances in the service of transforming the field of transformation itself.

10

Discovering a Generative Path to Organizational Change

Bill Veltrop

Business is in the process of transforming itself. The signs are everywhere. Business organizations are restructuring and re-engineering themselves at ever-increasing rates. Change has become our only constant.

The results have been mixed, at best. Most large-scale change initiatives take longer than expected, cost more than expected, are much more painful than expected, and simply don't deliver the expected benefits. Even when these initiatives are "successful" in re-engineering the infrastructure to eliminate waste, the organizations frequently become more machine-like.

Today's change initiatives are primarily based on a problem-solving view of organizations and change. They usually ignore the potential for *generative change*. Generative change is change designed to be life giving—change that builds in the organizational capacity not only to continuously improve *what is* but also to make evolutionary leaps to *what's possible*.

I am convinced it is possible to achieve a major breakthrough in the effectiveness of organizational change work—and do so in a way that helps create a new and more sustainable game of business. I see an incredibly large opportunity gap between what is and what's possible in the domain of organizational change.

This essay is written for a new kind of player in the game of organizational learning and change. These players are convinced that a radical breakthrough in effectiveness of organizational change work is essential, and they are hungry for ways to facilitate that breakthrough. They include both champions of change within organizations and external providers of organizational learning and change expertise. They are characterized by their level of commitment to consciously evolve themselves, their relationships, and the organizations they serve.

I call these players "Allies." They are individuals who recognize that we are all in this together—who appreciate that reinventing the game of organizational change demands that we learn to ally ourselves in new and generative ways. Today, these players are like puzzle pieces scattered within and around organizations.

The intent of this essay is threefold:

1. To sound a note that helps to bring Allies into relationship with each other so that we might explore how to creatively collaborate in this quest.
2. To sketch out an emerging organizing form—generative learning communities—as an organic approach to growing and spreading high leverage organizational learning and change innovations.
3. To highlight co-creative relationships as a prime source of energy and inspiration to support each of the above.

How do we know if we're Allies?

We will know we are Allies by our declarations and by our actions. For the most part we are players already involved in the work of organizational learning and change. We can be distinguished by the excitement we feel about the challenge of collectively bridging the opportunity gap—of exploring and pioneering new territory altogether.

Our beliefs are another clue. We believe that business can lead the global transformation that will reverse the nonsustainable path that business and society have been walking for so long. We are also convinced that this change can only be as effective as our own inner work. We've begun to experience the reality of "As within, so without. As without, so within."

On a more personal note, we will know each other by the amazing ways we begin to show up in each other's lives—by the seeming coincidences and synchronicities that bring us together.

Currently, we are mostly working in isolation from each other. This essay is a call for Allies to recognize one another and to begin to connect. We are on the same quest: looking for a path forward that fundamentally shifts the game of business.

Have you mapped such a path forward?

Not exactly. We're talking radically new territory. I've spent a couple of decades getting clear about the nature of this particular quest and I find it quite humbling. I'm convinced that no one has *the* answer or *the* map. The path forward will emerge from the collective initiatives and learnings of a large number of Allies who have moved to a new level of collaboration and co-creativity.

Although I don't have a whole map, I do have a number of ideas for evolving and sharing maps as we collectively step forward in search of the new game. Once we've created a network committed to supporting this evolutionary shift within and across organizations of all kinds, I see incredible potential for dramatic breakthroughs.

What makes you believe that such dramatic breakthroughs in organizational change work are possible?

I'm excited by the huge gap I see between the relatively low effectiveness of our current change initiatives and what is possible if we approach change in ways that are generative—life giving and self-evolving in nature.

Let me start by focusing on the state of current initiatives.

We've had a pretty mediocre track record so far. For instance, an A.D. Little study showed that two-thirds of the Total Quality programs in the United States had failed to produce "competitive impact." A Wyatt study revealed that while three-quarters of the respondents felt that restructuring had improved productivity, fewer than half of them were satisfied with the total results.

Why is the track record so poor?

There are lots of reasons. For example, too often these organization-wide change efforts aren't linked directly and strongly enough to business purpose and measures. Many are too single-minded: delivering just one type of solution throughout the organization, using single-solution "change architects," or focusing on only one or two of the primary stakeholder groups.

Mostly, they've tended to invest in improving the traditional paradigm rather than creating new ones. They've usually concentrated on problem-solving methodologies and ignored the potential of discovering and building on miracles that already exist.

They frequently proceed in ways that unconsciously erode rather than build trust. For example, it's not at all unusual for a management team to go through an exercise of creating an exciting vision and design for the future, and then shoot themselves in the collective foot by the way they orchestrate the work of change.

As I see it, *how* we approach the work of organizational change is all-important. If this work embodies the future we want, then we have a good shot at bringing that vision to life. If it doesn't, credibility erodes and negative beliefs are reinforced.

One big reason why the old paradigm is so sticky is our unconscious collusion in defining success almost exclusively in terms of financial wealth. I would invite us to think of *true wealth* as including all aspects of well-being: physical, mental, spiritual, and emotional as well as financial. "True wealth" is not at all easy to measure today, but we can develop that capability if we so choose.

Why is thinking in terms of "true wealth" so important?

Organizations exist to serve the needs of stakeholders: customers, investors, members, suppliers, local communities, government regulators, and even competitors. A larger circle of stakeholders ripples out from this first group and includes families, society, and future generations.

Many stakeholders are becoming increasingly conscious of their choices and of the consequences of those choices. In fact, I see stakeholder consciousness as an exponentially increasing and irreversible trend. For example, consumers are starting to choose products that are environmentally benign. Employees are beginning to select companies that are socially responsible. Special funds are catering to the socially and environmentally conscious investor.

This irreversible trend toward greater stakeholder consciousness will be a primary force in shaping the new game of businesses. Those enterprises that best appreciate this trend, and are most innovative in maximizing their contribution to the true wealth of all major stakeholder groups, will not only survive; they will thrive.

How does true wealth relate to achieving dramatic breakthroughs in change effectiveness?

We rarely measure the effectiveness of our organizational change work, and when we do we tend to focus primarily on the near-term financials. If we were able to look at change effectiveness in terms of its net contribution to the true wealth of all its stakeholders over time, the picture would be quite sobering.

I find it useful to define change effectiveness in terms of the true leverage of the change initiative, where true leverage is a ratio: all *true stakeholder benefits* divided by *true stakeholder costs*.

Organizational change work is extraordinarily risky business. The benefit-to-cost ratios can fall anywhere between zero and infinity. The figure below illustrates both my sense of where current initiatives cluster and also what I'm convinced is possible.

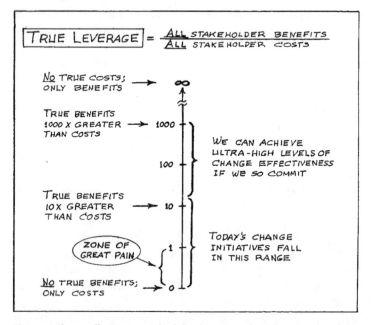

Figure 1: Change effectiveness can be defined in terms of *true leverage*, a benefit-to-cost ratio. Ratios lower than 1.0 indicate that the true costs exceed the true benefits.

How is it possible to realize the "ultra-high leverages" you indicate on your picture?

Traditional organization designs, measures of success, language, mental models, patterns of behavior, and the like can create a very subtle but highly effective "psychic prison" for members. This is especially true if fear is present in the system. Such systems seem perfectly designed to stifle innovation, mutual support, and sense of community. And traditional approaches to organizational change too often tend to exacerbate those fears implicit in hierarchical control, to stir up much resistance, and to incur great psychic costs.

We tend to forget that when not in the grip of fear, people love to grow, to develop, to have an identity, to belong, to contribute, and to make a lasting difference. We forget that everyone has a special gift and purpose and wants to find a way to realize his or her potential.

Organizational change that honors and respects the individual, gradually tearing down the walls of our psychic prisons, will unleash tremendous potential in individuals, teams, and the organization as a whole.

This is new territory. We have very little experience in large-scale change work that fully supports who we are and who we can be—individually and collectively. Furthermore, we grossly underestimate how we, the practitioners and champions of change, are ourselves trapped in old-paradigm thinking and patterns.

We need to challenge ourselves to move far outside our boxes by targeting for ultra-high leverage. We can and must make a shift in the work of organizational learning and change that is as dramatic as that from surface travel to air travel. And we won't invent the airplane by incrementally improving locomotive design.

Achieving the ultra-high levels of change effectiveness indicated in my picture above may seem as "impossible" as putting a man on the moon. But I not only believe that we are collectively up to the challenge, I also believe that the time is ripe and that going for such a goal will sharply accelerate the rate at which we reinvent the game of business.

How will that happen?

Just as a mechanistic approach to change will, at best, give us more efficient organizational machinery, a more generative or self-evolving approach will invite us to recognize and free up the life-giving forces present in that same organization.

The organization of the future, according to many people's vision, is a learning organization—one that is designed and led in a way that develops its individual and organizational capabilities so that it accomplishes its objectives in a changing environment. Free from unnecessary layers of hierarchy, it is nimble, responsive, and flexible. It supports local responsibility and accountability for results.

We need to go even beyond the above vision. If we're going to reinvent the game, let's do it with verve and with heart. Let's create the kind of learning organization that continually redesigns and evolves itself and its stakeholder relationships so that its contribution to the true wealth of those stakeholders keeps increasing as its environment changes.

To reinvent the game of business in ways that are swift and sure, we must reinvent the game of change, aiming for at least a ten-fold improvement (1000 percent) in change effectiveness. As indicated earlier, the key is to design our change work in a way that embodies the future we envision.

What's the secret of "embodying the future" in a current change initiative?

The first step is to approach the work of organizational learning and change with the same level of talent and expertise we would bring to bear on any other future-creating business strategy. A learning/change initiative that embodies the future can be designed and executed in a way that:

- Clearly focuses participating players on developing those organizational capabilities that are essential in realizing a compelling shared vision
- Builds trust and confidence every step of the way
- Is natural and organic in the way it grows and spreads
- Intentionally builds an empowering collection of processes, practices, tools, and stories
- Intentionally builds a sense of community throughout the organization and with its stakeholders
- Gives high priority to an organizational "nervous system" that supports knowledge work in general and this emerging learning/change community in particular
- Attracts the change innovators from all parts of the organization and supports them in making outlandish contributions to the initiative
- Focuses on accelerated development of change architect, change resource, and change leader capabilities
- Creates and evolves organizational design elements that are generative or self-evolving in nature—that is, self-improving, self-sustaining, and self-propagating

It's vital to intentionally set out to melt the iceberg of fear. This requires not only a very special change strategy, but also a special change infrastructure. Using existing infrastructure or forming yet another change team just won't cut it.

The concept of developing a generative learning community as both a change strategy and the primary change infrastructure has exciting possibilities.

What's a generative learning community?

A generative learning community, or GLC, is a sanctioned "skunkworks" for generating, incubating, and spreading high-leverage learning/change innovations. Its mission is to spawn and support self-evolving practices and processes throughout the formal organization.

The members of a GLC are a purposeful community of learners committed to evolving themselves, their teams, and their organization(s) in a way that best serves the common good. They find, attract, aid, and champion those going for breakthroughs in both business results and capability-building.

What might a GLC look like?

That depends on the organization. Let's say we're talking about a GLC formed to accelerate the rate at which the enterprise develops key change capabilities—for example, building a Total Quality culture, decreasing product development cycle time, and reengineering key business processes.

Members would select themselves, and could represent all levels and functions. Member selection processes would involve candidates clarifying their *offers*, identifying what's needed to fulfill these proposed commitments, and securing the support of their personal stakeholders: those who would be affected by their involvement in the GLC. A GLC enrollment team might aid this self-screening process.

All members would have access to a computer-based knowledge system designed to support GLC memory/knowledge management, communication, coordination, and learning. (See George Por's chapter, "A Quest for Collective Intelligence.") Through this medium and others, they would also have access to resource people who bring relevant expertise to the community and are committed to transferring this expertise to the organization in high-leverage ways.

The GLC could periodically sponsor learning carnivals designed to tell the "new story" as it is emerging; engage prospective members in the GLC culture and activities; celebrate breakthroughs in the invention and application of generative designs, processes, tools, and theory; and build a true sense of community and mutual support.

The GLC would be known more by the value-adding ripples it makes throughout the organization than by rhetoric about the group.

How would you go about starting a generative learning community?

The process is a bit like growing a garden or incubating a new life form. This would require special care and attention from the leadership group.

Success is most likely if the leaders of change:

1. Sharply focus on building those key organizational capabilities most essential to long-term business effectiveness.

It's dangerous to settle for anything less than a strong direct linkage between the work of change and what is essential to business sustainability.

2. Plant flowers rather than try to move the mountain.

Everett Rogers' extensive work at SRI on the diffusion of innovation provides us with a powerful way to look at organizational change work. He found that in any social change there is a normally distributed population in terms of readiness to change. The key to having change flow smoothly, naturally, and swiftly is to first work with the natural innovators, those who are already seeking change. Then support these innovators in enrolling those next most likely to change, the "early adopters." The early adopters will naturally attract the interest of the "early majority," and so on. Rogers' research has shown that when an innovation is adopted by 20 percent of the population, it's virtually unstoppable; it will move naturally through the rest of the organization.

One secret to growing a successful GLC is to design it to attract and support the "innovator-bees" and the "early-adopter-bees" and then let nature take its course. The nectar that attracts these bees is the opportunity to make a lasting difference while pursuing their particular individual passion.

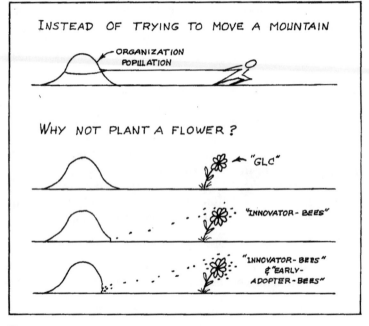

Figure 2

3. Concentrate on ultra high-leverage ideas, tools, distinctions, theories, designs, and practices that are generative—that not only have life in them but also tend to be self-evolving.

For example, traditional goal-setting/feedback loops have been vital processes for supporting organizational planning and control functions. Unfortunately, these traditional control loops can also tend to stifle the spirit of innovation. *Commitment-learning loops* can be designed and implemented in ways that elicit breakthrough commitments and harvest in-depth organizational learnings from the inevitable breakdowns. In addition to being self-evolving themselves, such loops can be used to weave the capacity for self-evolution into all aspects of an organization. They can also stimulate innovation and risk-taking throughout the enterprise.

4. Provide the knowledge infrastructure or nervous system that will support the GLC and the rest of the organization in becoming a community that learns as well as a community of learners.

Implementing a well-designed computer-based nervous system is absolutely essential to such a quantum shift in change effectiveness.

5. Provide the time, space, resources, and care to learn what it takes to incubate a successful learning community.

Many businesses have *spirit*—a special energy that helps align and unite the organization. To develop a learning community, especially one that is capable of evolving itself, requires soul as well. *Organizational soul* has to do with the quality of relationships and the sense of community present. It involves caring and respect, mutual support, and nourishment. Soul and trust go hand in hand; organizational soul grows cold in a climate of fear. It can become severely chilled when subjected to "flavor of the month" change programs and awkwardly managed "restructurings."

There is a measure of fear and distrust in most organizations in these downsizing days. If organizational soul is to be revived, a *safe space* needs to be created.

How do you create safe space?

Here's one possible approach:

Set aside a fixed time and space for learning/change innovators to use for testing proposals, building support, sharing learnings, sponsoring new technologies, and exploring new ways to approach learning and change. This time and place should be declared as safe space, in which people can explore what it takes to support generative learning and to begin to build community.

Before any embryonic innovation can fly, it needs to be incubated and hatched, then nurtured and fed until it has the strength to test its wings. I believe this to be more true for innovations in organization design and change work than for technological innovation. A safe space enables the incubation and nurturing not only of innovations, but also of a learning community that is generative.

Leaders can use this space to try out their wings as innovators and learners, to begin creating a new story through their actions. Potential resource people can be sponsored and introduced to the emerging GLC, and potential alliances can be explored at relatively low risk. The safe-space approach can be introduced and guided in a way that attracts innovators and early adopters and that evolves at its own pace.

You seem passionate about reinventing the game of business. What fuels your passion?

The stakes are very high. The old game clearly isn't working well enough for most of its stakeholders, and the effects not only reverberate through every aspect of our lives, but also ripple out to our children and their children. Shifting our global trends is absolutely dependent on our reinventing the game of business.

The concept of GLCs is incredibly exciting to me, and I see it sprouting in a variety of places. We need to creatively ally ourselves so that we build our collective intelligence and wisdom. One of the most powerful ways we can further the transformational shift is to consciously tap into the richness of relationship. Our more highly evolved social forms will be woven from *co-creative relationships*.

What do you mean by "co-creative relationships"?

Let me get very specific. Allies in my life include a number of the contributors to this book. My relationships with Geoffrey Hulin, Darla Chadima, George Pór, and Joel and Michelle Levey are bringing form to the concept of generative alliances. Also, my relationships with these and a number of other players, such as Marilyn Sammons, Prasad Kaipa, Donna Clark, Dick Eppel, and Brian Yost are the living laboratories for co-creative relationships.

Here are some tidbits I've been harvesting from the living laboratory of my relationships:

Limited View	Co-Creative View
Focus on overcoming limitations	Focus on unfolding other's unique/unlimited gift
See a limited being in need of development	See spirit/soul of other
Problem-solving mind-set dominant	Appreciative mind-set kept foremost
Buy into other's fears/worldview	Create largest/highest context
Deny shadow (uncomfortable, imperfect) side	Can honor and embrace the shadow
Stay in "either/or" mind	Embrace polarities/paradox: the "both/and" mind
Role-bound: parent/child, expert/client	Both seen as equals, as seekers
Force interaction into a method/model	Use other's process and self-authority
Stay logical	Evoke intuition
Stay in own head	Heart activity engaged
Mirror clouded by own projections/biases	Serve as "sacred mirror" for other
Ignore or downplay coincidences	Honor synchronicities
See breakdowns as failures or faults	See all happenings as sources of learning
Slip into judgmental self	Able to be in observer state
Minimize discomfort	Embrace discomfort as a friend and teacher
Constrained by unspoken fears	Grounded in speaking one's truth

All this is wondrously exhilarating to someone who has spent sixty years mastering the role of Lone Ranger!

And this brings us full circle.

In order to serve as leaders and co-creators of a new game of business, we need to master the art of evolving generative relationships within ourselves and with each other. Generative relationships can beget generative learning communities and generative learning organizations. Generative learning organizations will by definition stimulate and nurture generative learning communities and generative relationships.

As within, so without. As without, so within.

What skills and practices do we use to create community?

Part Three: Skills and Practices in Community Building for Organizations

How do we create these communities of learning and caring, where quality is generated out of fulfilling both the human needs as well as those of the organization, and one isn't sacrificed at the expense of the other? How do we resolve the dilemma? Or is there one?

These puzzlers are addressed by the seven authors in this segment, each offering a particular approach to developing community in organizations.

Marvin Weisbord describes his "future search" conferences, which have proven quite successful in creating organizational communities in recent years. Glenna Gerard and Linda Teurfs focus their essay on dialogue and the role it plays in developing community and transforming organizations.

Jim Rough reveals his community-building process—the "wisdom council"—which is particularly applicable to larger organizations. Elemer Magaziner advocates an opening of our hearts to accept human institutions as living systems so that they may achieve the joy of community. Finally, Darla Chadima and Geoffrey Hulin describe a return to an ancient and rediscovered practice of our ancestors that they have found valuable in creating community.

Marvin Weisbord managed a family business during the 1960s and has consulted to corporations and communities in North America and Scandinavia since 1969. He is a founder and co-director of SearchNet, a non-profit network that helps people learn the essentials of future search conferences through local self-managed service internships. His recent book, *Discovering Common Ground*, documents the use of search conferences around the world. He and Sandra Janoff also co-authored *Future Search: An Action Guide to Finding Common Ground in Organizations and Communities.*

11

Future Searches

Marvin Weisbord

"Future search" is my name for a remarkable conference that makes consensus planning possible among people with diverse interests. I coined the term while writing *Productive Workplaces* in 1987. A future search is an optimal planning event for ambiguous "problems without boundaries"—thorny dilemmas posed by the economy, the environment, technology, education, health care, and life in diverse communities.

How would you, for example, get sticky water rights issues out of the courts and into a forum of continuous dialogue among the parties as was done on the Upper Colorado River? How would you shake loose in a few weeks a Massachusetts state legislature bill critical to the future of small manufacturers that had been bottled up for several years? How would you bring together a common vision and action plan from diverse corporate cultures resulting from regional mergers in all four corners of the United States, as was done by Whole Foods Market? How would you take a stalled quality effort and enroll dozens and then hurdreds of people in continuous improvement over several years, as was done by Haworth, Inc. In each case the catalytic event was a future search conference.

METHODOLOGY

The method holds special promise for complex organizations. It has a sound theoretical base and a long history of success in many cultures. People who master the underlying principles can implement bolder action plans more quickly than before. Within hours they are able to build a temporary planning community of folks who have never worked together. In this essay I will describe the future search principles, methods that bring the principles to life, and the dynamics (and related feelings) you can expect during the conference.

Paradoxically, this structure holds special angst for executives. It triggers fears of losing control, opening up issues that can't be closed, having to hear demands that can't be met. It's important to acknowledge those feelings at the same time that we embrace the commonsensical principles. The future search conference takes us very quickly into uncharted territory. We cannot know what will happen until we get there. (Most people find they have more control, not less.) Basic future search principles are widely applicable to the day-to-day management of complex enterprises. Indeed, one principle, "getting the whole system in the room," has become a cornerstone of large-scale change strategies where speed and commitment are critical. The future search makes a good learning laboratory for this principle AND for containing the anxiety it stirs. We deal with the whole system at once. The three elements are:

- economics
- technology
- people

In the past, present, and future in every imaginable combination, we advocate that everybody owns all the data and be responsible for their own perceptions and plans. This is reality-based community building—at once simple and sophisticated. Alone, we are impotent to make a dent in the "big" issues. Together we can do things nobody thought possible. To sustain community within organizations we need information on the economic and social consequences of our actions.

Before I lay out the design, I need to differentiate a future search conference from other meetings that use similar procedures. Large meetings usually involve speeches, discussions, and "roll outs"—of missions, visions, strategies, training, and new structures. Nearly all assume an external diagnosis and prescription: This group needs information; that group needs team building; another group needs motivating. Such meetings are controlled from the podium. They often fall short of the aspirations we have for them.

Why should a future search be different? For one thing, we don't have a podium. Our conference is based on different assumptions. The first is that most of us can bridge barriers of culture, class, gender, ethnicity, power, status and hierarchy *if we work as peers on tasks of mutual concern*. The second is that to do this we must set up the conditions for a "whole conference" dialogue. Only then can we move toward complexity, make order out of chaos, and take responsibility for our lives. When we free ourselves from pressure to solve intractable problems we will find common ground none of us knew existed. If the planning task matters to all of us, we will then work successfully despite our skepticism and gloomy predictions. We must agree that instead of trying to change the world OR each other, we will include a more diverse group than usual AND change the conditions under which we interact. THAT at least is doable! If we do what is doable, we may discover how other "impossible" changes follow naturally.

BASIC PRINCIPLES

The conference depends on a set of mutually-reinforcing practices. Skip one and you have a different event.

- Get the "whole system in the room."
- Think globally, act locally.
- Work common ground and desired futures—not problems and conflicts.
- Self-manage discussions/action plans and take personal responsibility for implementation.

THE TASKS

Conference participation varies from thirty-two to seventy-two people for up to two and a half days. The purpose is always action on common ground toward a desired future for a company or unit, a local area, or an issue. The future focus can be finding a vision widely shared by all. Or it can be implementing a vision that already exists. Figure 1 shows the five tasks in their proper sequence. Tasks 1 and 4 are always done in mixed groups of eight or so, each a cross-section of the whole. Tasks 2 and 3 are done in peer groups called "stakeholders." Task 5, action planning, employs whatever structures make sense to participants. The sequence and table groupings are not optional. They set up a powerful set of dynamics that lead to constructive outcomes. Ambiguity, anxiety and confusion are critical by-products. So are fun, energy, and accomplishment.

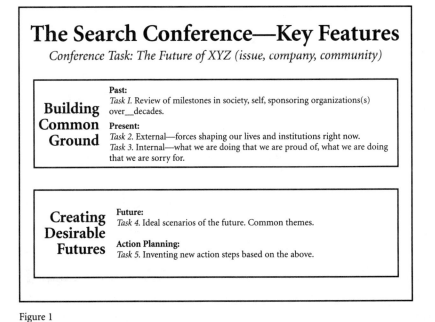

The Search Conference—Key Features

Conference Task: The Future of XYZ (issue, company, community)

Building Common Ground

Past:
Task 1. Review of milestones in society, self, sponsoring organizations(s) over __ decades.

Present
Task 2. External—forces shaping our lives and institutions right now.
Task 3. Internal—what we are doing that we are proud of, what we are doing that we are sorry for.

Creating Desirable Futures

Future:
Task 4. Ideal scenarios of the future. Common themes.

Action Planning:
Task 5. Inventing new action steps based on the above.

Figure 1

Task 1 establishes our history, differences, similarities, and shared values. It creates a sense of community, of being in the same boat, living on the same planet, subject to the same natural laws, needing many of the same things as everybody else. We accomplish this by reviewing the milestones in society, self, and the sponsoring organization over a number of decades. We emerge loaded up with information and eager to move on.

In Task 2 we focus on the present external trends shaping our lives and institutions. We pool our perceptions of world trends into a picture more complete than any one person had before. With other stakeholders we draw implications for the present and the future. There is no required shift in positions. Everybody hears all the other perspectives. "My facts" become "your facts" and vice-versa. The whole conference generates a "mind-map" of environmental trends. People often become awed and speechless at the complexity of their shared perceptions. Some may have a strong urge to run away. Instead, we actually touch the mind map. Each person affixes colored dots to those trends they consider most important. Then stakeholder groups explore what the map means to them. They describe what they are doing now about key trends and what they want to do in the future.

MAPPING THE ENVIRONMENT

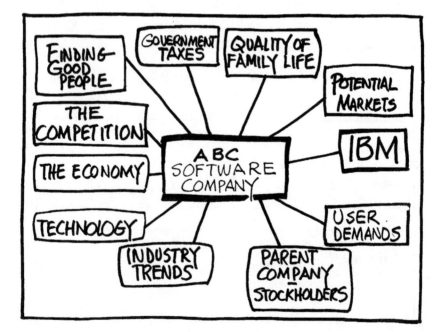

Figure 2

Task 3 calls for an assessment by each stakeholder group of what is going on right now—what they are proud of and sorry about in their relationship to "X." Each group's lists are viewed as "current reality," not problems to be solved. The purpose of this exercise is for the stakeholder groups to take ownership and responsibility, not engage in finger-pointing or blaming. At this point, we often hear some variation on the Pogo phenomenon, "We have met the enemy and they is us!" Here are some samples taken from several groups I have worked with:

Samples of Task 3 Work By Different Individuals

Manufacturers A

Proud: U.S. quality is re-emerging; manufacturing has begun to respond. Manufacturing creates real things: jobs, wealth, products, markets.

Sorry: We waited until a crisis occurred; we had to turn to too many foreign products; we had to eliminate good jobs; we tried to take too much from labor by resorting to temporary workers, reducing benefits and stagnating income.

Manufacturers B

Proud: We are able to change and adapt; we have a high level of skill and education; we are increasing efficiency and productivity.

Sorry: We failed to recognize the need to change and diversify sooner; we failed to invest in the long-term, which resulted in loss of jobs, technology, market share and confidence. Management-worker relationships are poor.

Workforce/Economic Development Agencies

Proud: We have a strong capacity for local/regional development; we have rich resources in this state; we have more private sector players and more input from regional groups for policy.

Sorry: We are reactive instead of pro-active; we are behind the curve because we do not anticipate workforce trends and needs; we compete for state turf, and we lack clarity of priorities.

Private Service Providers/Business Associations

Proud: We have strong capabilities; we have survived and achieved results.

Sorry: Management is recognizing and admitting to problems, but companies are not working together or sharing solutions; companies are not keeping up with customers' needs and with the requirements of world-wide market.

Figure 3: Samples of Task 3 Work

In Task 4, mixed groups devise ideal future scenarios. First, they build a list of desired futures drawing on what all stakeholder groups have said they want to do. Then they describe barriers to be overcome. Finally, they imagine that the whole scenario has been implemented. What does it look, feel, and sound like? They prepare a short dramatic presentation showing what has already happened five, ten or twenty years or more in the future.

By living our dreams as if they have already happened, we ground ourselves in what we really want and are willing to work for. We literally experience it in our brains, bodies, and psyches. We get to know what it feels like—so much so that we are much more likely to implement our dreams. More, we know in our bones that what we have dramatized is desired by ALL of us. All groups then identify common themes—key features that appear in every scenario. If we cannot agree on a feature, it is not "worked." Rather it is listed as a potential future. Usually there is 80 percent or more overlap among diverse scenarios. This unexpected congruence transforms our action planning. We know, often for the first time, where we and key others stand.

Thus in Task 5, action planning, we become more secure that we are working on a future desired by the whole spectrum of participants. We find capabilities we did not know we had. We take actions we did not believe possible. Having worked for three in time frames from three hours to three years with OD, MBO, TQM, and many other methods, I don't know a better way to spend sixteen hours than searching for common ground before making separate action plans.

WHY THIS PROCESS WORKS

Future search conferences are designed around common-sense assumptions. They build on skills and knowledge that people already have—without training, exhorting, or advising. They work simply by removing structural barriers between us that keep us from knowing, facing ourselves and our world, owning up, and acting. The process enables us to use the brains we were born with. It also allows us to explore and integrate technology and economics into the social fabric of our lives—a step essential for successful long-term planning. Thus future searches are likely to be renewing, productive, idealistic, practical, and surprisingly long lasting.

They are simple but not easy. Outcomes cannot be predicted. Along the way we face ambiguity that leads us to create a new worldview. No wonder, then, that sponsoring organizations sometimes get cold feet at the very thought of engaging in such an unpredictable process. For example: inviting people who don't usually meet; visiting the *global* context before confronting our local planning issue; working in self-managing peer groups, including strangers and people who have a history of conflict or failure; meeting for sixteen hours (excluding breaks and meals) over three days instead of trying to squeeze everything into one day; delaying action planning until we have a consensus on the future we all want. All these steps are essential to success, but they can be unnerving for the sponsors.

Organizations often assume *their* stakeholders are different. They won't show up, stay, or spend time talking about the past. They are too busy, too important, too knowledgeable to need a meeting like this. Even if their people came, they would never agree on the future. These assumptions are useful, but only if you test them. Folks new to this future search process may compromise key components before they have any experience, reducing both their anxiety as well as any chance for something new to happen. Keep in mind that when we stick to the basics we can make key breakthroughs; when we don't, we usually regret it. Future search conferences require a new openness to methods that build and foster hope, trust, and dignity among people.

FUTURE SEARCH GENEALOGY

Future search technology has an intellectual "genealogy" extending back to the 1920s. The simple tasks are built on a solid base of research and theory. I want to acknowledge key influences for which I am particularly grateful. The first is a summary of eighty-eight community futures conferences run by the late Ronald Lippitt and Eva Schindler-Rainman in cities, towns, and states throughout North America during the 1970s. They found that bringing a cross-section of community organizations together in one room—sometimes with as many as two hundred and fifty people—led to breakthrough problem-solving, even in time frames as short as one day. A key feature of these conferences was having people create "images of potential" (desired futures) rather than go head-on at the problems. This work led directly to my experiments, starting in the early 1980s, with getting the "whole system in the room" and focusing on the future, not the problem list.

Another key influence is the pioneering work of Eric Trist and Fred Emery with the "search conference," starting with a historic strategic planning meeting for Bristol-Siddeley Aircraft Engine Co. in 1960. For that meeting, Emery proposed an agenda he thought would create "conditions for effective dialogue" based on the consensus-building research of social psychologist Solomon Asch. Asch believed the following requirements were necessary to create these conditions:

- All parties are "talking about the same world," meaning that people back up their generalizations with concrete examples;
- All human beings have basic psychological similarities, for example, "laughing, loving, working, desiring, thinking, perceiving, etc." and if (a) and (b) happen, then—
- "The facts of one person's world become part of the other's and they develop a shared psychological field."

At this point, people become capable of a genuine dialogue on what to do. Its success would depend on how much the parties perceived increased freedom of choice along with greater understanding. If they did, reasoned Emery, then we could assume that they will experience their common dilemmas and/or shared fate and plan accordingly. Emery embraced Asch's admonition that, "Consensus is valid only to the extent to which each individual asserts his own relation to facts and retains his individuality; there can be no genuine agreement...unless each adheres to the testimony of his experience and steadfastly maintains a hold on reality."

Trist and Emery had the aircraft executives discuss the global context—first pooling all they knew and creating a systems view of their own industry and company. Much to their surprise, people didn't fight, run away from the task, or look to their leaders for solutions—all predictable dynamics of most task-focused meetings. This was a momentous discovery in human affairs. From Emery and Trist, I derived the importance of a global context, whole systems perspective, and people taking responsibility for their own plans.

Finally, to highlight the dynamics of the future search, I utilize a concept that has influenced organizational change practices widely in North America and Scandinavia. It is the creation of Swedish social psychologist Claes Janssen's "four-room apartment." It can serve as an explicit road map, marking a some-times difficult route for both participants and facilitators. Indeed, it is presented at the start of each conference. We acknowledge that some people have anxious moments at the complexity of their shared world. The idea that we move through all four "rooms" in our daily lives helps us accept what are, at best, feelings of anx-iety and, at worst, feelings of fear and impotence. In future searches, we validate all unwanted feelings and assure participants that these are natural experiences during this process.

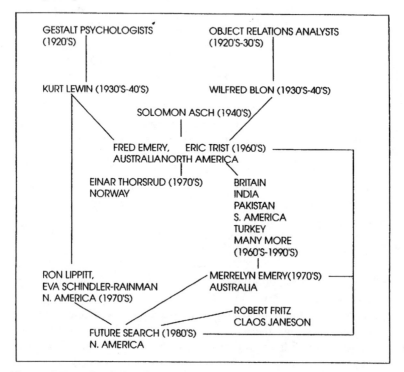

Figure 4: A Future Search Genealogy

In a future search we move through all the rooms. People generally start out in contentment, move into denial and hopelessness when they map the present, experience confusion as they sort out what they are doing and want to do, and enjoy renewal when they dramatize ideal futures. Indeed, we usually experience a dialogue between renewal and denial as people discuss what futures they can all agree upon. Always, we must choose whether to act on common ground or use the disagreements that remain as a reason for not doing anything.

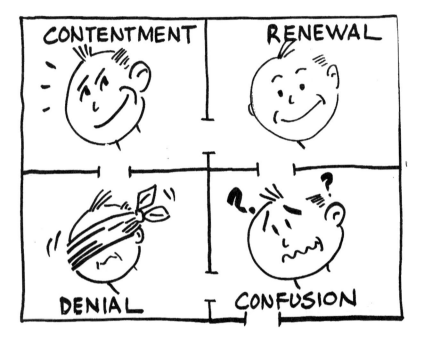

Figure 5: Four-Room Apartment

Indeed, we have learned that the passage to *renewal* originates with *denial via confusion*. You can't get there by any other route. In a future search conference, we allow this process to unfold. We do not try to "make" anything happen. We acknowledge everything that does happen as real, appropriate, and useful for our purposes. In short, we seek to "own up" to our feelings, not to change them.

During the journey, conflicts surface as a natural outgrowth of the information we confront. A radical aspect of the future search conference is our stance toward conflict. We nearly always find unresolved disagreements. We do not try to reconcile opposites—only to admit they exist. We own up to whatever comes to us as real and relevant. We neither avoid nor confront the extremes. Rather, we put our energy into identifying the widest common ground that everyone can stand on without force or compromise. Then, from that base, we spontaneously invent new forms of action, using processes devised for that purpose. People don't magically get better than they were. Rather, they tune in on different aspects of themselves—the more constructive and cooperative impulses.

Polarities take many forms. The most intractable are value conflicts centered in religious or ethical beliefs. The abortion controversy is an example. More often, we see disagreement over themes assumed to be held in common that turn out otherwise. In one community conference, one large subgroup wanted a strong statement on traditional family values as part of the "common ground." Another large subgroup was equally adamant that "family" include all people living together in a committed way, regardless of marital status or gender. Clearly, this was not going to be resolved in a few hours or, perhaps, ever. Both subgroups strongly supported a long agenda on jobs, housing, the environment, safety, and other matters. It was not necessary for them to agree on "family" to work together on common ground on many other pressing issues.

In summary, we seek to hear and appreciate differences, not reconcile them. We seek to validate polarities, not reduce the distance between them. We learn, innovate, and act from a mutual base of discovered ideals, worldviews, and future goals. Above all, we stick to business. We make the conference's central task our guiding star. Participants struggle in a safe environment with the issues, problems, challenges that confront them as a whole system. At our best, we can use the future search to take the focus off personality or political differences, problems and symptoms, and focus our energy toward building a sustainable and productive community.

In my enthusiasm, I do not mean to imply that this is easy work or that sixteen hours makes up for years of inertia or conflict. Searching is simple, but not easy. Planning how to get the right people in the room is hard work, often requiring more time than the conference itself. Having spent thirty years chasing elaborate technologies, I must caution you that future search methods are so straightforward they can be easily dismissed because of their simplicity. Yet they are profound enough to create great anxiety about control, conflict, and failure. Future searches create a strong sense of community among participants which allows them to be incredibly productive during their relatively short time together. Many individuals and groups have used the future search process with and without formal facilitation. Those who stick close to the method, embrace its bed-rock assumptions, and contain their own anxiety about success and failure, will surprise themselves with the productivity of the community that emerges.

Glenna Gerard
is a specialist in interpersonal communications with an emphasis on effective group development and leadership of collaborative work processes. She has twenty years of experience in business and education and has devoted much of her practice to working with dialogue in a variety of organizational settings. She serves on the affiliate staff of Interaction Associates and The Tom Peters Group.

Linda Teurfs
is an organizational consultant specializing in community building, interpersonal communication, executive coaching, and leadership. She has more than eighteen years of experience in corporate planning, marketing, and consulting, with a recent focus on building community through dialogue. She is on the adjunct faculty of the Center for Creative Leadership and the affiliate staff of Drake Beam Morin, Inc.

Gerard and Teurfs are founding partners of The Dialogue Group, which has been devoted to the research, development, and facilitation of dialogue since 1991. They have written numerous articles on dialogue and its contributions to community building, conflict and diversity work, and the learning organization.

12

Dialogue and Organizational Transformation

Glenna Gerard & Linda Teurfs

Suppose that we were able to share meanings freely without a compulsive urge to impose our own view or to conform to those of others and without distortion and self-deception. Would this not constitute a real revolution in culture and therefore eventually in society?

—David Bohm, *Changing Consciousness,* 1992.

The sciences of the 20th Century have brought us a profoundly new vision of how the universe works. Individual parts have definition and meaning only by virtue of the relationships between them. It is no surprise then that we find dialogue and community building at the forefront of organizational change efforts. Both are about creating cultures based on understanding relationships—relationships between people, structure, processes, thinking, and results.

For organizational change to be lasting, a shift of mind or change in consciousness has to take place. Because we are talking about cultural change, it has to happen at both the individual and group levels. Without such a shift, no restructuring effort will produce the kind of lasting change we are seeking.

Popularized recently through the work of the late David Bohm, dialogue is a group communication process aimed at exploring the nature and power of collective thinking and how it shapes the culture of a group. When we learned that one of dialogue's primary purposes is to affect a transformation in collective consciousness, we recognized its potential in the area of organizational change. While Bohm was working at a more global or societal level, we were interested in how it might be introduced specifically into organizational settings. We were not alone. Peter Senge devoted the better part of a chapter to dialogue in his book *The Fifth Discipline.*

Over the last several years we have explored dialogue in a variety of settings. We are seeing that it can serve as a bridge or how-to for community building and organizational transformation. Dialogue can help organizations create climates that lead to greater collaboration, fluidity, and sustainability. Its practice can provide the environment and skills necessary for creating a cultural shift toward high levels of trust and open communications, heightened morale, and alignment and commitment to shared goals.

BACKGROUND AND HISTORY OF DIALOGUE

The word dialogue stems from the Greek roots "dia" and "logos" and means "through meaning." It is a communication form for discovering the shared meaning moving among and through a group of people. "Shared meaning" forms the basis of culture. Dialogue involves becoming aware of the thinking, feelings and formulated conclusions that underlie a group's culture or way of being with each other.

Although new to modern-day organizational practices, dialogue has been around a very long time. It can be traced to the works of ancient Greece (for example, *The Dialogues of Plato*) and to forms of communication used by Native Americans and other indigenous peoples. Aspects of dialogue can be found within Quaker spiritual and business practice, and in counseling models such as that of Carl Rogers, as part of certain Eastern meditation practices and in the philosophical works of Martin Buber.

What is it about dialogue that gives such hope and evokes growing interest today? A fellow participant in dialogue once said, "Dialogue is about creating sacred space through conversation." That's a pretty powerful statement. Thinking about what values most cultures hold sacred—such as respect, trust, love, family, life, and the pursuit of happiness—it does convey the power and potential of dialogue. Dialogue is about creating an environment that builds trust, encourages communication with respect, honors and values diversity as essential, and seeks a level of awareness that promotes the creation of shared meaning (culture) that supports individual and collective well-being.

One useful way to describe dialogue is by contrasting it with discussion, a much more familiar form of conversation. The roots of discussion are the same as those of percussion and concussion, signifying "a breaking apart" or "fracturing" into pieces. The intent of discussion is usually to deliver one's point of view, to convince or persuade. Since points of view may differ widely, discussion often leads to divisiveness and polarization in groups. Opinions tend to be rigidly held on to and defended.

In contrast, dialogue asks us to "suspend" our attachments to a particular point of view (opinion) so that deeper levels of listening, synthesis and meaning can evolve within a group. The result is an entirely different atmosphere. Instead of everyone trying to figure out who is right and who is wrong, the group is involved in trying to see a deeper meaning behind the various opinions expressed. Individual differences are acknowledged and respected. What emerges is a larger, expanded perspective for all—what Bohm called an "impersonal fellowship," a term he took from the work of Patrick De Mare's *Koinonia*.

Dialogue informs and builds alignment without the need to pursue a specific outcome. Bohm often spoke of being struck by stories of hunter-gatherer tribes that came together frequently to talk without any agenda. In their day-to-day activities everyone knew what to do, what decisions to make. Bohm believed that it was during these seemingly aimless talks, that individual members of the groups became informed by the shared meaning they developed. Their alignment was a natural outgrowth of the shared meaning they created. In refining the application of dialogue for the business environment, we seek to create a modern-day equivalent.

THEORY OF DIALOGUE

> Thought has created a lot of good things. It is a very powerful instrument, but if we don't notice how it works, it can also do great harm.
>
> —David Bohm, *Changing Consciousness*, 1992

Bohm proposed that we live in a holographic universe. Every part of the universe both contains and contributes to the whole. If one part is affected by something (some change), it affects the whole and vice versa. Thus, we live in a relational world where the individual impacts the collective and the collective impacts the individual. The difficulty is that our thinking causes us to behave as though the opposite were true: that we live in a fragmented world where individual parts are separate from each other. Our thinking process works against our ability to perceive the interconnections and the whole.

An organizational example may help to further illustrate this. Several members of a cross-departmental team made assumptions around their input to a business plan. Because they didn't see their input as having real impact, they didn't put much effort into making it accurate. The head of the department, in contrast, took the data very seriously and was going to use it as the foundation for an important proposal she was to make to the board of directors. The discrepancy between her and the team members was discovered in a dialogue session the afternoon before it was to be presented. Had the department head made the presentation as it stood, she would have locked the department into parameters not in its best interest. The group was shocked to see the results its incoherent thinking could have produced if not brought to light. We have seen many such examples in our work with groups.

Bohm offers dialogue as a means to uncover and correct incoherence. By pooling our individual perspectives in an environment of non-judgment, a larger view of reality becomes possible. We can start to perceive the necessary link-

ages between our actions and the results we get. Through dialogue we can participate in collective thinking. We no longer have to take actions based on limited
understanding.

THE "TECHNOLOGY" OF DIALOGUE

The " technology" of dialogue as we have conceived it for organizational
settings consists of four main skill components we call building blocks and a set
of guidelines. We will first describe these skills and guidelines and then describe
how they work to enhance the day-to-day functioning of a group and lead to a
transformation of its culture.

Building Blocks

The building blocks involve learning a new way of being together and of
interacting. They involve skills that overlap and interweave in various ways. Often
for one to develop, the others need to be practiced.

Suspension of Judgment. Because our normal way of thinking divides
things up and creates what seem like ultimate "truths", it is difficult for us to stay
open to new and alternative views of reality. Our egos become identified with
how we think things are. We find ourselves defending our positions against those
of others. We close ourselves off from learning and do harm to our personal relationships. We can get into heated battles about who's right and who's wrong.

When we learn to "suspend judgment" we are able to see others' points of
views. We are able to hold our positions "lightly" as though they were suspended
in front of us for further consideration. It is not that we eliminate our judgments
and opinions—this would be impossible even if we tried. In dialogue we become
more open to other ways of viewing the same thing. Later, we may discover
whether our original perspective is still acceptable or needs to be expanded or
changed.

Suspending judgment in this way is the key to building a climate of trust
and safety. As others learn that they will not be "judged" wrong for having their
opinions, they feel free to express themselves fully. The atmosphere becomes
increasingly open and truthful.

Identification of Assumptions. The opinions and judgments we hold are
usually based upon layers of assumptions, inferences, and generalizations. When
we do not look at the underlying belief system behind our judgments, we all make
important decisions that lead to disappointing results. Unable to figure out why
we don't get the results we want, we may try adjusting our actions (based on the
same unexamined assumption set) and still not get the results that we want.

It is only when we are willing to peel away the layers of assumptions, that
we can see what might be giving us trouble: some incomplete or "incoherent"
thought.

By learning how to identify our assumptions, we are better able to explore
differences with others. We can build common ground and consensus, getting to
the bottom of core misunderstandings and differences. We have found assump-

tion identification to be extremely useful in understanding and working with diversity and conflict in groups.

Listening. Listening is critical to our ability to dialogue. Of the communication skills most often taught in schools: reading, writing, speaking, and listening; listening usually gets short shrift. For this reason, it is often overlooked and taken for granted. In this skill area we focus on how the way we listen impacts how well we learn and how effective we are in building quality relationships. Going far beyond active listening techniques, we focus on developing our capacity to stay present and open to the meaning arising at both the individual and collective levels. Bohm likens the mind to a quickly turning wheel. It is only when we slow it down that we can perceive the individual spokes. We bring attention to slowing our pace down so that we can listen and perceive at ever more subtle levels (this goes hand-in-hand with inquiry and reflection). We also work on overcoming typical blocks in our ability to listen attentively and to stay present.

Inquiry and Reflection. It is through the process of inquiry and reflection that we dig deeply into matters that concern us and create breakthroughs in our ability to solve problems.

> Our problems cannot be solved at the same level at which they were created.
>
> —Einstein

By learning how to ask questions that lead to new levels of understanding, we accelerate our collective learning. We gain greater awareness of our own and other's thinking processes and the issues that separate and unite us. By learning how to work with silence and slow down the rate of conversation, we are better able to identify reactive patterns and generate new ideas. It is this aspect of dialogue that can lead to what Bohm calls a more "subtle state of mind"—leading to a perception of common ground and a sensitivity to the subtle meanings around us.

Guidelines

Each time a group comes together to dialogue they commit to a common set of guidelines. These can be thought of as norms. As they are practiced over time, they become integrated at a tacit level of understanding. As the group matures, they may no longer be explicitly necessary (except as reminders).

A good way of introducing the guidelines is to first provide a demonstration. This is probably due to the natural way we learn to communicate—through the modeling we receive as children. We have found a short video presentation to be effective. It gives groups a "feel" of dialogue before they try it. After a demonstration the group can then be asked "What makes this different from other forms of conversation?" By generating the guidelines themselves, the group can take ownership of them.

Essential guidelines for dialogue include:

- Listening and speaking without judgment
- Acknowledgment of each speaker
- Respect for differences
- Role and status suspension
- Balancing inquiry and advocacy
- Avoidance of cross-talk
- A focus on learning
- Seeking the next level of understanding
- Releasing the need for specific outcomes
- Speaking when "moved"

How Dialogue Creates Community and Transforms Organizational Culture

Through the practice of dialogue, community is created and organizational culture transformed in three ways: behaviorally, experientially, and attitudinally.

Behavioral Transformation

Through ongoing practice with dialogue, participants learn how to be with each other differently. They practice skills and guidelines that encourage new norms. The more often they are practiced, the more dialogical communication is used beyond the practice sessions—leading to the actual state of community.

Experiential Transformation

Dialogue sets up the conditions of community. While groups new to dialogue will not be in full community when they first start out, the atmosphere induced by dialogue has the "experiential feel" of community. Individuals, thus begin to pick up at a tacit level what a culture based on community principles feels like. They incorporate it at an intuitive level.

Attitudinal Transformation

As group members experience the effects of dialogue, a profound shift takes place at the belief and attitude level. This comes about as a byproduct of the incorporation of new modes of behavior and learning the "feel" of what being in community is like. Attitudes of rigid individualism give way to attitudes of collaboration and partnership. Beliefs strengthen around the "value of the group as a whole."

A Practice Field

We can think of dialogue as though it were a practice field (a term coined by Senge) for building community. Once a group has had the initial introduction to dialogue's building blocks and guidelines, it is ready to begin. The more often the group comes together in dialogue, the faster it learns how to create and sustain itself in community.

Each group will have various ways and times of coming together for meetings. What is most essential at this beginning stage is that a regular routine be established according to the normal operation of the group. For example, if a group typically meets every other Monday for two hours, they might decide to dialogue for one hour before the start of these meetings.

It is also important that the head of the group and/or organization be aware of and be supportive of the transformative potential inherent in the process. A leader who is not willing to let go of position, rank and authority during the sessions will stymie and undermine the building of community. Ultimately, the leader will need to be able to support the vision of "shared leadership" both during and outside of the sessions, if community is to be built and sustained.

While the process of dialogue is being practiced during these routine times, the content can shift to reflect a group's most important issues. In a newly forming group, for instance, the content might be around the group's mission or purpose. In an already established group, the content might reflect the group's most pressing problems. By allowing this shifting of content, dialogue can enhance the group's functioning in several vital areas such as: decision making, problem solving, conflict work, strategic planning, issues of diversity, and organizational learning. These could also be considered practice fields that help integrate the dialogue process into day-to-day operations.

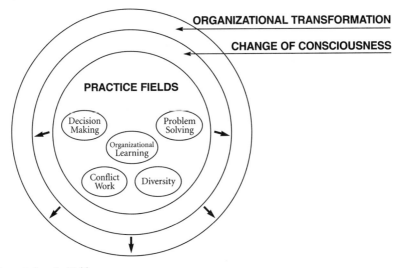

Figure 1. Practice Fields

It is critical that the content be relevant to real group needs. If the group does not see how dialogue improves their day-to-day operations, they may not be able to sustain the kind of enthusiasm and interest needed for ongoing practice to occur.

Over time, the group will learn to move between dialogue and discussion-based meetings—using both to their particular advantage. Typically, a group will set aside time for dialogue, followed by discussion (for decision-making purposes).

With practice, a change in consciousness occurs. Group members develop new attitudes about how to be and interact together. These usually include a greater honoring of individual differences, an increased sensitivity and caring for the group as a whole and individual members, and higher priority placed on trust and open communications. Eventually, these new attitudes lead to a transformation in the entire organizational culture. Group members act in the spirit of community both inside and outside the dialogue sessions.

PROBLEM SOLVING

Let's take a look at how dialogue might be integrated into a typical problem-solving cycle. In Figure 2 we depict the basic problem-solving stages groups go through: problems are identified, solutions generated and chosen, and actions taken.

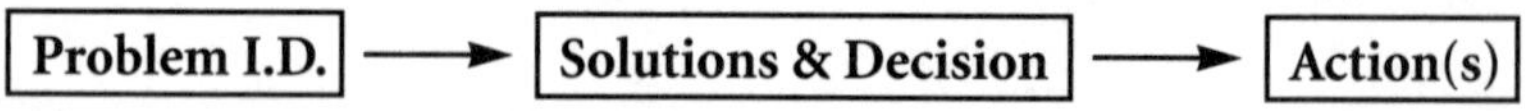

| Problem I.D. | ⟶ | Solutions & Decision | ⟶ | Action(s) |

Figure 2. Typical Problem-Solving Stages

First, a problem is identified in or out of a meeting context. Next, if the problem is important enough, a meeting is usually called to generate solutions and to make a decision. Once the decision is final, actions are taken to solve it. While this seems like a fairly straightforward approach to problem solving, it can be fraught with difficulties. A few common examples are:

- The problem is identified late and is now a crisis.
- The problem is not well understood; everyone solves a different problem.
- Not enough time is taken to generate a complete or lasting solution.
- There is a lack of commitment and alignment around the action—the implementers did not participate in the solution and may not understand it fully.
- Little learning occurs around what caused the problem in the first place, and the problem reappears.

If we assume that dialogue is being practiced routinely in a group, some of these difficulties diminish. Below, we spell out exactly how this happens at each stage. Although we start out with problem identification and end up with action, we do not wish to imply that dialogue always works in such a linear fashion. In any one session, for instance, several issues or problems in various stages may come into play. We describe the process in a step-by-step manner to show the general way that dialogue enhances problem solving.

Problem Identification. First, when dialogue takes place at regular intervals, emerging issues can be grasped quickly by all members. It becomes a kind of early warning device for the group. At the problem identification stage, dialogue can also help the group in sorting out which issues or problems are the most pressing for the group as a whole. Precious meeting time can be saved as the group learns to prioritize together.

Generation of Solutions and Decision Making. Next, as the group moves on to the solution generation and decision stage, dialogue can help to clarify the exact nature or definition of the problem (so the same problem is being solved by everyone), contribute to generation of a fuller solution set before decisions are made, and lead to insight on the implications of specific solutions.

Taking Action. Finally, as action is taken, members are more likely to be fully aligned and committed. They will all have had a part in identifying, sorting, clarifying, generating and reflecting on solutions. As results become available, dialogue can also serve as a feedback loop, alerting members to the fit between results and action. In this way organizational learning prevents problems from reappearing.

As groups progress in their ability to use dialogue, they will move to higher, more effective levels of problem-solving capability. They will begin to develop greater sophistication in their ability to identify and prioritize emergent issues, and their ability to reflect on and anticipate future conditions will continually expand. Such groups learn and operate on an ever-increasing, upward spiral of team effectiveness.

Dialogue and the Stages of Community

We've already spoken of the ways in which dialogue encourages community and organizational transformation. Let's look more specifically at what happens in groups practicing dialogue as they move through the various stages of group development. We will use M. Scott Peck's stage model of community.

Pseudo-Community

Dialogue sets up the conditions of community. In so doing it helps create the safety necessary for a high level of openness and disclosure right from the beginning. This can help give members a reference point for community. While members may still deny having major differences (a hallmark of pseudo-community), with dialogue they may be able to go very deeply into sensitive issues.

Chaos

Dialogue helps make the inevitable chaos stage seem not so "out-of-control" and fearful. As strongly held differences begin to be felt and disclosed, judgment is suspended, assumptions identified, all views expressed and listened to. As group members continue to dialogue their way through this stage, something often shifts: a new alternative may unfold; attitudes toward group differences that felt irreconcilable begin to dissipate; chaos becomes a source of creativity instead of something to avoid.

Emptying

Emptying is present right from the start of new dialogue groups and is continually deepening during each subsequent dialogue. Individual members agree from the beginning to suspend rigidly held positions. If they do not, there can be no dialogue.

Emptying can also be about healing. Groups often find it painful to move on to new ways of operating. For change to take place, people have to mourn what they are giving up. Dialogue helps by allowing emotions to be shared around the pain of letting old ways die. This speeds the ability of group members to move on and assures that difficult emotions are expressed in a timely manner and not allowed to fester.

Community

Through the ongoing practice of dialogue, groups learn to renew their visions and purposes for being together and to mindfully surface emerging issues and problems. Because dialogue is meant to be an ongoing practice, it is an ideal medium for maintaining a fluid and growing state of community.

DIALOGUE, COMMUNITY AND ORGANIZATIONAL SCIENCE
AT THE TURN OF THE CENTURY

We began our work with dialogue in hopes that it would allow us to work at deeper, more transformative levels with our clients; that by helping groups and organizations think and communicate differently, we could help them create lasting change within their cultures. We have not been disappointed.

David Bohm maintained that if we could become conscious of our thinking process we might be able to create a different kind of culture, one based on a holographic view of the universe. Such a culture would bridge the needs of the individual and the collective leading to increasingly deeper levels of community and adaptation to the environment. Two important challenges for us have been how to best facilitate people's ability to participate in dialogue and then how to help them continue the practice and experience all of the possible ways it can enhance the group.

Through introducing groups to the building blocks and guidelines and by encouraging them to continue in their practice of dialogue, we are beginning to observe enhanced functioning in practical, day-to-day ways. We are also observing changes taking place in the cultures of these groups. There are signs that dialogue has a ripple effect within organizations in which it is introduced. In other words, it can become contagious.

We conclude with two case examples. These are taken from our follow-up work with two different groups:

The first example involves a cross-functional team of seventeen managers in a sizable public agency. A two-a half-day training seminar was followed by four sessions that we facilitated—all over a three-month period. Team members practiced on their own for an additional six-month period. Over the course of the nine months they experienced three notable changes.

- They became aware of the profound impact their assumptions had on the results they obtained.
- They were able to catch emerging interpersonal issues and problems before they became full-blown personnel "crises."
- They felt a sense of community within the group that they characterized as increased respect, trust, and caring.

The second example involves a human resources group in a large, successful and progressive company. They were introduced to dialogue as part of a three-day retreat and planning meeting. The process was first used to identify assumptions pertinent to planning, then to gain a better understanding of the group's collective challenges and priorities. When they returned to their day-to-day activities, they continued to use the guidelines and building blocks in their meetings and their personal communications. As a result, they report they are able to work effectively in their current environment of almost daily organizational change. As the pace quickens around structural change, they are able to interact collaboratively and are able to stay focused on their goals.

For David Bohm, the purpose of dialogue was to consciously create cultures more in line with a relational, holographic universe. While Bohm, together with other new science theoreticians, has provided us with models, the hands-on work of organizational transformation remains. We believe that through the practice of dialogue, the fear of the unknown can become less paralyzing. Dialogue can provide us with a clearer pathway to making the organizational changes we so desire.

Jim Rough

has been a business consultant since 1971. As president of Jim Rough & Associates, he develops and teaches facilitative methods to help groups, individuals, and organizations transform. His work was featured in a 1992 *Industry Week* magazine cover story on The New Leadership. He presents his discoveries in the four-day seminar Dynamic Facilitation Skills.

He also speaks at numerous conferences and, for fourteen years, has been a faculty member of annual Creative Problem Solving Institutes in Buffalo, N.Y. Rough has published articles on empowerment, facilitation, and systems thinking. He is developer of An American Constitutional Invention, a breakthrough approach to societal change. His education includes a B.A. in physics from Occidental College in Los Angeles, M.S. and M.B.A. degrees from Columbia University in New York, and many years of independent study in Jungian psychology.

13

The Wisdom Council

Jim Rough

"I'm tired of all the small talk around here. I want some BIG talk for a change." These were the words of a manager before a meeting with his co-workers. His desire for meaningful communication with others is a step beyond the traditional working relationship where people are hired for their physical labor. It even goes beyond the work of professionals where people are hired for their minds. This manager's quest is for community. The BIG talk he seeks is not only desirable but a key ingredient in the search for corporate excellence. In fact, the authors of the classic business book, *In Search of Excellence*, characterized the single most important difference between excellent companies and the rest as "rich informal communication." Another way to phrase it might be "having BIG talk in the organization." I have developed a new process for creating community in large organizations through BIG talk. I have come to call it the "Wisdom Council."

RANDOM SELECTION

A Wisdom Council is composed of twelve to twenty-four people who are randomly selected to act as a microcosm of a larger population. The pool of possible participants generally includes everyone—managers, hourly employees, and salaried people. Like a jury, they seek an unanimous view. Unlike a jury, the group itself determines what they will discuss. It's like a "time out"—the members of an organization ask themselves how things are going and how they might go better. With the aid of a facilitator, these people enter into a high quality dialogue seeking collaborative breakthroughs. At its conclusion, the group issues an unanimous, nonbinding statement that articulates the informed wisdom of the people. This particular group then disbands, but each year, or each quarter, a new group is randomly chosen.

The Wisdom Council creates change the same way a crisis transforms an organization. It is the kind of time-out that happens in a game when a player gets hurt. The game stops, the energy shifts, and everyone remembers that we are all connected in ways that go beyond who wins and who loses. Caring and concern are shown, where only a moment ago there may have only been competition and self-interest. With a Wisdom Council, an organization symbolically enters into this structured, limited kind of time-out. People are encouraged to respond with creativity and open-mindedness so the organization is elevated to a new level of trust and capability.

In a county public works department, for example, a group of employees similarly met and determined that the critical issue for them was their overwhelming workload. At first, they talked about the need to hire more people. Then they decided that they really needed more time in the day. They achieved a breakthrough when they eventually realized that the underlying issue was that they didn't feel respected by the people they served. Each employee in the agency was independently working at a frantic pace to prove his or her own worthiness, despite a system they all felt was inadequate. Facing this issue and talking it through to a new resolution was a quantum step forward for the organization. It was healing to each person and to relationships between workers. Each person gained a greater sense of shared responsibility and many collective improvements were made.

Just acknowledging and facing critical issues like this with creativity has a powerful impact on the organization. In addition, a group's unanimous conclusions, when presented to the whole, possess power. In the example, the group expressed its new understanding about the need for mutual respect and suggested ways that people might earn that respect. Even people who were outside of the conversation were changed. Discussions about problems among co-workers, letters to the editor from citizens, and entrenched positions across the bargaining table were all positively influenced by the group's conclusions.

Another example illustrates how the statements that come from Wisdom Councils can make a difference. Employees and managers in the steam plant at a paper mill met and determined their key issue. At first, they listed issues like the need for better cleanup procedures, the need for more training, and the need for improved communication between and operators and the maintenance department. As the issues were categorized, it became clear to all that there was one overriding problem that everyone was afraid to mention. It was the ash that hung in the air of the plant.

Everyone knew that the mill had a competitive advantage because it was running at two times its design capacity and that ash was a natural result. All believed that nothing could be done without a major investment because the engineers had been studying the problem for years. The employee union and management had already tangled on the issue and everyone had backed away from a potential conflict. The black ash problem had disappeared from everyone's consciousness until this group brought it to the surface. Naming it in a statement to the rest of the mill sparked a new creative resolve and it wasn't long before two people invented a patentable device that solved the problem. The statement and the shared understanding of the issue's importance crystalized creative energy throughout the whole organization and spontaneous change was the result.

TRANSFORMATIONAL CHANGE

The Wisdom Council provides people at all levels in the organization with a symbolic opportunity to meet outside the hierarchy and to connect meaningfully on larger issues. It is a process for working on fundamental, deeply felt questions. "Is our organization really contributing something of value?" or, "Am I proud to work here?" are questions that might be dealt with. Rather than top management addressing strategic issues, in this scenario everyone deals with existential issues. As a symbol of the whole, each random group wrestles with the issues and reaches consensus that brings meaning to everyone.

The Council's power of change comes in three nontraditional ways. First, the existential crisis of BIG talk within the Council and the conversation it generates in the larger community elicit a transformational change. Secondly, the statement of unanimous wisdom of the group sparks dialogue and crystallizes creative energy. Thirdly, the periodic selection and disbanding of the Council establishes a learning process by which the community can evolve itself, reflecting on progress. Because the Council is all-inclusive and because it disbands immediately after presenting its results, it invokes a self-organizing process rather than a managed change process. Proposals, goals, action plans, and timetables may eventually result after it has disbanded.

When intelligent people stop to reflect on what really matters, change is created. Sometimes this change involves specific action items, but more often it runs deeper. It evokes subtle changes away from the need for extrinsic controls and toward the spirit of community. I believe Dr. Deming was talking specifically about this type of change when he said in his famous quality seminars, "We are destroying our people by the methods we use." He was talking about the system of extrinsic control and hierarchy vs. self-managed change and transformation, or what Deming called "metanoia." Managed change has obvious value in ensuring that specific actions are completed, but its overuse causes many problems. When used with people, they eventually either succumb to the control or rebel against it. In business, some people just wait for retirement. Some become bureaucratic thinkers seeking their own sense of control through rigid adherence to the rules. Still others opt out and profess to not care. Related problems like stress, burnout, rising health costs, and poor quality are secondary effects of people feeling manipulated. People under control feel estranged from community and from the impacts of their actions. Transformational change can eliminate many pressing problems as the spirit of community replaces the mechanisms of control.

THE STRUCTURE

The Wisdom Council is similar to other approaches of building community, yet fundamentally different. One special feature is that, even though only a few people participate in a particular Council, the whole community is involved vicariously. The random selection process and its short life span are particularly responsible for this. Anyone can be selected, and those chosen do not become an elite group. Each member speaks his or her own personal—and even spiritual—viewpoint without representing anyone else. Council members resume their normal activities immediately after disbanding.

Other group structures that are similar to the Wisdom Council, but not the same, are as follows:

- A *jury* because it assembles peers to reach unanimity on a decision for the whole community. However, a jury reaches a verdict on a predetermined issue through discussion and voting. The Wisdom Council picks its own issues and uses dialogue to evolve consensus.
- An *advisory board* in that it provides nonbinding guidance to an organization. The advisory board is not randomly selected. It meets over a long period of time and doesn't necessarily reach unanimity. The Council doesn't advise top management as much as it articulates the whole system view.
- A *survey* because it uses a random sample to identify the views of the total population. But in a survey there is no dialogue among participants. There is no vicarious sense of participation among those who were not selected.
- A *focus group* because there is a facilitated dialogue among a microcosm of a population. But a focus group does not choose the issue and doesn't reach unanimity.
- A *future search conference* because it seeks to involve the whole community in dialogue and to evolve the culture using a facilitated process. But the future search is a large group process particularly oriented toward developing a vision of the future. With the Wisdom Council, a smaller group containing few management people determines the topics based on members' own interests and energy.

QUALITY OF DIALOGUE

Beyond its unique structure, quality of dialogue is vitally important to a Wisdom Council. If members were to argue and develop a legalistic statement of compromise, or if people just complained about how awful things were and issued a statement that expected others to do something about it, much of the Council's power for change would be lost. The spirit of dialogue is essential. The late physicist David Bohm recently drew a distinction between a *discussion*, where people talk back and forth with one another, and a *dialogue*, where people meet without a predetermined agenda yet a "coherent culture of shared meaning" emerges. In the book *The Fifth Discipline*, author Peter Senge builds on Bohm's work, describing dialogue as (1) going beyond one person's understanding to a larger pool of meaning, (2) exploring complex issues from multiple points of view, and (3) inquiring in a way that people become observers of their own thinking.

In a Wisdom Council, this same spirit of mutual inquiry and emergent meaning is needed, but the group also needs to reach consensus on a specific statement. For a brief process, with people who have been randomly picked, the question is How can we ensure a spirit of creative dialogue yet also achieve an unanimous statement? In a trial jury, people are on their own to make a simple judgment on a predetermined issue. The need for a Council is for something more like a Quaker business meeting, where a deep and open spirit of inquiry exists, yet the group still reaches unanimous decisions. A facilitator is essential to achieving this blend.

FACILITATION

According to Senge and Bohm, dialogues per se are not suited to decision making. They envisage facilitative leadership and place emphasis on participant guidelines and taking time to be sure the guidelines are met. Examples of guidelines might be: drop all previously held assumptions, respect all views, and allow equal air time for all those who wish to speak. Bohm views the facilitator's role as limited to setting the stage and pointing out "sticking" points. Senge envisages more of a knowledgeable discussion leader, even contributing opinions at times. To reach decisions, Senge says that discussion is probably needed and suggests using both.

The Wisdom Council, on the other hand, needs a process facilitator who takes a more active role. He or she helps the group determine and meet the key issues, often in an organizational environment where they seem undiscussible; influences the group process so that dialogue, not discussion, is used; and helps to stimulate creative thinking where breakthrough insights, understandings, or new feelings can emerge. The aim is an emergent consensus, or a collective breakthrough, rather than agreement on a compromise. For this, one cannot rely on a step-by-step facilitation approach, nor exclusively on the self-management of participants. It is better to have facilitators with advanced knowledge of group dynamics and creative thinking who manage the group process. In this case the need for discussion is greatly diminished and usually restricted to fleshing out details.

Although exerting a strong influence on the process, this type of facilitator does not participate in the content. He or she ignores his or her views on the topic in order to help the group create its viewpoint. He or she is not concerned with "what" the group decides but with "how" the group talks and thinks together. Some pioneers of this type of process facilitation (aside from 300 years of Quaker meeting leaders) are Michael Doyle and David Straus, who wrote the book *How to Make Meetings Work*. The Institute for Cultural Affairs has developed facilitation tools for dialogue with large groups. The Guild for Psychological Studies has pioneered dialogue as a process of individual transformation for more than 50 years and the Creative Problem Solving Institutes have been advancing creative thinking for more than 40 years.

SIX FACILITATIVE PRINCIPLES

These approaches rely on a facilitator to help groups address issues with creativity and trust. Dialogue on crisis-level challenges leads to transformational changes. This is not "decision-making" and it's not "problem-solving." Instead, I coined the phrase "Choice-creating" to better describe it. This quality of thinking seeks quantum movements, changes of mind, and changes of heart. Key facilitative principles that go into Choice-creating are:

1. The facilitator orients the group toward developing lists (of issues, solution ideas, data, etc.) to avoid discussion. An opening sentence might be "What are some of the issues we might address?" This question asks for a listing instead of discussion. If someone starts to talk about one of the issues, the facilitator might head that off by saying "please turn your comment into another suggestion." In this way, discussion is averted and participants maintain a spirit of discovery.

2. The facilitator ensures that each person is protected from all forms of judgment. For instance, if one person has an idea and another starts to say why it won't work, the facilitator helps turn this judgment into a concern. Both people are protected and each comment is useful.

3. The facilitator helps people express themselves fully. For instance, if someone says, "There should be better communication," it is important to urge them to say more, to the point of risking and exposing real feelings. This expansion builds trust in the group.

4. The facilitator reflects back to the group what they are saying or what is happening. This raises the level of capability for self-management in the group and it helps all to listen and understand more fully what has been said. With reflection, members often change views of their own accord, allowing the group to spontaneously move forward. Simply by standing and writing ideas on the flip chart, the facilitator reflects to the group.

5. The facilitator supports the vital energy of the group. If some people are excited about an idea before the problem has been defined, for instance, the facilitator goes with their energy and asks them to articulate their solution. In this kind of setting, the group energy leads while the intellect follows.

6. The facilitator helps the group capture and acknowledge group movement. He or she might say, "It sounds like you are all in agreement about this part of the issue. Can someone summarize what you are saying here?" People often don't recognize their progress unless this progress is captured and articulated.

USING THE WISDOM COUNCIL

The Wisdom Council is a low-risk, low investment strategy for building community. This is not a top-down cultural intervention to be managed, but a small, limited structural addition that may generate system-wide, heart-felt change. In a formal sense, it has no power. But by creating an organization-wide dialogue and sparking ground-swell consensus, it has great potential for transformational change.

Organizations that are a part of the quality movement and wish to focus on real quality can find the Wisdom Council valuable. Some organizations install a Total Quality Management program that is exclusively focused on making quality measurable and more controllable. Such a strategy is a continuing part of an extrinsic control paradigm and not what the quality movement is about. As Peter Senge said in a recent keynote address, "If you don't understand that the quality movement is about intrinsic motivation, then you don't understand the quality movement." The Wisdom Council supports intrinsic motivation in people. It is a way for companies to ensure a vital quality effort.

Other examples of potential use are: A large university hospital might use this approach to overcome organizational barriers between doctors, administrators, and staff. A competitive software company might use it to call "time out" from their hectic pace and to build depth in the environment without losing competitive focus. For a large government agency it is a way to overcome the bureaucratic thinking that regulations and micro management encourage. In a manufacturing company one group of employees has proposed this approach to their management as a way to build and maintain a shared vision for everyone to invest in.

In these instances, the Wisdom Council helps to transform a hierarchical system. But in a different, more powerful application, the Wisdom Council might also be used to empower and give a new voice to the people of a democratic organization. An employee-owned corporation, a labor union, or a school, for instance, can use the process to create wise, democratic leadership. With a Wisdom Council in a high school, for example, the faculty and administration can assume a more facilitative role, helping students get what they want, instead of trying to control them toward predetermined aims. It can reinvigorate the learning environment.

When twelve students participated in a high school Wisdom Council, they developed six unanimous points. The points were focused on class sizes, the need for creative lessons, more meaningful requirements for graduation, etc. In the meetings students talked about serious matters. Some wanted harder classes. Others needed help to keep up. All wanted a safe place where they could be challenged to learn. At a presentation to the superintendent, principal, and city council, the adults expressed pleasant surprise. Many people had underestimated the level of capability and responsibility the randomly chosen students would demonstrate. The Wisdom Council was an initial step in building BIG talk with and among students.

A Wisdom Council builds a culture based on intrinsic instead of extrinsic motivation. By giving a voice to the wisdom of the students the whole system is brought into dialogue. In a similar application this process could be used to reinvent both government and citizenship. In fact, the Wisdom Council concept originally arose as a way to enliven responsible citizenship and to build community at the national level. In seminars where people were learning about facilitation skills, groups resembling Wisdom Councils addressed issues of their choice. They chose societal issues: the rising violent crime rate, the breakdown of families, the inequitable distribution of wealth, and the like. These groups sought simple, non-threatening ways to reverse the negative spiral of these problems. The break-through that emerged was the Wisdom Council concept as a constitutional amendment. By creating a national and wise "Will of the People," the Council would reinvent government as more facilitative than controlling. By building community and empowering responsible citizenship this process offers a low-risk, high-return way to deal with increasingly complex issues.

LARGE ORGANIZATIONS

From its initial conception as a constitutional amendment, it became clear that the Wisdom Council process can also be used to support participative leadership in most large organizations. It is a way to subtly move the system away from extrinsic control via rules and hierarchical structures toward intrinsic control through individual initiative and mutual trust. It doesn't directly confront the hierarchical system, but by establishing BIG talk it empowers the potential for transformation. It is best to structure the Council in a way that is consistent with this bottom-up power. Rather than being set up by the president of an organization to find out what people really think, for instance, it is more powerful to consider the Wisdom Council to be the people stopping to reflect on how their system is working. Structuring the context so that the Council is above the hierarchy enhances its transformational potential. The Wisdom Council best functions from the assumption that the ultimate authority is with the people of the organization.

Arranging the Wisdom Council requires coordination. A person or group needs to establish meeting rooms, identify facilitators, and schedule times. They need to help assure that everyone selected can attend. In any random selection process, it is critical that those selected participate voluntarily. The coordinators help the organization contract with itself so that people who are chosen will participate. It may be helpful to turn the selection process into a ceremony. Each person is eligible, so everyone should be aware and interested. It might be like a lotto drawing, or a large door prize. This enhances the sense of identification with those who are chosen.

During Wisdom Council meetings, the coordinators ensure that participants can be sequestered if need be, that they have accurate meeting notes, and that requests from the from the Council can be met. For instance, the group may ask for the opportunity to meet with experts or the organization's president, or to present their results to certain audiences. If top management does attend, it must be remembered that the real "top manager" is the Council in this setting.

Sessions may be videotaped and viewed. This can increase the sense of vicarious participation. At the conclusion, it is understood by everyone that the Council will present their results to the whole organization. At presentations, individual Council members need to distinguish when they speak for a unanimous Council and when they speak for themselves.

After the meetings and presentations, Council members have no further official role except possibly to help improve the process and to plan the next one. I suggest that a small committee of former members be created to oversee the Wisdom Council process.

SUMMARY

The Wisdom Council can be a powerful and valuable process for any large organization that is open to exploring growth through transformation. It can provide a basis for self-organization and self-management, and eliminate much of the need for extrinsic controls. It is a new concept for building community—ensuring that people address the issues that really matter and remain in dialogue. It helps everyone remember that, at the most basic level, we are just people and we are connected. The Wisdom Council ensures that there is room for BIG talk. It creates a time for "just folks" around the campfire. It's a way for the wisdom, goodness, and creativity in people to emerge and help in building community.

Elemer Magaziner
is the founder of Project Linguistics International, a training and consulting firm which has served clients such as IBM, People's Bank, GE, Pacific Bell, Hewlett-Packard, Longs Drug, DOD, the National Foundation for Consumer Credit, and the National Center for Manufacturing Sciences. Project Linguistics International also offers seminars such as The Innocent Leadership Program, a workshop for leaders who wish to move freely among paradigms.

He was born in Budapest, fled to Mexico in 1947, moved to the United States five years later, and now lives in Sedona, Arizona. He has a liberal arts degree from Reed College and a masters in mathematics from the University of Montana. Postgraduate work led him to a career in atmospheric research, where large projects, like a weather support system for the Apollo-Soyuz program, opened the door to program support, management, and administration. Magaziner is currently an international consultant, seminar leader, writer, and speaker.

14

The Way to Community

Elemer Magaziner

In every block of marble I see a statue,
See it as plainly as though it stood before me,
Shaped and perfect in attitude and action.
I have only to hew away the rough walls
Which imprison the lovely apparition
To reveal it to other eyes, as mine already see it.
—Michelangelo Buonarroti

Community, like beauty, is in the eye of the beholder. My vision of the world determines whether a group of persons before me deserves the title. I have known the joy of community at the sight of catatonic rush-hour commuters opening to the vulnerability of being pressed into a subway car. I have known the sadness of its absence even in the deep intimacy of the last day of a survival course. Community is to be found where we see it, not where we make it.

As we find ourselves in physical bodies that we may see our inherent beauty, so we find ourselves in groups of people that we may see the inherent connectedness in community. If we could imagine a world where our concerns were not the primary criteria for how things should be, we would find ourselves already in community. We could redirect the enormous energy we now dedicate to estimating and repairing the discrepancies between the universe and our expectations. We could see our task as "to hew away the rough walls" we have built in our minds "which imprison the lovely apparition to reveal it to other eyes." We could help each other remember that community is already who we are together.

The idea that community is to be found where we see it is powerful knowledge. Those who seldom see it know it to be rare, and must labor against the currents of human vicissitude to pursue it. Those who see it everywhere know it as the universe's natural consequence of organization, and joyfully receive it as part of the human condition.

Sculptors of community plainly see the community we are, "shaped and perfect in attitude and action." They beseech us to question the assumption that separateness is a reality. They encourage us to turn, from building ourselves into who we think we must become, to reminding each other who we already are. In the next century, sculptors will prove to be more effective than builders in the renewal of community.

THE CRISIS IN OUR CONSCIOUSNESS

> The crisis is in our consciousness, not in the world.
> —Krishnamurti

Twenty years ago, Apollo 14 astronaut Edgar Mitchell experienced the blue-white sphere of our planet from the perspective of a lunar orbit. As a scientist supporting the Apollo launches, I was blessed to be close to the wonder of the moment. In his eye, as the beholder of our home, he saw the Earth not only as a life support system, but also a mutual support system. From the stillness and emptiness of space, he saw the unbreakable bonds which unite us.

At this same time, Gregory Bateson was working on his manuscript of *Mind and Nature*, in which he writes, "What pattern connects the crab to the lobster and the orchid to the primrose and all four of them to me? And me to you?" Also at the same time, Fritjof Capra published *The Tao of Physics* in which he showed that Eastern thought and modern physics meet where unity is reality and separation is illusion.

Yet, twenty years later, our insistence on seeing separation still feeds the engine of civilization like some low octane fuel, and our institutions and organizations sputter and ping up the challenges of their responsibilities. But underneath the din and confusion of trying to make a better world is an irrepressible current urging us to admit that we must change our minds before we can change our habits.

But the supplies of sub-standard fuel are still plentiful. They have been depositing for centuries. Two hundred years ago, this country was founded on the notion of separating ourselves from those we disliked. We welcomed to our shores persons who saw two huge oceans as the solution to their problems. In *The Federalist*, James Madison expressed his belief that, "So strong is this propensity of mankind to fall into mutual animosities that where no substantial occasion presents itself the most frivolous and fanciful distinctions have been sufficient to kindle their unfriendly passions and excite their most violent conflicts... [the factions are] much more disposed to vex and oppress each other than to cooperate for their common good."

Now that there is nowhere to remove ourselves to, we struggle for new approaches while relying on the same fuel. President Clinton promised ethnic and gender diversity as a byword of his administration. Yet, when he assembled his Cabinet accordingly, *The Economist* issued a warning from abroad: "This cabinet, designed to 'look like America,' is in danger of representing the worst face of the country, interest group against interest group, all clamoring for attention."

We agonize over the shortcomings of our organizations, when the problem is what we feed them with our minds. We assume them to be inherently non-communities, and assign ourselves the responsibility of correcting this flaw.

COMMUNITY IS FOUND WHERE WE SEE IT

> Dear God
> It is great the way you always
> get the stars in the right places.
> Jeff
>
> —*Children's Letters to God*
> Compiled by Stuart Hample and Eric Marshall

In my mind is an unbreakable connection between "community" and Scott Peck. The excitement from reading *The Different Drum* visits me often, especially in my work as an organizational consultant. But I also remember a vague and gnawing discomfort that laced the excitement from the very beginning. I successfully dismissed the pesky intruder for several years, until an assignment to a large project with a major manufacturing corporation.

The program manager described the project as a large number of factions shooting at each other from deep foxholes. The management structure in the corporation at that time ensured that each faction was a sovereign entity, responsive above all else to its own agenda. The only incentive for participation was survival: the project had a large budget each could tap into. Using Peck's pseudo community, chaos, emptiness, and community as the phases in building community, I saw that the factions were already mired in chaos long before this particular project existed. Not only this, but in an engineering environment, advancement tends to be through individual accomplishment. Commitment to community seemed to me an impossibly remote outcome.

I sensed my pesky intruder skulking nearby. This time it was not to be dismissed. Determined to find it, I picked up *The Different Drum* and started reading from the beginning. There it was (the italics are my emphasis):

> "If we are going to use the word ['community'] meaningfully we must restrict it to a group of individuals who have learned to communicate honestly with each other, whose relationships go deeper than their masks of composure, and who have developed

some significant commitment...But what then does such a *rare* group look like?

"The problem is that the *lack of community* is so much a norm in our society.

"And in our society the occurrence of *community is still rare*—indeed, an *extraordinary happening* in the ordinary course of things."

That pesky intruder had been trying to warn me all of this time of the now apparent scarcity of consciousness of community. Not enough love, not enough money, not enough time, not enough freedom, not enough food—and now not enough community. My intruder was saying, "A belief in the scarcity of something important has never served you, Elemer. What makes you think this is any different?" In that moment, I switched from building community to sculpting community. Instead of laboring to make a community where we felt it had not existed, I spent my energy pointing out "the lovely apparition" to anybody who would listen. They carefully peeked out of their foxholes, at first just to see if I had lost my mind. But they too saw it, and this vision sustained them through the thick and thin of their four-year project.

The depth of cooperation, the high morale, and the permeability of organizational boundaries perplexed executive management. Accustomed to receiving a constant flow of crises to manage, they suspected people were concealing the organizational problems inevitable in a project this size. They hired an independent firm to audit the project. Their recommendation: use this as a model for other projects.

Sculpting community turned out to be more important and effective than I imagined. The ability to see community in every group, not as a future potential, but as an existing reality has served me more powerfully than any acts of building. I keep reminding myself that Michelangelo extracted, not built, *David* from what appeared to be a misshapen block of marble. The work in building community actually wastes our energy. When pursuing the potential of community in an organization, we misunderstand the word "potential." "Potential" means the work is already done, as in a stone we have lifted; all we do to release it is open our hand.

Opening Our Hearts to Organizations

When we realize that organizations are living systems, we begin to hold them not as exercises of the mind but as challenges of the heart. And when we do, a powerful premise emerges: Every organization is community, not by arbitrary definition, but by nature's design. This premise is nothing more than a natural extension of our belief in the wholeness of living things from the level of individual to that of organization.

Are we willing to extend this essential reverence for people to the next level of nature's hierarchy? Can we make the quantum leap to seeing our planet populated by organizations, not just ourselves? If we are serious about the health of our organizations , then the answer must be yes. Lifting our hearts to the level of our institutions is the journey we now interpret as "building community."

The journey is exquisitely simple, however, our legacy of blame and mistrust can make it a difficult one. Peck's model of the path into community (pseudo-community, chaos, emptiness, community) applies. The difficulty is in passing from chaos into emptiness. At the level of individuals, it means shifting our notion of love as a mandate for fixing our companions, to accepting them exactly as they are. This acceptance is the gate into community.

At the level of organizations, the meaning is the same: emptying ourselves of the habitual judgments, "feelings, assumptions, ideas, and motives— that have so filled [our] minds as to make them as impervious as billiard balls." It means releasing our compulsion to heal, convert, and fix our organizations. As long as we are not willing to risk this emptiness, Peck advises, chaos persists.

THE MIND'S PARADIGM FOR ORGANIZATIONS

> Our speech can build a world of peace and joy in which trust and love can flourish, or it can create discord and hatred.
> —Thich Nhat Hanh

> There is no blame.
> —Peter Senge
> A law of *The Fifth Discipline*

The rough walls that the sculptor of community hews away exist only in our minds. But changing minds is not an easy task. The thought that human beings become dysfunctional and dangerous when grouped into organizations is rooted deep in the present view of the world. This pattern of thought and language which says: Organizations, especially large ones, are inherently dangerous to our well being and as such are the cause of the mess on this planet, is the state of mind in which we try to create a better world. What an exquisite handicap: we must work together for the outcomes we desire, but in that act, we create untrustworthy human systems dangerous to our well being.

It is a macabre pattern in which we do not trust ourselves when we organize into groups. The larger the group, the deeper the mistrust. And we abstract these groupings until we can talk about them as if they were inhuman "systems." By the time the grouping reaches the size of a country, we call it "government," and completely forget that it is no more than "us." Now, safely removed from the reality that organizations' bodies consist of our bodies, we righteously attack, accuse, indict, and criticize. It may not be immediately obvious, but contempt for human institutions befouls us in our own eyes.

I just finished reading a new book which illustrates this point. Its subject is how leaders can be successful through deep integrity, fusing spirit, character, human values, and decency. On the jacket, a leading global futurist and professor of political science tells us that, because our institutions are becoming increasingly dysfunctional, we need to fortify ourselves against them with the ideas in the book.

The same book teaches that the new leadership calls for gratitude, optimism, respect, acceptance, appreciation, and even reverence. It says that a leader's state of mind needs to be one of grand welcome—an embracing, allowing, letting in. But this open heart appears to be reserved for persons. The author informs us that organizations contaminate people, that human systems do not support our living a more pure life, that large organizations are inherently prudent, shrewd, cautious, and cunning, and that organizations love to subdue our strength and limit our power.

This is the tone of much literature and conversations regarding the problems in the world. And we envision a future where this likely gets worse. We become outraged at the atrocities perpetrated by "the establishment." We form our own establishment to set things right, and our internal model of human organization replicates the object of our outrage. As Roger Sperry, the Nobel laureate observed, "Belief [is] the force which above any other shapes the course of human affairs."

Mountains of research and experience confirm that healing is not possible within a deep belief that we are broken, dysfunctional, and untrustworthy. How much power is there, then, in believing this about the human institutions we ourselves have created and are part of? It is certainly true that persons have, at times, disappointed and hurt us. It is certainly true that our institutions have also. But, without denying anything, where shall we stand so that healing may occur? Does treating our institutions with disdain make any more sense than despising ourselves or each other? Is it not time to follow Peck through emptiness into community, but this time, at the level of human institutions?

We have built mental walls around human institutions using language like this: Human institutions
- Are dysfunctional and becoming more so
- Love to neutralize our power and self-expression
- Are dangerous to personal and planetary well-being
- Do not support our needs
- Disregard our rights
- Pollute the planet
- Are base, corrupt, wasteful, and uncaring

Such a pattern as our paradigm can have, as Jeremy Rifkin once described, a "hold over our perception of reality so overwhelming that we can't possibly imagine any other way of looking at the world." We can no longer imagine that our organizations are or can be any other way. Community cannot be anything but extremely rare within the confines of mistrust of human systems. At worst, community is a curious and unlikely miracle; at best, it can be achieved only through hard labor against the tide of human tendencies.

THE HEART'S PARADIGM FOR ORGANIZATIONS

'What is real?' asked the Rabbit one day....'Real isn't how you are made,' said the Skin Horse. 'It's a thing that happens to you. When a child loves you ...then you become real.'
—Margery Williams
The Velveteen Rabbit

Sometimes we get very close to accepting human institutions into our hearts. In *Leadership and the New Science*, Margaret Wheatley writes about Peter Senge's work using systems thinking to understand the dynamics of an organization: "...the intent [of managing the system] becomes one of understanding movement based on a deep respect for the web of activity and relationships that comprise the system." This is an intellectual and roundabout way of saying the intent of leadership can become one of understanding based on a deep respect for organizations.

In *Reawakening the Spirit in Work*, Jack Hawley insists that we elevate this respect to reverence: "To put it simply: develop a reverence—no less than that— for: (a) the mission, (b) the products, (c) the customers, (d) the employees." If we shift from the mind's to the heart's concept, we can complete Hawley's list: (e) the organization itself. As in the children's story about the velveteen rabbit, caring about organizations makes them real and brings them to life in our hearts. In our hearts, we can see that organizations become communities not because we make them so, but because we love them.

We open the door, step right up to the threshold, and gaze in wonder at the living nature of human systems, but we don't quite step through. Perhaps we feel a little foolish and embarrassed extending our compassion to organizations, even though we have no reservation blaming them. "My own experience suggests that we can forego the despair created by [organizational events] if we recognize that organizations are conscious entities, possessing many of the properties of living systems," writes Wheatley.

We could boldly step forward and speak about human institutions as if they:
- Are, as the name organization implies, living systems
- Are not treatable as merely a collection of persons
- Respond to blame and appreciation just as we do
- Live up to exactly what we expect from them
- Become wounded or ill and, with support, can heal
- Are created by us according to our images of ourselves
- Have relationships with us and with each other
- Coexist interdependently with us on this planet

This pattern of thought and language about human institutions does not imply they are wonderful or they are dreadful, just that they are—well—human.

WHAT SHALL WE SAY COMMUNITY IS?

Scott Peck says about the true meaning of community: "In our culture of rugged individualism—in which we generally feel that we dare not be honest about ourselves, even with the person in the pew next to us—we bandy around the word 'community.' We apply it to almost any collection of individuals—a town, a church, a synagogue, a fraternal organization, an apartment complex, a professional association—regardless of how poorly those individuals communicate with each other. It is a false use of the word." Peck has a certain attitude regarding our nature, our culture, and our courage. However, we could take the position that to bandy around the word "community" is exactly what we should do. We could argue that it applies to every organization because of the intrinsic connectedness in all living systems. To bandy or not to bandy? What we need to ask is which approach yields the greatest benefit. It is not a matter of which assumption reflects the greater reality, but which is the most powerful place to start our journey toward community.

THE WAY TO COMMUNITY

It is no surprise that the way to community is an open heart. The age of compassion is increasingly stirring our thinking. Where power in the agricultural age was land, in the industrial age capital, and in the computer age information, the compassionate age thrives on acceptance. This acceptance overflows the boundaries of human concerns, and encompasses everything we perceive as a living "system."

Organizations, corporations, institutions, neighborhoods, governments, and all other groups which we belong to are living systems. Vine Deloria Jr., Professor of History and of American Indian Studies, teaches us that this idea has been a part of non-Western knowledge for centuries. He observes, "This idea that everything in the universe is alive, and that the universe is alive, is knowledge as useful as anything that Western science has discovered or hypothesized."

Our history of distrust—of ourselves and of each other—is dissolving into a recognition of human rights as a central issue of our time. However, we have not yet extended this respect and reverence to organizations, to our human institutions. At this level of nature's hierarchy, our suspicion and mistrust still closes our hearts. And yet, community occurs at the level of organizations, not of individuals. It is time we use our minds, not to relegate community into scarcity, but to accept it as the essence of organization. Let us stop trying to find our way to it, or build it. Instead, let us see community as something that can go away only in our minds.

Geoffrey Hulin

is an artist and entrepreneur and carries the wisdom of many challenging communication campaigns. He has produced and directed media and special events for organizations for twenty-two years. His passion is calling forward and passing on new stories—stories of promise and possibility—in ways that make a lasting difference.

Darla Chadima

is a master of context design with many years of experience creating provocative and powerful events. Her gift is seeing the patterns that connect us all. Her passion is the weaving of these patterns into the enduring cloth of community.

Chadima and Hulin are partners in The Whole Story..., a Santa Cruz, California, company dedicated to the vision and practice of wholeness in corporate life.

15

Rediscovering the Circle: Community in Balance

Darla Chadima & Geoffrey Hulin

"What is missing in your life?"
is the question we have asked managers during the last two years.
The most common answer:
"Balance."

Businesses increasingly turn away from compartmentalization and isolation to emphasize interrelatedness. Managers seek new strategies for balancing the needs of the individual with those of the business, making both company and employee healthier and stronger. Amid the quest for new answers, people tend to forget knowledge that has been around for millennia. Many of the current challenges we face in creating community in organizations have ancient solutions, or can be seen and understood in the echoes of ancient wisdom and practice. The way of the circle, which reaches back thousands of years, is the precursor of our modern ways of being together in business community.

Relax now as we take you, the corporate explorer, simultaneously into the future and back through time to a place of creativity and imagination. There you may experience balance and wholeness and see the possibilities for satisfying interaction with your fellow business community members. In this journey, we'll make use of both the healing wisdom of the ancients and a simple version of a modern business tool: the interactive computer.

As you read this essay, pause to reflect on any aspect of the whole or to savor the experience of tuning into the larger rhythms of the energy of the planet we all share.

Arriving at the Circle

Imagine you have been on a journey that has lasted many years. The purpose of your journey has been to find the keys to realizing a vision. The vision is of a time when corporations, as a powerful force for positive change on the planet, focus their contribution and connection on the whole of life.

After many adventures, you have come to a beautiful high meadow. In the middle of the meadow is a spacious circle of trees and in the center of the circle is a round table with a computer on it.

The screen brightens as you step into the circle, and the faces of an old man and woman appear. There is an integrity and power about them. They look right at you. The woman speaks: "Welcome, seeker of wisdom. We have been waiting for you. Come to the table. Make yourself comfortable."

You sit down in front of the screen, grateful for the chance to stop and rest. A gentle wind arises and the faces dissolve into a graphic image glowing on the screen in the early morning light.

The image is of a circle that includes four directions, east, south, west and north, with beautiful shadings of color in each—yellow gold in the east, deep red in the south, jet black in the west, and a shining white in the north.

In the center of the circle, the colors blend into a green diamond shape. Each of the directions is labeled, as is the center:

The man's voice continues: "Use the pointing device next to the screen to move around the circle. You can begin anywhere you wish, but I suggest you start in the east and work your way clockwise around the circle. End your journey by moving into the center.

"Each of the words in the wheel represents an essential element of community building. The elements exist in dynamic balance and interaction with each other. Each element—vision, change, nurturing, and action—must be dealt with fully and held in relation to the other three. Agreement is the vortex that allows the four elements to dance together."

You take a deep breath, reflect for a moment, and ask: "Before I start, would you mind telling me where this information comes from?"

The teachers' faces return to the computer screen. The old man speaks: "Not at all. Underlying this system is a body of teachings still taught the world over by many different 'carriers' of ancient, earth-based wisdom. These 'old' people knew about circles. By observing the earth and its patterns and rhythms, they saw ways of balance and beauty around them and modeled their communities in harmony with these natural patterns. In their oral tradition of teaching and learning, information was held in circular form or 'wheels' which could be overlaid on each other much like today's computer-based hypermedia. Looking into one particular area takes you deeper into the wisdom. Each wheel adds to your understanding of the whole."

The woman continues: "They also created processes ensuring that the wisdom and needs of the whole of life as well as of each individual would be heard.

THE CIRCLE OF COMMUNITY BUILDING

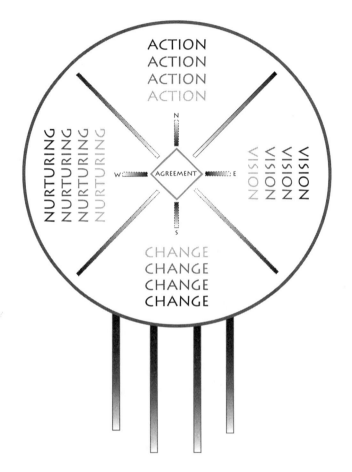

These same systems ensured that all perspectives would be considered and that the community would move forward in a balanced and harmonious way, having looked deeply into the issues that faced it. These ancients knew of the magic that occurs when people are truly a community. They knew the power of flying as a single flock of birds, of having a single collective intelligence. Yet they encouraged, even demanded, that the self-authority and intelligence of each individual be developed and brought forth. They danced a dance that moved between the wholeness of the individual and the oneness of the whole."

You experience a sense of anticipation. "Thank you," you say. "It feels good to have finally found the source of this information. It has been a long journey."

"Yes," says the old man. "Take a moment. Walk around the circle of trees in this meadow. Notice that there is a tree and a place of beauty in each of the four directions. Allow yourself to experience the magic of this place. This circle, and many others like it throughout the world, were built to be strong containers, capable of holding the challenging work that you are doing. Take your time."

Beginning in the east, you walk slowly around the meadow. As you walk, you notice a shift in your breathing, an openness to new information, a connectedness with whoever built this place. Refreshed, you walk back to the computer and sit down.

ESSENCE OF COMMUNITY

The woman's voice begins again. "Before we move on, we need to speak of community. What is community? What is it we seek to create?"

The following sentence, (attributed to Juanita Brown, President of Whole Systems Associates) appears on the screen:

"The essence of community is the sense of building a common destiny."

The old woman continues: "No matter who we are, where we find ourselves, or how much we 'know' about community, creating and experiencing community involves first making a choice. Unless this choice is clearly made and affirmed again and again in our daily lives, no amount of knowledge, no amount of wisdom, no amount of technology will create and sustain community. It depends, moment by moment, on looking at the person (or team, or country) next to us, and choosing to see our oneness or our separateness. If we choose to recognize our oneness, it is possible to join in the creation of a common destiny. If we choose to continue maintaining the illusion of isolation and separateness, community cannot develop.

"In our recent past, we have lived as if we are not connected, as if we do not share a common destiny. We act as if the water I pollute does not eventually flow into the well or water system from which you drink. It is as if the workers I lay off in the 'rightsizing' of my business do not become 'social overhead' to be paid for by all in the form of unemployment compensation, food stamps, Medicare, crime, homelessness, and so on."

The man continues: "We are an interwoven circle, a planetary web. As Chief Seattle said in the 1850s:

This we know:

All things are connected like the blood that unites us. Whatever we do to the web, we do to ourselves.

and as 20th Century physicist David Bohm has said:

The notion that all these fragments are separately existent is evidently an illusion, and this illusion cannot do other than lead to endless conflict and confusion.

(Both quotations appear on the screen)

"Scientists and wise people the world over more readily accept the view that the universe is an interconnected conscious whole. With this in mind, we continuously seek to marry the ancient wisdom of our ancestors regarding community with currently evolving technologies such as on-line networks, electronic media, collaboratives, and learning expeditions. This will allow communities to be created and sustained in ways that have not previously existed."

The sun is now high overhead. You take a drink of cool water from your canteen and reach for the pointing device. You click on the east, the place of vision. An image of fire appears on the screen.

Vision

The man speaks: "The east is the place of vision, creativity, spirit, imagination, and freedom. It contains the image of shared destiny we wish to create. Vision gives thrust, life, and fire to the community. It differentiates one organism from another."

You ponder his words as an eagle circles slowly, high in the sky.

Questions appear on the screen as you return your gaze to the computer.

The man speaks:

"Holding questions open is a key to learning and growing. We recommend that you enter into dialogue with your team and others concerning these questions, working with them until you reach clear agreement about your path forward.

1. What is the common vision that unites the community you seek to build? Is it one that everyone knows and agrees with and could clearly state without hesitation if asked upon being awakened from a deep sleep?

2. What is the process for determining the vision? In a community, everyone's gift is needed. How are you going to encourage the whole circle of people to step forward with their part of the vision—their understanding?

3. How do we weave the individual visions of the people into the common vision? What do we do with a vision that is very powerful for the individual yet has no place in the company? What do we do with someone who does not share any part of the vision?

4. What kind of time will be allowed for a vision to emerge and become seeded in your corporation? You will need to create a time of dialogue—meetings that encourage people to talk to and listen to one another, to reveal their deepest truths. When people truly share their visions, an intimacy is created, an intimacy that must be respected and allowed to grow.

The printer records the questions, and the woman takes up the thread: "Before we begin creating a vision, we must decide if we will proceed with integrity. It is not ethical to encourage people to 'tell their truth' and not have the courage to allow them to bring their visions into form. An organism, a living community is always capable of surprising us. To move forward with integrity, we must, as Angeles Arrien has said, be willing to do four things: 'show up, pay attention, speak our truth, and not be attached to any specific outcome.' All this while simultaneously maintaining community and getting the job done."

This is no small task, you think to yourself.

After a brief walk, you take a deep breath, sit back down and click on the red color. In the south of the circle is change. An image of flowing water breaking over rocks appears.

Change

You think of the increasing amount of change facing your team and corporations as a whole. You remember your friend Tom insisting that "people really love to change but resist being messed with."

The woman speaks:

"The south is the place of change, trust and innocence, power, danger, and emotional flexibility. Change shapes the shared destiny we are building and, if viewed positively, gives the community its sense of adventure, curiosity, awe, and wonder. It is in direct contrast with 'business as usual.' Change is one of the basic elements of community building. Realizing powerful visions requires that we change in order to create the future we desire to share."

The sunlight shines through the leaves of the ancient oak on your left. Questions about change appear on the screen with a reminder to hold the questions open, look into them, and not settle for quick answers:

1. What are the current attitudes toward change in your organization? Is it widely seen as a positive aspect of growth and evolution? Is it seen as a negative disrupter, to be avoided whenever possible?

2. How do we get all members of the community to be participants in the adventure of change? How do we help create change so that we are all moving forward together?

3. What means will be provided for people to communicate honestly about the effects of change? We must be able to openly acknowledge our thoughts and feelings as we are going through change. We must be able to say, "I'm scared" or "I'm angry" or "I don't want to move."

4. How do we create a climate for change? How can an attitude of openness, honesty and willingness be fostered?

The printer stops, and the man says: "Look, you've been at this for some time. Why don't you relax and play a game?"

"By myself?" you ask.

"No, if you look outside the circle of trees, you'll see a circle of children playing and learning a story. Go join them, and come back in an hour or so."

Gratefully, you get up and join the children. For the next hour you rediscover a sense of play and wonder while the children act out a story with their teachers. You come back refreshed.

Sitting down again, you click on the west area of the circle, the area of nurturing. An image of the earth, as seen from space, appears.

Nurturing

The woman begins: "The west is the place of nurturing, maintenance and balance, teaching, and healing. It is through nurturing that the shared destiny of the community can develop and survive.

The nurturing we seek is a balance between the good of the individual and the good of the corporation—a balance between a short-term and a long-term focus. It is a nurturing that considers the impact of an action upon the children for the next 100 years."

The questions for nurturing appear:

1. What kind of nurturing is needed, for the individual and for the well being of the community?

2. How willing are we to take the time to nurture?

3. How do we maintain and nurture people so that we take as good care of them as we do our machinery?

4. Who is responsible for nurturing?

Again, the printer prints out these questions. You imagine the lively discussions you will have with your team. You smile, stand up, and walk out into the circle, noticing again how the beauty of this place affects you—how it encourages you to slow down and feel the deep sense of connection to all that is around you.

You walk back to the computer and click on the north segment of the circle. An image of a large stand of poplar trees being blown strongly by the wind comes onto the screen.

Action

The man speaks:

"The north is the place of action, clarity, strategy, resources, and wisdom. It is the place of effective action in the service of shared destiny. There is a bias for action in our corporations and in our Western world. Action often precedes clear thinking and is frequently out of balance with the elements of vision, change, and nurturing."

The sun has shifted to the other side of the oak tree. A hummingbird dives from treetop height and halts a few centimeters from one of the flowers surrounding the circle. A flicker on the computer screen brings your attention back, and you see the questions related to action:

1. What is the most we can contribute to the good of the organization? What actions would that entail?

2. What is our action informed by? Before we act, what form

of inventory are we going to take and from whom?

3. What is our definition of effective? (Cheap, fast, profitable, short term, long term, effective for whom?)

4. Is our action consistent with our vision? Does this action bring our vision one step closer to form?

"Clear action comes from the courage of the heart and spirals around the wheel again and again. Action informs our vision, brings more change, and feeds on balanced nurturing."

You sit back in your chair and print out the questions. While you pick up the printed sheet, the word "agreement" begins to pulse on the screen, as if inviting you to click on the center of the circle. The teachers appear again on the screen when you do.

Agreement

"We come now to the center of the wheel. Agreement is the foundation of all relationship, and conscious relationship is the foundation of all community." The woman is speaking. "Behind all relationships are agreements. Many of the agreements in our communities and corporations today are not conscious ones.

Conscious agreement becomes possible once there is a shared vision. Without a shared vision, agreement often feels forced and superficial. Without some form of 'circle,' where people can speak and be heard from their own perspectives, deep agreement will never be reached. Think about your organization or community. What are your explicit agreements? Do you agree on the vision for your company? Do you have clear agreements about how change is handled in your community? Do you have any agreements about nurturing beyond giving or receiving a paycheck?"

The man picks up the thread: "Agreement demands clarity of understanding. We need to understand our own wants, needs, skills, and limitations—and the same qualities of those with whom we work. Agreements require constant revisiting because situations will change. Disagreement plays an important function in reaching agreement. In hearing disagreement we learn what we need in order to grow. Evolution depends upon the messages of disagreement coming forward. Once disagreement is brought into the open, dialogue can begin to move it into the next agreement. We can use the power of disagreement to learn and to enrich the fabric of our community as long as we hold the same vision."

The questions on agreement:

1. What are the fundamental agreements on which our community is based?

2. How is dissonance honored in our community? How can we find devices to help us hear disagreement—not to blame or punish but to honor and communicate?

3. In what ways do we see differences as a source of power for this community?

4. How do we share the power?

THE CIRCLE OF COMMUNITY BUILDING

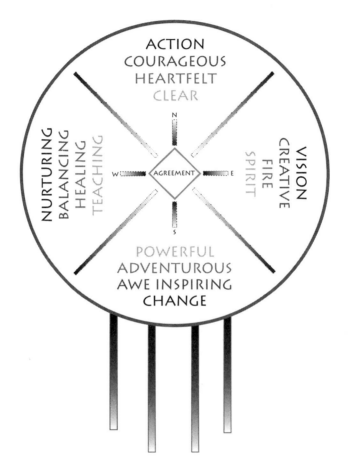

After the printer stops, you click on the screen. The image of the circle returns, displaying additional attributes in each of the four directions:

THE CIRCLE OF COMMUNITY BUILDING

You take a moment to reflect on the whole circle: "I'm amazed by how each of the directions connects with the others and how much I want to separate and isolate each area for attention and action."

"Yes, I know," says the woman. "It takes practice to envision the whole while looking into all the questions before jumping into action. The more you practice, the better you'll get."

"Remember" says the man, "this will take time and patience as well as powerful intention on your part. You are talking about a fundamental change in context within organizations."

The woman smiles before she speaks: "We have one last gift for you to take back to your team today. There have been many support systems throughout history helping to keep communities viable. We will briefly discuss one old form today to give you a sense of how things might change in corporations in the coming years.

Over the lifetimes of many generations, people developed and refined a process called the Council. This process required that all individuals contribute their points of view, always keeping in mind the good of future generations. Different viewpoints were not just tolerated but considered essential for reaching wise decisions. Rigorous listening and respect for all points of view was demanded. In The Council an issue was worked until a deep place of agreement was reached—a balanced, dynamic consensus. This requires study and experience to learn. Your questions will lead you toward this process if that is your destiny."

You notice that the light is low and that shadows dance in the circle of the trees. The children are nowhere to be seen.

The screen dims. You get up and pack your things, ready to begin your journey back to the world you have known, resolute in your dedication to be an increasingly effective and balanced proponent for change.

What is it within us that might stand in the way of our allowing
community to happen?

Part Four: Interpersonal Dimensions of Community

Eventually, all this technology for change gets down to personal challenges each of us must face. The theoretical, conceptual ideas—as lofty as they may be—need to be implemented if they are to have any real value in the world of commerce.

This section addresses our engagement in this process—changing our mind-sets, our long-held assumptions about how things need to be. The five essays in this part examine the personal "re-thinking" that needs to occur in those of us who wish to see change happen.

Susan Campbell advocates making learning and meaning as important as profits in her opening essay. Rondalyn Whitney considers an essential element of developing community to be genuine heartfelt caring for others.

Jordan Paul examines trust and respect as building blocks for effective communities, while Craig Fleck expands upon the principle of creative tension and identifies five basic tensions that exist in business. Concluding this segment, Jim Ewing compares the modern business organization to a tribal clan, calling for a non-traditional form of organizational leadership.

Susan Campbell,
Ph.D., is an independent organizational consultant, trainer, and speaker
with offices in Belvedere and Rohnert
Park, California. A nationally recognized authority on change and conflict
management, she consults with Fortune 500 companies as well as smaller
organizations from both the public and private sector. Formerly a faculty mem-
ber in the Applied Behavioral Sciences Graduate Program at the University of
Massachusetts, she is now on the adjunct faculty at the Saybrook Institute in
San Francisco. She is the author of five books, including *Beyond the Power
Struggle: Dealing with Conflict in Love and Work, The Couple's Journey:
Intimacy as a Path to Wholeness,* and her most recent, *From Chaos to
Confidence: Your Survival Strategies for the New Workplace,* to be published
in 1995.

16

A Sense of the Whole: The Essence of Community

Susan Campbell

In 1981 I received a research grant from the Tides Foundation to study the ingredients of healthy community. I spent a year traveling through the United States and Canada, immersing myself in thirty cooperative business organizations that displayed a strong commitment to the spirit of community. These groups were chosen because of their stated commitment to bringing forth a new standard for work—one that emphasized participative decision making, compassion, caring, and shared commitment.

The purposes of this research were to observe how these businesses were embodying the preceding principles and report my findings to the general public via the book *Earth Community: Living Experiments in Cultural Transformation.*

While each organization differed in its specific business purpose, all of the groups in my study had similar ideas about what makes a community healthy and what the new business-as-community looks like.

Everywhere I traveled, I saw people living and working with a sense of the whole in mind. This sense of the whole was exemplified by four essential principles:

Community Ownership
Meaningful Work
Ecological Sustainability
Respect for Differences

These four principles promoted a shared experience of belonging and contributing to something larger than oneself. This is the essence of community.

When this "we-feeling" is present, people can accomplish amazing things. The feelings of trust and support that come from this sense of community creates a profound synergy. The businesses that showed the highest levels of morale and productivity were those that not only espoused these values but lived them as well.

COMMUNITY OWNERSHIP

All of the groups I visited were engaged in some form of economic enterprise. Each worker was part owner of the business and part worker. In some cases, the shared ownership was financial. In other cases, ownership was conferred through the fact that the community owned and ran the business, so if you belonged to the community, you felt responsible for the success of the business. The spirit of shared ownership was felt by everyone, young and old. This led people to put forth more effort with more enthusiasm than they had in their former occupations. To quote from one of my research participants: "I feel like I'm working to support not just myself but everyone in the community. And I feel like I have their support also. If I do a good job, everyone benefits, so we all care about helping one another do better. But not in a 'supervisory' way. It's a real caring about doing our best and helping others do the same."

This man's disclosure reveals the value gained from a sense of cooperation. It illustrates the heightened sense of significance that people feel when they are part of a group effort.

Sharing Mundane Tasks

The typical distinctions between management and labor did not exist in the shared-ownership organizations/communities. There was a core leadership team of two to five people in every group, but these leaders could often be seen pitching in on the most mundane tasks. The group's leader would of course have different duties and responsibilities from those who mainly worked in the kitchen, but leaders did not limit their activities to management tasks. Most groups had a system of rotating the less desirable duties among all members.

I recall visiting one well-known community founded by a world-renowned author, someone whose work I had admired for many years. At the appointed hour of our meeting, I entered the main cafeteria where our interview was to take place. I found him contentedly vacuuming the floors. "Let's have the first part of our meeting here while I finish up my chores," he suggested. I followed him around, notebook in hand, for an hour as he vacuumed, dusted, and gave me a tour of the building all at the same time. Instead of apologizing for his preoccupation, he seemed proud of it. He told me he liked "getting out of his head, away from his desk, and into another role."

Shared Leadership

Shared leadership responsibility is another aspect of shared ownership. The essential leadership tasks in any community are to allow more and more people to share in getting the job done, to invest them with responsibility, to foster cooperation, and to find ways of using every single member's talents. Empowerment is essential to the new workplace and requires a sophisticated level of people skills.

The groups I studied were structured for empowerment. Value was placed on giving community members increased responsibility. For example, the role of staff meeting facilitator would often be rotated to a different person each work. Similarly, I experienced in several communities the ritual of leaving ten or fifteen minutes at the end of each meeting for "group self-reflection." During this part of the meeting, participants would ask themselves such questions as:

- How do we feel about this meeting? Pleased or disappointed, energized or depleted, cohesive or divided?
- How well did we maintain our purpose?
- How do I feel about my own participation in the meeting?
- How well did we use and respect each person's contribution?
- Are we leaving the meeting with any ill feelings that might decrease our effectiveness?
- What and whom do we appreciate?

Reflecting together on these questions at the end of every meeting gave participants a sense that others cared about their feelings and observations and that they could influence the course of future meetings. It was also an excellent vehicle for learning how to make their meetings more effective.

Letting Go of Control

One of the biggest impediments to community ownership I observe in my corporate clients seems to be the fear of relinquishing control. Business owners and leaders are traditionally seen as the only ones who really care about the bottom line—because it's *their* business. But consider the possibility that everyone in the organization might really care about the financial success of the business. If we believe this to be possible, and it appears to be so from the evidence here, we can then create ways to structure our collective efforts so that everyone feels his or her talents and input are vitally needed.

The old "boss-employee" contract is no longer effective because companies need so much more from employees than they did in the past. They need employees willing to change and grow to be more effective on the job. They need employees to risk personal criticism in order to inform leaders about what is really going on in the marketplace. And they need employees to work up to their fullest capacity.

MEANINGFUL WORK

In order to feel fulfilled, people need to feel they are doing meaningful work that contributes to the good of the whole. Those organizations where people seemed to feel enhanced rather than depleted by a day's work had all made this principle of "right livelihood" an important part of their vision.

In these groups, I saw people taking an active, creative stance toward their work rather than the passive, reactive stance I often see in businesses where people feel exploited or demeaned by what they do.

E. F. Schumacher, in his book *Good Work*, elucidates this concept of right livelihood, one of the steps in the "Eightfold Path" to enlightenment according to Buddhist tradition. In this view, one's way of supporting oneself can be considered right livelihood if:

- it gives you a chance to develop your abilities
- it enables you to overcome ego-centeredness by joining with others in a common task
- it brings forth goods and services needed for a becoming existence.

The same theory is echoed in the philosophy of Indian economist J.C. Kumarappa: "If the nature of work is properly appreciated and applied, it will stand in the same relation to the higher faculties as food is to the physical body. It nourishes and enlivens the higher man/woman and urges him/her to produce the best he/she is capable of."

Reframing the Purpose of Work

In the groups I studied, each community's economic philosophy fulfilled these provisions, and the people felt nourished by their work. After watching how long and hard everyone worked, I asked a member of one California community, "Does anyone ever get burned out on their work? You all seem to go at it with such vigor!" To this he replied, "Sometimes we get tired, but never burned out. Burn-out occurs when you're in some sort of conflict about what you're doing. We are totally committed to the work we do, body and spirit, so there's never that little voice inside asking, 'What am I doing here?'"

These people enjoyed their work as much as they enjoyed their leisure time. Unlike their previous work experiences in mainstream companies, this was not felt to be exploitive because profits ranked second in importance to people. Creative activity was given priority over consumption. People were encouraged to be innovative, to express themselves in their work, rather than conform to prescribed ways of doing things. Emphasis was on the worker, the work process, and the meaningfulness of the work.

"We feel meaningful work is a basic human need," asserted one community member. "We operate on the principle that people need work not only for income, but for self-expression, self-discipline, and a sense of participation." This woman's comments show the ideal of right livelihood in practice.

Making Learning and Meaning as Important as Profits

Most businesses do not inspire trust and commitment. From my talks with both CEOs and employees, I observe the trust gap getting wider. Companies need to strike a new deal with workers—a contract which honors employees' needs for self-expression and social significance. This will foster an ethic of continual self-improvement—something which today's "learning organization" cannot function without. How can an organization continually learn and adapt to rapidly changing market conditions unless workers themselves are continually learning and adapting?

Reframing the meaning of work along these lines represents a profound cultural change for most organizations. We must take steps to insure our vision is aligned with real human and environmental needs if we hope to do this. We must also design the work process with human learning in mind. Then we must show workers by our actions that their learning is as important as their output.

Most organizations already have the necessary feedback mechanisms in place for assessing needs. The employment interview, the performance review, the job assignment process, various employee surveys, and informal conversations— these sorts of vehicles can be used to assess our progress in helping workers feel a sense of right livelihood. When workers feel included and cared about in this way, commitment to company goals is the natural result.

ECOLOGICAL SUSTAINABILITY

A sustainable way of life recognizes that the Earth's resources (food, water, air, minerals) are finite and the growth of all living systems is limited. These limits are dictated by the size of the Earth and the input of energy from the sun. We humans need to attend to the amount of traffic the Earth can bear while still nourishing a quality of life fit for continued human development.

Most people know the difference between a sustainable way of life and one that is based on short-term thinking or overconsumption. When our lifestyles are aligned with principles of sustainability, we feel more secure and self-respecting. When they are not, we often feel vaguely uneasy.

Aligning Organizational Goals with Planetary Needs

For many years I have conducted public seminars where managers from a variety of organizations spend one or two weeks in a retreat setting developing communication and leadership skills. Typically, as the trust between group members grows, people who work for corporations whose philosophy is misaligned or rooted in unsustainability confess these feelings: "I hate that I have to work for a company that (pollutes the environment, makes nuclear weapons, etc.). But that's the only way I know how to support my family."

These managers feel conflict over earning a living in a way that damages their self-respect. It is easy to understand their feelings of shame, confusion, ambivalence, and anger. As a result, their pride of workmanship is practically nonexistent. Working for a paycheck in a way that does not support the good of the whole is emotionally draining and spiritually debilitating. An organization does not earn a worker's commitment under these conditions.

Contrasting this with those communities that practiced ecological sustainability, I saw people working enthusiastically from dawn until dusk without tiring.

Business organizations are just beginning to consider how their purposes can support human evolution and planetary well-being. We are starting to recognize that work is not just economic. It is both economic and spiritual. It fulfills needs for significance and meaning as well as needs for food and shelter. Just as in the ancient Buddhist tradition, we may find that the key to accomplishing more without burning out lies in aligning one's activities and goals with higher values and truths.

Openness to Stakeholders' Feedback Fosters Trust

What if a company is pursuing goals that seem unsustainable—at least in the eyes of some members? What does this do to morale and productivity? In some of the communities I studied, this issue had caused quite a bit of controversy. The important factor in determining whether members' full commitment could be sustained was the degree to which they felt heard and respected by management. When leaders were willing to listen to critical feedback from stakeholders, those stakeholders continued to participate with enthusiasm. When such feedback was ignored, discouraged, or punished, morale suffered noticeably.

Fostering Bioregional Identity

One way to foster ecological awareness in community members is to help them see themselves residing in a particular bioregion. A bioregion is to ecology what a state or nation is to politics. Instead of identifying primarily with a political subdivision, community members were encouraged to see themselves as part of an ecological niche or watershed—each with its own combination of natural resources, climatic, and geographical conditions.

Such bioregional stewardship promotes a sense of global responsibility and relatedness to the whole. It fosters the ability to "think globally while acting locally," or to nourish and heal the whole by attending to that aspect of the whole that is within one's domain (one's body, one's psyche, one's own backyard). This identification with the larger community of which we are a part, if fostered in mainstream organizations, helps workers feel more connected to that "something larger than oneself" that lies at the heart of peoples' spiritual longing.

RESPECT FOR DIFFERENCES

People who see their business and personal relationships as vehicles for learning are less attached to outcome than are people who see the same as sources of comfort and security. Increased value on learning, instead of control, is essential if one is to truly respect people who see things differently. A commitment to learning from differences, rather than trying to force agreement, was shared by all the groups in my study.

Methods for Learning from Differences

The groups whose work relationships were most productive and harmonious were those that had instituted regular procedures for communicating about, learning from, and clearing away relationship tensions and conflicts. Several of the groups used a format called the "Clearness Committee." The

Clearness Committee is an old Quaker ritual in which all community members belong to a three-person support group. This group acts as a sounding board for interpersonal differences and tensions. By meeting regularly with one's Clearness Committee, each person is supported in taking responsibility to learn from those people and situations that concern them most, thus clearing away the internal and interpersonal tension associated with the relationship. Your committee's function supports your learning without taking your side.

When I compare this to the typical lunchroom gossip that serves as an outlet for frustration in many of the organizations with whom I have consulted, I see a crying need for people to have a more constructive venue for dealing with their daily frustrations.

Those committees who used the Clearness Committee process spent much less time in disagreement and debate in meetings. Gossip was practically non-existent. Having one's own three-person listening post added the opportunity for self-expression, clarification of feelings, and a sense of being heard that all people need. This strengthened each person's sense of trust and belonging in a way that transferred to the organization/community as a whole.

Community Promotes Communication and Commitment

Most businesses I have worked with share similarities with the "dysfunctional families" described in popular magazines and self-help books. One of the differences between a healthy system and a dysfunctional one is the way the group deals with the unique needs and views of the individual members. In a dysfunctional system, certain members benefit at others' expense. Only these more powerful or feared members get their way. Others conform or comply due to a fear of rocking the boat. One problem with such a system is that you never really know what people are thinking because minority opinions are never raised. Thus, people mistrust one another, and important information that may be needed for critical decision making is unavailable.

Certainly it is no simple matter to evolve from dysfunctional to healthy. It is not easy for those in power to share it, or for those who have invested more of their hard-earned dollars to invite others into the business as partners. Yet these sorts of changes must and will take place if we are to survive and thrive in a workplace where the best and the brightest will not tolerate disrespectful and condescending treatment.

People long to participate with others in meaningful, useful work. People long for the sense of community that many only hear stories about from their grandparents. It behooves American business to search for ways of creating such a sense of community in the workplace.

What is most apparent from those groups where a sense of community is already present is the tremendous power that is unleashed when people feel they are a vital and respected part of a meaningful collective enterprise. People want community. They need to feel connected to something larger than themselves. They want the opportunity to give and receive, to teach and learn, to help and be helped. Work is no longer a nine-to-five proposition. It is a person's vocation. If we can re-vision our business organizations as communities, where workers are supported in expressing these deeper aspects of themselves while pursuing financial goals, we will unleash an energy source that we are only beginning to understand.

Rondalyn Varney Whitney learned the power of deep roots and interconnections from her mother and father's extraordinary examples and her community's caring gestures. During her tenure as CEO of Sweet Service Corporation, her team's caring community led to a tripling of sales and an unprecedented reduction in employee turnover.

A native of rural West Virginia and a former teacher and consultant, Whitney has developed courses on Caring, Angels in Business, and The Art of Business and lectured to entrepreneurial women on such issues as Valuing Ourselves and Pricing Our Services. She is a widely published poet and student/practitioner of occupational therapy. She lives blessedly in San Jose, California, as Zachary's mom and Whit's partner.

17

Caring:
An Essential Element

Rondalyn Varney Whitney

All things are connected like the blood which unites one family.
Man did not weave the web of life; he is merely a strand in it.
Whatever he does to the web he does to himself.
—Chief Seattle

Community cannot be built in an organization or anywhere else without a bedrock of caring upon which to hoist the first beam. We cannot build cohesion among human beings without caring.

The real challenge for building community in organizations is to find the courage to flex and grow, to bend and not break in the precarious balance between individual and organizational growth and well-being. What occurs in the process is a strong, healthy system—a community. When any of us look at building a community, we must first grapple with our own definition of caring.

The definition of caring I espouse is "to simultaneously be in behalf of the growth and well-being of another." When caring is the act of attending to the growth and well-being of another, it forces decisions that require deep looking and courageous action. Caring for others ultimately facilitates growth in ourselves.

What I know about community building in organizations comes from my experience with and belief in the interconnections of things and people, and my knowledge that interdisciplinary harmony enhances all focused efforts. It comes from my trained observations, first as a poet and consultant, later as an entrepreneur and occupational therapist (COTA). People want to make a difference, contribute to others, and grow throughout their lifespans. To some, the stereotype of "business" evokes images of cold, impersonal, suited robots. But in my experience, people in business, taken as individuals, want to care and are committed to meaningful lives. When businesses fold, the people feel sad because their dreams went unfulfilled. When layoffs occur, a hole is left and people feel it in their hearts. When business is built on caring, people are fulfilled, and miracles can happen.

We long for a sense of purpose in our occupations, beyond a bottom line, beyond a fad. There is reaching toward a pure sense of growth, a wellness that spawns deep roots and wings that propel us toward self-satisfaction. Our careers are uncertain and the world as a whole volatile. We long to play, to love and be cared for, and to feel as if we are growing, that our lives make a difference and that we belong. It is asking too much of a human being to get into a cold car each morning, suffer traffic, and arrive at an office where no one smiles with familiar greetings. That life is what makes grey skin and robs the sparkle from our eyes. We all want rosy cheeks when we are ninety and eyes that radiate grace.

People who create a sense of community and caring at work experience this deep sense of satisfaction. People love it. It makes them happy. Community evolves as people develop a sense of being appreciated, of belonging, of deeply caring and being cared for. We feel uplifted when we see teamwork blossom where none existed before. Community is inspired by collaboration, sharing beliefs in the present and mutual hopes for the future. As a customer or employee, it is invigorating to play and work around this energy.

PREPARING FOR COMMUNITY

In order to care for others, you must first care for yourself. You must be responsible and see to it that you are well enough to care for others. We care for ourselves when we create a sense of balance in our lives and develop a sense of safety in our worlds. It is unreasonable to expect ourselves to attend to issues of global or community importance when our attention is on personal survival. It is essential that we prepare ourselves as caring ones before attempting to create community.

Developing caring habits parallels the process of developing physical muscle strength, range of motion, and endurance. When building a weak muscle, one inhibits abnormal patterns of movement and facilitates normal patterns of movement. In developing overall physical fitness, we lift weights to strengthen, tone, and sculpt. In developing overall caring selves, we lift our hearts beyond expectations, strengthen our concentration, tone our courage, and dance with grace.

One begins training by exercising at the current level of strength. If I can lift twenty pounds with my biceps eight times then I work toward lifting it ten to twelve times. When I reach twelve repetitions, I add more weight onto the barbell. Then I lift twenty-five pounds eight times. Again I build toward twelve. When my muscles quiver, freeze, and cannot complete the repetition, it is known as failure of the muscle group.

Moving to the maximum level of performance, not just risking failure but courting and striving for it, is the process by which we develop our muscle strength and overall physical endurance. Failure is the only way to measure maximum performance. After I push my muscles to failure, I need to allow them to rest and recover before beginning again. This prevents injury. Building muscle strength is an example of growth; appropriate rest breaks are an example of balancing growth with wellness. Both rest and pushing to failure are required for wellness. This process of balancing allows us to maintain wellness and still be prepared to grow instantaneously in response to environmental demands.

We need strong caring muscles in order to build a community. We need courage to respond and faith to care, knowing the results may look and feel like failure. Practicing growth increases our ability to move in response to our environment, and this prevents the pain of stagnation and of regret. This takes conscious effort. A muscle only develops when we work to the point of failure, rest, and try again. Only in this way does the muscle becomes strong and able to endure. In committing to long-term wellness, we need to develop muscles of caring in order to succeed on the path of caring.

I have experimented with several different ways to develop the muscles of a caring one. When I feel like I am failing in my relationships, I look at where I am stuck, where I (or we) stopped growing, and figure out a way to stretch. Would it be growth for me to say I am angry or to hold my tongue? Would it be growth to help someone avoid failure or to let them learn the natural consequences of their behavior? At what point is my intervention caring and at what point does it rob another of growth? Do I just need to rest in order to heal and restore my own inner willingness to try? Do I need a coach? Someone to cheer for me to push out just one more inch of caring, one more repetition, to risk one more failure? I find growth in any experience. Failure is an opportunity to develop strength, not the birthplace of regret. By naming this place of potential grace amid confusion, we can deal with failure rather than flee from it.

In addition to developing strength in preparing for community, we need to develop an internalized sense of safety. Being authentic in community requires being vulnerable, exposed. I have found it useful to set up a few individuals to be caring ones in my life, people who have the freedom to tell me ugly truths that I will not see myself, as well as point out my beauty when I feel colorless. These are people who I know will push me forward in their commitment to my growth as well as stop me and hold me when I need to rest. This community allows me to risk failure as well as experience the profound exhilaration of touching human hearts in my caring. Having people in my life who know how to love me, care for me, and return me to wholeness allows me to live with my heart open.

In order to care for others, you must first care for yourself, making sure you are safe and have the necessary strength for the journey. Similarly, in order for an organization to have an impact outside itself, it must first care for itself, its members. The organization must be well enough and healthy enough to direct its energy outward. We care for an organization when we focus on the overall growth and well-being of the organization, the environment, the culture, and the individuals. Caring does not, however, mean giving out warm fuzzies at the expense of financial well-being. It would not be caring to exchange fiscal responsibility for authentic caring.

One of my favorite examples of courageous caring is the case of the Tylenol tampering. The president of the company considered the overall well-being of the individual consumer, employees, and the organization and pulled the product off the shelves. That ultimately cared for everyone. Call it good management or creative problem solving—what matters is not the label, but the willingness to focus on the overall system and demand a balance of growth and wellness for the entire community. Taking product off the shelves cost the company in the short term, but ultimately it sent a strong message of caring and transformed the breakdown (tampering) into a breakthrough (caring). It takes courage to risk vulnerable exposure, but I believe it builds healthy relationships and consequently healthy communities.

Encouraging Caring and Growth

There are signposts along the way to community evolving. Just like physicists first study the trails of particles and their actions in order to discover a particle's existence, we can observe evidence and discover the development of community. Building a community occurs when caring can be observed. Evidence of caring includes individual growth, growth in the community, and growth in the human species.

One way to build community is simply to begin caring. If we spend more time in conversation, demonstrate caring expressions and actions, others will mirror us. Mirroring is an observable, predictable phenomenon in group dynamics. People working together tend to mirror one another's behavior. People on teams begin to speak with common language, to assume one another's gestures. Given that mirroring occurs in a healthy organization, why not care and let people mirror that? Mirroring builds commonality. Mirroring our environment is healthy and a powerful component in building a community. As we mirror one another, we develop new behaviors,and our attitudes transform.

In a functioning community inventiveness manifests in both relationships and the results of problem solving. This dual inventiveness is easy to see in high performance teams. A high performance team needs to invent some skills for itself. In order to do this, members stretch their thinking outside of the normal ways of operating, to look at what growth would be for themselves as individuals and what growth would be for the organization or community. They need to painstakingly attend to the task of developing beginners' minds. As they solve their problem they invent a new way of relating within the structure of the organization, and revitalize the larger team. They generate a newer, stronger sense of being useful, and of belonging. That sweeps through the entire environment.

Beginners' minds are luscious arenas for breakthroughs. Polaroid Corporation's instant camera was created from such creative simplicity. Edwin Land's daughter asked, after he snapped her picture, "Where is it?" Land invented the instant camera and transformed photography.

Activities are another way to build common experience, and bonds will naturally occur. When we focus our attention on an activity, there is room to shift, stretch, and get to know those around us. We learn, for example, that the person to our left is not good at closing sales contracts, but she will stay up until midnight to make sure the customer's order is done right. We begin to see what we can count on one another, and the strings of connectivity are laid.

We develop our values within community and find ways to maintain these values. One team I participated in valued maintaining and capitalizing on our diversity. The team members included a scientist, a poet, a financial officer, an accountant, and a software engineer. Needless to say, our perspectives and uses of language were vastly different. Rather than compromising our values, we agreed to invent a common vision and to create individual visions reflecting the group vision. Collectively we agreed to "reach beyond how we now know how to be." Personally I aspired to create "exponential unfoldment." We honored our diversity and we achieved results. Our values required we invent a way to do both. Our commitment to care for and honor each other's uniqueness led to our group developing into a true community. We were and are still, five years later and thousands of physical miles apart, safe with one another, caring for one another, honoring and feeling honored by our relationships with one another.

Borrowing Lessons from Occupational Therapy

> Don't pray for the rain to stop.
> Pray for good luck fishing
> when the river floods.
>
> —Wendell Berry

Occupational therapy (OT) is a model of a community based on caring and increasing function within an individual's environment. The pioneers of OT examined society's treatment of illness and developed a methodology to care for people while encouraging them to pursue meaning in their lives.

Occupational therapy concepts have overreaching applications into caring, community building, beauty, and business, while having good practice techniques for enabling growth. OT offers well-researched, practical techniques for assessing status, fostering growth, and identifying what components must be included when treating a dynamic system. Whether someone is diagnosed with a stroke or schizophrenia, or is building a community in an organization, there are ways to help people make the most of their strengths.

My job as a therapist is to foster growth in others by enabling them to witness their success. Caring is the act of encouraging successful growth and long-term well-being. Occupational therapy assists people in being the utmost they can be. Our work creates healing that is authentic, long lasting, and deeply satisfying.

Occupational therapy examines the actions and activities that build a community because it includes systemic thinking, observation and analysis, and caring. Trained in the distinctions of activity analysis and observation, occupational therapists capture the essence of mastery, communicate it, and reproduce it in others. This discipline simultaneously accounts for the person's environment, the cultural influences acting upon the person, the roles they assume day to day, and the degree of true meaning and purpose in their lives. From there, occupational therapists design treatments that close gaps in the client's ability to function. Such work provides a template we can overlay on our organizations, permitting us to map progress, encourage growth, and monitor wellness.

CHALLENGES TO BUILDING COMMUNITY

Just as there are signs that community is present or emerging, there are also signs that indicate when community is missing. When it is missing, our longing for it can be exhausting. It is not the exhaustion of self-satisfaction, like after a great run, but the bone-tiredness that fills your body when you've spent the day trying to do your job but were thwarted by traffic jams, locked file drawers, busy signals, and rudeness.

B. R. Hasselkus and V. A. Dickie recently published a study in the *American Journal of Occupational Therapy* that addresses which activities and attitudes build or thwart community in business. Community becomes thwarted and dissatisfying when members cannot create harmony, when individuals are thwarted or controlled by institutional structures and policies or when they do not feel valued by the community at large. When members who feel like they can make a difference are blocked by a lack of support, they struggle with feelings of personal rejection.

Have you ever asked someone to go out on a limb for you and when he does, you've run in the other direction? In building community, we have to find the courage to stay around and see what is there at that moment when someone, at our urging, scoots to the edge of a skinny branch. Stepping onto a limb, taking a risk, is a dance in faith along a precipice. If we are to be caring individuals, we must wait and be prepared to step in when help would enable growth, and stand back when intervention would prevent growth. This takes courage, but it is the only path that leads to community.

What stops us from caring? It hurts to care. It takes discipline, rigor, and a willingness to grow to become a caring being. It is difficult to put aside our preconceived ideas about what shows care for others, to keep our hearts open and to let in another's joy, pain, and love. But it is essential. Sometimes it hurts to watch a stroke patient struggle with a button. I have learned that if I intervene, I am not truly caring. I am not fostering their growth and wellness. Instead, I am robbing them of their own lessons and their sweet taste of victory. It is caring for me to stand and watch the struggle and to allow for their failure. And it hurts. Sometimes the person cries. Sometimes I cry. Sometimes I think my heart will break open from watching a patient attempt to walk, dress, regain their sense of self-competence. Caring hurts. This is the hardest part of becoming a caring one.

Caring sometimes creates tension between moral and ethical behavior. For example, when I enter a patient's room to provide occupational therapy for a hip replacement, and notice they are fixated on needing to move their bowels or perhaps they are disoriented by a bad dream, do I leave the room and wait for the nurse or psychologist to arrive? Do I ignore their present state, superimposing whatever treatment agenda I have for them? Some might argue it is unethical for a non-licensed person to listen to and offer feedback on a dream, or beneath my profession to fetch a bedpan. I have found that it promotes greater healing if I find the extra time to pause, to listen, and to care. I listen to dreams, change bedpans, and allow myself to grow attached.

BENEFITS OF BUILDING CARING COMMUNITIES IN BUSINESS

We nurture the tree of our business concerns by caring. The fruit it bears is: quality products, productivity, job satisfaction, lower turnover, lower health care costs, grace in aging, more energy left over to appreciate the beauty of humanity. When we work in a spirit of community the customer is better served. Human beings feel more generous when our own sense of spirit is cared for. We have enough, then, to share. We must move beyond the social standards that require us to justify our actions with logic and linear analysis. If we are ever to transcend our animal origins and grow toward our angelic potential, we must develop a reasoning ability that expands beyond the tangible and grapples with the spiritual essence of humanity.

Compassion, from its Latin origins, means to have passion with, to suffer with, to bear up from under the emotions present in the intimate connection of another. Think about passion in your life. How do you feel when passion is present? How do you feel when it is absent? Passion is from the Greek *pathos*, to suffer, to feel deeply. Mariah, the angel of birth, says to us, "You may go to the earth and enjoy becoming flesh, practice the longing for oneness, but you will forget your divine purpose. Passion will be your anchor. When steps toward your goal become difficult, you will feel more pain as you stray from your path than you feel when you stay true. This is our gift. Now, go be human."

What would occur in our lives if business were comprised of passionate, caring people? It would be beautiful, like a work of art that triggers feelings too deep and mysterious for words. Our day-to-day lives would extend beyond our personal awareness and open to the aesthetic perception of the vastness and ultimate fragility of the universe. Each day would spring from the sense of unutterable depth and profundity at the brevity and the privilege of human life.

CONCLUSION

Community building is easier when we just care for each other. People long to touch others' hearts. Even when it is frightening, we still long for it. What is required is a safe space in which to care. Community can be that safe place. It makes us happy to belong. Researchers rediscover this all the time. Newborns need to touch; children need careful, loving boundaries; elders require intimacy; and we all need to belong in our daily occupations.

By caring, we comfort our aching. Caring makes couples, teams, communities, and humanity purr. Organizations must be willing to care in order to emerge as communities. We must be allowed to invent, touch, and nurture buds of growth.

Our world cannot advance to the place we envision unless we develop a more caring approach in our relationships. Lack of caring is the root of many of our world's conflicts. It is time to expand our way of measuring success to include well-being for the earth and all its inhabitants. There is an old wisdom, "If the tree is sound the fruit will be good." If people are caring, a community will prosper. To the extent that we can be people who love our neighbors as ourselves, we will foster community and promote shared success.

My definition of caring comes from angels like Mariah. This angel was so enraptured with the human spirit that she dedicated herself *ab aeterno*, to eternity, to stand at the moments of creative transformation that buffet the soul between fear and longing. She eases the soul into human castings, teaching toes how to wiggle while still in the womb. I began to wonder why she would want to stand at that threshold. My answer was that she knew easing a soul from divinity to flesh embodied the practice of authentic caring.

Mariah, The Birth Angel

Each day she goes to birthing rooms
reassures the descending spirits
Those souls schooled while
in heaven
growth-spurts, solids, trees—

She helps them pour themselves
into human castings
small fingers, small encumberments,
new bodies, flesh, she
teaches them to wiggle toes while they're still
in the womb.

In the womb she
answers their final questions
Does gravity hurt?
Must I forget everything?
Tell me again what feet are for?

She touches each infant
just before he slides from the womb
rests her finger on his upper lip
imprints him with her hallmark divot
below the nose
and whispers
forget now.

—Rondalyn Varney Whitney

Jordan Paul,
president of Effective Communities
International, a consulting and training
company based in Sausalito,
California. He is also founder and chairman of the non-profit Foundation for
Community Partnering and a psychotherapist, author, lecturer, and motivation-
al speaker. He has been a personnel specialist for Litton Industries and a high
school teacher, and has co-authored four books with Margaret Paul, including
Do I Have to Give Up Me to Be Loved by You?

Paul is a nationally known expert in conflict resolution. He has assisted
individuals and organizations in building high levels of trust and respect both
in their work and personal communities. In Effective Communities International,
he has brought together a multi-talented consortium of highly skilled professionals to develop programs for teaching the skills for effective leadership, that
is, how to build trust and empower constituents.

18

The Personal Elements of Effective Communities

Jordan Paul

An effective workplace depends upon healthy relationships among people. We cannot ignore the requirement for good relationships or endure unhealthy ones and expect to create healthy communities in our organizations. Good relationships are the foundations for effective communities and are built on trust, respect, and learning.

TRUST

The effectiveness and satisfaction of everything we do is determined by the level of trust in our relationships. Mistrust drains vitality, creativity, productivity, and joy. It leaves a wake of cynicism, protections, and indifference. Attempting to relate in a sea of distrust is like trying to swim through water that is being polluted with more and more debris.

Every new relationship begins a new "community"—moving to a new town, starting a new job, falling in love, bringing a baby into the world. At these times we often feel excitement, passion and optimism. But if day-to-day interactions erode trust, these feelings cannot be maintained. Low trust spawns adversarial relationships that must slosh through the muck and mire of defensiveness. Stalemates, resistance, rebellion, boredom, arguments, and power struggles weave a picture that bears little resemblance to the tapestry that existed before trust was eroded.

As our society becomes increasingly complex, trust becomes more and more important. Yet many people believe that trust should be added to the list of endangered species. Without trust, people withhold or distort the truth and communication breaks down. Relationships then become adversarial, problems mount, and solutions remain more and more outside of our individual or collective capabilities. Whether we are trying to make our family life satisfying, our career successful, or our community more peaceful, the journey requires more and more effort and we experience an increasing number of failures.

Businesses suffer when labor and management do not trust that the other cares. Families suffer when kids believe they will not be respected if they tell their parents the truth, and parents do not trust that their children are telling them the truth. Relationships between men and women suffer when we do not trust that we will be respected for our different styles. Education suffers when students do not trust that their teachers care about them more than the subject matter they are being taught, and teachers do not trust that students will work hard unless they are threatened. Effective communities cannot occur when people do not trust their politicians, doctors, lawyers, auto mechanics, or law enforcement officers.

RESPECT

Respect is the requisite behavior for building trust. Disrespect is the single most important cause for the erosion of trust. "I don't trust you," almost always means "I don't trust that you will treat me respectfully."

Trust grows when feelings, thoughts, and actions are mutually respected. Knowing that we will be accepted and valued helps us feel at ease. Knowing that we will be treated respectfully, even when our actions conflict with the expectations of others, encourages trust.

For respect to be given more than lip service, being respectful must be as important as our tasks and goals. This may seem like common sense, but it is not at all common. Deeper examination will illuminate how rarely it is practiced and the significant difference it makes when incorporated into our lives.

In building a successful business, teaching a lesson, getting a job done, or winning a game, the means used to accomplish these tasks and goals are almost never considered to be as important as the ends themselves.

When the means are not given equal importance as the goal, the means are often disrespectful. Parents often teach their children how to to be careful, be respectful, use proper language, have good manners, be responsible, and so on in ways that are often disrespectful to the child. Consider the long term consequences to a business when employees, customers, or the environment are not respected. Consider the long-term consequences to yourself when your own behavior has been disrespectful to your emotional or physical well-being.

Almost all relationship breakdowns, depression, deteriorating health, and business/career failures result from a history of disrespect and distrust. Only when we recognize the inevitable and enormous price that is paid when people or our environment are disrespected, will we be open to adopting a new paradigm in our organizations, large and small.

LEARNING

Respect is the behavior, trust is the result, and learning is the vehicle that makes it all happen. If the wonderful accomplishments we have realized from this "great society" are to continue, we need to learn from our mistakes and chart a substantially different course. As the ancient Chinese saying warns us, "If we don't change our direction we'll end up where we're headed." Openness to learning is the means for accomplishing this course correction. Once we've committed to a new course, continual learning is necessary to make ourselves and our communities more effective.

Significant and meaningful change often requires reevaluating deeply held beliefs. The courage to learn about ourselves and others is essential. Feedback and support are needed to make appropriate decisions and course corrections more quickly.

But learning becomes blocked by fears of reprisal, being taken advantage of, being criticized, or not being heard. Important information is held back or distorted and discussions fall into the same unsatisfying patterns. When afraid of being disrespected, we close up and defend ourselves. When we try to get others to change, power struggles erupt that feel like "do or die" battles. When we are busy protecting ourselves, there is no openness to learning and examining areas that need to change is nearly impossible.

Talking without an intent to learn is unsatisfying and counterproductive. Curiosity is our natural state. When learning is free from the fear of negative consequences, such as failure and punishment, we can give and receive feedback on how we're doing and how we can improve.

The major learning necessary to build effective communities centers around building trust. This requires learning more about trust and respect.

LEARNING ABOUT TRUST

If you are not yet convinced that a high level of trust is essential to the well-being of yourself and your community, consider some of the costs when there is a low level of trust.

In a system where neither party has a great deal of trust, the cost of adversarial battles is enormous. Consider the costs of negotiating a problem when each side sees the other as the enemy and believes they have to fight to be treated fairly. To protect against being disrespected, enormous amounts of time and money are spent jockeying for position. Decisions become stalled in endless negotiations. Every possible outcome must be accounted for and written in voluminous documents. The lawyers' clocks run constantly, and the hidden overhead costs are astronomical.

Now consider how different the negotiations would be if each side trusted that the other genuinely cared about their well-being and was committed to finding mutually respectful solutions.

Adversarial relationships between labor and management are just one example of a heavy price business pays when there is a lack of trust. When employees do not trust that management really cares about them, management becomes the enemy. As Frank Sonnenberg says in *Managing with a Conscience*, "Without trust, marriages fail, voters become apathetic, and organizations flounder. Without trust, no company can ever hope for excellence."

Consider the difference if a sexual harassment incident occurs in a workplace where there is respectful treatment and high trust—as opposed to circumstances where there is low trust. Where trust is high there is a good possibility that with good mediation the incident could be resolved with a minimal cost. Important learning for all concerned would take place, wounded feelings could be healed, and trust would actually increase.

Where trust is low, the victims do not trust that they will be treated respectfully. They believe the only way to get fair treatment is through the legal system. The cost, even if the lawsuit never goes to trial, is enormous and, no matter what the outcome, the residue is an environment where trust is lowered.

No system can continue to accommodate the costs of adversarial relationships. The consequences mount as trust is eroded, defensiveness is increased, and inevitable future problems are set up. Nobody ever really wins. Difficult situations in your life can often be traced to a lack of trust. Typical examples are power struggles, communication difficulties, broken agreements, excessively long negotiations, and lying or the withholding of information.

In my work in business, family, and education communities, I have observed the inevitable consequences resulting from low and high trust. By comparing those results you can begin getting an idea of the enormous price we pay for low trust. Here are some examples:

Results of Low Trust	Results of High Trust
Diminishing productivity	Increasing productivity
Defensiveness	Openness
Hostility	Friendship
Power struggles	Cooperation
Alienation	Connection
Depleted energy	Increased energy
Feeling insatiable	Satisfaction
Anxiety and tension	Peacefulness and tranquility
Limited creativity and visions	Expanded creativity and visions

LEARNING ABOUT RESPECT

The following example of a respectful interaction was reported to me while I was serving as a consultant with the Aspen Police Department:

An Aspen police officer pulled up behind a car that was stopped in the middle of Main Street. Turning on his flashing lights he motioned to the driver to move to the side of the road. As the woman drove to the curb she "gave him the finger," according to the officer's account.

Anger immediately boiled in his body. Armed with self-righteousness, he decided that she needed to be taught a lesson in manners. Noticing how her rigid body bristled as she girded herself for an expected attack, he approached her cautiously.

As she rolled down the window, he sensed a sadness behind her armored body. As soon as he felt this concern, his anger drained. He said compassionately, "You must be having a really difficult day." Her tension dissipated and her eyes filled with tears as she recounted the very painful events of the day to a new friend.

Whenever I tell this story a common question is "Did he give her a ticket?" Whether he issued her a ticket or not is unimportant. What is important is that a potentially adversarial circumstance was defused by a respectful interaction, and both parties left the interaction changed for the better. By maintaining his commitment to being respectful, this officer was able to serve far beyond the normal call of duty.

Anyone or any organization who makes respect an integral part of their mission and their lives embarks on a fascinating and challenging voyage. For example, when the Aspen Police Department began exploring this area, the problems created by disrespectful behavior, both with the citizens and within the department itself, began to surface. The areas of distrust and the cost of that distrust became apparent. It also became obvious how much easier and more satisfying their job would be if people had more trust of each other. In some areas, however, a tradition of distrust was deeply ingrained.

Once respect was accepted as a common mission, the idea of making respect as important as their tasks was introduced. Doing their job in ways that were respectful to themselves and the alleged lawbreakers became as essential as the task of stopping people who were breaking the law. That brought up plenty of resistance and a lot of questions. The most common response was "I've never thought about that." Then followed questioning about what a respectful response would be in many different situations.

They discovered that although suspected lawbreakers were usually treated respectfully, this was not always the case. It became a challenge to learn from situations that produced disrespectful behavior and to find answers to such questions as:
- What would have been respectful behavior in that situation?
- What got in the way of behaving respectfully?
- What needed to happen to be able to respond respectfully?

Without making respect essential, these questions would, in all likelihood, never have been asked or answered.

Respect is a principle held in common by most people. It is the essence of the "Golden Rule." A variation of this value is central to every major religion. Yet, although respect is often talked about, there are not many good models for respectful living. There are many examples of disrespectful behavior that are justified or condoned when the cause is believed to be "right, just, honorable, worthy or important." Religions have done it, governments have done it, and you and I have done it when we have hit or yelled at our children, or attempted to manipulate our business associates, family, or friends.

We would like to believe that we can treat ourselves, others, and our environment disrespectfully and not suffer any negative consequences. But disrespect is subject to the universal law that "for every action there is an equal and opposite reaction." In every relationship, whether it be with ourselves, others, or the environment, any disrespect has a negative effect.

Every relationship can accommodate some disrespect. But continued disrespect results in negative consequences for all aspects of the relationship. Even though negative consequences may not show up immediately, an accumulation of small damages eventually results in major consequences. For example, the human body is negatively affected by even a small amount of cigarette smoke. That damage, however, will not be serious unless the behavior is continual.

In interpersonal relationships, on-going disrespect eventually results in a diminution of trust, caring, self-esteem, and goodwill. Disrespecting a co-worker in order to teach a lesson may not have serious consequences when done occasionally. But consider the consequences of routine disrespect to the manager and to the employee. Disrespecting people may produce a "well-behaved" workforce in the short term. But the long-term results will not look so good when these employees get fed up and start "acting out" their resentments.

With short-term focus, we not only do not see down the road, but when we get there, we usually do not connect the problems we are having with the choices we made only a short time before. There is no doubt that many "successful" business have been created with a primary focus on profits and little regard for employees, the environment, and even, customers. But there is always a heavy price tag.

Although most of us care a great deal, we can behave disrespectfully more often than we like. When our expectations are not met, all of us, at times, resort to disrespectful behavior. When upset, disappointed, or sad we can withdraw into indifference or attempt to get others to change by making them feel guilty or afraid. These manipulative behaviors are disrespectful because they devalue others. Attempting to get others to change and do things our way dishonors them because it denies the appropriateness of their own behavior. Who has not cajoled, criticized, blamed, threatened, or isolated another person to get them to conform to what we thought was "right" or to get what we wanted? None of these behaviors is respectful.

In attempting to accomplish important tasks and goals, fears of losing something that we believe to be necessary for our well-being are often activated. Common fears are of losing control, money, another person, or our reputation. Many times we are not even aware that an underlying fear has been activated. We just react with a behavior that was developed in childhood as a survival mechanism, and is now a deeply ingrained and habitual. Even though our reactive behavior is usually disrespectful, our primary intent is not to hurt others, it is to protect ourselves from having to confront a dreaded loss.

Not a Time for Self-Blame

Becoming aware of disrespectful behavior is the first step toward stopping it. The task of acknowledging and learning from our existing ways is made inordinately more difficult when we make ourselves wrong for our behavior. Self-blame keeps us stuck. Acknowledging the past often brings up feelings of sadness over hurting others or ourselves. When we make ourselves wrong we do not want to acknowledge those situations. When we deny and repress past and present behavior we cannot learn from it. We then lose an important opportunity to change our future.

As you read this chapter and interpret your life through the lens of respect, try not to be self-deprecating when you find areas where you have been disrespectful. Respectful behavior is a guidepost, not an expectation of perfection. Each of us can find many situations where our focus on accomplishing a task or goal became more important than being respectful to those around us and even to ourselves.

To move past blame, it is helpful to remember that there are always very important reasons for behavior. We may be unaware of other behavior choices, or too afraid to make them. Even though the behavior we choose is disrespectful, we are not bad, wrong, worthless, or unlovable. We are protective and doing the best we can at that moment. This does not condone disrespectful behavior to others or to ourselves. But making ourselves or others wrong is not helpful in stopping the disrespect. To maintain dignity and self-respect we must learn to accept accountability for the results of our choices without negatively judging ourselves.

Deeper Understanding

Although the idea of respect has appeared throughout this chapter, deeply understanding its meaning may prove to be challenging. An in-depth learning about respect would include:
- What is respectful to ourselves, others, and our environment
- What is disrespectful to ourselves, others, and our environment
- What beliefs create the fears of loss and block respectful behavior
- How to resolve these beliefs

On the surface, understanding what is respectful and disrespectful may seem easy, but disrespect is so much a part of everyday life that we have lost the awareness of what it really means.

Without respect as our guiding value, a great many disrespectful beliefs and resulting disrespectful behaviors infiltrate and permeate our lives. For example, most of us would agree that having fun at someone else's expense is disrespectful. Yet a great deal of humor does just that. Jokes about people of a particular ethnic or racial group, sexual orientation, or gender may be laughed at by people not in those categories, but any demeaning stereotype is disrespectful. Anything that criticizes another person, such as sarcasm, is an underhanded way of putting someone down and is disrespectful.

There are other subtle forms of disrespect, but the one from which a lot of others spring is codependency. Codependency is a good example of how complex respect is to understand and the devastating effects disrespect wreaks on a community.

Codependency—Bane of Community Effectiveness

Codependency is a system formed out of neediness by a "taker" who needs to be taken care of financially or emotionally and a "caretaker" who needs to be appreciated for what he or she is giving. Those who have participated in co-dependent systems have probably been perplexed by the anger and unapprecia-tion that inevitably surfaces. The implicit expectation of takers is that if they can get enough of what they want they will be happy. The implicit expectation of caretakers is that if they can give another person enough of what he or she wants, he or she will be happy and satisfied and appreciative.

The basic flaw in this thinking is that, typically, people believe that they need "things" like money, love, sex, or affirmation to feel fulfilled. But things are never what people truly need to feel fulfilled and at peace. Therefore, the care-taker can never give enough to satisfy the taker. Codependence is a no-win sys-tem because we can never get enough of that which we do not need. Everyone in the system typically feels frustrated and self-righteously blames the others for their unhappiness.

Doing things for others is respectful and caring, as long as it doesn't foster dependency. Whether that dependency is on a substance like alcohol or drugs or on someone taking care of us emotionally or financially, it is the dependency that leaves us feeling weak and disempowered. Anytime we feel dependent on some-thing or someone outside of ourselves, we are like a child dependent on our par-ents for our sense of well-being. This is normal for a child, but in a healthy mat-uration process we move from dependency to independence. Therefore, anything that encourages dependency is disrespectful.

Caretaking fosters dependency because it carries with it the subtle mes-sage, "I don't have the faith that you can do this for yourself." When we believe that people are capable, we assist them in learning what they need to become independent.

We only need things that build our sense of self-worth. We need self-esteem; we don't need to be taken care of and kept dependent. The more we feel confident in our ability to meet our basic needs, the more we are free to interact interdependently. Without self-esteem and confidence we fear being engulfed (losing ourselves) or abandoned (losing another). To protect ourselves from these two deep fears of loss we are stuck in behavior that erodes effectiveness— control, manipulation, and withdrawal. Communities become bogged down with problems created by overly independent or dependent people.

Our welfare system provides a good example of the problems created by codependence. The intent behind welfare is honorable, but codependence creates insurmountable problems both for the caretaker and for the taker. Providing only money and food without opportunities to participate in meaningful work encourages dependency on the system. It puts recipients in the position of children dependent on their parents for support. A disrespectful system has produced disempowered care-receivers who feel distrustful and resentful, as well as drained caregivers who feel distrustful and unappreciated. Creating an effective welfare system would require continually making sure that whatever is implemented is respectful to all concerned.

In dependency or independence we are stuck needing to get love and respect. Maturity occurs as we learn how to meet our basic needs for security so that we are better able to give love and respect. When we are free from the fear of loss we can relate interdependently. Then we can discover our highest possibilities for creativity, productivity, and satisfaction and the more effective we, and our communities, can be.

LEARNING RESPECTFUL BEHAVIOR

I have used the example of codependency to illustrate how complex this issue of learning to be respectful can be. There is a lot to learn. Here are some examples:

- The subtle ways we try to change others and why trying to change another is disrespectful
- The fears and difficulties that arise when we let go of control and allow others the freedom to be themselves
- The faith it takes to let go of attempting to control others
- How we disrespect ourselves and how to better meet our own needs
- How to maintain our intent to be respectful even when another person is behaving disrespectfully toward us

Since respectful behavior is not generally well understood, learning about it may prove more challenging than you might imagine. One dictionary definition of respect is "to treat something as sacred." The general definition I like is, "Respectful behavior nurtures the well-being of oneself and others." The following list compares some specific respectful and disrespectful behaviors:

Respectful Behaviors	Disrespectful Behaviors
Honoring. Being aware of and considering other person's boundaries—their right not to have anything done to them that they do not want done, or that violates their sensitivities.	*Manipulation.* Attempting to control people and things. Not considering what others want, think, or feel, thus violating their physical and/or emotional boundaries.
Accepting. Appreciating differences by valuing and supporting the choices and feelings of others.	*Punishing.* Imposing or threatening negative consequences—hitting, yelling, or silence when upset with another.

Respectful Behaviors continued

Empathy/Compassion. Feedback that acknowledges and understands the feelings actions, of others. It follows from knowing that all behavior is motivated by important reasons.

Being Inclusive. Inviting others to participate in discussions and decisions about things that affect them.

Cooperation. Considering and valuing each person's thoughts and feelings thing or win at the when working on tasks and goals

Faith. Maintaining one's caring while allowing others to solve their own problems, especially in the face of difficulties. they are capable of doing for themselves.

Humility. Remaining unattached to beliefs. Having strong ideas but holding them lightly enough to remain open and flexible.

Open to Learning. Desiring to learn about oneself and others when differences occur Having faith that solutions which do not compromise anyone's integrity emerge from exploration and learning.

Disrespectful Behaviors continued

Criticizing/Judging. Making others wrong for their thoughts, feelings, or words. Communicating that another is stupid, a jerk, crazy, weird, etc.

Being Unavailable. Making other things more important than being fully present and really hearing another.

Egotistical Competition. Interactions where there is a need to prove some-expense of another.

Caretaking. Enabling dependency by taking responsibility for others and continuing to do things for them that

Unsolicited Sharing. Expressing feelings or pushing information and advice that has not been asked for and is not wanted.

Arguing/Debating/Persuading. Attempts to win, get one's way, be right or prove a point by convincing others to change their beliefs and behavior.

Learning is always respectful. The moment we open ourselves to learning, all disrespectful behavior stops and does not begin unless we close ourselves off again.

LEARNING—A CONTINUING PROCESS

A person once said to me, "Once you say that you understand something, you are closed to learning." That has always struck me as an intriguing thought. By acknowledging that there is always something more to learn, we stay open to learning. As we deepen our learning about what is and is not respectful we will continue to evolve.

Becoming more respectful is a journey, not a destination that we reach. Consider what it would mean to see yourself and others as always being "reinvented." One of my favorite posters is of a boy and a girl, around the age of eight, each saying, "Be patient, God hasn't finished with me yet." I always think that each of us needs a reminder of this no matter what age we are.

The longing for a sanctuary, a place where we feel safe, dwells within each of us. When our workplace is dedicated to the unfolding of our souls it fulfills this desire. It becomes a place where we enjoy spending time and using our best resources to contribute to insuring that it thrives. Making every community in our lives more respectful is a formidable challenge. But when living in a safe community becomes a high priority, you can begin in the areas in which you have some leverage—your business and your family.

Craig Fleck
has twelve years of experience in
counseling, group facilitation, and
consulting in support of organization-
al change. He works as part of an informal network of consultants who regularly collaborate on client engagements. He feels the most creative and sustainable work is done in partnership with colleagues and clients. He special-
izes in program design, team building, leadership, and vision development.

Fleck has lived in an intentional community in New Hampshire since
1983. This lifestyle offers him a foundation of experience to draw upon when
working to build communities of caring learners in organizations. Integral to
sustaining the experience of community is clarity of personal purpose, hence
he co-designed the Life Purpose Process, a series of one-on-one facilitated sessions that connects people with their life purpose and assists them in manifest-
ing that purpose.

19

Embracing the Paradox of Current Reality

Craig Fleck

Squeeze a pair of handgrips together. Hold the position for ten seconds. Hold it for twenty seconds. The longer you hold the tension the more concentration and mental focus you require. Hold it a minute and it will be difficult to think of anything else. Tension is so uncomfortable, so stressful, that most people try to avoid it, deny it, or shorten its duration. Yet it can be a tremendous source of strength and health for a business community—if it is employed creatively.

The notion of dealing with tension in positive ways is not new. Robert Fritz, in *The Path of Least Resistance*, dealt with the creative nature of tension, which Peter Senge took into the domain of organizational learning with his book, *The Fifth Discipline*. Creative tension, as they describe it, is an interplay between what could be in the future and what is now; it becomes a positive force for change when we articulate a vision of the future and then anchor ourselves in current reality. But there is another kind of tension that, because of the extreme pace of change, is putting increasing and unyielding pressure on our organizations today: the kind which arises simultaneously between two aspects of our current reality.

For example, an organization may be struggling between two concurrent desires: responding appropriately to a changing external situation and maintaining a stable environment that has been developed internally. Both are important, but they appear to be in conflict. Understanding and dealing with such a paradoxical situation is crucial to the ability of an enterprise to move forward creatively. Senge states that "an accurate, insightful view of current reality is as important as a clear vision." Unraveling the paradox can begin to give us this accurate and insightful view.

In nature, tensions play themselves out in natural rhythms: a rise in food supply leads to a rise in population, a decline in food supply leads to a decline in population. The balance most frequently happens before crisis is reached. In a business dealing with the paradox of current reality, it is easiest to feel the tension in a situation when it has reached crisis proportion. The challenge is to perceive the tension earlier, determine what kind of tension it is, and deal with it before the crisis starts.

FUNDAMENTAL PARADOX IN BUSINESS

Five basic current-reality tensions that continually appear in business are as follows:

- whole and part
- order and randomness
- external and internal
- sameness and change
- task and process

By understanding the dynamics of these tensions and how they affect our organizations, we build a foundation for making better long-term decisions, for counteracting drastic imbalances, and for preventing crises.

Whole and part tension is the interplay between purpose and the components which achieve that purpose or function. When should we focus on company purpose and when on individual need? Both are necessary for healthy functioning. Tension may also appear between different parts of the whole. In such a case, the whole affects each part and vice versa.

Order and randomness is the tension between a structured format and a more spontaneous approach. How much should we follow established policy and procedure and when should we allow room for the unknown to emerge? It may be fine to have a set policy and procedure to address a situation, but if it is inflexible, it may get in the way of something beneficial that is seeking to happen.

Internal and external is a matter of boundaries. One of the most fundamental boundaries determines what is inside and what is outside the sphere of consideration. The overall framework for a decision is affected by how we draw these boundary lines: Are we making a decision for the health of our department, the company, or the community? Another boundary determines inclusion and exclusion. Which people do I include in this decision and which people do I leave out?

Sameness and change is the interplay between the way things are done now and new possibilities. Should we continue to do what has been successful, or should we do something new which may increase our capability to handle what is coming? This tension comes into play whenever we go through a reorganization, consider a new training program, or update our technology. Will the change actually increase our capacity or is it just a dressed-up version of something we already do fairly well?

Task and process is the tension between getting things done and creating an environment in which things can get done. Another way to look at this issue is to define it in terms of getting results versus building relationship. When is it right to push forward toward resolution of an issue or completion of a project, and when would it be better to slow down and turn our attention to interpersonal dynamics that may be affecting creativity or implementation?

Part of what allows community to thrive is its attention to these tensions and its effectiveness in dealing with them. The tensions represented between each of these pairs can create a powerful synergy, producing more together than either individual component can accomplish in isolation. We lose this synergy when the focus is one-sided. It is important to be conscious of the interplay of the tensions and not fall into a rote pattern.

ATTRIBUTES OF THE TENSIONS

As with breathing, there is a natural rhythm to these tensions which oscillates from an emphasis on one side to an emphasis on the other. Just as a problem would arise if we were to decide only to inhale, a basic problem with respect to these tensions occurs when organizations get into a rut, making decisions on only one side of the tension.

For example, a company may have an unwritten rule that whenever the pressure is on to complete a project, employees are expected to work overtime until the crisis is averted and the project is completed, essentially sacrificing their personal lives. This would be an example of making a constant choice in favor of *internal* (the company) instead of *external* (the family). This is not a problem as an isolated incident, but if the organization develops a trend toward this sort of crisis management, the unwritten expectation may begin to build resentment on the part of the employees, increase tension at home, and eventually lead to less productive, less creative staff—thus increasing the likelihood of more crises. The very strategy used to deal with crises actually gives rise to more!

Tensions are seldom separate or isolated. When we make the decision to work late, it has an impact on our family (*internal* and *external*). The reason we make the decision is to please management which expects us to put in extra time on an important project nearing deadline (*whole* and *part*). Management thinks that way because "That's the way it's done around here" or "If you want to be a success, you put in the necessary time. Besides, I do it that way!" (*sameness* and *change*). As in all systems, nothing stands in isolation. All the five tensions are interrelated and any in-depth change in one will alter the interplay in the others.

The five basic tensions are so close to us, so much a part of what we do at work, that we often don't notice them. But it is critical for us to attend to them if we are concerned with the long-term health of the company. When we suddenly realize that, because we are overstaffed or have not talked directly to our customers in a very long time, our bottom line doesn't look good, that gets our attention! By then, though, we're already in crisis.

The following chart shows some of the places the five tensions show up in our businesses:

Internal/External
Business/Customer
Work/Home, family
R&D/Market need
making/Empowerment

Order/Randomness
Hierarchy/Matrix structure
Policy/Situational response
Top-down decision

Sameness/Change
Old method/New method
Current reality/Vision
Current size/Expand
or downsize

Whole/Part
Corporate/Divisional
Management/Employee
Year's profit/Quarter profit
Majority/minority (diversity)

Task/Process
Doing/Being
Results/Relationship
Action/Reflection

The paradox inherent in these situations is that both elements may need to be addressed at once, often in seeming contradiction. How can we both change and stay the same? How can we simultaneously be action/results-oriented and reflective?

In the complexities of today's business environment, we have little choice but to embrace the paradox. Charles Handy argues in *The Age of Paradox* that "managers have to be 'masters of paradox,' turning the horns of dilemmas into virtuous, not vicious, circles." J. Stoppford and Charles Baden-Fuller, in their study of rejuvenating businesses—"Rejuvenating the Mature Corporation"— report that the successful ones live with paradox: "Firms need to be planned, yet flexible, be differentiated and integrated at the same time, be mass marketers while catering to many niches, must introduce new technology, yet allow their workers to be the masters of their own destiny…in short, they have to reconcile opposites, instead of choosing between them."

Dealing with the paradox of current reality successfully requires us to move beyond either/or thinking and focus on both polarities as valid and necessary. Since we have been conditioned to think in either/or, right/wrong patterns from childhood, this is not an easy task.

For example, there is a tendency to go to extremes when implementing new programs. I have witnessed many organizations beginning to apply consensus-based decision making, in which the parties involved, through joint inquiry, create a solution together that everyone can support (as opposed to having a decision in mind and getting "buy-in" for it). Frequently, such organizations attempt to change from no decision being made by consensus to all decisions by consensus. This creates difficulty and frustration for a number of reasons. For one thing, the skills required for unilateral decision making and those for consensus are vastly different; one requires expert knowledge and experience as a base, and the other calls for deep communication and team skills. Also, considering the time pressures of today's business environment, trivial decisions and those requiring specialized expertise do not lend themselves to consensus. When utilized inappropriately, consensus gets a bad name.

How Organizations Handle Tensions

Most managers in a crisis feel pressured to resolve tensions quickly. As a result, they habitually seek resolution almost entirely on a traditionally favored side of a basic tension. Once a policy is set, it is applied to all related situations for ease and consistency of implementation.

But making rote choices threatens the long-term health of the organization. Although one-sided decisions seem to alleviate tension, they only bring temporary relief. Choices without regard to the rest of the system lead to imbalance and reduced capability. Connection with the natural rhythm is lost when the focus of decisions and actions is only on one side of a tension, particularly in times of crisis.

Suppose, for example, an organization needs to institute new innovations or methods continually to keep a competitive advantage. Consistently favoring *change* over *sameness* can undermine employee confidence in management's commitment. Without employee confidence, programs are quickly labeled "flavor of the month" and not taken seriously. Soon, any of the benefits of a new approach are lost and with it the competitive advantage.

The challenge is to maintain the tension long enough to perceive what new response may be required in this situation. In business, we often try to "sell" decisions by convincing each other. This approach tries to circumvent the development of creative tension by providing an obvious choice. A strong sell can lead to difficulty later on because we're approaching an issue as if we already know the answer, rather than saying "I don't know" and entering into joint inquiry and discovery. If a decision is "sold," it may not be supported in the long run because both sides have not looked at the tensions involved. If you acquiesce just to make a decision, it is likely that your heart will not be behind the implementation.

In today's environment of dynamic and rapid change, the decision-making parties often cannot be certain their solution will work. This uncertainty provides the opportunity for continued curiosity: How *will* this turn out? It can keep feedback moving within the system if people keep their attention and communication open. When we have to sell, we have to act as though we are certain the proposed action will work. This certainty subtly discourages follow-up and feedback, closing our attention to other options.

I recall working with an organization that was implementing a new change process. Developed and initiated from "the top," this process was a forum in which people lower in the system could question, challenge, propose eliminating useless work, and suggest new ideas and solutions. Initially, this idea generated some short-term successes, but then the participants began generating such long lists of changes that more work was being created than eliminated. People complained, among themselves, of being overloaded (this was a downsizing organization). Since the idea had come from the top, however, they felt a subtle pressure to continue without even tracking the effectiveness of the actions implemented. Although the process had been designed to promote upward feedback, employees felt constrained from giving feedback about the process itself!

TENSION AND COMMUNITY

People who have lived, studied, and written about community report that true community flourishes in an atmosphere of vibrant and dynamic interchange, in which people are open and honest about their needs and wants. Expression of a full range of feelings is not only possible but encouraged. A vibrant, vital community is a place where intimacy thrives, diversity is welcomed, learning is an ongoing interest, and there is a strong sense of both individual and collective purpose.

Before community can fully emerge, copious amounts of tension are inevitable as individuals argue for their diverse points of view. All the fundamental tensions put in an appearance during this phase. Making creative use of these tensions requires a pause in which all the elements influencing a situation are allowed to mature, without being squashed by quick decisions. A community-in-process holds tension creatively, acknowledging that cycles are important and that, if the time is not right for a decision, forcing it will not help matters.

An organization that operates as a community could watch the tensions over a period of time, using them as barometers to assess the organization's overall health. Members might perfect an issue, asking the question: "What are the fundamental tensions in operation here?" Other questions that may reveal the nature of the tensions in a specific system might be: "What is the normal way we deal with these tensions?" and "What are the crucial parts of this system and how do they interact?" "How does this issue fit into our overall purpose?" These questions are most effective when asked of a wide variety of individuals connected to the issue, not only "overseers," but also laborers, suppliers, and customers. This wider perspective is a basic tenet of systems thinking; you cannot see the whole system from one point of view.

After decisions are agreed upon and actions taken, feedback and public reflection are required to gauge and ensure success. This is done most effectively in an environment that is safe and open enough for honest, candid feedback—one that supports community. Such an environment only happens when difficult issues and conflicts are put on the table and dealt with free of political posturing. If someone brings up an "untouchable" issue or subject and is immediately shut down or ignored, particularly by his or her manager, the message is clear: it is not safe to address these tough issues. Candidness needs to be coupled with an appreciation for the diversity of perspective that individuals bring.

Paradox can be dealt with effectively only by forging a larger view that encompasses the two poles of tension. Actions taken from that larger perspective can open up creative options that were previously invisible.

Holding the tension does not necessarily mean being inactive; it means paying attention to both sides over time and watching how your choices affect the dynamic interplay between them. If the organization constantly decides on one side of a tension rather than the other, a caution flag should go up and the larger principle considered from a long-term strategic perspective.

This is a common dilemma business often faces: if we don't act quickly, we may lose important ground; if we act too soon, we may not be acting strategically for the long term and end up redoing a short-term fix. To explore where the balance of a tension currently is, you might ask: "If we continue to resolve this only one way, what is likely to happen?" and "What other key tensions are affected that haven't been considered?"

The greatest ally to holding tension is curiosity—asking questions that expand the understanding of the system. This is the fuel that drives the development of learning organizations and allows operation from a systems mindset. The next greatest ally is tolerance for discomfort—a willingness to pause and live with conflict and uncertainty while looking more deeply into the issue. For any of the five basic tensions, repeated choices on one side will eventually cause stress on the other.

If we have a pain, we usually think first about stopping it, and only then about what has caused it. The measures we use to eliminate or reduce pain often can mask the cause or distract us from the search, like a toothache we put off dealing with by taking aspirin until it's abscessed. The challenge is to stay alert and aware while we are uncomfortable long enough to have a new option come into consciousness.

Waiting is the most challenging part, as it is of any creative process. There is a great temptation to act decisively on what we think we know now, which does not leave room for intangibles like feelings, emotions, the energy surrounding a situation, and intuition. These intangibles are exactly the data that provide clues about the nature of the system we are addressing. By waiting and opening our awareness we can perceive many previously invisible factors and set up conditions for systemic solutions to emerge.

A CASE OF OVERCAPACITY

Rhino Foods was in a fix. Recent analysis showed that an anticipated drop in orders would lead to an overcapacity of workers in production. This was not good news. A small food service company dealing with frozen dessert products, Rhino had developed purpose and principles statements that reflected the spirit of discovery, creativity, and commitment to its people, and had also cultivated a strong network of relationships with suppliers, customers, and the surrounding community. Laying workers off was a most unpleasant prospect.

The issue here primarily reflected a tension of *internal* and *external*: carefully built internal community and stability versus external factors that affected the bottom line. *Whole* and *part* also came into play: individual versus company survival needs.

Ted Castle, Rhino's founder and CEO, rejected the easy and obvious solutions: laying off unneeded workers for the interim and hiring them back when orders picked up, or maintaining current worker capacity, taking the losses, and counting on future sales to make up the difference. Neither of these solutions reconciled the paradox: responding appropriately to the changes from the external business environment and simultaneously maintaining internal integrity.

Castle determined not to simply decide unilaterally what would happen, but to draw on others in the company for information and inspiration. Instead of making a quick decision, he chose to hold the tension and allow as broad a representation of employees as possible to be involved in addressing the situation.

At the weekly company-wide meeting, he described the situation and presented a process plan. A volunteer task force, open to all employees, was established. Half the company participated. After three weeks of some gritty sessions, the following solution emerged: Rhino would initiate an exchange program in which certain Rhino employees would go to work temporarily for other local companies. (One, a customer, had specialized needs.) This created a win-win situation for all concerned The outside companies received trained, skilled workers for a specified time period, Rhino's workers continued to receive paychecks (from the other companies), and Rhino Foods avoided significant losses while maintaining the internal stability that had made it so successful. The Rhino employees returned to Rhino as soon as production warranted.

The company held the tension long enough to find a way to reconcile the different aspects of the paradox. The solution emerged, in part, through blurring the lines of what was internal and what was external. Other crucial factors were Ted Castle's patience and unwavering commitment to his employees and the employees' trust that the company actually would empower them to deal with their employment destiny.

Specifically, here is a summary of the process Rhino followed, which can apply to a wide variety of paradoxical situations in business:

- Clarify desired outcomes, guided by your purpose, values, and vision.
- Be open and candid in disclosing the situation.
- Mobilize the widest resource available; specifically involve those with as many different perspectives as possible.
- Expand the domain of the tensions involved. For example, at Rhino, this meant expanding the external side of the polarity—that is, including other companies, some of which were partially responsible (through reduction of orders) for the situation, as part of the possible set of solutions.
- Frame questions that expand your understanding of the system and provoke new thought and perspective. One of Rhino's questions was, How does a company deal with worker overcapacity in a way that adds value to the company?
- Be patient; stick with the process.
- Make your decision or choice based on new elements that emerge while you hold the tension—particularly elements that reconcile the paradox.

- During and after implementation, actively seek feedback.
- Evaluate, review, reflect, modify, and innovate based on this feedback. Continue to keep the feedback loop alive. Notice and record your learnings.

Rhino Foods gives us one example of the benefits holding tension can have. As our organizations begin to function as creative communities and strive to sustain that atmosphere, embracing the paradoxes of current reality will become more natural. When we build our awareness and capacity to hold both sides of a tension, we increase our ability to make systemic business decisions that promote the long-term health of the organization and those who give life to it.

Jim Ewing
established his private consulting practice in 1978 and later founded Executive Arts, Inc., a design, education, and services enterprise. He has served a wide spectrum of individual and organizational clients ranging from San Diego city government to high tech engineering, manufacturing and marketing organizations such as TRW, Unisys, Apple Computer, Navistar, Centex, BP, and Smith Kline Beecham. After graduating from Cornell University in Electrical Engineering, he held various positions in industry, beginning with technical systems engineering management at TRW.

Ewing and his family have spent the last two years in Scotland on an extended assignment with the Exploration wing of British Petroleum, which is in a continuing process of restructure and renewal. He has designed transition processes for the initiation of new organizational 'tribes'; has trained internal pros in the use of his transition, coaching, and group process methodologies, and is developing new ways for traditional staff people to add value to 'tribal' productivity.

20

Gaining the Ear of the Clan
Jim Ewing

It is no longer news that competitiveness in the world marketplace requires the nimble, flexible structures that can cut through traditional organizational boundaries. From independent production teams to stand-alone profit centers, companies are installing small, focused, integrated productivity units, peopled with talented players drawn from diverse organizations.

These groups behave more as business 'clans' than projects. My *Webster's* defines 'clan' as a "narrowly exclusive group of people usually held together by a common, often selfish, interest or purpose," and "a number of people having something (as habit, interest, occupation, or age) in common."

Business clans are organized closely around the work to be done and the assets needed to do it. They are constructed on clear investment and return equations. They tend to be self-contained in the breadth of knowledge and experience necessary to deliver physical, technical and financial results. They develop their own identity, spirit, ways of work, rules, financial structures and ethos, in order to maximize their operational effectiveness. These groups are set up with interests, commitments and rewards all their own. Thus they can appear independent and even rogue-like, operating outside the traditions of their sponsors.

Successful clan members tend toward the self-assured and communicative. They have a personal vision which does not rely on permanent employment with any one entity. Rather, visions tend to include open-ended investments of time and energy in teams and activities which are high on interest and reward, including appropriate breaks for kids, adventure and personal and professional development.

When genuinely free to manage themselves, clans build shared, communicative power structures utilizing transparent, fast information systems and communication tools. They strive for efficiency in thinking, explicitness in feeling and simplicity in actions.

Clans, organized outside of traditional organizational structures, do not take the imposition of top-down control easily. Hence, the very senior managers who champion the clan creation must change their traditional leadership strategies if they are to succeed in having influence.

A Corporate "Profit Community"

Larger firms are increasing their profit capacity by organizing, investing in and managing many of these clan-like productivity groups.

My dictionary defines community as "an organized aggregate of persons who are responsible for a prevailing social order." I take the liberty of changing the word "social" to "business." In this sense, the highest level corporate managers, those responsible for the financial health of the corporate entity, are increasingly required to have influence and impact as "profit community" leaders in a culture of business clans. This requires abilities associated with   complex social community guidance rather than traditional, privilege-based, autocratic command and control skills.

The Symphony and the Jazz Band

A music analogy is helpful to explore the transformation to business clans and the profit community.

Business clans operate more like jazz groups than they do symphony orchestras. Meanwhile, the very large, traditional organizations most in need of clan structures, are predicated on a symphonic model of performance.

Picture the symphony. Director on a raised platform. Tidy groupings of instruments. First-, second-, and third-chair players in specific seating arrangements. A completely documented score. An interpretation of the score to the liking of the director. The score itself, the invention of one person, usually long dead. Formal dress. Individual players devoting every thought, emotion and action to the composer's score and the director's interpretation. Rehearsal, rehearsal, rehearsal.

Done right, the symphony is a magnificent, breathtaking, emotional, even spiritual ritual. It is created from consummate technical musicianship, structure, and organization in unquestioned service of the personal vision of two people, the composer and the director.

The symphony is not, however, a nimble, flexible, risk-taking, innovative, customer responsive, self-empowering crap shoot.

The bigger an organization gets, the farther the upper managers are removed from the actual work being accomplished. When this separation goes beyond a couple of management levels, the managers tend to see the business in abstractions. Product lines, operating groups, laboratories, and other convenient arrangements of human effort and assets become the violin, brass, percussion and other orchestral voices in the strategic financial symphony played out in the marketplace. From the high view, these voices are scored, arranged and directed to create an ongoing satisfaction in the marketplace which must, first and foremost, generate return for the investors. The shareholder expectation of symphony-like coordination and control comes with the executive role. Given human nature, the executive manager traditionally reflects the same expectations downward into the organization.

The clan, of course, is responding to a different reality in the marketplace. Chaos reigns. Anything can happen and probably will. If we can think of it, it will be in our face tomorrow afternoon.

The improvisational jazz ensemble is far closer to the style the clan must adopt to deliver the efficiency and responsiveness the current environment demands.

Imagine seven or eight musicians arranged as they prefer, without musical scores or music stands. They wear clothes which suit the setting and their mood. The group has agreed on a tune to play, which is defined by a key and a set of chord changes in time. These interactive disciplines are so basic and inviolate they can be held in each player's mind rather than written in a score. The "leader" sets a beat and provides a countdown to the start of the music. At crucial points, he or she signals major changes in key or rhythm. At the end, the leader tells everyone when to finish, and when that time comes, they do.

The players carry on the unfolding dialogue of technically skilled, spirited and expressive human beings. They listen to one another and reflect internally on what they hear, as much as they speak through their instrumental voices. Rehearsal is really practice in listening, reflection and speaking. The goal is nothing less than the highest level of personal challenge, interaction, learning and performance.

Skilled jazz players move between player groups with ease, taking on a shared identity quickly. They rely on highly interactive communication to succeed. They are valued for their ability to express themselves powerfully in the moment and their ability to relate and interact effectively and quickly with other players.

They are not valued for their ability to keep leaders happy or comfortable. Their allegiance to their current musical clan is balanced with a dedication to their own flexibility and capacity. Success of the clan depends on experimentation, learning, risk taking, individual experience and expression beyond the individual's previous limits.

THE EXECUTIVE DILEMMA

The best senior people struggle mightily and with great craft to perfect the symphony of resources at their command. Usually, it is the human factor which defeats the best plan. Their score changes before the ink has a chance to dry. The third chair violin section is cheering on the kettle drummer who is hopelessly in love with the first cellist. Cost reductions have forced the director to produce sounds from sections of 30 players instead of 110. And those 30 are playing with half their attention on the score, while the other half is spent looking over their shoulders for the next wave of cost reductions. So, who's watching the director?

Sound familiar? If you are an upper middle manager in most big organization in the 1990s, it probably does.

Imagine that in order to compete effectively and survive financially, our local symphony orchestra decides to organize a small jazz group composed of members of the symphony, contract labor from small, local jazz groups and players from a competing symphony. It will be cost effective, immediately responsive to audience interest, and easily redeployed in different sizes and structures.

Symphony leadership method imposed on the jazz group seems stultifying and oppressive to the players. Jazz seems risky, unconventional, undisciplined and reckless to the symphonic parent.

Yet, the symphony parent must find a way to manage the jazz group to its highest powers, to repay the parent symphony investment.

The senior managers with the necessary experience and judgement to be entrusted with the corporate nest egg grew up in symphony method. These are the very people risking it all on the clans. They have put themselves in great personal jeopardy by inventing the clans without sure knowledge of "how to control the damn things," as one manager put it.

FROM LEADERSHIP TO GUIDESHIP

It comes down to this: how to assure the corporate investors a predictable, reliable, controllable profit community by managing disparate, roguish bands of self-directed, independent players.

As clans are defined and grow, they find their own processes for arriving at the best options, choices and directions, or they do not succeed. The successful clans, therefore, increasingly do not need or want direction from above.

Thus, the leap for the corporate manager is from command and control, power-centered, privileged leadership to what I've branded organizational "guideship," which works more on the principles of social community leadership and influence building, rather than those of benevolent dictatorship. The Guide exists to optimize the productive life of the clan and improve portfolio performance. Guideship is sitting with the many clans, providing information, options, visions, thinking and feedback in the best interest of clan reality. It is making requests instead of giving orders. It does not expect compliance. It does expect the unexpected. It is far more coordination than direction. It holds that the only 'big picture' which merits feeding and focus, is the big picture held by those closest to where the work gets done, the value gets added, and the profit is generated.

I offer the following four Guideship practices to increase the Guide's access and influence. While investing the Guide with more of what he or she requires, these practices also enrich the clan's powers and will be appreciated, even sought after by the clan.

The first practice derives from an essential first assumption (the EFA, to the aficianados of the acronym): the clan is a learning organism, continually in search of ways to achieve better conditions for itself.

The second practice is one of dedication to a new mission: enrich the clan's big picture before your own.

Third, the practice of non-judgment: join the conversation in the clan as a free person, without secret agendas, without labels, without a priori schemes.

Fourth, the practice of inquiry and visionary challenge: draw out and enable the diverse voices of the clan into higher service to the clan and the profit community.

THE CLAN IS A LEARNING ORGANISM

Taking the traditional view of the clan as a rationalized unit of productivity is not particularly useful to the Guide. It fails to get at the free-standing, creative nature of the beast. Standing up for the clan as a self-generative, improvisational engine of value creation is closer to the mark. The Guide's job is to increase the best that the clan can do for itself. While the clan may not actually be a learning organism at a given moment in time, the Guide must act from this assumption.

This premise will show up in your effort to organize the clan on an honest basis, with a clear and challenging mission, learning-oriented performance standards, and a fair and flexible reward system. You populate the clan with the healthiest people you can find, and the smallest number, to maximize flexibility, sustainable performance, and personal health. Finally, you work to unburden the clan from needless bureaucratic interference and red tape. In operation, you seek maximum knowledge, freedom to innovate, the best tools and the best information for the clan, so it can learn as rapidly as possible.

WHOSE BIG PICTURE IS IT, ANYWAY?

The Guide's corporate 'orders' must be re-created as part of the clan's own interest and growth process rather than arriving at the clan as a top-down demand. Profit community leaders can best engage the clan within the terms of the story the clan has constructed, no matter how believable or unbelievable the story may seem. The only big picture that counts is the story the clan owns and uses for internal motivation.

In the Western social democracies, the "clans" (neighborhood groups, trade unions, state education delegations, main street business alliances, corporate special interest groups, political action committees and so on) rarely fall in line with anything like a direct order from the mayor, the governor, or any other over arching potentate. Short of calling out the National Guard, the mayor has no direct, fear-of-losing-one's-job power over the clans.

The social clan's special, focused interests are their potentates. Each has its own life, its own big picture, its own identity and destiny. The collective view is some kind of shared answer to the basic questions which each member strives to answer for him or herself: Who am I? What's my purpose here? How am I doing?

What's in this for me? Where am I headed? Where should I be going? Where did I come from? What should I be doing right now?

So it is in the business clans. Because they are diverse and very focused, their big picture may have little pragmatic relationship to the big picture of the corporate investors.

The Guide's efforts to take the clan's big picture as primary, to bring broader experience, information, thinking skills, and some roll-up-the-sleeves service to the clan may well evoke exceptional performance without directly introducing the corporate agenda. The clan will draw the Guide's corporate big picture into their reality, through the Guide, in direct measure to the value which the corporate information base holds for the clan's local success.

GETTING TO NON-JUDGMENT

Achieving non-judgment depends on managing your own fears of what will occur if the clan carries on, being no more and no less than what it is. We all have fears. Failure, embarrassment, loss of future earnings, loss of security, loss of information sources, loss of rank, power, position, face. If you believe that the clan's behavior and performance can wound you along any of these lines, or you are attached or addicted to certain privileges or outcomes in your business life, be careful. No matter how skillful you think you are at portraying a smooth, cool facade, your righteous judgment will pervade your interactions.

The senior outsider perspective is destructive if it is delivered with the least hint of judging anyone or anything in the clan to be wrong or right.

To get started on the path to non-judgment, tell the truth to yourself about judgments already made and likely to be made. Make your concerns and vulnerabilities known to the clan. At the least they need to be aware of what it is in their reality that triggers your fears. I know this suggestion will bring up more issues regarding vulnerability, loss of personal power, and so on. In the long run, are you more powerful as an explicit, authentic, person, or as a facade of invulnerability? You must answer that. Take your time. Borrowing a line from the Course in Miracles, "Authenticity is a required course. You may take it now, or take it later. You will take it."

Having assessed your vulnerability, don't be a hero. Handle the work to be done in areas where you are relatively free of fears and addictions. Ask someone else to handle the parts you have trouble with. Recognition and acknowledgment of fears and judgment does more, over time, to dissipate them than anything else in my awareness.

THE CLAN'S STORY IN THREE VOICES

Non-judgment is in hand. You have accepted the first assumption. You realize that the clan's big picture is paramount. So, how to talk to these people and make a positive difference?

Clan members, like all of us, want meaning in their lives. They want enough power. They want to know they count for something. Every one of us has a life story which gives us a reason for being who and what we are. A reason for acting. The Guide's job is to build on the quality and dimension of that story, to increase the promise and possibility held in the story, and to enhance clan members' powers to act from within their enhanced story.

Clans work out their story in three voices. I picture these three voices as circles, below.

- Voice One, the voice of experience, speaks our current view of reality and the status quo. Voice One stands for predictability and no surprises. It has our complete life experience on its side. The stand for the status quo is threatened by real change. So, Voice One is the seat of loss, worst fears for the future, and avoidance and denial behavior in the face of transition. Voice One cries out the grief of an ending, foresees the absolute worst that could transpire, and walks us away from change. Voice One keeps the status quo circle, the innermost and smallest, in shape and in check.
- Voice Two, the voice of curiosity, speaks the possibility, the potential, the ideal outcomes, and ultimate opportunities in our future path. Voice Two expresses the release of attachment to the past. It explores and wanders in the unknown, searching for clues and patterns. Voice Two walks us into the experiments and initiatives necessary to explore the dimensions of change. Voice Two pushes the largest circle as far out as possible. This is the "Maybe So" circle.
- Voice Three, the voice of resolve, speaks for taking appropriate risks and establishing appropriate controls in service of realizing appropriate rewards. Voice Three creates the middle circle, a pragmatic stretch from the status quo, in service of the possibility. I call this the "Forward Ho" circle.

Each of us feels, thinks and acts from a preferred voice most of the time. We tend to have a second voice as a back-up style with a least-expressed third voice bringing up the rear.

Similar personalities making up the clan can add up to a dominant voice. Or, a situation may drive the group to express its story through a single voice.

If Voice One dominates the clan, we may be seduced by the apparent security of the the status quo circle. In this case, Voice One becomes an end in itself, rather than a partner in learning and growth. Anyone expressing the "Maybe So" possibility of Voice Two may well be heard as a heretic, anarchist or just simply mad. "Forward Ho" will be heard as over-active, with lots of "reasons" put forth about excessive risks, unworkable methods, and puny rewards.

Voice Two seems to dominate when we are young, when we believe we have little to lose. The "Maybe So" circle becomes the focus. The "status quo" attitude will sound like infinite wet blankets, "yes buts" and barriers to great ideas. Voice Three is apt to be heard as an attempt to kill the ideation and exploration practice, to close out options, a rush to judgment, conformity, and overemphasis on results.

Voice Three tends to dominate when life gets serious, we sense the stakes are extremely high, we think we have already heard all the good ideas, the status quo is no longer good enough, or the time is getting short with much demanded of us. In this situation, Voice One will sound like endless worrying and negativism, while Voice Two may come through as pie-in-the-sky, diversion from the work to be done.

Each voice has a limited perspective which also limits ability to perceive and act. A balanced, informed dialogue of the voices is the fastest route to awareness, completion, innovation and commitment.

VALUE-ADDED, BALANCED INQUIRY

Balancing the voices requires a patient, non-judgmental inquiry, asking open-ended questions from the perspective of all three voices. Inquiry is about exploring and noticing. It does not matter whether the clan answers your questions directly. It matters that they engage the question, no matter what comes out in response. What's important is to cover all three voices in the inquiry. Hanging up on any one will limit the possibility.

Raise the questions as part of whatever reason you came to see the clan. It does not matter whether it was your need or their request. The inquiry process is a value-adding role for you.

SOME QUESTIONS TO GET YOU STARTED

The following are a few direct questions to access the voices:

Inquiry into Voice One: Stability and Status Quo

- What do we seem to be losing?
- What are we doing to keep everything safe?
- If things go on without change, what will happen to us?
- If the changes, which seem to be occurring, continue, where will we wind up?

Inquiry into Voice Two: Invention and Possibility
- What are the ultimate opportunities in this?
- What experiments are we running these days?
- What are we not doing right now, to make sure we learn something new?

Inquiry into Voice Three: Risk for Reward
- What are we committed to?
- What is at risk?
- What disciplines are in place which limit our risk and help make the most of our investments?
- What is on the line? What resources have we invested fully in our future?

REFLECTION

As you begin to understand the current structure of the clan's experience through the answers to questions of feelings, thought and action, you may begin to construct a way forward that the clan does not see. Your perception may constitute a value to the clan's awareness and perspective as well as offering direction and guidance for them. The value derives from your unique worldview, through which you have fairly reconstructed the clan situation. Reflecting your perception by making up a story based on the three voices can be mightily influential.

I prefer to tell the story beginning with Voice One, which is one of the status quo. Then I involve the feelings, concerns, and behavior that appear to take us away from productivity. Next comes Voice Two, a reflection on the experiments, concepts, behaviors, and practices increasingly being left behind, as well as the possibilities in view. Finally, Voice 3, my perception of where the clan is investing in the realization of something truly new.

The critical issue is to tell the story as a learning story, in terms that are as close to the language and culture of the clan as possible.

When the clan agrees you have the story right, you have succeeded in creating an opening to retell the story by yourself and by the clan, stretching the various elements in new directions. These are like simulations, building on the existing reality, introducing new ideas and frameworks of thinking. You are as free as anyone to suggest the direction of the story, and to request the clan to engage it.

Your influence is felt as your guidance into richer and more possible stories reveals new schemes for a story that better suits the clan.

*How is the use of technology enhancing or detracting from
a systemic sense of community?*

Part Five:
Technology—A Tool in a New Role

Computer-based technologies can be valuable allies in establishing and maintaining community, as the next three essays demonstrate. This is particularly applicable in a world where we are geographically separated. Peter and Trudy Johnson-Lenz address the need to begin acting for the common good, showing us how computer-augmented learning can serve this purpose.

Jerry Michalski points out the advantages of connecting with each other electronically, while George Pór sees the advantages of developing collective intelligence for organizations and human systems.

These forms of "virtual community" are modern applications of traditional modes where geographic proximity usually provides the glue that binds people together.

Trudy & Peter Johnson-Lenz

are founders of Awakening Technology, a knowledge and consulting company whose mission is to bring spirit into computer-augmented collaboration and learning.

They are internationally recognized pioneers in using computers for interpersonal and group communication. In 1978 they coined the now popular term "groupware." They take a whole systems approach, emphasizing purpose, values, processes, and collaborative culture as keys to effective and satisfying on-line work.

They consult with organizations in the private and civic sectors, conduct workshops on this chapter's themes, and facilitate groups using groupware tools.

They have published popular articles, professional papers, and book chapters, and have spoken at conferences in the United States, Canada, Europe, and Japan. Their work has been featured on NBC, the BBC, and in *The Wall Street Journal, Christian Science Monitor, Omni,* and *Time.*

21

Groupware and the Great Turning

Peter and Trudy Johnson-Lenz

Conversations are the way knowledge workers discover what they know, share it with their colleagues, and in the process create new knowledge for the organization. The panoply of modern information and communications technologies—for example, computers, faxes, e-mail—can help knowledge workers in this process. But all depends on the quality of the conversations that such technologies support.

—Alan Webber, "What's So New About the New Economy?"
Harvard Business Review, January–February 1993

Our overarching purpose at this critical time in history is to create a sustainable future for our species and planet. Our collective survival depends on learning to act for the common good and taking responsibility for the whole. To do this we must discover how to tap our collective intelligence, learn together, and sift and weave our knowledge into the meta-patterns of wisdom—that life-essential, deep knowing that can guide us.

The personal key is the intent to learn from what we discover when we listen to others and listen deeply within. The collective key is transforming our organizations into communities that evoke and support the deepest learnings of which we are capable. Both conversation and reflection are essential. We need to take time to tap our inner knowing and to make sense of and integrate the challenging complexity of multiple perspectives. Each of us sees a part of the truth. When we share our truths with each other we can see more deeply, like two eyes see in three dimensions.

OUR COLLECTIVE SURVIVAL

The very same skills of separation, analysis, and control that gave us the power to shape our environment are producing ecological and social crises in our outer world, and psychological and spiritual crises in our inner world. Both these crises grow out of our success in separating ourselves from the larger fabric of life.

—Fred Kofman & Peter Senge, "Communities of Commitment: The Heart of Learning Organizations" *Organizational Dynamics,* Autumn 1993

In the beginning was the matrix, the undifferentiated web of life.

EMERGENCE

After billions of years, human culture emerged from the earth.

DIFFERENTIATION

During the scientific and industrial revolutions we differentiated ourselves from nature and developed our technological power to understand and manipulate the physical environment.

DEVELOPMENT

The rise of the scientific method and rationalism in Western culture was fueled by the separation of our logical and spiritual lives as we learned to observe the cosmos objectively, rather than participate in it. To develop Western culture fully, we had to "forget" our essential relatedness to ourselves, each other, nature, and the Mystery of creation.

Now, according to cultural theorists Charles Johnston and Duane Elgin, we are roughly at the halfway point in our evolution. Our technological capacity is highly developed, but our environment is stretched to its limits, and we are more alienated from each other than we will ever be.

GREAT TURNING

Our collective survival depends on what Craig Schindler and Gary Lapid call the Great Turning. We are beginning to "re-member" our essential connection with all Life.

RECONNECTION AND INTEGRATION

Our challenge is to simultaneously awaken the participative, holistic consciousness we have forgotten and hold it in creative relationship with our vast scientific and technological powers. The process of creation involves both differentiation and integration, distinction and wholeness. We need analysis as well as awe. To navigate the Great Turning we need both the linking/thinking power of the technology Peter Russell calls our "global brain" and the grace of a profound global mind change.

GLOBAL BRAIN, GLOBAL MIND

> This instrument can teach, it can illuminate; yes, and it can even inspire. But it can do so only to the extent that humans are determined to use it to those ends. Otherwise it is merely lights and wires in a box.
>
> —Edward R. Murrow, about television

We are now laying the foundation of a new social architecture made of fiber-optic cable, silicon chips, high-speed switches, display screens, and software through which digital information travels as pulses of light. As part of the Great Turning, it is one embodiment of interconnectedness. "Reach out and touch someone," "the information superhighway," and "we bring the world to you," are literally becoming true. Every day millions of people worldwide use the Internet, an early version of the electronic global brain that connects our small planet.

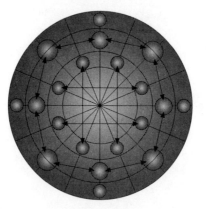

The advent of "information at your fingertips" may give it to us instantly, but we already suffer from too many disconnected facts, words, and images; too many phone calls, faxes, messages; too many demands on our time and attention. Out of context information confuses. As futurist Robert Theobald says, as information doubles, knowledge is halved, and wisdom is quartered. We must choose what we want, with whom we connect, and for what purposes. To really use our global brain, we need a global mind change.

The emerging electronic planetary nervous system is an expression of nature's impulse to ever-greater complexity and intelligence. Through it we may become smart enough together to respond quickly, wisely, and resiliently to the profound challenges of our time. But this silicon and fiber-optic "body" will not realize its potential without healthy organizational and community life breathing the spirit of interdependence, partnership, and collaboration throughout it.

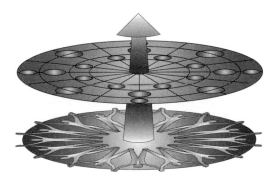

GROUPWARE

Instead of asking, "What is the information that matters and how do we most effectively manage it?" companies must start asking, "What are the relationships that matter and how can the technology most effectively support them?"

—Michael Schrage, "In Information Technology, the Key Is Good Relationships," *The Wall Street Journal,* March 19, 1990

Esther Dyson, an industry consultant, says managers must think carefully about how their company interacts before embracing groupware, lest they simply automate relationships that didn't work to begin with. "Everyone says groupware creates a flatter, more democratic organization, but that really only happens if the organization is ready for it."

—John Wilke, "Shop Talk: Computer Links Erode Hierarchical Nature of Workplace Culture," *The Wall Street Journal*, December 9, 1993

Corporations and organizations are beginning to use groupware to increase their ability to think collectively and act quickly and coherently in turbulent times. In 1978, we coined the term to refer to the potent combination of intentionally chosen *group* process and soft*ware* to support it. Today most people use it to mean any multi-user software that supports group work, coordination, information exchange, and learning. Groupware comes in many diverse forms. Here we focus on a few that support collaborative learning.

People meeting at the same time in the same place may augment their conversation with groupware. It can be an aid to discussion, such as using keypads to indicate individual opinions or preferences while the computer graphically displays the whole group's responses. It can be a sophisticated electronic meeting system where everyone uses networked personal computers and a facilitator guides the group through cycles of generating, organizing, and evaluating ideas.

Other forms of groupware support teams meeting at different times and places over networks connected through the telephone system or over the emerging "information superhighway" of the Internet. It can be a simple electronic bulletin board for posting news; a network of computer conferences where diverse stakeholders in virtual corporations discuss projects, clients, and markets across different time zones; or a global corporate memory system spread over several continents, with multi-media "maps" of organizational issues and knowledge in text, graphics, voice, and video, continually accessed and updated by knowledge workers, customers, and suppliers working together.

Since groupware is an electronic embodiment of collaboration, introducing it is a process of orchestrating both technological and cultural change. Organizations expecting a technological "fix" have learned this the hard way. Some companies threw out an early groupware system for coordination because it was more suited to a culture with well-established procedures than the more open-ended information exchange they needed. Another rejected a popular electronic meeting support system, even though it saved time and money, because it allowed more democratic involvement in decision-making than this traditional command-and-control organization was ready for.

Just as word processing does not make good writing, even with spelling- and grammar-checkers, groupware, no matter how sophisticated, will not create good collaboration by itself. Groupware introductions fail or backfire when they are not supported by participatory planning, pilot projects, team-oriented cul-ture, and plenty of training.

PURPOSE AND INTENT

The human is the determiner, the one who through self-reflexive consciousness and intent may cocreate many different worlds. So our experience will be sacred or secular partly according to the purpose and intent we bring to it.

—Peter Reason, "Reflections on Sacred Experience and Sacred Science," *Journal of Management Inquiry*, September 1993

Groupware can have different results, depending on the group's intentions and commitments, purposes, processes, and style. The same system can be used for deeply reflective dialogue or acrimonious argument. Electronic mail can con-tain messages of encouragement and coaching or standardized bureaucratic memos. Electronic meeting systems can support fuller conversations that consid-er all voices and viewpoints or march a group through an agenda to reach a quick decision.

Like any technology, groupware is an extension of our faculties and capabil-ities, a tool that accelerates, amplifies, and magnifies the interactions and behaviors it supports. If our purpose is security and control, it will amplify that. If we intend to learn and discover, it will help us do that, too.

In some organizations electronic mail is routinely sent to large numbers of people "for your information only" and to create electronic paper trails. The result is clogged mail boxes and information overload. On some public systems, people have devised "bozo filters" to screen out communications (private and group) from those who are vicious, obnoxious, or otherwise annoying. Michael Schrage reports on the use of software "agents" in groupware systems to act on one's behalf, such as making appointments, scheduling resources, collecting information, and the like. These agents may be programmed to act deceptively, just as human assistants might make excuses or withhold information for the benefit of their bosses rather than the whole organization.

As Jordan Paul notes in this anthology (see page 209), learning depends on trust and mutually respectful behavior. If e-mail becomes junk mail, bozos are fil-tered, and software agents deceive, then trust in the system and on-line commu-nity seriously erode.

LEARNING COMMUNITY

Learning communities are a place of truth-seeking and speaking without fear of reprisal or judgment. They are a place where curiosity reigns over knowledge and where experimentation is welcome. Developing the capacity to live with "not knowing" when it naturally arises, to learn to be in relationship with oneself and to be reflective rather than defensive in nature is the leverage

for learning, and the leverage for learning in community.
—Stephanie Spear, "The Emergence of Learning
Communities," *The Systems Thinker,*
June/July 1993

Groupware consultant and writer Susanna Opper says that groupware is the enabling technology of the learning organization. The key to realizing this potential is an organizational culture that supports inquiry, reflection, and collaborative discovery—a learning community.

Community is a verb, a process, not an end state. As described elsewhere (see page 14), M. Scott Peck has identified four stages of community making: pseudo-community, chaos, emptiness, and true community. There is overlap between the stages, and not everyone is in the same stage at the same time. Whether a group reaches true community depends on its intent and commitment. And even when it does, it will inevitably slip back into pseudo-community, and thus around the cycle again. This is a natural part of the process.

Deep conversation happens in true community. It thrives on "truth seeking and speaking," respectful listening, and reflection. All voices are heard and included in the dialogue. Deep learning depends on deep conversation. It challenges strongly held assumptions. It takes time, committed intent, and an atmosphere of trust and safety. Fear, doubt, judgment, blame, and defensiveness get in the way, keeping us from seeing clearly and embracing errors in thinking and behavior in order to learn from them.

Many kinds of computer-supported communities are developing on public computer networks and within corporations. They are *virtual* communities, existing in essence and effect but not in physical form. Instead of being place-based, they are located across time and space as communities of affinity and interest with shifting memberships. Many never progress beyond Peck's stages of pseudo-community and chaos. However, with the intent to learn, a supportive culture, appropriate groupware tools, and facilitation, virtual communities can become *virtual learning communities* where powerful and deep conversations occur. In our work with groups, we've discovered some simple skills that are keys to those conversations.

Skills of Relationship

Show up in all ways.
Pay attention to what has heart and meaning.
Tell the truth without judgment or blame.
Do not be attached to outcomes, but be open to outcomes.
—Angeles Arrien, *The Four-Fold Way*

The more each member of a community practices the following skills, the more it will function as a learning organization, with or without the benefits of groupware.

- *Presence*—being aware of your inner and outer experience; taking time to listen, reflect, and express what is true for you; being *present* to yourself and in the group.
- *Self-differentiation*—communicating your experience (what you are thinking, feeling, and wanting) in the group; standing for what you know.
- *Active and reflective listening*—listening with empathy; paraphrasing what has been said well enough so that others feel heard; listening for deeper understanding; listening to your own listening
- *Capacitance*—Charles Johnston's term for increasing the amount of "aliveness" you can hold; holding multiple, conflicting points of view in creative relationship, seeing the larger truth in an apparent paradox or polarity; being "big enough" to stay with the questions in a spirit of inquiry and discovery—living with "not knowing."

Presence and self-differentiation increase group intelligence by differentiating its members' experience—making the power of diverse views potentially available to the group. Active listening and capacitance realize that potential by *integrating* that diversity into a creative whole.

ARTS OF FACILITATION

A safe environment that enables truth to be expressed opens the way to real healing and is profoundly transformative...in ways that go beyond what we can measure and, ultimately, it is such experiences that are often the most motivating and valuable to people.

—Dean Ornish, "Opening Your Heart: Anatomically, Emotionally and Spiritually," *Noetic Sciences Review,* Winter 1993

Facilitation increases group intelligence by encouraging the process of differentiating and integrating individual knowledge into collective wisdom. The more at least one person takes responsibility for the whole through one of these roles, the more a group will learn, with or without groupware support.

- *Vessel Holder*—holds an image of the whole, allowing people to find their way within it; maintains an environment of open exploration, curiosity, reflection; holds the space open to live with the questions rather than grasp for easy answers.
- *Protector*—maintains psychological safety; upholds mutually agreed upon guidelines and community commitments.
- *Navigator*—guides the group through chosen processes to achieve its goals; suggests possible directions for exploration; orchestrates competing factions learning from each other.
- *Learning Facilitator*—poses issues or questions for consideration; asks for other ways to frame issues; probes to get participants to expand or build on responses; provides additional information or ideas as appropriate; models learning behaviors by reflecting and commenting on the learning

process itself.

- *Weaver*—integrates and synthesizes key points and themes; sees patterns, makes connections; organizes information into collective knowledge and wisdom.
- *Evocateur*—sees and asks, "what's needed, what's missing, what has not been said?"; raises issues based on inconsistencies or gaps; draws out members; gives permission/authorizes members to risk speaking truth from the heart.
- *Fool*—breaks the frame of the group's focus as necessary to free it from limiting perspectives; through humor creates fluidity essential for learning by seeing the paradoxes and absurdities of life.
- *Guide/Shaman*—experienced traveler who can take the whole group through dangerous passages to a deeper level.

INDIVIDUATING AND TEAMING DYNAMICS

In Buddhism, the metaphor of Indra's Net…has been used over the generations to exemplify how not one thing is separate from any other thing even though things are different from each other. At each intersection in Indra's Net, there is a shining and distinct jewel. Sustaining the light from all the other jewels, each jewel reflects all the jewels in the Net and has no real or separate self nature. A single jewel and all other jewels thus exist in a pattern of presence and mutual activity.

—Joan Halifax, *The Fruitful Darkness*

Group intelligence is greatest when everyone brings everything she knows to the group. This requires that people be themselves—unique and differentiated. It also requires that the group respectfully holds the diversity of individuals in creative relationship for something greater to emerge. Group learning requires both differentiation and integration—the paradox of Indra's Net.

Groupware is a new organizational and architectural medium. Just as physical architecture influences the dynamics of community within it (see Ann Roulac's essay on page 243), virtual architecture shapes the dynamics of virtual community. Groupware for collective learning needs to support both differentiation and integration, action and reflection, the parts and the whole which is greater than any of them. Unfortunately, in our highly individualistic society, many groupware systems have only a strong individuating (differentiating) dynamic. A few have a teaming (integrating) dynamic. Both are needed.

Individuating dynamics:

- emphasize individual autonomy
- enable individual user preferences
- encourage work by personal rhythms—"my time/my place/my way"

- differentiate a system into separate individuals

Electronic mail and most bulletin board systems have strong individuating dynamics. A graphic user interface that allows you to do anything you want, in several places at once, and view things in any order is individuating.

Teaming dynamics:

- emphasize relationships and responsibilities
- embody community commitments
- encourage interaction with others
- enable collaboration and learning with/from others
- integrate individuals into teams
- tap collective intelligence

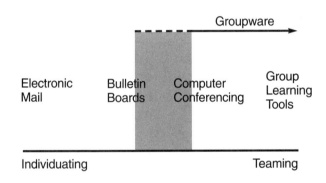

RANGE OF DYNAMICS

Computer conferencing and new groupware tools that support group learning have teaming dynamics. Their architectures shape and focus the flow of attention and conversation into coherent patterns that generate knowledge.

GROUP LEARNING TOOLS

Fragmentary thinking becomes systemic whenever we recover "the memory of the whole," the awareness that wholes actually precede parts.

—Fred Kofman & Peter Senge, "Communities of Commitment: The Heart of Learning Organizations," *Organizational Dynamics,* Autumn 1993

Two kinds of groupware tools with teaming dynamics are essential for supporting knowledge-generating conversation. Group thinking tools augment a group's ability to generate and evaluate ideas. Group memory tools organize and hold the knowledge that is created. Other tools with teaming dynamics worth noting include group graphics, interactive modeling, simulations, flexibly arranged virtual meeting spaces, and facilitator agents.

Tools for group thinking are part of electronic meeting support systems. In addition to face-to-face conversation, people use networked personal computers to generate, organize, evaluate, and communicate ideas together. Because everyone can enter ideas into the collective group mind at once ("parallel processing"), many more comments are generated. Each person has much more air time than in a regular meeting. The option of making comments anonymously encourages everyone to contribute, challenge assumptions, and try out "risky" ideas. Tools for evaluating and prioritizing provide quick feedback about group preferences. A facilitator guides the group through its process, mixing conversation, computer tools, and other methods as appropriate. Overall, computer-augmented meetings are faster, and participants are generally more satisfied with the quality of the decisions.

Group thinking tools embody the whole creative cycle that begins with generating and differentiating ideas and ends with integrating them into useful knowledge.

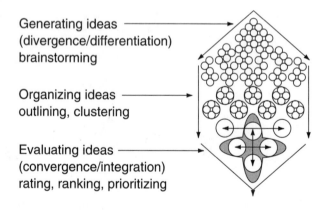

Generating ideas
(divergence/differentiation)
brainstorming

Organizing ideas
outlining, clustering

Evaluating ideas
(convergence/integration)
rating, ranking, prioritizing

CYCLE OF GROUP THINKING

Memory is essential for learning; otherwise issues continue to be revisited and rehashed, and new people involved later in a project may be unaware of assumptions and rationales for choices and decisions. One form of computer-supported group or organizational memory is an issue-based information system (IBIS) with "maps" of the issues addressed, positions considered, and the arguments for and against each.

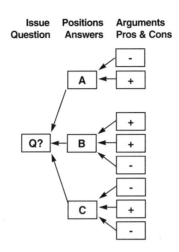

ISSUE MAP (ORGANIZATIONAL MEMORY)

Computer-supported issue maps can transform the nature of conversation from adversarial discussion to collaborative learning. It's common in meetings for someone to hold and push for a position again and again. In contrast, when it is electronically displayed for all to see, complete with detailed arguments, that person may feel heard and step back from his position enough to enter into a dialogue and learn with others.

Groupware tools for group and organizational memory:

- include all points of view
- record how and why decisions were made
- provide continuity between meetings
- support continuous updating of issues
- weave information into knowledge

Newer systems offer graphic hypertext environments for creating, organizing, and displaying an organization's remembered conversations, issues, and decisions. This is ongoing, dynamic, living knowledge. Elsewhere in this anthology, George Pór writes about community nervous systems (see page 271).

Groupware for thinking and memory can shape, hold, and augment organizational learning. But it cannot make it happen without a shared intent to learn

.

INTENT TO LEARN

To create trusting relationships, we need to communicate with the aim of learning, or mutual understanding, not control.... When you trust that whatever life deals to you, you can handle it, then you can let go of your need to control the events of your life.
—Susan Campbell, *Survival Strategies for the New Workplace*

Most of what happens is beyond our control. However, with practice, we can learn to control how we respond. Susan Campbell says this shift in mindset from security/control to learning/discovery is the key to organizational learning (see page 189).

Developing the self-mastery to be truly open to learning from whatever happens requires facing our fears of failure and loss of control, rather than avoiding them. It always seems easier to salve our symptoms by working longer, using the latest management techniques, trying a new and improved groupware system, or whatever. And yet, even though we may get short-term results, we always pay the price each time we avoid grappling with the deeper issues (see "Quick Fixes to Community", page 419).

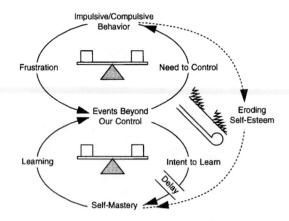

LEARNING THROUGH REFLECTION

The intent to learn also opens up the power of learning in community with others. When we listen with genuine respect and curiosity to another, we open a safe place in which his or her truth can be freely given into the space of relationship. As we learn, through reflection, to develop our capacity to learn from whatever happens, we open up the possibility of learning through conversation with others.

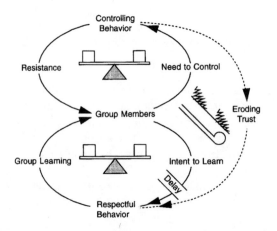

LEARNING THROUGH CONVERSATION

By reflecting on the frustrating consequences of controlling behaviors, we begin to realize that we yearn to trust something other than events and people out of our control. To truly work together, we need to know deeply that we are part of, not apart from, something greater and enduring. Joel and Michelle Levey elsewhere in this book (see p. 105) offer us an array of tools for inner work and quality of mind in community which, over time, deepen the connection with our Greater Self. Only this deep wellspring of compassion and wisdom has the capacitance to carry us through the narrows ahead.

MAKING THE GREAT TURNING

In its barest terms the social challenge...is to achieve sufficient long-term cooperation among the human family to ensure the survival and basic health of the species and planet. The question of questions is whether humanity will actually reconcile itself to working together to build a sustainable future....

In giving birth to a sustainable species-civilization, humanity will probably move back and forth through cycles of contraction and relaxation until we utterly exhaust ourselves and burn through the barriers that separate us from our wholeness as a human family.... Numerous times we may go to the very edge of ruin as a species, hopefully to pull back in time with new levels of maturity and insight.

—Duane Elgin, *Awakening Earth*

To make the Great Turning, we can draw from three wellsprings of largely untapped collective intelligence:
- connecting with and trusting our Greater Self
- using our many differences creatively to respond to complex challenges
- using rapidly evolving technologies to augment our capacities to think, learn, and work together.

Connecting with our Greater Self gifts us with a fearless intent to learn and the compassion to reconcile and use our differences to create a sustainable future. It is the key to unlocking the awesome power of our silicon brains and fiber-optic nervous systems. Technology may provide high-speed chips and channels for knowledge-creating conversations, give us flawless electronic memories, and support more responsive, resilient organizations and communities, but we must make the choice to use it with heart and spirit.

Each of these moves us beyond our separate selves into fuller engagement with others, nature, and the Mystery of creation. Used in concert they represent the birth of something entirely new on the planet.

Jerry Michalski
is the managing editor of *Release 1.0*, a monthly newsletter that covers the future of communications and computing technologies. He has particular interests in the emerging personal electronics market, unified messaging (telephony, voicemail, e-mail, paging, video), wireless communications, advanced user interfaces, groupware, software design, text processing, information navigation and representation, neural networks, and voice processing. He is also concerned with the social effects of technology, and has written about such topics as virtual communities.

Prior to joining *Release 1.0*, Michalski was a vice president with New Science Associates, Inc., a retainer market-research company focused on analyzing emerging technologies for use by large corporate clients. He also served as senior consultant in the Strategic Management Consulting practice at Price Waterhouse and manager of Computerized Freight Rate Systems for Mobil Oil Corporation's domestic operations. He earned an M.B.A. in international business from the Wharton School of the University of Pennsylvania and a B.A. in economics from the University of California at Irvine.

22

The Role of Technology

Jerry Michalski

Depending on your point of view, technology is either destroying our way of life by obliterating all meaningful connections between people, or opening new possibilities for connection, new ways of building communities that can enhance and enrich our non-technological lives. There's much truth to both points of view.

This essay explores ways in which technology can aid community building and maintenance. It explores unique and compelling aspects of the new media at our disposal—from telephones to TVs, computers and communications networks—and suggests ways that they may help us connect with each other. It particularly explores ways in which these media can help or hinder the establishment of trusted relationships and safe places, which are essential to creating a sense of community.

A PESSIMISTIC VIEW

It's easy to blame technology for many of society's ills. "Advances" such as the automobile, air conditioning, and television have driven us away from each other and into our living and family rooms. Our environments have been designed around these technologies: Roads and parking lots run where parks and walkways ought to. Advertising treats people as lab rats to be conditioned, and trains them to consume. Television and print media are the primary vehicles for those messages. Crime is up, and it's on the local news every evening. Many people feel alienated and afraid—their diminishing social and work circles increasingly reflect and reinforce the isolation. They stay (or are kept) in their own neighborhoods, avoid people unlike themselves, and form defensive gangs and cliques. This process, especially the lack of contact and familiarity, increases the level of fear. All of this decreases the shared sense of community.

Communications technologies present the opportunity to open an electronic back door in many people's homes and workplaces, through which they can go out and meet each other. As they meet, intentionally or not, they have an opportunity to become familiar with each other, perhaps meet in person, and begin to lose their fear of one another. The electronic world includes many people with evil on their minds. However, even people with evil intent can experience things online that affect them elsewhere. We hope that this possibility can lead to greater peace.

However, there is no guarantee that technology will be taken down this path. Its designers seem more concerned with putting private malls along the information superhighway than with setting up plazas where people can meet and play. So this essay ends with a call to arms, encouraging interested parties to get involved with the design of the information infrastructure.

A Starting Point

Before we go any further, though, here are some working premises:

Nothing compares with meeting face-to-face. Although this essay is about technology, the richness of "F2F"—the online world's shorthand for "face-to-face"—is impossible to replicate electronically. Even the highest-fidelity videophone image cannot transmit a person's presence, the subtle changes and shifts that occur from moment to moment. Each technology has its own merits and flaws. The idea is to complement F2F, not replace it. The extent to which technology is designed to facilitate and enhance and even enrich human interaction will be its measure of success.

A community and the feeling of community are two different things. Sometimes they occur together, sometimes they don't. The dictionary defines a community as any labeled group of people, be they left-handers, Catholics, Manhattanites, or jugglers. But labels don't bring about a feeling of community, which has more to do with issues such as trust and commitment than with labels. We sometimes refer to the feeling of community as "communion."

Community is essential to the future of business organizations, not just neighborhoods. The downsizing and restructuring of industry are more than temporary symptoms of an economic slowdown; they are evidence of a substantial change in the structure of our work lives. As companies struggle to become smaller and more agile, they become more "virtual:" some workers are contractors, others strategic allies; companies collaborate more often, sharing expertise. These loose and ever-changing relationships can only succeed if the historic binding agent—loyalty—is replaced with trust. The difference is subtle.

Balance is critical. Just as we balance our private and public lives, work and play, we will also find a healthy balance between a virtual, electronically mediated existence and the so-called real world. Living in virtual space at the exclusion of the physical world is deforming and unusual. Most healthy electronic communities—work or private—meet occasionally in person to establish and reinforce their presence.

The technologies that we use today are very, very primitive; they have a long way to go. Most of them impose a considerable burden on the user (what's a stop bit? what's parity?). Sometimes the complexity and the limitations help foster communion, either through shared experiences in overcoming the technology (whew, can you believe how hard this thing is to use?) or by hiding aspects of ourselves that might otherwise get in the way of finding shared meaning with others (such as skin color, accent, disabilities, or dress). A text interface hides practically all of these attributes, though it can't mask bad spelling.

The feeling of community emerges when people are present, open, and willing to be vulnerable. As we describe in the next few pages, the online world today makes it particularly challenging to create such "places." For example, in many cases the only way to know that someone is present is for them to type something into the system. If they do type something, there's no way to make sure that they are who they claim to be. So how is a participant to know that it's safe to speak?

At the same time, the online world offers unique opportunities. People who might never want to speak to each other if they met in person can become close friends online. Introverts don't have to wait for pauses in the conversation and wrestle for the floor: They can type whenever they want to and their comments will be fit into the stream of comments. And a president's words are no larger or more important looking than a clerk's. The medium has a democratizing effect.

STATE OF THE ART

People who use electronic communications successfully usually have to buy moderately expensive equipment and master some arcane knowledge. The most notable exception is the telephone, which doesn't cost much and is quite simple. The fax machine's success is due in large part to its similarity to and use of the phone system.

Once people are online and have mastered the fundamentals of moving around in this medium, they find themselves in a whole new world. Some people find it sterile, boring or confusing and don't return; others become addicted.

Depending on the service they use (e.g., America Online, CompuServe, or a local Internet access provider) and the software they run, people can view color weather maps collected straight from orbiting satellites, find flight information and book trips, trade stocks, collect software and data, send messages to other people practically anywhere in the world (called electronic mail or e-mail) and share ideas in electronic conferencing systems and so-called "chat rooms."

It is these last few functions—e-mail, conferencing and chat—that lead to people meeting each other and building relationships online. Because they are the tools of communication, these are the most crucial capabilities for creating a feeling of community in an online world. Technologically, these tools haven't changed much since the 1970s, but they are going into a period of great change now.

E-Mail, Conferencing, Chat—and the Internet

Think of e-mail as electronic post cards that you can send, quickly and easily, to one or more people. Several years ago, the number of people you could send a message to was limited by the boundaries of whatever system you were on, such as CompuServe. Now the Internet, an informal network of networks, has become the glue that links most of the individual islands to each other. It is easy today, for instance, for a student at a European university to send a message to a CompuServe subscriber (or vice-versa), or even for an office worker to send an e-mail message to a colleague with a wireless pocket computer. This is a mind-expanding capability.

With a few exceptions, e-mail is most appropriate if you want to send a message to up to about a dozen people. You have to know all the recipients and their e-mail addresses. Computer conferencing is an excellent way for a much larger number of people to hold a discussion. Conferencing systems, which resemble publishing more than a phone call or post card, include bulletin-board systems (BBS) and document-sharing systems such as Lotus Notes, which has become popular in business.

Bulletin-board systems are usually organized into conferences (e.g., Health, Humor, Politics, the Grateful Dead, Investments), which are divided into topics (e.g., Hypochondria, Contagious diseases, Watch for the nasty flu going around, Holistic medicine), each of which has a string of messages contributed by participants, in chronological order. Participants can post new messages whenever they want, and it's usually easy to read old messages and get a feeling for the history of any topic.

Unlike e-mail and most conferencing systems, chat rooms require that participants be online at the same moment. Chat rooms usually accommodate up to thirty people. Online services have many such rooms, each with a label that identifies the kind of discussions going on inside (e.g., Beginners, Bikers, The flirting zone, Kids). People can set up private chat rooms if they want to. Often the the conversations in the chat rooms are barely above babble, yet people frequent them avidly. Online services love chat rooms, because participants have to be online to use them, which means their meters are running.

E-mail, conferencing systems, and chat rooms can be pretty hard to learn: They are early versions of what promises to be a richer, more creative and aesthetic communications infrastructure.

Community Building Online and in Real Life

Technology and social behavior coevolve. That is, as technologies such as telephones, pagers, answering machines, and faxes become widely adopted, people adapt to them and change their behaviors. They screen their calls, for example. As the technologies mature, their designers often adapt them to the way people use them.

In order to discuss this interplay between technology and human behavior as it affects community building, it is useful to interpret the online world in terms of the facets of community that M. Scott Peck describes in *The Different Drum*. These are:

- Inclusivity, commitment, and consensus
- Realism
- Contemplation
- A safe place
- A laboratory for personal disarmament
- A group that can fight gracefully
- A group of all leaders
- A spirit

I will focus on the most recent communications technology to emerge: online data services. Although these services are likely to change quite a bit over the next few years, they are already very useful, and are full of lessons about human behavior.

Inclusivity, Commitment, and Consensus

A great benefit of the primitive and chaotic nature of today's online networks is its homogenizing effect: Everyone is in the same, large boat and looks pretty much the same. Individuals can personalize the name by which others see and address them, but beyond that, there's not much to tell them apart. That means people who might avoid each other if they could see or hear each other have an opportunity to make contact.

These networks have geographic reach unlike any other medium or setting. People whose paths may otherwise never have crossed can meet, and can do so regularly and build relationships over time.

People often get very intimate online, very quickly. They disclose things to apparent strangers that they might not disclose easily to their partners. Simple interactions can result in an astonishing amount of trust and intimacy—though it can sometimes be deceptive. After all, unless the parties describe themselves to each other, there's no telling what they look like or what they really do. Their gender, race and religion may be completely concealed. For example, the host of a popular CompuServe forum is deaf, blind and mute, but the text interface makes her seem like anyone else. Plenty of people pose as things they are not.

Not only is it easy to achieve deceptively intimate interactions online, it's also easy for participants to avoid responsibility and bail out. The technology offers many excuses, ranging from "My computer was broken," to "I just haven't had time to log in" and "I couldn't afford the service, so I closed my account." But when people spend a lot of time together online, participating can lead to an emotional high. Leaving can be emotionally painful and serve as a punishment, like shunning or ostracism in some non-technological communities.

Cost is still a barrier to getting on these networks, though there are some favorable signs. The question of who can access this medium is high on national and international agendas. Locally supported Free-Nets are popping up in many cities. Prices are falling, and any old computer will do.

Today's text-only online networks are great equalizers, but as they establish more order, people may collect in well-defined groups and erect high walls for safety. Electronic polling and voting may replace the chaotic and organic process that dominates now, which is best exemplified by the Internet. Nobody owns it. Freewheeling discussions abound on it. Its direction is created by consensus and approved by a few committees, after considerable deliberation.

TECHNOLOGY AND COMMUNITIES

Realism

Online life may seem artificial, but it's very real. Despite some poorly designed systems, people help each other, they fall in love, they get into fights of amazing proportions. People meet to discuss and share information about every imaginable avocation and activity: they share tips, advice, jokes and recipes; they help each other solve technical problems; they dream about the future and share their poetry. Parents discuss child-rearing and seek help in emergencies.

There's amazing richness and variety of contact between people online. In his book *The Virtual Community*, Howard Rheingold gives many eloquent examples. There are men- and women-only online conferences. There are anything-goes conferences with names like Weird and Plain Wrapper. Many people flirt in chat rooms that are open to the public, then escalate to personal e-mail messages. These relationships sometimes lead to face-to-face meetings—and occasionally to weddings.

Not all of these liaisons are innocent and happy. Some subscribers misrepresent themselves and cause damage. Some harass others and become problems for the system operators, who must decide whether or not to take disciplinary action, which usually involves kicking the abusers off the system. Other system operators let the community self-regulate.

Real-life crises have their counterparts online, and events from the physical world are broadcast more quickly than usual. In one particularly troubling and poignant event, a person deleted all his postings—a form of virtual suicide—a few days before committing suicide. His action shocked his online community and led to much soul-searching and long, eloquent eulogies.

Contemplation

Real-life tragedies such as this cause much discussion about the communities that exist in online networks. So do the sheer magnitude of the medium and its implications. The online world is just as complex as the physical one, yet it has few rules and norms. Everything is being reinvented for the new medium: law, advertising, etiquette.

One thing that needs to be reinvented is silence, which is hard to convey with text, especially when the meter is running all the time. Community building requires spiritual spaces, and silence is often an integral element. Longtime researchers and practitioners Peter and Trudy Johnson-Lenz (see page 243) have conducted much practical research on silence and rhythm in the online world. They have designed simple text interfaces that help create appropriate containers for conversations involving spirituality, trust, and respect. The approach can be as simple as presenting a screen when a participant is about to enter a space that asks her to take a moment to center herself and focus on the topic being discussed inside.

A Safe Place

That kind of safety is rare today. The way the online world is arranged, almost all places are potentially unsafe. Some people roam these virtual places looking to help others; some are out to harm. There's no way of knowing in advance which is which. There are many people online trying to fix, convince, or convert others. Many participants are out to prove their superiority through expertise.

It's also easy to be misunderstood online, because many of the cues that are usually obvious in a F2F meeting or even on the phone—tone of voice, pace, modulation, inflection—are missing altogether. Someone can intend a message to sound coy, but it can be read as angry; they might intend a compliment, but be misunderstood as being ironic, angry, or deprecating. The resulting barrage of nasty e-mail messages, known as "flames," can seem disproportionate to the originating interaction. Because of the medium's limitations, it takes no time at all for tempers to flare and lots of time for tempers to cool.

Creating safe places online takes time and effort, but it's possible. Therapists lead online counseling sessions. Twelve-step and other support groups find the medium's 24-hour availability is a great boon: Members having a tough time can log in at any time and connect with others.

An Imagined Online World

TrueNet has trusted communications. People are definitely who they say they are. Its spaces mirror the spaces we have in the physical world, along with their expectations. For example, only people you invite can come into your online "home." Your "neighborhood" is safe for kids. If you want more randomness or adventure, you can go to the virtual main street, park, or jungle.

TrueNet has special sections where people can meditate together or just hang out, without worrying about the cost of connect time. They can stay in a virtual place all day long if they care to. In a separate zone, people can adopt pseudonyms, but whenever you "see" them online in that zone, visual cues signal that they aren't using their true names, so you can take appropriate precautions. Imagine an asterisk by their pseudonym, or a red hat that their online character must wear.

A LABORATORY FOR PERSONAL DISARMAMENT

Anonymity online is full of wonderful paradoxes. On the one hand, an environment that guarantees anonymity helps people avoid responsibility for their actions and increases the likelihood of misrepresentations. On the other hand, anonymity offers a way for people to discuss things they fear. People who are afraid to ask questions that might be traced back to them (how do you put on a condom? where do I get an AIDS test?) might ask them if they are guaranteed privacy.

More interestingly, anonymity makes the online world a very fruitful laboratory for personal and social experimentation in the spirit of *The Different Drum*:

> An experiment is designed to give us new experience from which we can extract new wisdom. So it is that in experimenting with personally disarming themselves, the members of a true community experientially discover the rules of peacemaking and learn its virtues. It is a personal experience so powerful that it can become the driving force behind the quest for peace on a Global Scale.

Pseudonyms allow people to try out different roles, with surprising consequences. It's quite an eye-opener for a male to don a female persona and begin receiving pesky instant messages from other males. People can walk in others' shoes, intentionally or not; unintentional lessons can be more profound than any lecture or punishment. It is likewise a shock for someone to flirt with someone else, only to find out they are not of the sex they thought—call it the Crying Game Syndrome.

There are also intentional social experiments, where participants agree to adopt certain rules of conduct, such as posting at least once a week or not criticizing each others' ideas. Online is also a good place to try out economic or legal theories, to run simulations with real people instead of equations, and to start the whole process over again for a new group, or just for fun.

Two More Imaginary Online Worlds

Your World allows subscribers to design their space and the rules they live by, within limits: the space is generally realistic (no bug-eyed monsters, please). No business is allowed in *Your World*, which has no memory. That is, the system encourages real-time communications, and wipes the slate clean every three months. People come to *Your World* to learn things firsthand. They want to discover legal systems and invent languages and social norms.

The Rubber Room has few rules, and those are regularly broken. Creatures of all sorts roam the halls/parapets/marshes. Some are automatons, some are people in disguise. Games and fantasies abound. Video is the principal means of communication. People who are really good at special effects are highly prized in *The Rubber Room*. In fact, many 3D-jays (what else would come after DJs and Vee-jays?) have huge cult followings.

A Group That Can Fight Gracefully

Communicational competence online involves mastering "netiquette," the set of social protocols that digerati—the digitally experienced—observe when communicating online. Examples include reserving CAPITAL LETTERS FOR SHOUTING, placing a ">" before lines you are quoting from other participants (it's very easy to quote others in the online world, so attribution is important), and giving advance warning about very long postings so others can elect to read them if they want to.

Not all such rules need to be explicit, though some rules are. For example, in the Manhattan online service called Echo, participants are asked to avoid personal invective: "Attack the idea, not the person" is the policy, and people risk being ejected from the service for violating the rule.

Although the online world has its share of messy fights, there are also numerous cases of groups interacting with grace and respect, while discussing difficult and sometimes personal issues. Members of online communities watch out for each other and help newcomers ("newbies" in online jargon) learn the ropes.

A Group of All Leaders

We've already described the democratizing nature of online networks. Online networks allow people to share their gifts and celebrate them. They allow ordinary people to publish their favorite stories and poems. They allow meek, shy or low-ranking people to become recognized authors or heroes in a crisis.

Television is a broadcast medium. Telephones are used mostly between two individuals. If one person on the phone doesn't participate, there is no purpose to the call. The online environment offers the best of both. Many people can hang out online without necessarily contributing (people who read but don't post are called "lurkers"). There is a sense of participation with an audience.

Moving from the audience into the middle when it's appropriate, then back out again, is a dynamic that is an important aspect of community building. Sociologist Jean Lave and education researcher Etienne Wenger describe the phenomenon as "legitimate peripheral participation" and note that it is essential in developing what they call "communities of practice." For example, when workers tell stories in a lunch room, many members of the community can listen and learn, and anyone can chip in with solutions or suggestions. The best practices emerge from the group's interactions.

Online technology allows many people to monitor conversations and to jump in when they have something to offer. Researchers at the Xerox Palo Alto Research Center (PARC) are experimenting with such a system for business use called Jupiter. In Jupiter, which includes audio and videoconferencing, colleagues can hang out in "rooms," leave documents on virtual tables, and have a sense of constant, appropriate contact. Such support may prove essential for telecommuters.

Spirit

Spirit is the last feature of community that Peck describes, and it's the most evanescent. It has to do with the way a group takes delight in its existence and with the extraordinary aspects of being in community with others. The online world offers a setting for such feelings. Its vastness can be awe-inspiring, like seeing pictures of the Earth from space. It can be frightening or overwhelming. To deal with these feelings successfully, participants often learn to let go of the need to read and know everything. They learn to rely on each other to find and bring interesting things to the conversation.

The online experience can also be a narcotic, substituting for real-world interaction. Participants are transported out of the world of everyday frustrations and concerns into a world they can design.

PLAN OR BE PLANNED FOR

Technologies are not value neutral. They reflect their designer's intentions, and many of the national information infrastructure's designers are bent on building a better way to sell goods and services, rather than a better way to communicate. The rules of the road and its underlying design affect whether the feeling of community can emerge in ways both subtle and direct.

Thinking through technologies' implications is essential. In his book *In the Absence of the Sacred*, Jerry Mander provides a great example of the pervasive effects the automobile has had on our society. He enumerates the ways that the automobile has changed our environment, from the way land has been paved everywhere to the emergence of assembly-line jobs and the pollution from ubiquitous fossil-fuel-powered vehicles. Then he invites the reader to consider whether we would have let automobiles evolve the way they have if we had been able to imagine some of those events earlier.

Clearly the car has shaped our lives dramatically since it became popular. Now computers are doing so. Yet few people question the course that computer technology is taking, aside from irritated (and justifiable) comments about how difficult it all is. Partly we abdicate responsibility because we are made to feel powerless and dumb. That need not be the case at all.

Don't stand by and let others design things for you. The social value we will be able to derive from the technological environment over the next century is up for grabs. It could remain organic and social or get paved and sterilized. We urge you to participate in its design and development.

An Optimistic View

Communications technologies have presented a huge opportunity. The back door opened by technologies helps us become more familiar with one another. Through this familiarity we can overcome fears (and biases, stereotypes, and misconceptions), which are the major contributors to strife and hatred. This is how some of these technologies might lead to a broader, more lasting peace.

Things you can do:
- Try the tools, they can be powerful.
- Learn how to use e-mail and proselytize.
- Learn and support the ethic of the Internet.

George Pór
is president of Organizational
Learning Systems, located in Soquel,
California. Organizational Learning
Systems is a network of consultants to business, government, and research
organizations dedicated to building community in the workplace. He is the
author of many articles on the role of information technology in organizational change, published in five languages. The focus of his current research,
development, and consulting work is the intersection of virtual communities, the
Internet, groupware, corporate memory systems, and intellectual capital.

23

The Quest for Collective Intelligence

George Pór

Think about the organization where you work. Is it only a collection of individual intelligences or does it have a collective intelligence? Organizations that will succeed in these times of accelerating changes will be social organisms with a collective intelligence to guide them through turbulence and transformations.

Organizations can thrive on the key evolutionary challenge of our age, identified by Douglas Engelbart as "the increasing complexity multiplied by the increasing urgency," only if they develop a high level of collective intelligence, or intellectual capital. Maximizing the organization's human and intellectual capital is its key to success in the new, knowledge-based economy.

An organization develops collective intelligence the same way bodies do—by growing and using a nervous system.

FROM ORGANIZATION TO SOCIAL ORGANISM:
GROWING A COMMUNITY NERVOUS SYSTEM

Back in 1970, Engelbart, a visionary for using computers to augment individual and collective intelligence, warned: "Today's environment is beginning to threaten today's organizations, finding them seriously deficient in their nervous system design...The degree of coordination, perception, rational adaptation, etc., which will appear in the next generation of human organizations will drive our present organizational forms, with their clumsy nervous systems, into extinction." His prediction is coming true.

Only a community—a social organism—equipped with a robust and agile nervous system will be able to anticipate and continually respond to the shifting concerns and needs of its members and stakeholders. (A "stakeholder" of a biological organism is any other organism in its habitat affected by its existence. "Stakeholders" of a community are all the individuals and organizations that have a stake in its success.)

The nervous system's evolution—both in living or social organisms—defines how effectively it can perform the following four functions:

- Facilitating the exchange and flow of information among the subsystems of the organism and with its environment.
- Coordinating the harmonious action of the subsystems and the whole.
- Storing, organizing, and recalling information as needed by the organism.
- Guiding and supporting the development of new competencies and effective behaviors.

The main function of a workplace community's collective intelligence is to provide the social organism with guidance in times of accelerating complexity and chaos. It serves to sustain the community by continuously augmenting its competence in rapidly responding to vital challenges and possibilities, as they emerge.

The nervous system in a social organism is the network of conversations that enables it to coordinate its actions and learn from its experience. To picture a network of conversations in a small company with 100 employees, imagine an animated flowchart with 100 small circles. Arrows of different sizes and colors link the circles to indicate the length and media of communications—phone calls, memos, reports, and various meetings—in a single day. Then imagine how this flowchart of conversations would look in a corporation of 10,000 people working on a large number of projects simultaneously, many of which require ongoing conversations among geographically scattered employees, suppliers, and customers.

For any organization to have all its members speak their minds in a few hours, the development of its collective intelligence calls for "electrifying[its network of conversations—for developing synergy between its people network and its computer network. An "electrified" nervous system is the infrastructure needed for the self-organization and self-improvement of a community's collective intelligence. The four enabling functions of this nervous system are the same as in biological systems:

- Communication
- Coordination
- Memory/knowledge management
- Learning

A collective intelligence system is a dynamic, living "ecosystem" for individual and collective learning, in which emergent patterns of meaning, coordination flows, insights, and inspiration interact, cross-fertilize, feed upon, and grow on each other. Those who want to grow such a system will first have to consider each of the above functions.

COMMUNICATION SUBSYSTEM

Although the richest in multi-sensory signals, face-to-face meetings are a poor mode of communication when ongoing, many-to-many communication is required, or when speed of action is important and the community needs to process and evaluate simultaneous input from multiple internal and external sources.

To meet these challenges, the communication subsystem has to include the *virtual space* of conference calls or video conferences, which allow "same time/different space" meetings.

When conflicting schedules prevent simultaneous participation, or when continuous access to the shared mind of the community is crucial, then you add the *virtual time* technologies of e-mail, electronic bulletin boards, and computer conferences which allow "different time/different space" meetings. "Virtual time" means that a server or host computer receives and holds everyone's input. It stores and forwards messages to all community members whenever they want to access them.

For a leadership team committed to equipping the community for sustainability, the single most important piece of the enabling infrastructure is a "different time/different space" computer conferencing system. Combined with the appropriate facilitation, this technology can connect not only the minds but the hearts and spirit of its users. This potential is of vital importance because under pressure, high stress, or challenges or in breakdowns, the sustainability of the community depends on the quality of relationships among its members and with its outside stakeholders.

When setting up a conferencing system as the backbone of the intelligence infrastructure, it is essential to give special attention to including every member of the community. Without adequate access they cannot fully participate in the concurrent feeding and use of the collective-intelligence ecosystem. This is an unnecessary and unacceptable waste of the community's human capital and self-organizing capacity. Whatever weakens diversity in the ecology of the collective mind weakens the intelligence of the whole system.

Another critical factor determining the effectiveness of the nervous system is the seamless integration of real-time conversations held in a meeting room and those held continuously in the virtual room of computer-mediated meetings. For example, a management team that meets both in person and on the electronic network needs to discover for itself what is the best mix of these and other media—phone, fax, e-mail, videotape, and so on—for each of the major tasks that require collaboration.

Input from one medium can serve as output to another and vice versa. If the signals don't travel quickly and easily between the face-to-face and electronic domains, any breakdown in the network of conversations can result in a breakdown in community, performance, and learning. Here's an example of how an "electrified" management team—or other groups of knowledge workers—can avoid communication breakdowns and accelerate breakthroughs:

- During the face-to-face meeting, use any of the popular software programs for electronic brainstorming, collaborative scenario writing, or group decision making.
- Leave ten minutes at the end of each meeting for discussing what the team as a whole has learned.
- Print out the record of meeting notes taken on a laptop and give a copy to all participants so they can further reflect on the team's deliberations and on the next action while their impressions are still fresh.
- Post the meeting minutes on the communication network for future reference and access by all those who need to know, who will be affected by the deliberations, or who have a contribution to make in turning them into action.

COORDINATION SUBSYSTEM

To coordinate is to "bring into proper order or relation so as to have harmonious action" (*Webster's Dictionary*). Imagine what would happen if a community of you and me wanted to produce some kind of harmonious action—for example, a way to share and deepen the key insights that each of us gained as we were reading or writing this book. If only the two of us were involved, the only coordination tool we would need is the telephone.

However, if that community included not only you and me but also many other readers and writers of this anthology, then first we would need to develop some basic agreements about how to share our learning insights with each other. As Darla Chadima and Geoffrey Hulin say in their essay (see page 175), "Agreements are the foundations of the community's coordination system."

We would want a system that allows us to minimize our time and money spent on coordinating the action, yet lets us produce powerful learning outcomes both for our ad hoc learning community and for each of its members. Fortunately, computer power has dramatically decreased the cost of coordination, thus increasing the possibility of collaboration and community. Collaboration researchers Paul Cashman and David Stroll reported these benefits:

- "Higher quality work can be done because of the more diverse knowledge, experience, skills, and views that can be brought into any project from more parts of the community, over more extended time, and faster, when speed is important.
- "More complex processes can be coordinated, because they can be specified and agreed upon or, alternatively, they can evolve organically. They can be examined, since they are in an explicit form.
- "More work can be done (due to increased complexity which is now manageable)."

I would add to this list the following benefits of today's coordination technologies:

- More accurate mapping of the community's intellectual capital and more collaborative decision making, particularly when the complexity of the

decision or planning requires the coordination of a large number of inputs.
- Closer coordination and management of the relationships with the community's external stakeholders: customers, suppliers, and other groups.

The tools for a high performance coordination system include:
- The electronic, interactive version of the community's policy manual, mission statement, and other documents containing agreements by which the community wishes to live.
- Project planning, co-authoring, and work-flow automation software.
- Software for creating learning feedback loops and signaling anomalies in all the major activities of the organization. (One example: a simulation program that calls attention to potential breakdowns in marketing channels.)

Memory/Knowledge Management Subsystem

"Knowledge," as used here, is the organization's capability to answer a new challenge or an opportunity. "Memory" is its capability to retain an appropriate answer to a specific challenge or opportunity over time. Knowledge and memory are two aspects of the same subsystem of the community's nervous system.

Without using computer technology, a community can neither organize large volumes of data into information nor refine information into knowledge by structuring it for supporting the action. Engelbart was also the first to paint the picture of an electronically augmented community memory system:

> An active community would be constantly involved in dialogue bearing upon the contents of the last formal version of its [electronic] Handbook—comments, errata, suggestions, challenges, counter examples, altered designs, improved arguments, new experimental techniques and data, etc.
>
> *This human-resource sharing has explosive potential*—I look to it with a biological metaphor as providing a new evolutionary stage for the nervous system of social organisms, from which much more highly developed institutional forms may evolve that are much improved in: awareness of self and environment, situational cognizance and response, visualization of the future, problem-solving capability, etc. (Emphasis added.)

Unlike a paper-based knowledge system, an online system allows updates and additions from its creators and users on an ongoing basis. Blurring the reader/writer and user/contributor distinctions, it can become a busy mental gym for the collective mind, the place where the community keeps raising the fitness level of its collective intelligence.

A memory/knowledge system has two main functions: to support a sense of collective identity and to support the community's learning by enabling the rapid sharing of recorded experience and other knowledge resources. Without an explicit organizational memory system, the community's sense of identity is only anecdotal. For new members it may take years to piece together all the relevant stories from which a sense of the organization's identity may emerge.

A computerized system for managing the community's knowledge assets and memory should provide easy access to shared documents and lessons learned in the past. A well-designed system is not merely a repository of files and archives. It also includes the rationale and assumptions upon which actions were based so that they can be examined and improved for more effective future action. For example, an electronically indexed collection of videotaped interviews, explaining the conditions that allowed successful teams to shorten the time needed for moving from breakdowns to breakthroughs, will enable troubled teams to accelerate their learning by reviewing those lessons and using what is applicable.

The system should also indicate, as Nancy Dixon points out, "where specific organizational memories are located. For example, who knows about a particular issue or process? Who has been through it before? How does this situation compare to the one five years ago?"

In organizations that value and encourage both individual and collective learning, the benefits of a memory/knowledge system will be highly valued, monitored, and measured. In contrast, in organizations where the antidotes to learning—bureaucracy and fear—dominate relationships, there will be great resistance to any systemic, recorded form of community memory. That's because members engaged in coordinating their actions will most likely scan the memory/knowledge management subsystem for information needed to upgrade current standards of trust, interdependence, and accountability.

What does it take to build a memory/knowledge system?

First, leaders who understand and support how the system benefits the community.

Second, a small but competent design team with at least one member trained in knowledge management.

Third, competence in organizing and facilitating the evolution of the community's shared knowledge on an ongoing basis.

The core component technologies that a community needs to acquire for building its knowledge system include:

- Document linkage systems, frequently implemented in hypermedia: a technology for organizing and representing knowledge as a navigable web of information nodes connected with links that show their relationships. Nodes can have textual, graphic, audio, or video elements, and any combination of them.
- Argument management systems that use hypermedia for graphically mapping complex issues and the multiple positions organization members hold about them. An example of such systems is "CM-1," which stands for Corporate Memory 1. Users of CM-1 can map a complex design or decision rationale as it emerges through their conversation so that it can be reviewed and collaboratively improved before committing large amounts of resources.

Both the document linkage and the argument management systems should be well indexed and cross-referenced for easy access by people with various information retrieval needs, skills, and strategies.

- Search and browsing tools for retrieving information from vast repositories of documents created with different software applications and residing in various online networks.

LEARNING SUBSYSTEM

As you read this or any other book, you may acquire new information, refreshing insights, and even inspirational ideas. But how will you know whether you *learned* something? What is learning, anyway?

You knew that you had learned to ride a bike when you actually rode one. I recall the delightful new sense of freedom I felt when I first shouted, "Look mom, no hands!" It is with this image in mind that I use "learning." As Larry Victor defined it, it is "a process leading to an irreversible alternation of the structure of a system that leads to the modification of the repertoire of potential behaviors, experiences, and improved cognition of the system."

We learn as we become more capable of responding to the new challenges and opportunities that life throws at us all, both as individuals and as communities. We learn to learn as we become capable of responding faster to those challenges and opportunities.

A community cannot be sustainable, and cannot endure the challenges from its environment, if its nervous system is not equipped for explicitly supporting the collaborative exploration of this question: How can the community as a whole increase its competence in learning to learn?

Part of the answer is to design and grow a robust learning system that keeps evolving as long as the community is committed to lifelong learning.

Unlike the memory/knowledge system which supports the content of the collective mind, the learning system supports its operations.

To envision a learning system in action, let's say your team is responsible for redesigning the collective intelligence infrastructure of your community. You want to gain access to the best thinking and practices in the design of community nervous systems around the world. You subscribe to an online service called, say, "Collective Intelligence Systems," which is tailored to the needs of designers of intelligence infrastructures in medium to large communities. At your fingertips, you have in this electronic library hundreds of books, conference proceedings, benchmark reports, and interviews with senior designers of collective intelligence.

What makes this learning system so valuable to you is not only its voluminous content, but what it allows you to do with it. You can, for example:

- Combine key words pertinent to your quest and search an ocean of information in a few minutes.
- Enjoy stories on videoclips about recent breakthroughs in the use of intelligence infrastructure for community building.
- Watch filmed demonstrations and tutorials on how to use all the learning

tools and processes of the service.

- Record your experiences and reflections on using the service in the electronic "Visitors' Journal." Others who feel inspired will respond to you, widening the pool of relevant conversations and meaning.
- Use the "patterner" tool for graphically representing and linking important patterns of information you discover that may shift your team's thinking about the task into a new phase.
- Articulate and test hypotheses for various designs of your intelligence infrastructure with the "simulator" tool.

None of these capabilities is a technological pipe dream. They can all be developed on the foundations of existing technology.

The learning subsystem of the community's nervous system is responsible for supporting the learning objectives and processes of the community, including the objectives and processes of improving the infrastructure of its collective intelligence. High performance learning communities plan for, and commit resources to, the articulation and periodic reassessment of the community's short- and long-term learning needs.

As more members of the community discover the rewards of the learning journey, they contribute to expanding and nurturing their shared intelligence and the infrastructure that supports it. The stronger the infrastructure, the more support it provides to each individual's learning journey.

Systemic Wisdom

Having an adequate *intelligence* infrastructure is a necessary but insufficient condition for a community's long-term viability. The sustainability of social organisms also requires the exercise of systemic, collective *wisdom*.

Collective wisdom can be seen in the balance of nature's ecosystems. It is also present in the potential of your organization or community to anticipate its next crisis. As David Spangler wrote, "It is this embracing, blending with, inhabiting, joining kind of knowledge that represents wisdom for me. I am not wise about something just because I have a lot of data about it; I am wise about something because I am one with it in some manner."

As learning is the "becoming" aspect of knowing, wisdom is its "being" aspect. Maintaining a dynamic balance between them is a vital competence. To thrive, a community must have both the wisdom to ask the right questions from itself at the right time, and the infrastructure for tapping into its own collective intelligence for responses.

Imagine an organization caught in the struggle between the economic necessity of laying off hundreds of employees within six months, and its sincere commitment to them as people. A management team aware of the social overhead of layoffs wouldn't just slough off those members of the company that it can't justify economically. From the place of connectedness, of being one community, they would look for creative breakthroughs that could meet the contradictory requirements of the situation. For example, they may ask themselves, What can we do, in a short time, to increase our peoples' skills base, and so increase their chances of finding new, rewarding work here or elsewhere? How can we redesign our working relationships from "all or nothing" to a continuum of connectedness?"

THE QUEST CONTINUES

Before we can live in a learning society, in which the unfolding of each individual's and community's full creative potential is the highest value of the whole, we need a critical number of learning organizations to embrace that vision. I spot signs of such trends. For example: "Johnsonville Foods (Sheboygan, Wisconsin) changed its management style to allow the people who do the work to make decisions relating to their own jobs," according to Linda Honold writing for *Training* magazine. "One of the keys to this transformation was *changing the focus of the company from using people to build the business to using the business to build great people.*" (Emphasis added.)

Imagine if each community engaged in the process of growing its collective intelligence could tap into and contribute to the collective wisdom of all communities in transformation. A global electronic network of active practitioners of organizational innovation and learning is not only a possibility, it's a condition for accelerating both the evolution of the field and the learning curve of communities in transformation.

This possibility has just begun to turn into reality. If you want to learn about, and be part of, the latest developments in collective intelligence as they unfold through global computer networks, let me know.

The quest continues.

*Since we know from systems dynamics that structure drives behavior,
what is the impact of organizational structures on community?*

Part Six:
Structural Dimensions of Community

This segment is dedicated to forms and structures that support the development and continuing evolution of community—those guiding principles, contexts, models and, yes, even the buildings that support true community.

John Gardner leads off this section, identifying ten ingredients for a healthy community. Amitai Etzioni explains the communitarian concept that he has pioneered over the past several years. John Nirenberg follows with an examination of the history of democratization, seeing workplace community as the next evolutionary step. Robert Mang identifies a framework for building sustainable communities—from ecosystem to governance.

David Goff provides readers with highlights of his research on the effectiveness of community-building workshops. Terry Anderson and Ed Klinge focus on what is needed to create self-sustaining, self-determining communities. In the final essay for this part, Ann Roulac shares her father's legacy as a master builder, synthesizing the tangible and intangible elements of community.

John W. Gardner

directs the Leadership Studies Program of Independent Sector, a nonprofit coalition of over 800 corporate, foundation and voluntary organization members. A former president of the Carnegie Corporation and the Carnegie Foundation for the Advancement of Teaching, he was Secretary of Health, Education and Welfare (1965–1968), chairman of the National Urban Coalition (1968–1970), founding chairman of Common Cause (1970–77), and a co-founder of Independent Sector. Gardner is presently the Miriam and Peter Haas Centennial Professor of Public Service at Stanford University.

A graduate of Stanford and the University of California at Berkeley (Ph.D. in psychology), Gardner was a captain in the Marine Corps assigned to the Office of Strategic Services during World War II and has served on the Scientific Advisory Board of the Air Force. He has been a member of the Board of Directors of Shell Oil, New York Telephone Company, American Airlines, Time, Inc., the Metropolitan Museum of Art and Stanford University. He is the author of *Self-Renewal, Excellence*, and *On Leadership*.

This essay was previously published in a booklet for Independent Sector, "Building Community," and is being published with permission of the author.

24

The New Leadership Agenda
John W. Gardner

Where community exists it confers upon its members identity, a sense of belonging, a measure of security. Individuals acquire a sense of self partly from their continuous relationships to others, and from the culture of their native place. But with today's mobility, and with family and community disintegration, many of those anchors for the sense of self no longer exist.

Without the continuity of the shared values that community provides, freedom cannot survive. Freedom is not a natural condition. Habeas corpus, trial by jury, a free press and all the other practices that ensure our freedom are social constructions.

Strong and resilient communities can stand between the individual and any government that tries to impose dictatorial solutions from the right or left. Healthy communities constitute one kind of intermediary structure. Undifferentiated masses never have and never will preserve freedom against usurping power.

A community has the power to motivate its members to exceptional performance. It can set standards of expectation for the individual and provide the climate in which great things happen. It can pull extraordinary performances out of its members. The achievements of Greece in the 5th Century B.C. were not the performances of isolated persons but of individuals acting in a golden moment of shared excellence. The community can tap levels of emotion and motivation that often remain dormant. Humans need communities—and a sense of community. A journalist resident in Los Angeles said of the youth gangs in that city: "Regrettably, they provide a sense of community that some of the kids can't find anywhere else." Part of an anti-gang strategy is to make sure the kids can find it somewhere else.

It would not be wise to end this recital of the positive attractions of community without some words of caution. First, there is such a thing as too much community—as a number of extremist cults have vividly demonstrated. For the community where evil flourishes and freedom perishes, disintegration is a favorable outcome!

Second, psychological research has shown there is a measure of constraint upon the individual in all social action, and therefore in all authentic communities.

In the thinking of some writers, a belief in the importance of communities is associated with a strong anti-government bias. This is understandable to the extent that Federal and state governments have often undermined the strength of local communities. But one can seek to restore local communities and still recognize that vital and effective government at state and federal levels is essential, and can be so designed as to strengthen community at lower levels.

THE BREAKDOWN OF COMMUNITY

The historians, sociologists and anthropologists who did the first studies of peasant or tribal communities were immensely taken with the social cohesion, the wholeness, the solidarity of these human groupings, and for a long time they (and their readers) tended to idealize that image of community. Few communities in the United States today offer anything approaching that standard of cohesiveness. But many communities in our country have within the memory of living persons supplied some of the same benefits that those earlier communities provided in full measure—security, a sense of identity and belonging, a framework of shared assumptions and values, a network of caring individuals, the experience of being needed and so on.

The breakdown of community is not a uniquely modern phenomenon. No doubt it occurred in antiquity when the collision of tribal cultures in an urban setting shook the unshadowed faith of the tribesman, or when the unsettling tales of traders from far places planted seeds of questioning in comfortably parochial minds.

But those were occasional happenings. With the Renaissance and the rise of transportation and communication, the breakdown of communities began to become a common experience—not yet devastating but common.

Progressively, the traditional community has been stripped of its autonomy and deprived of many of its functions. Today we see the weakening and collapse of communities of obligations and commitment, and of coherent belief systems. We see a loss of a sense of identity and belonging, of opportunities for allegiance, for being needed and responding to need—and a corresponding rise in feelings of alienation, impotence and anomie.

Causes

It has been the fashion of late to single out our individualistic culture as the sole cause of the breakdown—and indeed it must bear a share of the blame. Excessive competitiveness and emphasis on individual performance have eroded the sense of community as individuals compete fiercely for advancement or recognition. For example, in the harsh competitive environment of our best schools and colleges, even successful students often feel alone, and those who aren't successful suffer even more.

But we are dealing here with a trend that has emerged over centuries on every continent. Deep and far-reaching forces have been at work. There is no single cause.

Consider the rise of the nation state. From the beginning, it was more or less continuously at odds with all lower-level unities—the family, the tribe, the guild, the township. It is precisely in those lower-level unities that community and the sense of community were preserved.

Another powerful force for change over the centuries has been the steadily increasing capacity of transportation and communication to dissolve local belief systems and disintegrate local cultures. The extraordinary mobility of the individual today poses a stiff challenge to community.

Consequences

We need not attempt an exhaustive list of causes. We are all familiar with the consequences. Families fall apart. People suffer isolation, alienation, estrangement. More and more lost and rootless people drift through life without a sense of belonging or allegiance to anything. Too many of them lack any supportive network. The rise of the so-called "support group" is no accident. Where can individuals turn to still their anxieties when there is no longer a web of reciprocal dependencies? The casualties stream through the juvenile courts and psychiatrists' offices and drug abuse clinics. And quite aside from individual breakdown, a great many of our contemporaries, freed by the disintegration of group norms, torn from their natural home in a context of shared obligations, have gotten drunk on self.

When a community disintegrates, the consequences for its members can be destructive. Certain intellectuals of the 1960s cried, "Life is absurd." Life is indeed absurd when the web of community meaning is shredded, when belief systems are shattered, when there remains no supporting framework of values. Sociologist Daniel Bell charges that in modernist culture, "There are no sacred groves that cannot be trespassed upon or even trampled down."

We have seen all the disorders of men and women torn loose from a context of community and shared values. Individuals often experience it as a loss of meaning, a sense of powerlessness. They lose the conviction that they can influence the events of their lives or the community (non-community) in which they live. And one striking consequence is a diminution of individual responsibility and commitment.

I have sketched a bleak picture. It is most readily observable in disintegrating metropolitan areas. The affliction is less acute in some rural communities, particularly in the midwest.

Those in the upper range of the economic and social scale are less conscious of the need for community. The consequences of community breakdown are far less vivid and violent in the areas where they live. They don't feel the same immediate threat to their lives and safety. Perhaps for those reasons, some social analysts think of community breakdown as chiefly a problem for the lower socioeconomic levels. But the breakdown is evident at all social levels and the consequences, though less violent, may be just as devastating. Social disintegration is no less malignant when it occurs in an environment of physical comfort. Many of the gifted transgressors whose criminal activity has shattered public confidence in Wall Street and Washington have come from backgrounds characterized by affluent disintegration.

Regeneration

Disintegration of human communities is as old as human history. Disease, natural disasters, conquest and absorption into emerging urban centers were the most common causes. But there were always processes of regeneration at work to counter disintegrative forces. As old social grouping broke down, new groupings tended to form. Humans are community-forming animals.

I made the point earlier that family and community are the generators and preservers of value systems. It is their generative rather than their preservative function that deserves our closest attention. A society can do much to preserve, disseminate and celebrate existing values; but to cope with change, the process of value generation must go on continuously. The regenerative powers of human society have not weakened. The capacity of humankind to create and re-create social coherence is always there—enduring and irrepressible.

A number of sociologists who studied our great cities in the middle years of the 20th Century were convinced that they were witnessing the final disintegration of community. But later studies have revealed that the capacity of communities to survive or reappear in altered form had been considerably underestimated. William F. Whyte's 1955 study of street corner society and Elton Mayo's studies of the workplace in the 1920s and 1930s revealed authentic community-building impulses in unexpected places. Studies of the American soldier in World War II revealed similar processes at work. As a rule, the dissolution of a human community or a group of communities is not the end of the story. Some communities restore themselves in altered form. Wholly new communities take shape.

But today communities are being continuously undermined and we cannot be optimistic about the outcome unless we take deliberate measures to abet the regenerative processes and slow the destructive processes. What is needed is the active nurturing and rebuilding of community—in a spirit that honors both continuity and renewal.

Individual and Group

An understanding of the mutual dependence of individual and group has existed below the level of consciousness in all healthy communities from the beginning of time. But that understanding survives faintly, if at all, today. The contemporary self, insatiable in its quest for autonomy, all too often rejects custom and tradition, and looks with contempt at the imperfect institutions of its own society. No society can survive such abandonment by its members. A sound society provides the individual with nurturing in infancy, a secure environment in which to mature, a framework of meaning, a sense of identity and belonging—and sometimes much more. In healthy societies the individual gives something back—at the very least, allegiance and some measure of commitment to the society.

There will always be a tension between the needs of the individual and the needs of the group. Both must be honored. There would be no gain in letting the pendulum swing to excessive emphasis on the group. We seek mature and morally responsible individuals, proud of their individuality but ever conscious of group obligation. We have seen the specter of 20th Century totalitarianism, and we have seen the depersonalizing effect of a large, intricately organized society. The pressures toward conformity are real. The idea of community must leave room for the angry voice that says things aren't working right.

Young people, as they are maturing and becoming individuals responsible for their own actions, should be maturing as members of the community. Ideally, one fosters individual initiative but expects that a certain amount of that initiative will be expended on shared purposes.

To make this possible, we shall first have to rehabilitate the idea of commitments beyond the self. This reverses a century of fruitless search for happiness in an ever more insatiable shattering of limits so that the self might soar free and unrestrained. Commitments involve self-discipline and constraints, but they are freely chosen constraints.

We have learned through hard experience that without commitments, freedom is not possible. Something has to hold the society together. If that "something" is not dictatorial rule then it must be a commitment to the freely devised constitutional framework and web of custom that characterize the open society. We must freely grant our allegiance to the society that gives us freedom. Montesquieu said a Republic can survive only as long as its citizens love it.

Liberty and duty, freedom and obligation. That's the deal. You are free within a framework of obligations—to your family, to loved ones, to community, nation, species; in Shaw's words, to "the posterity that has no vote and the tradition that never had any"; to your God, to your conception of an ethical order. The obligations you accept may be different from mine. But it is not in the grand design that we can have freedom without obligation. Not for long.

The mutual dependence between individual and group is ancient. But today the survival of our communities—and our survival as social beings—requires that we alter somewhat the nature of the relationship. Historically, the society supplied most of the continuity and coherence through its long-established belief systems and nurturing institutions. In return the individual gave allegiance but—except in time of war—it was truly a rather passive allegiance. One accepted one's culture as an infant accepts its cradle.

Passive allegiance isn't enough today. The forces of disintegration have gained steadily and will prevail unless individuals see themselves as having a positive duty to nurture their community and continuously reweave the social fabric.

Note that the task is not one of uncritical reaffirmation; it is a task of renewal. And the process of renewal encompasses both continuity and change, reinterpreting tradition to meet new conditions, building a better future on an acknowledged heritage and the wisdom of experience. That calls for loving, nurturing critics.

The Traditional Community

Setting about the contemporary task of building community, one discovers at once that the old, beloved traditional model will not serve our present purposes well. Nostalgia for "the good old days" will not help us through the turbulent times ahead.

The traditional community was homogeneous. Today most of us live with heterogeneity, and it will inevitably affect the design of our communities. Some of the homogeneity of traditional communities was based on exclusionary practices we cannot accept today.

The traditional community experienced relatively little change from one year to the next. The vital contemporary community will not only survive change, but, when necessary, seek it.

The traditional community commonly demanded a high degree of conformity. Because of the nature of our world, the best of our contemporary communities today are pluralistic and adaptive, fostering individual freedom and responsibility within a framework of group obligation.

The traditional community was often unwelcoming to strangers, and all too ready to reduce its communication with the external world. Hard realities require that present-day communities be in continuous and effective touch with the outside world, and our values require that they be inclusive.

The traditional community could boast generations of history and continuity. Today, only a few communities can hope to enjoy any such heritage. The rest, if they are vital, continuously rebuild their shared culture and consciously foster the norms and values that will ensure their continued integrity.

In short, much as we may value the memory of the traditional community, we shall find ourselves building anew, seeking to reincarnate some of the cherished values in forms appropriate to contemporary social organization. The traditional community, whatever its shortcomings, did create, through the family, through the extended family, and through all the interlocking networks of community life, a structure of social interdependency in which individuals gave and received support—all giving, all receiving. With this no longer available, we must seek to reconstruct comparable structures of dependable interdependency wherever we can—in the workplace, the church, the school, the youth-serving organizations, and so on.

Forms of Community

Communities take many diverse forms today.

1. Traditionally, we have thought of a community as a geographically coherent and bounded place that was the scene of both work and home life. Such communities survive, but they aren't what they used to be. The small town of today is linked into economic networks that girdle the globe. The mobility and transience of its population makes cosmopolitanism inevitable. And every day, thanks to the media, the excitement and anxieties of a troubled world wash through it like a spring flood.

2. More common today is the pattern in which people form a geographically coherent residential community, but have widely scattered places of work. This pattern, common among suburbs and bedroom communities, has been criticized by social commentators. Some flatly regard it as falling outside the definition of community; but it has to be counted as one of the forms that community is taking in the contemporary world. Some suburbs are communities in the best sense of the word.

3. There are some sites of common activity—work, worship, education, and so on—where people associate regularly but come from widely scattered residential sites. For a good many people these are the most authentic communities they know.

4. There are dispersed communities in which neither the residences nor the worksites of members are contiguous. The members might be scattered all over the nation (or the world) but are held together by occupational, religious or other bonds. Religious orders are perhaps the oldest example, professional societies the most common contemporary example. Perhaps dispersed groups can never achieve the full richness that we associate with the word community. Maybe they can survive as communities only if the members receive their initial indoctrination in face-to-face settings in which deeper bonding can occur—and if they periodically gather for "retreats" or reunions to reaffirm the bond.

Among the groupings that may or may not be communities (depending on the presence of ingredients I discuss later) are:

Geographically defined units (cities, towns)
Families and extended families
Religious congregations
Schools and colleges
Workplaces
Union locals
Clubs, lodges, hobby groups
Professional groups
Political groups or parties

Voluntary groups, for example, youth service organizations
Neighborhoods

The earliest communities studied—tribal and peasant communities—involved bonds of reciprocal dependency that were usually unchanging and unchangeable. The bonds were not a matter of choice. We have moved steadily toward choice. Present-day communities are characterized by ease of exit.

In the contemporary world, membership in one particular community does not preclude membership in other communities. Indeed, it is probably the norm that individuals have outside ties and interests, and many are full-fledged members of two or more communities (for example, one where they live, another where they work).

Inadequate Models

Humans still have a powerful impulse toward community. How can we enable that impulse to express itself? Let me mention first some models that are of quite limited value in the next steps we must take.

First, the Utopian community. Throughout the 19th and 20th centuries, small Utopian communities have been created by like-minded idealists. Though some were able to serve the purposes of their founders, they have never managed to create patterns capable of being widely replicated, and all too often they developed cult pathologies.

Another model of limited value is the community of shared struggle. Bonding commonly occurs among individuals who are fighting a significant battle shoulder to shoulder—a strike, a protest, a natural disaster. Nations have been born in struggle, as have labor unions, political parties and veterans' organizations. More commonly, the community born of struggle fades swiftly when the battle is over—unless those involved create the institutional arrangements and non-crisis bonding experiences that carry them through the year-in-year-out tests of community functioning.

Finally, a model that is decidedly useful but also decidedly limited is provided by small group bonding experiences. Ever since the National Training Laboratory began experimenting with small group behavior after World War II, it has been apparent that certain types of small group activity produce rather remarkable emotional bonding among the participants. It emerges from the shared confessions that occur in therapeutic or self-help groups. It occurs in the "ropes and rock climbing" exercises that are now a familiar part of many leadership training programs. It can produce a powerful effect. But it is a bonding experience, not a community.

Such short-term small group experiences gain part of their power from the fact that people interact directly and personally with a minimum of the structure, rules and roles that generally hold human give-and-take within a web of constraints: all the bonding impulses of the human psyche without the restrictions! Very attractive. But as many a commune of the 1960s and 1970s discovered, an early demise is virtually certain for communities that fail to develop the structure and processes for successful group maintenance.

THE INGREDIENTS OF COMMUNITY

I have spoken of the building and rebuilding community, but so far haven't said what we might expect as a result of our rebuilding. Let me be specific. I think of community as a set of attributes that may appear in diverse settings—a school, a congregation, a town, a suburb, a workplace, a neighborhood. I'm going to list ten attributes of a community that would be viable in the contemporary world. There is no value neutrality in my description of the ingredients—but I believe the values explicit in these pages are widely shared. My interest is not in depicting Utopia. My interest is to get us away from vague generalizations about "community" and to identify some ingredients we can work on constructively.

One of my purposes is to provide a list of characteristics against which observers can measure any setting in which they find themselves. Many readers, as they review the list, will be asking themselves what steps might be taken in their own setting. So at the same time that I describe the ingredients, I shall be suggesting—under the heading Steps Toward Solutions—some of the ways in which those ingredients might be made to emerge—methods of building community. I do so with some hesitation because my thought at this writing are preliminary and incomplete—but they may lead to more developed ideas as the subject is pursued further.

Some methods buy community at too high a price, and I shall not advocate them. It is always possible, for example, to build community by creating (or exaggerating) an outside threat. Many cults force new members to divest themselves of old ties and to cast off old identities. Many totalitarian societies create community by cutting off other options for their members.

1. Wholeness Incorporating Diversity

We live in a world of multiple, interacting systems. On the international scene, nations function interdependently or collide. In the city, government officials, business, labor, ethnic groups and community organizations find—or fail to find—ways of living together. Russia seeks a way of dealing with the Ukraine, Canada a way of dealing with Quebec. Los Angeles copes with its multiple cultures. One encounters religious congregations that are split along class, racial or doctrinal lines.

In our system, "the common good" is first of all preservation of a system in which all kinds of people can—within the law—pursue their various visions of the common good, and at the same time accomplish the kinds of mutual accommodation that make a social system livable and workable. The play of conflicting interests in a framework of shared purposes is the drama of a free society. It is a robust exercise and a noisy one, not for the faint-hearted or the tidy-minded. Diversity is not simply "good" in that it implies breadth of tolerance and sympathy. A community of diverse elements has greater capacity to adapt and renew itself in a swiftly changing world.

But to speak of community implies some degree of wholeness. What we seek—at every level—is pluralism that achieves some kind of coherence, wholeness incorporating diversity. I do not think it is venturing beyond the truth to say that wholeness incorporating diversity is the transcendent goal of our time, the task for our generation—close to home and worldwide.

"Wholeness" does not characterize our cities today. They are seriously fragmented. They are torn by everything from momentary political battles to deep and complex ethnic rifts. Separate worlds live side by side but fail to communicate or understand one another. The list of substantive issues facing the city are not the city's main problem. Its main problem is that it can't pull itself together to act on any of the issues. It cannot think as a community or act as a community.

As we look at the world's grimmest trouble spots, wholeness incorporating diversity seems a hopeless quest. But there are a good many cities and even nations where markedly heterogeneous populations live and work together quite peaceably.

Steps Toward Solutions

To prevent the wholeness from smothering diversity, there must be a philosophy of pluralism, an open climate for dissent, and an opportunity for subcommunities to retain their identity and share in the setting of larger group goals.

To prevent the diversity from destroying the wholeness, there must be institutional arrangements for diminishing polarization, for teaching diverse groups to know one another, for coalition-building, dispute resolution, negotiation and mediation. Of course the existence of a healthy community is in itself an instrument of conflict resolution.

A clear part of the problem—particularly in our cities—is the fragmentation of leadership. Most leaders are One Segment Leaders, fattening on the loyalty of their own little segment and exhibiting little regard for the city as a whole. Indeed, sometimes they thrive on divisiveness. But in any city there are leaders capable of a broader perspective, capable of joining with leaders of other segments (in and out of government) to define and solve the larger problems of community. Such networks of responsibility can serve as a kind of constituency for the whole.

In our pluralistic system, each group is given the right to pursue its purposes within the law. Each group may demand recognition, may push for its rights, may engage in the healthy conflict of pluralism—but then, in a healthy community each group will reach back to the whole community of which it is a segment and ask "How can we help? How can we sing our part in the chorus?"

The nonprofit or voluntary sector can be a significant ally in accomplishing wholeness that incorporates diversity. It is a natural arena for diversity, but it is also capable of the "knitting together" that brings us back to some semblance of wholeness.

2. A Reasonable Base of Shared Values

To require that a community agree on everything would be unrealistic and would violate our concern for diversity. But it has to agree on something. There has to be some core of shared values. Of all the ingredients of community this is possibly the most important. The values may be reflected in written laws and rules, in a shared framework of meaning, in unwritten customs, in a shared vision of what constitutes the common good and the future.

To say that the community is characterized by those shared ideas and attributes puts the matter too passively. It will be more truly a community if members see it as an active defender of the shared ground. There should be a sense of social purpose. In our own society we expect that the community will not only respect but actively pursue such ideals as justice, equality, freedom, the dignity of the individual, the release of human talent and energy, and so on. Thus programs in education, civil rights and the like build community. Rampant crime, fraud and corruption tear it down.

The community teaches. If it is healthy it will impart a coherent value system. If it is chaotic or degenerate, lessons will be taught anyway—but not lessons that heal and strengthen. We treasure images of value education in which an older mentor quietly instructs a child in the rules of behavior, but that is a small part of a larger and more turbulent scene. The child absorbs values, good and bad, on the playground, through the media, on the street—everywhere. It is the community and culture that hold the individual in a framework of values.

None of this should be taken to mean that healthy communities should suppress internal criticism or deny their flaws or agree on everything.

Steps Toward Solutions

If the community is very lucky—and few will be in the years ahead—its shared values will be embedded in tradition and history and memory. But most future communities will have to build and continuously repair the framework of shared values. Their norms will have be explicitly taught. Values that are never expressed are apt to be taken for granted and not adequately conveyed to young people and newcomers. Individuals have a role in the continuous rebuilding of the value framework, and the best thing that they can do is not to preach values but to exemplify them. Teach the truth by living it. All of us celebrate our values in our behavior. It is the universal ministry. The way we act and conduct our lives is saying something to others—perhaps something reprehensible, perhaps something encouraging.

Today we live with many faiths, so we must foster a framework of shared secular values—liberty, justice and so on—while leaving people free to honor diverse deeper faiths that undergird those values.

3. Caring, Trust, and Teamwork

In some of the primitive tribes studied by anthropologists, the group was almost wholly self-sufficient. The community was responsible for all of the functions essential to human life: the provision of food and shelter, the resolving of internal conflicts, common defense in a hostile environment (human and other), the passing on of survival skills as well as provision of a context of meaning, allegiance, identity and emotional fulfillment.

Today the community has been stripped of many of these functions by federal and state government, by distant suppliers, by media external to the community and so on. All the more important then that we give attention to the functions that remain. Prominent among those remaining functions is providing the climate of caring, trust and teamwork that ensures the accomplishment of group purpose.

The members of a good community deal with one another humanely, respect individual differences and value the integrity of each person. A good community fosters an atmosphere of cooperation and connectedness. There is recognition and thanks for hard work, and an awareness by the members that they need one another. There is a sense of belonging and identity, a spirit of mutual responsibility. There is the altruism that is so consistently urged by major world religions. There is trust and tolerance and loyalty. Everyone is included. There is room for mavericks, nonconformists and dissenters. There are no outcasts. Obviously, this describes an ideal community, perhaps beyond our reach. The best communities we know have a long way to go.

But even the approximation of such an environment is powerfully rewarding to individuals and can counteract the tendency of members to drift away that afflicts most American communities today.

Research shows that much of the basis for positive and generous adult relationships traces back to a warm and nurturing environment in childhood. But there are measures that can be taken at the adult level.

Steps Toward Solutions

In seeking the goal of caring, trust and teamwork, the first necessary step is to give all subgroups and individuals reason to believe that they are fully accepted. It is essential that ethnic minorities, women, newcomers, the disabled and so on— all feel that they count. We know how to fight that battle and should not let up.

Another step—equally crucial—is to institutionalize arrangements for dispute resolution. Conflicting purposes and values are inevitable in our pluralistic society, and part of the normal functioning of a healthy community. Indeed, groups that have been denied just treatment by the community find it necessary to precipitate conflict. But without processes for conflict resolution we can never achieve the "wholeness incorporating diversity" that we seek. Some systems for resolving disputes have been institutionalized over centuries. Our courts, our representative political institutions and the economic marketplace resolve many conflicts. Some cities have community boards to deal with neighborhood disputes, commissions to work on racial harmony, or other instruments to diminish polarization.

Beyond that, there is an impressive array of measures that may be taken to resolve disputes. Every competent legislator knows the modes of building consensus and forming coalitions. Wise political leaders have learned the methods of collaboration and compromise.

The arts of reconciling conflicting purposes should be taught in every school and college in the world. Young potential leaders should be exposed to real-life situations—a political campaign, internship in a legislature or action in a community organization—where they learn the arts at first hand. The goal is not to abolish conflict, which is inevitable and even healthy, but to achieve constructive outcomes.

The third step is based on shared tasks. When individuals invest (time, energy, whatever) in their community, their bond with the community is strengthened. If they give something to (or give up something for) the community, they feel closer to it. Community problem-solving activities build community.

A healthy community will provide ample opportunities for the individual to participate in community efforts. Beginning early, boys and girls should take some responsibility for the well-being of any group they are in—a seemingly small step but without doubt the first step toward responsible community participation, and for that matter the first step in leadership development. Through volunteer community service experiences outside of school they will learn how the adult world works and will have the experience of serving their society. Every organization serving the community should find ways to involve young people.

There should be an Experience Corps through which older citizens can engage in volunteer work. A Volunteer Technical Assistance Center should help every nonprofit institution in the community learn the rather complex art of using volunteers effectively.

Finally, a healthy community creates a considerable variety of bonding experiences. I have already mentioned some, e.g. the common task, but there are many others: shared social activities, ceremonies, celebrations, rituals, the honoring of exemplary figures, retelling the community story and so on. Across the broad expanse of urban America today, the chief community bonding experiences are probably provided by religion and sports. Yes, sports.

4. Effective Internal Communication

Members of a well-functioning community communicate freely with one another. One of the advantages of the small group is that frequent face-to-face communication is possible. In large systems (cities and corporations, for example) much conscious effort is needed to maintain a free flow of information among all elements of the system, and to combat the we-they barriers that impede the flow.

Steps Toward Solutions

In a healthy community, groups that find themselves in disagreement feel free to express their views. That is essential. But groups that fall into habits of fierce mutual accusation generally diminish communication—a condition that can be reversed by techniques of conflict resolution if both sides are willing to use them. A tradition of civility helps. A common language helps.

There should be formal provisions for communication among subcommunities, but even better is a rich web of personal acquaintance cutting across the boundaries of subgroups. In cities and towns, local government and the media have a positive responsibility for effective communication with the community. But they cannot be counted on as the only means. There should be active and continuous communication among a variety of organizations and agencies in and out of government. Nongovernmental organizations can develop effective information-sharing networks.

For the community as a whole, there should be occasions when members gather for what the National Issues Forums sponsored by the Kettering Foundation call "public talk". There must be common meeting grounds. In cities or neighborhoods there must be organizations willing to provide meeting spaces or to serve as conveners. And communication includes listening!

5. Participation

A two-way flow of influence and communication is dictated by our value system. Our society requires a dispersed network of leaders spread through every segment of the organization and down through every level. And beyond this wide network of identified leaders, there will be, in a vital community, a large number of individuals voluntarily sharing those leadership tasks that lend themselves to sharing, e.g. achieving a workable level of unity, motivating, explaining.

If the system under discussion is a community functioning politically, one would want to add that beyond this voluntary sharing of leadership tasks a very large number of people will be expected to participate in such matters as voting, attending town meetings and so on.

There are those who are opposed to the very concept of "a leader"—and there is much in human experience that makes their attitude easy to understand. But leadership in the mode I've described is not the sort of coercive or exploitative process that we've seen so much of in human history.

For a city perhaps the most important requirement for effective leadership is the continuous collaboration between city government and all the segments of private sector leadership, profit and nonprofit. Private sector groups are coming to recognize that such participation is a positive duty.

The citizen voting or speaking out in public meetings is participating, but so are the parents who rear their children with a sense of community responsibility, so is the teenager who volunteers to tutor disadvantaged children. The healthy community has many ways of saying to the individual "You belong, you have a role to play, and the drama has meaning." It is this more than anything else that accounts for the sense of identity so characteristic of community members.

Steps Toward Solutions

Among the conditions that enhance the possibility of participation are the following:

A. A community culture that enables all members and all subgroups to feel accepted and confident that their needs will be considered.

B. Civic education as to how local government works, and why it sometimes doesn't work.

C. Voter registration and "get out the vote" drives.

D. Strong and active neighborhood groups and civic associations.

E. Free and responsible media of communication.

F. An open and responsive political process—restoration of trust in government by making it worthy of trust!

G. A sound educational system that includes preparation for effective leadership and participation.

H. Avoidance of the delusion that experts and professionals will solve all problems—what some have called managerial liberal ism—making citizen action unnecessary.

I. Forums in which community members can "work through" (to use Daniel Yankelovich's phrase) the key issues facing them. Yankelovich points out that the superficial poll responses that are labeled public opinion are not at all the same as public judgment, which can only result from public dialogue.

J. A strong tradition of voluntary public service.

Let me elaborate on paragraph "G" above—education for effective leadership and participation. The overwhelming emphasis in contemporary education on individual performance must be supplemented with education in the accomplishment of group purpose. Some of the new cooperative education programs achieve that result. At some point in high school and college, one or another form of community service or political internship is helpful.

Many other institutions in the community can help with the task of civic education. Any citizen group, any advisory commission, every civic task force is a potential training ground for leaders and community builders. In addition, the community should have one or another form of "community leadership program" of the sort sponsored by the National Association for Community Leadership or the American Leadership Forum. All segments of community leadership must be represented in such groups.

It would be wrong to conclude a discussion of participation without mentioning some of the complexities of the subject. First, participation is never total, and those who do participate are always a self-selected group. Some have a higher than average self-interest in participating, some have more of the energy that participation requires, some are more zealous (or dogmatic) on the issues, some thrive on emotional intensity and combative talk, some have more of the physical or psychological stamina required for interminable meetings. Whatever the basis of selection, the result is not a representative sample of the community.

Among those who do participate, there will be a small group of activists who come to dominate and a large number who play less directive (or downright passive) roles. One cannot change that reality. One *can* design the system so that the small guiding group is required to act openly and is held firmly accountable by the others.

6. Affirmation

A healthy community reaffirms itself continuously. It builds its own morale. It may face up to its flaws and tolerate criticism, but basically it has confidence in itself. No group, no matter how well-established, can take such affirmation entirely for granted. There are always young people to instruct and newcomers to welcome. Even a group with no history or tradition to build on can reaffirm its identity, its purposes and its shared values. Individuals are generally members of more than one community and there are competing demands upon them. The communities that survive the competition are likely to be those that press their claims.

In an earlier era communities celebrated their beginnings, their roots. But in few American communities today can a majority—or even a sizable fraction of members—claim any link with the community's history. The story of most communities today is acceptance of wave upon wave of newcomers who over generations found a way of living with the culture, influencing it as they accommodated to it. The drama and pride of our communities has been the coming together of many cultures—with consequent enrichment of all.

Steps Toward Solutions

Of course, a healthy community provides innumerable and ever-present affirmations of shared purpose just by being intact and vital. Everything from its nursery tales and its legendary figures to its structures of law and custom are forever conveying messages of instruction and reinforcement. Its history speaks, its symbols speak. It affirms the framework of meaning so important to community membership.

Normally, communities have ceremonies and celebrations to reaffirm the symbols of group identity, to recognize and reward exemplary members, to provide bonding experiences. In addition there should be more formal measures to further civic education, not just in the schools and colleges but in the churches, youth organizations and civic groups. It is everybody's business.

In thinking about the task of affirmation, we face the question of how far one carries a good thing before it becomes a bad thing. It is appropriate in a martial community such as the U.S. Marine Corps to pursue the matter somewhat obsessively. But for the normal community, excessive affirmation may create more pressure for conformity than is compatible with creativity.

7. Links Beyond the Community

The sound community has seemingly contradictory responsibilities: it must defend itself from the forces in the outside environment that undermine its integrity, yet it must maintain open, constructive and extensive relations with the world beyond its boundaries. The public school, for example, must be in some respects a haven for its students, capable of shutting out some of the most destructive aspects of city life, but it can maintain itself as a strong institution only through extensive community relations and constructive dealings with the school district and state.

A vital community inevitably distinguishes itself from its surroundings to some degree. If there were no boundaries at all, community members would not know where they belonged. But every community must combat the self-absorption that increases its distance from others. Total self-absorption is not acceptable. Impermeable boundaries are not acceptable. But it would be wise to admit that this question of appropriately permeable boundaries bristles with difficulties and paradoxes.

Primitive tribes could exist in relative isolation (though external forces such as trade or colonial administration cropped up frequently enough). But the community of today is decidedly not isolated. It is linked for good or ill with regional, national and world economic events; it is affected by state and federal laws and programs; and the media give it large daily doses of the outside world.

The most familiar situation for a community is to be nested in a larger community—the relationship of a neighborhood to the city, of the city to the metropolitan area, the state and the nation. Generally speaking, the larger unit will gain in health and vitality as the communities within it grow strong and vital, provided the constituent communities recognize their responsibility to, and need for, the larger whole. Those who have worked to restore grassroots community strength have made admirable contributions, but they sometimes succumb to a self-centeredness that leads them to ignore the larger systems in which they are nested. In a city such as Miami, for example, strong segmental communities sometimes appear to undermine the coherence of the larger whole. In the past three or four decades, a number of newly-independent African countries have had difficulty establishing a national community because of the strength and divisiveness of tribal communities.

Steps Toward Solutions

The relationship of the community to the world beyond its boundaries is an example of the problem of wholeness incorporating diversity. The community seeks to preserve its own integrity while reaching out to play an effective part in a larger whole. In the most desirable outcome, the community's leaders will establish collaborative ties with leaders of other subcommunities. The well-functioning city has ties with its metropolitan area and its region—and with state and federal governments. It is alert to national or regional economic or demographic trends that may impinge on it. Not only city government but leaders in the business and nonprofit worlds should participate in establishing the broader links.

The same may be said of the community development groups, neighborhood organizations and grassroots communities now flourishing. They can and should define their own problems and exercise their own initiative in working toward solutions. But, finally, they must have recourse to larger networks—and must play their role in strengthening the larger systems.

There is no way for them to survive without many kinds of linkage into larger frameworks. And even if they were to survive they would be incapable of registering their concerns and playing their role without such linkage. Many of the policies that affect the neighborhood are decided in the state capital or in Washington, D.C.

8. Development of Young People

Those who will lead the community four decades hence are scampering off to school today. Any community that seeks to ensure its continued vitality will not only enable those young people to develop to the full, but will prepare them for their future roles, instilling the shared values, fostering commitment to shared purposes, and teaching them to preserve and renew the common heritage.

Steps Toward Solutions

Beginning in elementary and high schools, girls and boys should learn to take some responsibility for the well-being of any group they are in—a seemingly small step but, as I pointed out earlier, the first step toward community participation and leadership development. Cooperative education methods can help. On the playing field and in group activities in and out of school, teamwork can be learned. Through volunteer and intern experiences they learn how the adult world works and have the experience of serving their society. Every organization serving the community should find ways of involving young people.

9. A Forward View

A healthy community should have a sense of where it should go, and what it might become. In an earlier era, when many communities experienced little change over decades, the idea might have made little sense. The answer might have been "We're not going anywhere. We're happy where we are."

In theory, a community doesn't absolutely have to have a goal or "vision" beyond survival, physical and spiritual. It doesn't have to be "going" anywhere. But in practice, if it drifts it may have changes forced upon it that it would not have chosen. Today change is a given—for good or ill. So the question becomes "Where will the currents of change take our community if we fail to act? How can we intervene to ensure a better outcome for our children and our children's children?" An answer to these questions can provide a vital goal and focus of motivation for the community. Far from pursuing such a goal, many of our communities today are laying up trouble for their children—in debt, in deteriorated infrastructure and so on.

Steps Toward Solutions

The conventional community approach to the future is to think in terms of a planning commission. Because over the years such commissions have tended to get bogged down in routine activities, the preference recently has been for ad hoc exercises such as LA 2000—short-term, intensive, wide-focus efforts to identify future problems and prepare for them. But such exercises should be supplemented by many dispersed institutional efforts. Local academic institutions should be engaged in continuous research relevant to the future of the community and its region. Various segments of the community—business, agriculture, education and so on—should be examining economic and demographic trends relevant to their future.

10. Institutional Arrangements for Community Maintenance

Every community has institutional arrangements for group maintenance. In a city the most conspicuous arrangements are those we call government. In a nonprofit organization it is the board of trustees, the director and staff, and perhaps some volunteer committees. The forms are infinitely varied. Unwritten codes of conduct play their role.

There are marked variations from one community to the next in the extent to which the institutional arrangements are characterized by structure and control. We can't accept the extremes. Excessive community control does not accord with our ideal of individual freedom and responsibility. At the other extreme is a degree of anarchy that does not permit (or invite) the emergence of shared values, that tolerates a degree of disorder wholly incompatible with a sense of community.

Between the extremes we can tolerate considerable variation in the degree of structure and control.

In a democratic society, a high proportion of the population has some role in the maintenance system. In a town, for example, there are leaders in town government and in the private sector. There are lower level leaders in every segment of the community. And there are a considerable number of individuals throughout the system who "share leadership tasks" on their own initiative, working to maintain group motivation, to heal rifts, to do volunteer work, and so on. And then there are the many members who participate by voting, by setting an example of appropriate individual behavior, by nurturing younger members.

Steps Toward Solutions

Some of the writers who are most concerned to restore a sense of community today are not inclined to pay much attention to government, but its role is critically important. If it doesn't work, it must be made to work. We cannot take it for granted. It has to be made an instrument of community and of participation, worthy of respect and trust. Politicians are much maligned, but the best of them, skilled in mediating among disparate groups, can make a significant contribution to community.

There must be continuous collaboration between local government and the private sector. There must be an infrastructure of neighborhood associations, churches, citizen groups, youth-serving organizations, and professional groups. Today some of these groups are genuinely interested in the community as a community, but most are highly specialized, each existing in its own little niche, rarely if ever thinking about the fate of the community as a whole. They must learn where their civic duty lies. They are an important part of the fabric of the community.

One of the most important functions in community maintenance is training and development of those who will ensure the continuity of maintenance. For this, the mingling of the generations is crucial. Young people should, from an early age, learn how their community functions and how it can be kept functioning.

CONCLUSION

Social theorists have pointed out that among the first acts of totalitarian dictators coming to power is to undermine the private associative links of the citizen, so there is nothing left but the State and a mass of separate individuals, easily dominated. Such theorists argue (correctly) that the close-in loyalties—to family, school, church, lodge, union, neighborhood and community—are essential to the health of a free society. Not only do such loyalties make the rise of an absolutist state far more unlikely, but they are teaching arenas for the arts of community that we need so desperately at national and world levels.

At first glance it would seem that no other nation has—or could have—a richer diversity of associations than the United States has. We have taken pluralism to its limits. So what's the problem? Why aren't we in great shape?

The answer is that the conditions of contemporary life have leached out the ingredients of community from a great many of these potentially nurturing associations. How many congregations have we seen in which the element of community is so thinned out as to be nonfunctional? How many schools have we seen that might be splendid communities but in fact don't even approach that condition? How many neighborhoods that might be coherent human settlements are not?

I had occasion recently to spend considerable time with the local branch of a famous social service organization, committed in its public pronouncements to serve its clients humanely. I have reason to believe that the agency uses its funds carefully, and provides its services dutifully. But the rich opportunities it has to provide an experience of community to clients who desperately need that experience are squandered. It is a station for the delivery of social services, but one might find more sense of community among the patrons of the nearest motel.

Another problem is that even for those of our associations which are in fact communities, there is often a reluctance to play their role in relation to the larger wholes of which they are a part. I know of one small business enterprise whose officers and employees constitute a satisfying little community, but they have little or no interest in the disintegrating city in which they are located.

Returning to a point made earlier, I think of community as a set of attributes that may or may not be present in a particular group or social system. I have tried to describe those attributes so that people can assess any particular institution or social system of which they are a part—school, congregation, village, workplace, neighborhood, whatever—and judge whether it is in fact a community.

We must seek to regenerate the sense of community from the ground up. How can people work to make their metropolis a community when most of them have seldom experienced a sense of community in any familiar setting? Men and women who have come to understand, in their own intimate settings, the principles of "wholeness incorporating diversity", the arts of diminishing polarization, the meaning of teamwork and participation will be strong allies in the effort to build elements of community into the metropolis, the nation and the world.

It would be a grave mistake to imagine that—in a great burst of energy—

we can rebuild our communities and then turn to other tasks. That assumes a degree of stability we once knew but may never see again in our lifetime. We can never stop rebuilding.

The communities we build today may eventually be eroded or torn apart by the crosscurrents of contemporary life. Then we rebuild. We can't know all the forms community will take, but we know the values and the kinds of supporting structures we want to preserve. We are a community-building species. We might become remarkably ingenious at creating new forms of community for a swiftly changing world.

Amitai Etzioni
is the first University Professor of The George Washington University and 1995 president of the American Sociological Association. He has served as the Thomas Henry Carroll Ford Foundation Professor at the Harvard Business School, Senior Advisor in the White House, and guest scholar at the Brookings Institution. He is the founder of the international Society for the Advancement of Socio-Economics and editor of *The Responsive Community: Rights and Responsibilities,* a quarterly journal.

He is also the author of fourteen books, including *The Moral Dimension: Toward a New Economics and The Spirit of Community: Rights, Responsibilities and the Communitarian Agenda.* He also contributes frequently to the news media, through articles in publications such as the *New York Times, Washington Post,* and *Wall Street Journal,* and through appearances on network television.

Etzioni founded the Center for Policy Research, a not-for-profit corporation dedicated to public policy. A 1982 study ranked him as the leading expert of thirty who made "major contributions to public policy in the preceding decade."

This essay was first published as a chapter in *The Moral Dimension* (Crown Books, 1993) and is reprinted with permission.

25

Back to We:
The Communitarian Nexus

Amitai Etzioni

It's hard to believe now, but for a long time the loss of community was considered to be liberating. Societies were believed to progress from closely knit, "primitive," or rural villages to unrestrictive, "modern," or urban societies. The former were depicted as based on kinship and loyalty in an age in which both were suspect; the latter, however, were seen as based on reason (or "rationality") in an era in which reason's power to illuminate was admired with little attention paid to the deep shadows it casts. The two types of social relations have often been labeled with the terms supplied by a German sociologist, Ferdinand Tönnies. One is *gemeinschaft*, the German term for community, and the other is *gesellschaft*, the German word for society, which he used to refer to people who have rather few bonds, like people in a crowd or a mass society.

Far from decrying the loss of community, this sanguine approach to the rise of modernity depicted small towns and villages as backward places that confined behavior. American writers such as Sinclair Lewis and John O'Hara satirized small towns as insular, claustrophobic places, inhabited by petty, mean-spirited people. They were depicted as the opposite of "big cities," whose atmosphere was said to set people free. Anonymity would allow each person to pursue what he or she wished rather than what the community dictated. It was further argued that relations in the *gesellschaft* would be based not on preexisting, "ascribed" social bonds, such as between cousins, but on contractual relations, freely negotiated among autonomous individuals.

Other major forms of progress were believed to accompany the movement from a world of villages to one of cities. Magic, superstition, alchemy, and religion—"backward beliefs"—would be replaced by bright, shining science and technology. There would be no more villagers willing to sell their wares only to their own kind and not to outsiders—a phenomenon anthropologists have often noted. Old-fashioned values and a sense of obligation were expected to yield to logic and calculation. Social bonds dominating all relations (you did not charge interest on a loan to members of your community because such a charge was considered indecent usury) were pushed aside to make room for a free market, with prices and interest rates set according to market logic. By the same token, the network of reciprocal obligations and care that is at the heart of communities would give way to individual rights protected by the state. The impersonal right to social services and welfare payments, for instance, would replace any reliance on members of one's family, tribe, or ethnic benevolent association.

The sun, moon, and stars of the new universe would be individuals, not the community. In a typical case, the U.S. Supreme Court ruled that the Sierra Club had no legal standing to argue for the preservation of parkland as a community resource. Rather, if the Sierra Club wished to show standing, it would have to demonstrate that particular individuals were harmed.

Throughout 20th Century America, as the transition to *gesellschaft* evolved, even its champions realized that it was not the unmitigated blessing they had expected. Although it was true that those who moved from villages and small towns into urban centers often shed tight social relations and strong community bonds, the result for many was isolation, lack of caring for one another, and exposure to rowdiness and crime.

Criminologists report that young farmhands in rural America in the early 19th Century did not always work on their parents' land. However, when they were sent to work outside their home they usually lived with other farmers and were integrated into their family life. In this way they were placed in a community context that sustained the moral voice, reinforced the values of their upbringing, and promoted socially constructive behavior. It was only when these farmhands wet to work in factories in cities—and were housed on their own in barracks without established social networks, elders, and values—that rowdy and criminal behavior, alcoholism, and prostitution became common. Even in those early days attempts to correct these proclivities were made not by returning these young people to their families and villages, but by trying to generate "communitarian" elements in the cities. Among the best analysts of these developments is James Q. Wilson, a leading political scientist. He notes that associations such as the Young Men's Christian Association (YMCA), temperance societies, and the Children's Aid Society sought to provide a socially appropriate, morality-sustaining context for young people.

Other experiences paralleled those of the factory hands. The migration to the American West, for example, is usually thought of as a time when individuals were free to venture forth and carve out a life of their own in the Great Plains. Actually, many people traveled in caravans and settled as communities, although each family claimed its own plot of land. Mutual assistance in such rough terrain was an absolute requirement. Mining towns and trading posts, however, in which rampant individualism often did prevail, were places of much chicanery. People who had mined gold often lost their stakes to unscrupulous traders; those who owned land were driven off it with little compensation by railroad companies, among others. Fly-by-night banks frequently welshed on notes that they themselves had issued. An unfettered market, one without a community context, turned out to lack the essential moral underpinnings that trade requires, and not just by sound social relations.

In many ways these frontier settlements—with their washed-out social bonds, loose morals, and unbridled greed—were the forerunners of Wall Street in the 1980s. The Street became a "den of thieves," thick with knaves who held that anything went as long as you made millions more than the next guy. Moreover, the mood of self-centered "making it" of the me generation spilled over into large segments of society. It was celebrated by the White House and many in Congress, who saw in an unfettered pursuit of self-interest the social force that revitalizes economies and societies. By the end of the 1980s even some of the proponents of me-ism felt that the pursuit of greed had run amok.

By the early 1990s the waning of community, which had long concerned sociologists, became more pronounced and drew more attention. As writer Jonathan Rowe put it: "It was common to think about the community as we used to think about air and water. It is thee. It takes care of itself, and it can and will absorb whatever we unleash into it." Now it became evident that the social environment needed fostering just as nature did. Responding to the new cues, George Bush evoked the image of a "kinder, gentler" society as a central theme for his first presidential campaign in 1988. The time was right to return to community and the moral order it harbored. Bill Clinton made the spirit of community a theme of his 1992 campaign.

The prolonged recession of 1991–1992 and the generally low and slowing growth of the American economy worked against this new concern with we-ness. Interracial and interethnic tensions rose considerably, not only between blacks and whites, but also between blacks and Hispanics and among various segments of the community and Asian-Americans. This is one more reason why the United States will have to work its way to a stronger, growing, more competitive economy: interracial and ethnic peace are much easier to maintain in a rising than in a stagnant economy. However, it does not mean that community rebuilding has to be deferred until the economy is shored up. It does indicate that enhancing we-ness will require greater commitment and effort from both the government and the people if community rebuilding is to take place in a sluggish economy.

THE NEW COMMUNITY

Does this mean that we all have to move back to live in small towns and villages in order to ensure the social foundations of morality, to rebuild and shore up we-ness? Can one not bring up decent young people in the city? Isn't it possible to have a modern society, which requires a high concentration of labor and a great deal of geographic mobility—and still sustain a web of social bonds, a Communitarian nexus? There is more than one sociological answer to these queries.

First, many cities have sustained (or reclaimed) some elements of community. Herbert Gans, a Columbia University sociologist, observed that within cities there were what he called "urban villages." He found communities where, generally speaking, "neighbors were friendly and quick to say hello to each other," where the various ethnic groups, transients, and bohemians "could live together side by side without much difficulty." Gans further noted that "for most West Enders [in Boston]...life in the area resembled that found in the village or small town, and even in the suburb." Even in large metropolises, such as New York City, there are neighborhoods in which many people know their neighbors, their shop-keepers, and their local leaders. They are likely to meet one another in neighbor-hood bars, bowling alleys, and places of worship. They watch out for each other's safety and children. They act in concert to protect their parks and bus stops. They form political clubs and are a force in local politics. (Jim Sleeper's *Closest of Strangers* provides a fine description of these New York City communities.)

In some instances members of one ethnic group live comfortably next to one another, as in New York City's Chinatown and Miami's Little Havana. In other cities ethnic groups are more geographically dispersed but sustain ethnic-community bonds around such institutions as churches and synagogues, social clubs, and private schools. In recent decades a measure of return to community has benefited from the revival of loyalty to ethnic groups. While the sons and daughters of immigrants, the so-called second generation, often sought to assim-ilate, to become Americanized to the point that their distinct backgrounds were lost in a new identity, *their* children, the third generation and onward, often seek to reestablish their ethnic identity and bonds.

How does one reconcile the two sociological pictures—the James Q. Wilson concept of the city as *gesellschaft*, with little community or moral base, and the Herbert Gans image of *gemeinschaft*, of urban villages? The answer, first of all, is that both exist side by side. Between the urban villages, in row houses and high rises, you find large pockets of people who do not know their next-door neighbors, with whom they may have shared a floor, corridors, and elevators for a generation. Elderly people especially, who have no social bonds at work and are largely abandoned by their families, often lead rather isolated lives. In 1950 14.4 percent of those sixty-five years of age and older lived alone; by 1990 the per-centage stood at nearly 31 percent.

Also, to some extent a welcome return to a small-town life of sorts has been occurring in modern America. Although not all suburbs, which attracted millions of city dwellers, make for viable communities, as a rule the movement to the suburbs has enhanced the Communitarian nexus.

In addition, postmodern technology helps. More people are again able to work at home or nearby, and a high concentration of labor is less and less neces-sary, in contrast to the industrial age. People can use their computers and modems at home to do a good part of their office work, from processing insurance claims to trading worldwide in commodities, stocks, and bonds. Architects can design buildings and engineers monitor faraway power networks from their places of residence.

It used to be widely observed that Americans, unlike Europeans, move around so much that they are hard-pressed to put down real community roots. On average, it is said, the whole country moves about once every five years. These figures, however, may be a bit obsolete. For various reasons, in recent years Americans seem to move somewhat less often. One explanation is a growing desire to maintain the bonds of friendship and local social roots of their children, spouses, and themselves. In effect there is little reason to believe that the economy will suffer if this trend continues, and it may actually benefit from less shuttling around of people. Surely the Communitarian nexus will benefit.

Finally, there are new, nongeographic communities made up of people who do not live near one another. Their foundations may not be as stable and deep-rooted as residential communities, but they fulfill many of the social and moral functions of traditional communities. Work-based and professional communities are among the most common of these. That is, people who work together in a steel mill or a high tech firm such as Lotus or Microsoft often develop work-related friendships and community webs; groups of co-workers hang around together, play and party together, and go on joint outings. As they learn to know and care for one another, they also form and reinforce moral expectations.

Other communities are found in some law firms, on many campuses (although one community may not encompass everyone on campus), among physicians at the same hospital or with the same specialty in a town, and among some labor union members.

Some critics have attacked these communities as being artificially constructed, because they lack geographical definition or because they are merely social networks, without a residential concentration. Ray Oldenburg, author of *The Great Good Place*, decries the new definitions of community that encompass co-workers and even radio call-in show audiences. "Can we really create a satisfactory community apart from geography?" he asks. "My answer is 'no.'" But people who work every day in the same place spend more hours together and in closer proximity than people who live on the same village street. Most important, these nongeographic communities often provide at least some elements of the Communitarian nexus, and hence they tend to have the moral infrastructure we consider essential for a civil and humane society.

In short, our society is neither without community nor sufficiently Communitarian; it is neither *gemeinschaft* nor *gesellschaft*, but a mixture of the two sociological conditions. America does not need a simple return to *gemeinschaft*, to the traditional community. Modern economic prerequisites preclude such a shift, but even if it were possible, such backpedaling would be undesirable because traditional communities have been too constraining and authoritarian. Such traditional communities were usually homogeneous. What we need now are communities that balance both diversity and unity. As John W. Gardner has noted: "To prevent the wholeness from smothering diversity, there must be a philosophy of pluralism, an open climate for dissent, and an opportunity for subcommunities to retain their identity and share in the setting of larger group goals." Thus, we need to strengthen the communitarian elements in the urban and suburban centers, to provide the social bonds that sustain the moral voice, but at the same time avoid tight networks that suppress pluralism and dissent. James Pinkerton, who served in the Bush White House, speaks eloquently about a new paradigm focused around what he calls a "new *gemeinschaft*." It would be, he says, neither oppressive nor hierarchical. In short, we need new communities in which people have choices and readily accommodate divergent *sub*communities but still maintain common bonds.

WHAT CAN WE DO?

To strengthen the Communitarian nexus requires four measures, each of which deserves some discussion: changing orientation, changing the "habits of the heart"; working out conflicts between career needs and community bonds; redesigning our physical environment to render it more community friendly; and fostering volunteer endeavors that do not trivialize and squander our commitments to the commons.

Investing in the Communitarian Nexus

We constantly, whether we are conscious of it or not, choose how to invest our psychic energy, allocate our time, and invest our resources. Some who are under the spell of modernity, and who try to live up to the image of *gesellschaft*, choose to invest ever more of themselves in the pursuit of "making it": to gain a raise or a promotion, to advance their careers or profits one more notch, then another. To the extent that these efforts become their dominant pursuit, one to which all others are subordinated, "making it" becomes a self-defeating endeavor because it is inherently Sisyphean in nature. There is no point of satiation. It is an intrinsically *un*satisfying activity. Like other addictions and obsessions, the more one takes in, the more one requires—and the less one enjoys the process. Regardless of how much you earn or gain, there are always higher salaries and ranks to aspire to, always some Joneses ahead of you in the race. When financier Michael Milken was making $550 million a year, more than some nations, he cheated to make some more.

Social science findings leave no doubt that genuine inner satisfaction cannot be attained in this way. As a matter of fact, people whose incomes are higher are not happier than those whose incomes are lower. As Diane Swanbrow, who summarized the relevant data, observes: "Although poverty clearly makes people miserable, studies consistently show that having more than enough money to meet your needs doesn't guarantee more happiness." She also notes that as the real income of Americans rose dramatically from 1946 to 1978, Americans reported no increase in happiness. Indeed, the proportion of those who reported that they were happy with their fate and those who were discontented did not change.

Also, there is little difference in personal contentment among countries, regardless of their socioeconomic conditions, according to a cross-national study by political scientists Ronald Inglehart and opinion research Jacques-René Rabier. For example, the United States and Great Britain were neck and neck in satisfaction scores (7.57 vs. 7.52), despite the fact that the average income in the United States was twice that of Britain when the study was conducted. Moreover, Northern Ireland and Ireland, both with rather low GNPs per capita, ranked higher in satisfaction scores (at 7.77 and 7.76) than either the United States or Britain. Japan ranked second to last in satisfaction scores in the Inglehart and Rabier study, "beaten" only by Greece, with a *much* lower per capita GNP.

Further, R. A. Easterlin, in a review of other data from nineteen countries, concluded that "richer countries are not typically happier than poorer ones... By and large, the evidence indicates no relation—positive or negative—between happiness and national income." In short, once your elementary needs are sated, chasing money won't make you more content.

People are better off when they combine their self-advancement with investment in their community. The observations made earlier about children and spouses hold for relatives, friends, and neighbors: people who have several significant others with whom they have meaningful, stable, affective relationships—especially when they share a sense of we-ness with one or more groups of people—are psychologically much better off than those who do not.

There are many well-known ways to develop, cultivate, and nourish these relationships. Popular self-help books for singles are full of advice that applies to couples as well: join a church group, do some volunteer work, go fishing or bowling together with other couples. Preparing dinners for guests has become less popular as many people work full days outside the home, but Communitarian meals (in which all participants contribute a dish) are growing in social acceptance. These are all small steps that, at least potentially, enhance not merely one-on-one relations but we-ness as well.

The problem is not listing ways to enhance the Communitarian nexus, but to make the commitment to connect and sustain the effort, despite some initial awkwardness. Community facilitators may be a modern necessity. Here I do not mean quick-buck dating services that often exploit the lonely, but individuals who organize social activities in which interpersonal and social bonds can be initiated. These may range from church choirs to weekend outings, from groups that discuss books to groups that organize charity events.

The best social events do not merely develop social bonds, but also serve a Communitarian purpose, from organizing neighborhood crime watches to running soup kitchens. Groups that focus directly on the social relations themselves, like parties for singles aimed at fishing for dates, are often less socially constructive; more effective groups are those where members focus on bettering others and allow social networks to evolve as a by-product. Even investment clubs and bridge groups seem to do better than most meet-a-mate pot lucks.

True, some of these social activities can be fairly shallow; this is especially the case when get-togethers are limited in scope, intensity, and regularity. Thus a onetime evening of folk dancing at the local church is not nearly as socially constructive as a folk dance group that meets every week. Even the best book club is not as involving as an Alcoholics Anonymous chapter. (The same holds for many organizations that follow the AA pattern, from groups that help people cope with cancer to those that support those who have children or spouses who are addicted.) Centers for senior citizens are particularly effective because beyond fostering one-on-one relations, they often encompass group activities and provide a continual, often daily, community space.

It is sociologically naive to sit back and wait for new communities to spring up. It is often necessary, and there is nothing artificial or otherwise improper, in recruiting or training organizers and facilitators of we-ness. (One way this is done, for instance by the Montgomery County Volunteer and Community Service Center, is to provide an office that trains volunteers and helps them find opportunities for service as well as occasions to get together with other volunteers to exchange experiences, to recognize achievements, and—to socialize.) Sure, some group leaders may be tedious, overbearing, or a bit pompous. But such human frailties are far from unknown among leaders of natural communities. When all is said and done, the more individuals dedicate themselves to fostering a Communitarian nexus, the more their fellow persons will join in and bring about the revival of communities where they are waning.

Harmonizing Careers and the Communitarian Nexus

Under the spell of the curse of either/or that befuddles much of our thinking, many young people view their alternatives as either a career of self-centered aggrandizement ("making a million before you are thirty") or a life of social service and self-sacrifice. Joining a religious order provided a dedicated and ascetic existence in earlier times; more recently, joining the Peace Corps provided an outlet for such altruistic aspirations.

The sociological fact, though, is that one's interests in finding a career and serving the community can be fused in many ways, avoiding the two extremes of a life of self-aggrandizement and one of self-sacrifice. Former president Jimmy Carter, unlike several other ex-presidents, provides a fine role model that shows one can earn a decent living without being consumed by attempts to swell one's bankroll. He does not sell his time to the highest bidder, or help Japanese corporations promote their wares, or spend his retirement days playing golf. He set up a center to study many key international problems; helped negotiate peace in Ethiopia; and builds housing for the poor in several cities, without starving, although he must do without stretch limos and his wife without tiaras and designer dresses. As a result, Carter is now widely recognized as our best former president and bakes in the appreciation of many Americans. He must feel at the end of the day the special glow of an inner affirmation of having done right and good.

For the rest of us, nursing, teaching, and social work all provide careers that are reasonably rewarding in the traditional sense of a career and, at the same time (if carried out with dedication), often contribute directly to the community. A physician does not have to choose between tucking tummies and lifting breasts in Beverly Hills and family medicine in the Gobi Desert. There are many medical pursuits, such as emergency medicine, in which a doctor can lead a rewarding life that is also of service.

Similarly, lawyers' choices range beyond specializing in fanning conflicts between spouses (and turning them into protracted divorce proceedings that run up the legal bills) and spending their lives as public defenders. Lawyers who spend much of their lives *resolving* conflicts between clients will find themselves socially constructive and still able to pay the rent.

When *gesellschaft* was considered all the rage, when modernity reigned, it was considered good corporate policy to move managers around frequently. As a consequence, social bonds of all kinds—of the extended family, friendships on and off the job, relations with neighbors, and those of young people in schools— were disrupted regularly to serve real or imaginary corporate and career needs. Moving as often as once every three years was far from unknown. In recent years, however, it has become evident that many companies may do quite well, and perhaps even better, if their employees are moved around less often, allowing them to cultivate rather than uproot their Communitarian roots.

In general, there is a need for corporations to become not only more family friendly, but also more community friendly. I do not mean merely to contribute to the local Red Cross, children's museum, and chamber music society, but to examine their policies from a community standpoint. Moving corporate headquarters to another town fifty miles away may lower a corporation's office-space costs, but it will also severely disrupt the social bonds of many employees. And the savings in costs may well be less than the losses due to a decline in morale and increases in tardiness, absenteeism, and resentment that such disruptions often engender.

Closing plans that are the mainstay of a community sometimes cannot be avoided, but such closing should not be undertaken capriciously or abruptly. Affected communities should be accorded an opportunity to help the corporation solve its economic problems or to find buyers for the plant (including its workers), if it is to be sold rather than transferred. At least the employees should be afforded some time (and, if at all possible, financial help) to assist them and their community to adapt. Even those who are opposed to government controls as a rule may see merit in new laws that slow plant closings by corporations that are grossly insensitive to community needs.

Communitarian Design, Architecture, and Planning

To make our physical environment more community friendly, our homes, places of work, streets, and public spaces—whole developments, suburbs, and even whole cities—need to be designed to enhance the Communitarian nexus. Although paying attention to the effects of architecture and city planning on the

Communitarian nexus is hardly a new idea, it is a consideration often given short shift. An era dedicated to a return to we-ness would value and promote design that is pro-community.

A systematic study of the numerous ways to proceed is a major topic for future Communitarian studies. Here are some places to start, places others have been and more need to turn:

On a small scale: *Provide people shared space to mingle.* It does not require a grand social science study to note that when chairs are placed in the empty spaces in many public buildings next to the elevators, people are often found there "visiting." The same holds true for other places to sit, from park benches to lounges in public libraries. Sure, there are some sterile places (such as the huge, wind-swept plazas among the high-rise buildings in downtown Minneapolis) in which probably no set of benches could foster sociability. These are the exceptions, however, that do not disprove the rule.

Sandboxes and playgrounds don't work just for kids. Some of my best friends are those I met when I watched over my sons' play in the sandboxes of Riverside Drive in New York City. The streets adjacent to Riverside Drive, which had no strips of park to accommodate such play areas, had much less social life.

Even high-rise buildings can be made more community friendly. Just having in-house services, such as self-service laundries and barber shops, offers residents some places to get to know one another and to "hang out." Some have in-house restaurants, in which tenants (and outsiders) can eat. Community swimming pools, tennis courts, and such simple sports facilities as basketball hoops or volleyball nets are socially constructive. If you set aside rooms to play cards, dominoes, and chess, more often than not they fill up, demonstrating the unstated need for social connectedness.

On a larger scale: *Plan developments in ways that enhance rather than hinder the sociological mix that sustains a community.* For instance, earmarking a proportion of a building's units for senior citizens, by providing small units with small kitchens and by enhancing safety devices, will ensure the presence and comfort of elders. They, in turn, provide a group of adults who are on the premises during the workday and when children come home and make it easier for families that wish to attend to their parents to be able to maintain their extended families rather than institutionalize elders prematurely in remote nursing homes.

Whole developments are now being designed around courtyards, rather than buildings set row upon row. Public and social spaces are set aside for the role that traditional plazas served. An old chocolate factory in San Francisco (Ghirardelli Square) and a railroad station in Washington, D.C. (Union Station), have been converted into bustling social spaces, in which people interact merrily, safely, and in constructive ways. Numerous shopping malls are opened early to allow senior citizens safe and heated (or air-conditioned) spaces to walk. Pedestrian pockets, in which automobiles are banned and people can stroll and promenade and visit with one another, are springing up in many urban centers.

Thirty years ago a student of urban planning, Jane Jacobs, recommended that buildings be integrated into the street. She argued that windows be kept low and face the street, so that mothers would be able to prepare dinner and keep a watchful eye on their children. By the same token, the streets would be safer and encourage people to hang around together. Similarly, she pointed out that short blocks, with corners dedicated to shops, favor sociability. Wide pavements encourage children to play in front of their houses. Vest-pocket parks and gardens are more community friendly than grand ones or those designed for decoration and effect. In London, for example, one often finds sets of buildings that together form a pleasant enclosed space used for a garden. Those who live on the block have keys to the garden gates and can send their children to play in the shared safe area.

Extreme attempts to be community friendly are found in totally planned towns such as Reston, Virginia; Columbia, Maryland; Roosevelt Island, New York; and Irvine, California. Here, schools, libraries, bike paths, and social spaces have all been carefully located to enhance community. Not all of these arrangements are successful. Some, in fact, are excessively regimented and costly. Others presume that people will give up the use of their cars.

Recently several designers of what are called "new villages" have called attention to the fact that existing zoning regulations reflect the days when workplaces were smoky, ugly factories that were kept out of suburbs. Now these designers see a need to integrate residential units with workplaces, interspersed with shops. This reorganization is said to allow people to walk, within a quarter of a mile, to most places they need to be. It would reduce the use of cars and enhance the formation of social webs—the basis of community.

These ideas may leave some wrinkles to be worked out. Having carried groceries for one-fourth of a mile, I would prefer in my old age to have them delivered if I am to give up the use of my car. But surely they indicate directions that are to be explored if the design of space is to support a community rather than be a hindrance.

COMMUNITARIAN ACTION: MAKING IT COUNT

So much has been written about Tocqueville's America, the land of voluntary associations and activities, that the notion that Americans are much more active Communitarians than Europeans has become a sociological cliché. Indeed, in America there are many tens of thousands of associations that promote block parties, babysitting pools, lodges, and clubs. One is tempted to bless them, saying, "May they grow, flourish, and multiply," and let them be. However, for them to sustain the *gemeinschaft* elements in a society that tends toward *gesellschaft*, it is essential that Communitarian activities not be trivialized.

We must learn to distinguish between activities that provide at least a reasonable modicum of opportunity to serve the commons and those that provide all too facile a way to discharge our obligation to the commons. True, for busy homemakers with a full-time paying job and a houseful of children, making some cookies for the PTA might be all they can do. Usually, though, the community must ask people for greater and more consequential contributions.

Peter Drucker, one of our leading pundits, made a strong case that in the 1990s we will need to rely even more on voluntary efforts than in the past. He expects that attempts by governments to provide for numerous social needs will continue to suffer both a shortage of funds and what seems to be a congenital inability to provide services that match in quality those that voluntary associations regularly render.

It will not do simply to urge people to turn off lights to help conserve energy or require New Yorkers to request a glass of water in restaurants (rather than being routinely served one) to save water. Plugging the leak in one of New York City's many old water mains would save more water and electricity than such "public services." It might be argued that the purpose of such measures is public education, to sensitize people to the need to conserve. However, phony devices are not educational. Most of the public realizes that the benefits of these measures are slight at best (and phony at worst), which adds to their alienation from public authorities and community causes. Public education should endeavor to find ways to highlight genuine steps the public can undertake that are truly helpful.

Trivialization is particularly likely once politicians try to use American Communitarian inclinations to avoid having to make major public commitments. President Bush's 1988 election slogan of seeking a gentler and kinder society was quite welcome and timely, following eight years of unabashed celebration of conspicuous consumption and greed. However, when his rhetoric yielded largely to the "thousand points of light" program, it became something of a joke, even among many of his supporters. The "points" are too often awarded for activities that entail rather little service, such as some visits to a nursing home by a few members of the community. Commendable, to be sure, but hardly worthy of presidential honors.

I have long supported a year of national service for young Americas. As a result I have attended more than my share of meetings on the subject, and I am still a member of a national secretariat that promotes national service. In these meetings I have noticed a curious development. Every few years someone comes forward and suggests activities that are to qualify as "national service" that are less taxing and less of service than those previously suggested—such as going downtown from comfortable suburban homes to assist in public libraries for a few hours. (Some would even reward such "national service" with college fellowships.) As I see it, it does not serve us well to squander our Communitarian approbations. The term *national service* is best reserved for those who make a significant contribution of time or effort.

Serious community endeavors that deserve our appreciation are illustrated by the following two prime examples, chosen from the scores that could be given.

Nearly half of the nation's 486,000 emergency medical technicians (EMTs) are unpaid volunteers. Volunteer EMTs do virtually everything professionals do: they monitor the victim's vital signs, provide an initial diagnosis, stop bleeding, transport the victim to a hospital, or call for emergency helicopter evacuation.

Volunteers have completed an extensive training program (sometimes taking as long as 120 hours) and are usually trained to perform CPR (cardiopulmonary resuscitation) and administer first aid. EMT volunteers must be willing to see other persons suffer greatly, even die, and cope with the resulting trauma; they must be willing to risk themselves to pull people out of fires or overturned cars. Many towns and villages still have only voluntary ambulance crews and EMTs.

Similarly, the Seattle CPR program highlights what community service is all about. To appreciate its importance, you must take into account that medical studies show that victims of heart failure will have a much stronger chance for survival if they are resuscitated in the field. Indeed, the main result of having to wait for an ambulance crew for medical service to be initiated is often a dehumanizing and costly death. In contrast, victims who received CPR from citizens, without waiting for an ambulance, are *twice* as likely to recover as those who had to wait for professional care.

Given these facts, if you mush have a heart failure, try to have it in Seattle. Unlike the residents of most cities, as many as 40 percent of those suffering out-of-hospital heart failure in Seattle have their resuscitations begun by bystanders, *before* they are moved to a hospital. By 1988 Medic II, which trains citizens to perform CPR, had certified more than 400,000 Seattle-area residents. Between them, the good citizens of Seattle have already saved hundreds of lives and sustain many others on a much more meaningful level.

These are but two examples of how dedicated individual effort benefits the community. Staffing telephone hot lines for those who are suicidal or runaways, running kitchens or clinics for the homeless, shelters for battered women, being a PAL to a child from a disadvantaged background—these are among many genuine community services.

In Conclusion

The 1990s are going to be difficult economic times. Beyond the usual ups and downs, we face an economy whose growth rate has been slowing down for decades and that has accumulated mountains of debt that it used largely to enhance consumption rather than investment—in short, an economy that will not return quickly to a high growth pathway. In this context it will be even more important for members of communities to reach out and help one another and those of less endowed communities.

Even if the American economy performs much better than it has since the early 1970s, there is a need to restore stronger social bonds, not merely friend to friend but among groups of people, the Communitarian nexus.

John Nirenberg, Ph.D., founded the Center for Workplace Community, based in Denver, Colorado. He is a social scientist, consultant, and professor. He is the author of several books, most recently *The Living Organization: Transforming Teams into Workplace Communities*. Nirenberg has a long-standing commitment to helping organizations and individuals explore the power of workplace community as a way of sustaining high performance in organizations. He speaks widely on the subject of workplace community and helps top-level managers build vibrant, living organizations that are both effective in achieving their goals and in creating satisfying places in which to work.

His clients include organizations in the United States, Southeast Asia, and Australia.

26

Workplace Community: The Struggle for Legitimacy

John Nirenberg

Frank is an engineer in a high tech firm in Silicon Valley. He got excited about building workplace community and sent a memo around his department asking people to join him for an informal discussion of the idea. Before the meeting was held, however, the human resources department heard about Frank's plans and immediately ordered him to stop or face the first step in a formal disciplinary hearing for insubordination. Frank stopped. He now works elsewhere.

Brenda is a dean at an urban university experiencing serious infighting and turmoil following the appointment of a new provost who has dramatically upset the academic culture. Brenda decided that workplace community was a way of rebuilding her department's morale and sense of purpose. She arranged a workshop for the faculty and staff of her school to explore how they could maintain positive work relationships given the turmoil being generated from above. She was successful. Her department stabilized and developed a camaraderie that helped them weather the storm. Their relationships are now open, communicative, and show mutual good will.

Frank and Brenda demonstrate two inescapable truths: First, introducing community into a typical organization is fraught with the perils that befall any challenge to the status quo. Second, community building requires a strong personal commitment.

Brenda and Frank's experiences are telling in yet another way: the organization either tolerated their efforts or crushed them. Therein lies the fatal flaw facing all organizational reforms: The inherent nature of the system is designed to reflect the centralized power and decision making at the pinnacle of a hierarchy that responds solely to the interests of the CEO as the representative of the board of directors. It is the CEO's will and values that permeate the organization. This occurs because all subordinate officers are ultimately beholden to the CEO for their tenure, their future prospects, and their very livelihood. The character and personality of the CEO will become that of the organization. Because of their position, managers begin to anticipate the thinking of the CEO and act upon that presumption. That is how managers are expected to behave and how they earn approval, promotions, and raises.

The rise of corporate power and its tendency toward total control over those who must work in them was noted almost fifty years ago by one of America's foremost captains of industry. In 1948, Theodore Quinn, chairman of the board of General Electric, declared that these "brute economic monsters" are "leading our country just as surely as the sun sets to a brand of totalitarianism which is a perversion as far from individualism, civil liberties, and the democratic process as Russian Communism."[1]

In a world where democracy is breaking out in some of the unlikeliest places, in a world more committed now than ever before to the idea of liberty, it is sadly ironic that Americans willingly surrender themselves to corporate tyranny.

- How have we come to accept the sacrifice of over half of our waking consciousness devoted to earning a living without the slightest thought to the propriety of the relationships in the workplace?
- How have we come to totally surrender ourselves to an impersonal workplace bureaucracy that defies our influence and distributes power so unevenly?
- How have we come to accept and legitimize the powers of unelected, unaccountable bosses to pursue profit-making without considering the quality of work life for those they manage?
- How do we continue to justify all business decisions made solely for the financial bottom line, believing these actions fully discharge management's responsibility to all stakeholders?

Frank didn't want to leave his friends and work associates, his career and benefits, his car pool. He was humiliated and demeaned by an arbitrary and unassailable use of power that totally destroyed his efforts to build a better organization. And where were his friends? Too intimidated to stand up for him, they were silenced by fear for their jobs. At least Frank had the dignity to defend his self-respect and took his talents elsewhere. Yet, ninety-nine percent of all organizations do not honor the kind of initiative that Frank displayed. It is simply too challenging to the way things are. It threatens the "powers that be" with a loss of control.

Contemporary community-building efforts survive only so long as they are granted permission or are allowed to exist due to a benign tolerance. Unless reformers engage in political processes to redistribute power and accountability, community building will experience a tenuous existence and become just another management fad, at best.

I look at our organizations from the conviction that they are the major influence on our day-to-day experience of community and that the issues we face in the workplace greatly influence not only the quality of our work lives but the overall quality of our lives. Thus, as we turn our attention to the workplace as a locale for building a meaningful sense of community, a new political frontier will emerge. In building community in our organizations we must redefine our workplace relationships. Being dismissed as simply another "factor in the production process" will no longer be acceptable to people devoted to doing good work. Just being a "human resource" to be used and discarded by organizations will no longer be acceptable. If we are to visualize our organizations as communities we need to convey a sense of organizational citizenship to each person in them. In building workplace community we need to grapple with the issues of personal efficacy and establish a new understanding of the relationship between the individual and the organization as well as the nature of all workplace interpersonal relationships.

With this new realization—that organizations are indeed arbiters of our way of life, and that individual employees must have the right to influence their destiny at work—a new era of corporate governance will dawn. Then, the process of building workplace community can be initiated and will stand a chance of success.

A New Milestone in American Democracy?

The call for workplace community is the latest in a long litany of pleas for workplace reform. In this century it began with Upton Sinclair's 1906 expose of the meat packing industry in his explosive novel The Jungle. It was one of the catalysts that ushered in the progressive era in American politics. Many reforms were fashioned and real change occurred because the movement led to a change in the structures of our lives through the political process. Exhortation alone was not enough. Shortly afterwards, social scientists began showing the importance of positive human relations on productivity in the workplace and their research and prescriptions to management became known as the "human relations school" of management thought. More recently, participative management, humanistic management, eupsychian management, Theory Z, excellence, and, currently, self-directed work teams have declared the traditional organizational system inappropriate for contemporary needs. Yet, the traditional system persists. Instead of ushering in a new system, each reform has faded in its turn.

One case dramatically demonstrates both the difficulty in challenging the status quo and the myth that managers will respond to scientific evidence that productivity improves with community-building efforts. A 1992 Fortune article reported that "The Gaines pet food plant in Topeka Kansas, just celebrated 20 years of self-management. For two decades under three owners...Topeka has always placed first when its labor productivity was compared with that of other pet food plants within its company." Why haven't the other plants followed the twenty years of evidence that the self-managed plant was most productive? Management intransigence. The need to crush change, even when it is demonstrably best for profits, is due to management's attachment to the powers and perks of office. It is the rare manager who can turn away from the seductive trappings of power for which they have vied throughout their professional careers.

By now it should be evident that lasting workplace reform has not and will not take root upon the initiative of the owners and managers of American enterprise. Except for the occasional workplace experiment and noblesse oblige of an enlightened chief executive, all lasting reform has been instigated by legislatures, courts, or unions.

The call for workplace community, in spite of a so-called societal transformation to a "new paradigm," enjoys no better chance of success from within than the myriad techniques and philosophies that have come before it—unless it includes fundamental changes in the structure of organizations, the re-design of their internal relationships, and the reformulation of assumptions about one's appropriate role in the workplace.

WORKPLACE COMMUNITY IN THE LONG VIEW

The good news is that the relationship between the individual and societal institutions has been on an inexorable journey from autocracy to democracy. Though there have been dark ages and various regressions, there has been fairly consistent movement toward granting rights and entitlements to individuals who were once denied them. (See Figure 1: Milestones In Democratization.) Owners and managers of modern organizations are just the latest in a long line of dominating forces that have assumed powers over individuals in the neo-feudal realms we call businesses. Undoubtedly the future will witness the extension of democratic principles into our workplaces and the conversion of bosses to "work partners" as a way of resolving the individual—organizational conflict. As in the civil body, it will not happen without a deliberate effort; and, building workplace community will only come about when organizations are accepted as being legitimate venues for exercising one's civic responsibilities.

Today, it is the corporation that assumes the hands-on governance of people at work. It is called "management," but no matter what one calls it, this relationship fundamentally establishes an imbalance of power over individuals' lives. If one accepts a job, it is assumed he or she will abide by the employer's terms of service that include obedience to a boss who is unaccountable to the subordinate. As can be readily deduced (and verified through a massive literature on work and the conditions of labor) the corporation and its managers have an influence over each worker similar to that of dictators, monarchs and undemocratic governments from which humankind struggled for millennia to wrest its fundamental liberties in the first place.

The rise of the corporation with proprietary privileges extending to the purchase and management of people, as if they are like any other resource, surely seems to place humankind back into a dependent position whose livelihood once again is determined by a fundamentally totalitarian social structure: corporate bureaucracies. Until very recently, the corporation was immune from

Figure 1: Milestones in Democratization

- Glorious Revolution in Britain establishing parliamentary supremacy, 1688
- US first modern republic, first nation of choice, 1783
- Separation of Powers, Checks and Balances, 1789
- French Revolution and emergence of constitutional government, 1789
- U.S. Bill of Rights, 1791
- Modern corporations established mid 1800s
- Slavery ended in the US., 1863
- Voting rights for black males, 1870
- Feudalism ended in Japan, 1871
- Regulation of corporations begun, 1896
- Direct election of senators, 1913
- Voting rights for women, 1920
- Trade unions safeguarded, 1930s
- Right to economic security established, 1930s
- Collective bargaining instituted, 1930s
- Court-ordered school desegregation, 1954
- Due process at work, 1960s
- Equal opportunity guaranteed for women, minorities and those over 40, 1964
- Right to a court-provided legal defense (Miranda Decision), 1966
- Occupational Safety and Health Admin., 1970
- Environmental Protection Agency, 1970
- Consumer protection/product liability, 1970s
- Vote extended to 18-year-olds, 1971
- European communist states hold elections, 1989
- Americans with Disabilities Act, 1990
- Soviet Union collapses, 1991
- Gay rights, children's rights, animal rights, Earth rights, workers' rights, minimum guaranteed income, organization as polity leading to corporate citizenship, 199? - 20??

adherence to basic constitutional requirements such as free speech, due process, and the right to organize. Even now, expressions of individual rights as they are understood in the larger community are not secure within the vast majority of organizational environments.

Thus, in order to allow the real feeling of community to blossom in our workplaces, we will first need to alter the structure of our relationships and the distribution of power within organizations. A new social contract articulating each person's rights and responsibilities will be required.

While great pains were taken to cautiously assign powers to our political leaders with many checks and balances, and separations of responsibilities, to guard against what is believed to be the inevitable corruption of those in office, we have neglected to address the full scope and use of executive power as it is applied to people in the workplace. Only now is this issue coming to the fore as the sexual harassment of women, just one form of abuse due to the imbalance of power in workplace relationships, dramatically grabs our attention.

Men have been suffering workplace abuse for years as well. For example, they have been moved around a corporate domain like a pawn on a chessboard. For years IBM used to be called "I've Been Moved" by many employees because men aspiring to a lifetime career were sent to distant parts of the far flung corporate empire at a moment's notice. Failure to move was seen as a career, and sometimes a job, limiting decision. Of course the men's (only recently have women also felt this abuse as well) families were expected to be supportive throughout the years spent hither and yon.

As long as people must work to earn a living and organizational rewards and power are unfairly distributed, the struggle between the individual and the corporation will continue. Each manager must become accountable to the governed and each individual accountable to the whole. Building community indeed means including everyone in the shared process of governing. Each person must have an equal say regarding internal managerial issues and policy while compensation, or the role one plays in an organization, will be a matter of assessing the individual according to acquired skills and how they are best applied to the tasks at hand.

Charters or constitutions will be necessary to specify institutional structures that will guarantee employee participation in decision making and a procedure for amending the process, when necessary, through a consensual mechanism. Community cannot be created unless employee rights to privacy, due process, free speech and the right to not being harassed for political or sexual favors are all guaranteed.

Can a democratic society that traces its foundation to a war over the right to self-determination force people to work without a role in policy and decision-making, especially when it affects their livelihood? John Stuart Mill wrote: "The principle of freedom cannot require that mankind should be free not to be free. It is not freedom to be allowed to alienate his (or her) freedom." Yet, when it comes to life in organizations, we all too often do exactly that. Fortunately, leading edge companies are forging a future that promises to correct this unfortunate state of being and, through building a shared community of interest among managers and employees, find they are better able to reach their economic objectives. As welcomed as they are, their efforts have not yet been institutionalized. They can still be revoked at any time.

One family brewery, for example, recently turned to an outside individual to be CEO. His first two acts almost caused a revolution. Upon his arrival, after the company had devoted a long time instituting teams, he unilaterally declared that there was "no time for that anymore." Attention first had to be placed on "improving the profitability picture" as if teamwork and profitability were unrelated! Second, to get new ideas he believed it was necessary to "churn up the organization." His plan was to fire the bottom 10% of performers each year. It was this particularly nasty and totally misguided effort that the brewery owners refused to agree with. "After all, we have been like a family here for generations." While this second act was reversed, the CEO remains at the helm. Still, the efforts of the organization development department to build self-managing, high-performing teams was obliterated over night and the very productivity sought by the new CEO was reduced even further. The organization is in disarray. So much for noblesse oblige.

It is for that reason that workplace community cannot genuinely be created until serious attention is drawn to the "traditional law of the master-servant relationship which, in the main holds that management can fire an employee for cause, for no cause, or for cause morally wrong," as Ewing wrote in 1981. Since the early 1970s this tradition has come under fire. But as long as all power emanates from the pinnacle of the organizational hierarchy with no checks and balances, and no consent of the governed, the imbalance of power will continue to result in abuses and community-building will be stifled.

With the adoption of a bill of rights, "rights then become not what one can give a worker, but what no one can take away," as Ramsey Clark reminded us. The second area of concern moves away from merely protecting oneself from corporate abuses and the infringement of personal rights to the issue of establishing an equitable role for each person, or their representative, in the mechanics of corporate governance. It is not difficult to see how employees would consider full participation in the decision-making process a logical extension of their "rights" since their livelihood for the most part now depends on decisions by people far removed from them in the organization.

As the struggle to win these rights unfolds, enlightened personnel practices, government regulations, and union-management agreements influence the extent to which companies welcome workplace community.

SELF-MANAGING TEAMS AS A PRELUDE TO COMMUNITY

As with all human endeavors, the past is prologue; the vistas and prospects for change are indeed vast. The recent self-management movement has been gaining much attention lately, besides its positive impact on productivity, because it asserts that employee rights must include a measure of control over one's work by the individual. Its goals are to secure, in addition to rights, respect, a proprietary feeling about one's work, and equality of treatment and opportunity for employees as organizational citizens. People have to know there is hope for them. As Einer Thorsrud, an advocate of self-management said 20 years ago, "If we are not successful in giving meaning to their lives, then we may see the terrible turmoil of the end of technological society....If you don't make changes in the way people work, an increasing number of companies...will find that there are simply no more people to do the work for them, even when these people are going hungry."

To implement a self-management program is to begin the transformation of organizations into communities, to articulate new relationships among people and to enable each worker to make decisions about his or her life. Ultimately, a self-management program abolishes the dichotomy between manager and worker. It enhances the growth and development of individual, company, and society alike. As we have seen, however, these programs must be designed so they are not what "can be given a worker, but what no one can take away."

To succeed in achieving workplace community both a new managerial and a new workers' consciousness are required. All organizational members belong to and benefit from the company. "Labor is an asset to be enriched rather than a production input to be consumed and discarded once no longer needed," wrote Adizes and Borgese in Self Management. Each person should be willing to take personal responsibility for the success of the organization and develop a sense of responsibility to society at large. Unfortunately, conventional management co-opts the agenda and summarily dismisses the employees' ability to contribute beyond the task at hand. Therein lies much of the reason that each reform and progressive management technique has failed—almost as if an organizational immune system is at work preventing their success. Labor, on the other hand, has too frequently abdicated their responsibility for the success of the organization and focused too narrowly on settling wage and benefit issues. Until both parties realize that a mutual concern for the success of the organization is required, the insidious and destructive competition between them will cripple them both.

MAKING WORKPLACE COMMUNITY A REALITY

Once organizations are seen as communities, it is quite possible that political activism will spread from city halls, statehouses and the streets of Washington into the boardrooms, executive suites, offices, and shop floors of the nation. This consciousness revolution could succeed in altering the fundamental structure of business organizations for the first time since the advent of the Industrial Revolution.

A few years ago this was unimaginable. Today, the evidence of a mounting readiness is widespread and abundant; examples are everywhere. Ubiquitous professional meetings and networking events find agendas filled with speakers and workshops on "Dealing With Downsizing: Are You Next?"; "Are You Fulfilling Your Potential at Work? How To Revitalize Your Career"; "Leadership Through Empowerment"; "How to Build Self Managing Work Teams"; "Counting Your Own Hours; Creating Your Own Benefits," etc. Even CEO's are being bombarded from their traditionally conservative and reactionary business and trade organizations to re-examine the place of the corporation in the larger community and to acknowledge the legitimacy of including stakeholders as well as stockholders in the corporate decision-making process. The pain of organizational life is endemic in the system and the symptoms can no longer be ignored.

THE MOVE TOWARD WORKPLACE COMMUNITY HAS MANY FRONTS

A self-styled study group of middle managers is circulating underground white-papers on reforming and redesigning organizations to become more responsive to individual needs and to honor our humanity in the workplace. American corporate employees, middle managers, white collar employees and labor, are becoming intolerably restive like East Europeans before the collapse of communism. They are no longer willing to suffer the numbness that comes from being part of the status quo when the future demands so much more; when to continue business as usual is to defy one's own common sense that the times call for a change. Not surprisingly, union membership has reversed a fourteen year decline and added 200,000 new members to their rolls in 1993.

Furthering the impetus for change, computer workstations now provide individuals access to vast on-line networks throughout the nation and most of the industrialized world. Tune in to "The Well," an electronic network based in the San Francisco Bay Area, for example, and you will become part of an endless conversation about many subjects including changing the nature of our organizations and the future of economic life on the planet. These discussions result in frequent informal meetings that raise the consciousness among individuals who then generate reform efforts within their companies.

Others fed up with business as usual but unsure of how to stem the tide of organizational abuse have withdrawn their energy and have become virtually "retired on the job"—part of an army of employed going through the motions until they intellectually starve their organizations into reform or until community-building enters the next phase and they can find a way to purposefully act to reform their organizations.

Pressures from within these networks increase the likelihood of regulation becoming an acceptable way of changing the reluctant organization. Equal employment opportunity (most recently for the disabled), worker's compensation, environmental and safety issues, have all been regulated into organizational life because of the commitment of unions and external networks. It is only a short step to including issues of governance, participation in decision making, compensation, and myriad other issues facing the organizational community, on the regulators' agenda.

Of course, organizations can choose to make community happen. When community-building consciousness fully permeates the organization, companies may voluntarily change. However, being reminded of Jefferson's dictum that "...Mankind are more disposed to suffer, while Evils are sufferable, than to right themselves by abolishing the Forms to which they are accustomed," workplace community building will be as difficult a force to move forward as the status quo will be to move aside. Building workplace community will take some kind of activism similar to that which has resulted in establishing each of the democratic milestones we have achieved so far. It is the employees, not the investors and managers, who have the most to gain. Therefore, employees will need to actively pursue a change in the structure of their organizations either through internal means or through the external political process in order to give community building a chance to succeed. In times that are "sufferable" these activists will also need one more thing: a great deal of personal courage.

Robert A. Mang

has broad experience in business and public policy. He founded Heritage Homes and Investments of Palo Alto, a California real estate investment and development company, was a principle owner of ReloAction, a corporate relocation service company, program director of the National Committee on U.S.-China Relations, and senior program officer of the Salk Institute's Biology and Human Affairs Program. He is currently a consultant for strategic planning and organizational development.

In a civic capacity, he chairs the World Business Academy's Sustainable Economy Project, is chairman of the International Rivers Network, and serves on boards of the WBA and Living Structures, a Santa Fe environmental development company. He also chaired a Santa Clara County Housing Task Force, was a commissioner on Bay Vision 2020 (a nine-county San Francisco Bay Area regional planning panel), and president of Greenbelt Alliance.

He and his wife Pamela live in Santa Fe, New Mexico.

27

Principles for Sustainability

Robert A. Mang

> I needed to get out of the mindstuff that took me upward…I needed to get down to Earth…Later I would understand that magic lives in the ordinary world, in the details of our everyday lives. It is in those simple moments that we can really appreciate the magic of this world. When Buddha realized enlightenment, he touched the Earth. This gesture connected him to the world, it made him the world's relation. I needed to "touch the Earth."
>
> —Joan Halifax, *The Fruitful Darkness*

Community is an act of Will—not individual willpower, but a collective or higher order Will. It requires commitment to engage in a dynamic natural process that enables coalescence of diversity toward a common purpose. A sustainable community is life giving for generations. It includes people and place engaged in value-adding, reciprocal relationships. It evolves in harmony with changing demands on its internal and external environments. It can range in size from neighborhood to village, city, or region, depending on the capacity of its people to remember their purpose as a community and to be conscious of their impact on others in their universe.

A society passes laws and uses law enforcement in an attempt to maintain internal order. Community is different. Its order is derived from internalized principles that guide its behavior. The development of principles is fundamental to our becoming able to be conscious and to manifest effective and sustainable order. The more we are able to expand our capacity for consciousness, the more diversity and complexity we are able to coalesce into community and thereby evolve into higher order value.

These ideas describe a real community that, today, embraces a city of 1.5 million people. The city is Curitiba, capital of Parana, Brazil. A very brief story illustrates the importance of committing to a place, the potential realized from coalescing diversity toward a common purpose, and adhering to the principle of working for reciprocal, value-adding relationships.

CURITIBA AND ITS BEGGARS IN COMMUNITY

When Jaime Lerner became mayor of Curitiba in 1973, he and a small team of serious, dedicated citizens and planning professionals had already spent years developing a vision and a set of comprehensive principles for changing Curitiba from a typically corrupt, poor Latin American city, being overrun by immigrants from the interior, into an inspiring community. Their success is reflected in the fact that Curitiba has since become widely known as "The Ecological City."

One of the first acts of the city's new leadership was to create a major outdoor pedestrian mall to rejuvenate Curitiba's downtown. Not surprisingly, the city's numerous beggars also found the mall a pleasant place, much to the dismay of the merchants and to the detriment of their businesses. In our current juridified society, the solution to this problem is normally "pass a law to prohibit begging." Then we spend a great deal of money on police monitoring, court time, and jail space to enforce the new law.

Curitiba's leadership responded in a profoundly different way. It did not start by viewing the presence of beggars as a separate "problem to be solved." Their principle was "everybody counts for potential value." They worked to rejuvenate the whole of a community. The last thing they wanted was to pour any of their precious resources into an effort that would alienate a large, dispossessed segment of the population from taking responsibility for improving the city. Instead, they focused on realizing the potential of everyone in their community. They saw "the problem of beggars" as a symptom of a deeper systemic lesion that needed a network of mutually reinforcing programs to heal. Each program entailed fewer costs than conventional approaches, but had ramifications on multiple levels. The principles they employed might be summarized as: Don't alienate. Create! Create new, value-adding relationships, among very different people and between people and place, that are reciprocally maintaining.

The story began, not with the question of what Curitiba should do to eliminate beggars from the mall, but with what the beggars could do for the city. A recycling program had been set up to address litter and waste disposal concerns. It was working well in middle- and upper-class neighborhoods, but the lack of streets in the *favelas*, shanty towns which were home to many of the beggars, made them impassable to the heavy recycling trucks. The city offered to pay *favela* residents for bringing recyclable materials to central collection points. So successful was the program that former beggars and their families were soon fanning out throughout the city collecting litter.

The beggars were paid, not in money, but in food coupons or tokens on the new public transportation system. The food coupons were redeemable at local farmer's markets, set up by the city to support the small truck farmers struggling to make a living on the outskirts of the city. The transit coupons were used to transport them to jobs that were previously inaccessible to them.

The results of the whole effort to eliminate beggars on the mall were manifold. Benefits included a net financial gain to the city from the sale of the recycled waste and a food-generating program that cost less than enforcing an anti-begging law and fed the entire population of poor people. There were also newfound skills for job seekers, mobility for poor people on the new transit system, new local transit products for export, new jobs for unemployed, and an attractive and successful pedestrian mall that now extends for forty-nine blocks with no beggars.

Curitiba transformed itself from a blighted, sprawling, corrupt city into a life-giving, sustainable community. It used *reciprocal maintenance* as a standard to test every proposal. This is only a part of the Curitiba story, but it is sufficient to illustrate the order and value that come from the commitment to creating a sustainable community. It demonstrates what can be accomplished by consciously developing a clear, common purpose; by developing and using these principles instead of juridifying the process; and by seeing the potential value of coalescing diversity into value-adding relationships. The new spirit created among its people is still palpable and inestimable a decade later.

Elsewhere, Community Is Crumbling

Over the course of the past decade, I participated in a difficult and inspiring process with a group of San Francisco Bay Area business, environmental, and civic leaders aimed toward developing a comprehensive, nine-county regional planning system. Simultaneously, I made my living as an infill real estate developer and later as an organization development consultant. Currently, I chair the World Business Academy Sustainable Economy Project.

From these different perspectives and experiences, I have learned a great deal about community and its absence and have concluded that much of the increasing social alienation and ongoing deterioration of our natural environment would not be occurring had we not lost our commitment to community. Passing more laws and spending unprecedented sums of money on law enforcement, environmental cleanup, and more infrastructure—including very expensive health, education, transportation, waste disposal, and flood control systems, all born of noble intent—have not been very effective. Notwithstanding these prodigious expenditures and efforts, our society and environment continue to deteriorate at what now appears to be an accelerating rate. Our systems are falling apart because, in our rush to achieve great affluence and knowledge, we have lost our connection to the earth and sun on which we totally depend, and we have become flabby in our ability to stay committed to value-adding, reciprocal relationships with each other and to all of life.

PURPOSE

The first step toward reversing this randomness that stresses our sense of life is to develop a shared purpose in our shared place, a collective sense of what is significant and must be sustained. A community's purpose can be as primal as survival and protection, as intermediate as self-development, and as transcendent as service to a greater good beyond itself. Depending on how many levels of added value the community's purpose embraces and integrates, a community is less or more whole and sustainable.

Nature teaches us that natural communities integrate three levels of value—the nature of an entity, its proximate environment, and its universe—into a common purpose. A community's *nature* deals with the survival and fulfillment of a single species. For example, the wolf is a predator of the caribou.

Its *environment* reveals a reciprocal nurturing among diverse species, often including transcendent service that further develops and enriches the common, immediate environment. The relationship between the wolf and the caribou enable each to maintain its population at a level appropriate to the environment they share.

Its *universe* encompasses the universe of a species, which the species also impacts and contributes to, through ages of time. This level enables an evolution of the ecosystem's organizational value to the whole. The wolf, caribou, trees, soil, rivers, fish and other species cooperate to sustain a natural community that nourishes a fishing village hundreds of miles downstream and continues to evolve to a higher order of value in its universe.

This is depicted graphically in Figure 1. The graphic was adapted from a concept developed by Charles G. Krone.

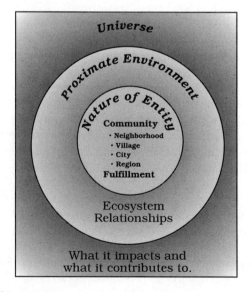

Figure 1. Purpose of Community

COMMUNITY AS PLACE

Any community becomes sustainable when it is integral to its ecosystem and serves all of these three levels of value. The ecosystem defines the boundaries that serve as a reference point for defining the community's proximate environment and its universe. Every creature within this eco-community plays a role, but humans carry the added burden of choice: to be consciously committed to the ongoing process of community in that place or not.

It is important to understand that identity, so vital to an enduring community, springs from a common agreement about boundaries. Most of the villages and cities that have endured and contributed to the qualities of our civilization, from Florence to Kyoto to San Francisco to ancient Baghdad, were formed by natural boundaries. In the absence of natural boundaries, Curitiba, London and numerous other cities in Europe, Portland in the United States, and Damascus in Asia Minor have deliberately bounded themselves by greenbelts to manage sprawl and maintain the proximity of their people on a human scale. Contrast the quality of life in those bounded cities with Los Angeles, São Paulo and Tokyo where there are no conscious boundaries.

Boundaries enable pride of place for the qualities they contain. They provide the crucible that requires us to deal with the messes we create, rather than dismiss them by moving away. By being conscious of our identity, we have much more control over our own destiny. As we center on our own place and identity and become less dependent on products from remote places, we are less likely to be victims of some far away faceless demand that depletes our natural resources and burdens us with debt. Nor are our consumption patterns as likely to make us unconscious victimizers of others whom we shall never meet. Community in place enables us to self-organize and self-regulate the impact our human desires have on others, on our surroundings, and on our progeny.

Much has been written and demonstrated through workshops and retreats about community as a spiritual experience. Such an experience, while inspiring and true in the moment, is not sustainable unless it connects us consciously to our impact on a place through time. Furthermore, it tends to support the currently held assumption that community can be mobile. In fact, there is ample evidence that the human species is not yet conscious and integrated enough to be a "mobile community." Modern corporations, constantly changing the places of their employees, owners, and production, or "electronic communities" that share no place outside the mind, are not, and cannot be, sustainable communities. Both create bonds in different forms—one as an organization, the other as a network. Both bonds are undeniably valuable, but because they are not connected to place or nonhuman nature, they tap into only a part of our whole being and, if taken as a substitute for sustainable community, they ultimately destroy it.

IMPACT OF CONTEMPORARY BUSINESS ON SUSTAINABLE COMMUNITY

Most of the United States and large portions of other industrial nations and the developing world are becoming, at an increasing rate, dysfunctional non-communities. A large part of this, I believe, is directly related to the dominant impact modern business and technology have had on the rapidly changing structure of our values, our thinking, and our relationships.

There is a subtle, but strong relationship between the imperative of the short-term, bottom-line nature of current business practices and the breakdown of community. To succeed today, corporate executives believe they must make drastic physical changes in their businesses—uprooting and relocating key employees or whole factories, merging or selling entire companies, changing management, moving headquarters, downsizing, or expanding. Each is based on "good business reasons" and further reinforced by the encouragement of the finance system. The fact that all of these decisions are commonly being made by many corporations continuously has had an untold deteriorating impact on our human commitment to sustain community in almost every part of the globe.

When we are able to step back and look at the growing evidence, we see fairly clearly that our expanding world economic system has become value depleting rather than value adding, in spite of the fact that we deeply wish it otherwise. Places where people live and work, their surroundings, and even some global ecosystems that all our lives depend on are in decline, largely because of the dominating and pervasive impact of our collective business activity— the very activity on which most of us depend for our livelihoods. At the same time, it is clear that because it is so adaptive and pervasive worldwide, business is the singular institution on this planet that has the potential to turn this regrettable situation around.

THE SACRED AND PROFANE

As businesspeople, it is time to stop denying our relationship with the sacred—the natural environment from which our wealth springs—and the profane—our cities which we have allowed to fester to gangrenous proportions at our peril. Business is faced with a choice of radical and painful restructuring imposed by the pressures and increasing costs of the failure of community or transformation into a different, more healthy form that integrates with and nurtures community. We must recognize that we are caught in a system driven compulsively by finance, growth, and litigation that, like a well developed cancer, is rapidly separating us as whole persons from being able to pursue a common, harmonious, sustainable life. Once we can see that, we can then begin to reorder the economy, governance, our systems of technology, culture and the ecosystem into an appropriate system that regenerates community, and thereby begins to reverse the entropy we now find so overwhelming.

The steamroller of the late 20th Century post-industrial political economy has become more powerful than our vision and ability to bring our human activity into balance with the dynamic forces of nature—human and nonhuman. Returning to community is a more effective, less costly way to deal with our current situation than what we are currently doing, both in business and in government. Business has both a large responsibility and much at stake in this profound effort.

FRAMEWORK AND PRINCIPLES FOR A SUSTAINABLE COMMUNITY

Given the complexity involved in restoring community, and all the changes such an effort would portend for our current systems, the big question facing all of us is How to even begin to think together about it?

During the course of negotiating differences and forging consensus toward a Bay Area regional planning system, the various parties discovered, after we began to know and talk to each other as individual people, that we shared a hierarchy of values about the relative importance of different systems of life in the region. Once we saw this, it made reconciling our different agendas much easier. Everyone agreed that maintaining a healthy economy was essential. Also obvious was the view that an economy wouldn't be very healthy if the ecosystem died. So, all agreed, the ecosystem was more essential than the economy. It was not a question of either one or the other. The economy was still essential. It just wasn't the most fundamental system from which to build our collective picture about how all the elements fit together.

Because the effort was limited to a land-use planning system, our informal model dealt only with place. Since then, I have developed it into a more comprehensive framework as a way to provide a structure for thinking together about building a sustainable community. It is depicted graphically (see Figure 2) and described below along with some principles at each system level. The principles should be thought of as providing a step-translation from the abstraction of values toward the development of a collective vision about how a particular sustainable community would look. Community principles are also valuable to remember as touchstones in reasoning and dialogue, and as mentors in the community's decision making.

SUSTAINABLE COMMUNITY EMERGES FROM AN ECOSYSTEM

The ecosystem, a living community itself, is the dynamic foundation upon which all else rests and from which every other element of a sustainable community is built. Within its boundaries, a host of diverse organisms and matter at a variety of levels interact, forming increasingly complex interdependencies and interrelationships between and among each other. Each organism contributes to others in some life-nourishing way and, in doing so, adds value beyond the ecosystem to its universe. The ecosystem, nourished with light from the sun, offers the potential for reversing entropic processes. No known life form, including human, exists without it.

Eco is derived from the ancient Greek word for house or household. Thus, an ecosystem is the "household system" that enables a sustainable community to be "home."

Figure 2. Framework for Building Community

Principles for guiding a sustainable community's behavior related to its ecosystem include:
- A sustainable community understands the nourishing interdependencies and interrelationships within its ecosystem.
- It continuously maintains consciousness of the impact its human activities have on the health and evolution of the ecosystem.
- The boundaries of a sustainable community are its ecosystem; the human habitat is seen only as a meaningful and significant *part* of the community.

SUSTAINABLE CULTURE EMERGES FROM THE ECOSYSTEM

Rooted in, developing from, and nourished by the fertile ground of the community's ecosystem, culture is the invisible womb that holds the human community together at its core. Through generations, it nurtures continuity of the human life unique to a particular community. It gives rhythm to our life and significance to our being part of a community. The language and music of meaning; the motion, feeling and tastes of rituals; the vision and textures of sacred symbols; and the wisdom and odor of taboos form the dimensions of culture.

The depth of the values and beliefs of a community's culture shapes how well a community reconciles adversity and appreciates the richness of diversity within it. The quality and consciousness of a community's culture profoundly influences whether our social conventions and relationships—gender, family, education, business, justice, religions—will work or not.

Principles for guiding a sustainable community related to its culture include:
- The culture imbues a sustainable community with a sacred sense of its uniqueness, its connection to its place, and its continuing value-adding relationship within its universe.

- A sustainable community is able to see the potential in diversity and develop the capability to harmonize itself in the aim of becoming something new and valuable.
- The culture of a sustainable community drives its members to seek the essential quality of their activities in order to recognize and eliminate waste—physical, energy and social—by transforming it into higher value "food" for development.

SUSTAINABLE ECONOMY INVITES RECIPROCAL VALUE ADDING

Economy, from its Greek origin, means managing the household. The economy of a sustainable community requires a dynamic balancing of reciprocal, value-adding transactions between the culture and its ecosystem. Managing the household includes guiding the transformation of matter and energy from the ecosystem into products and services that enable the culture to enhance, uplift, and sustain the community. It also includes responsibility for nourishing (giving food back to) the community's ecosystem through time. The market system can be the medium for managing the household if it serves the values of the whole community—ecosystem and culture. The ecosystem, when managed appropriately, yields bounty. The culture, when guided by reciprocal, value-adding transformations and transactions, connects us to our Source. The role of the economy is to manage and guide accordingly, to manifest well-being.

The notion of managing the market system by an "invisible hand" had authenticity the way Adam Smith conceived it. But the "invisible hand" has since been amputated from its body—the values and well-being of the community it was supposed to serve. Smith's view is in stark contrast to the current "economics of growth," where earth and its communities are being drained to fuel economic activity.

The economy of nature offers an instructive and different model. Nature is constantly transforming waste into nourishment for a succession of higher order beings. With intention, business can work similarly with regard to higher order community.

Some principles for guiding an economy of a sustainable community include:

- Transactions and product transformations in a sustainable economy are reciprocally maintaining and value adding.
- To the extent a community extracts and uses the ecosystem's yield, it returns greater enrichment to its source in the ecosystem. (For example, the soil becomes richer from growing and harvesting food through permaculture, in contrast to our current agro-industry practices that deplete the soil.)
- An economy of a sustainable community nurtures the further development of the community's human capability to serve—now and beyond our life time.

- A sustainable community economy looks for creative ways to replace its reliance on importation of products.

Import replacement is fundamental to the creation of wealth and healthy sustainable "cities," as Jane Jacobs persuasively demonstrates in her book *Cities and the Wealth of Nations*. By continually developing its own capability to produce products that replace a region's dependency on imports, a regional community and its component businesses build a stronger and more sustainable economy and a more stable social and political structure.

INFRASTRUCTURE SYSTEMS SUPPORT FUNCTION AND DEVELOP ASSETS
Infrastructure is an inclusive term for all of a community's physical and social support systems. Communications, transportation, land use, utilities, health, education, market and finance systems enable a community to function well and to further develop its assets. In a sustainable community each system is designed to meet needs and manifest the value of the economy, culture, and the ecosystem. The economy couldn't manage the household if there were no infrastructure.

When traffic congestion begins to overwhelm our streets, instead of automatically deciding to build a new freeway, a sustainable community would ask, "What systems failures are contributing to the congestion?" The city of Portland asked that in the late 1970s. Instead of simply building a new freeway to connect and accommodate further urban flight, Portland's civic, environmental, and business interests got together on a community infrastructure plan. The result, fifteen years later, is a highly developed sense of community in one of the most attractive and vital downtown urban centers in the United States.

Principles for infrastructure in sustainable community include:
- Education, communications, transportation, finance, and other support systems are designed to increase potential and manifest value for the whole of the community.
- A sustainable community views its problems systemically and designs its infrastructure proactively.

GOVERNANCE TO CREATE SUSTAINABLE ORDER
Finally, we discover the relative value of governance. Unlike the institution of government that imposes an order on society based on an adversarial process where everyone looks out for him or herself and comes up with the lowest common denominator agreement, governance in a sustainable community is a derivative, self-organizing process. Governance engages a community, through formal and informal interactions about long-term planning, decision making, and managing the community's relationships.

Self-organizing is the way of the natural order. It is not, however, a conscious process for most historical human societies, and it is certainly not the model we are familiar with today. Yet it is present in real communities, of which there are still many. It requires greater capability than is currently our standard of attainment in our unsustainable society. The ethic, resources, and systems to support and develop this higher level of capability in its people are imbedded in the sustainable community's culture, economy and infrastructure. In return, governance, in pursuit of common purpose, serves the other systems.

Principles for governance in a sustainable community include:

- Governance in a sustainable community relies on self-organizing and aspires to achieve social and economic order in a way that is non-juridical.
- A sustainable community develops its information media in a way that is engaging and enlightening, rather than passively entertaining and demoralizing.
- A sustainable community nurtures and supports its governance process through development of its people toward capability to
- interact thoughtfully and compassionately toward value-adding agreements and order.
- create and maintain reciprocal relationships, and
- sustain commitment to freedom to create higher forms of service for the common purpose.

Is the Vision Possible?

"To touch the Earth." This is only the beginning of a vision of how we can begin to reverse the accelerating deterioration in our natural and social systems by creating regional sustainable communities in the 21st Century. The whole vision has to be created by all of us. A very big order, it calls for a caring commitment over extended time, against well-entrenched inertia. Nonetheless, it is difficult to envision a more worthy endeavor.

David Goff, Ph.D., teaches at the Institute of Transpersonal Psychology where he employs large group processes to promote community and personal development. His graduate research into the psychological sense of community is the first study to describe psychological dimensions of group consciousness.

In addition to performing research, writing, and practicing psychotherapy in Palo Alto, California, Goff directs A Foundation for Interdependence, which is dedicated to developing a psychology of interdependence. The Foundation integrates mainstream psychotherapy, transpersonal psychology, and new social learning technologies to create learning communities that catalyze personal empowerment and cultural transformation. It offers workshops, training seminars, ongoing groups, social rituals, and organizational consultation.

28

Getting Along Together: The Challenge of Communitas

David Goff

Amidst the mayhem and destruction of the Los Angeles riots in 1992, Rodney King expressed what may be a core question for our time: "People, can't we all just get along?" His plea gives voice to the urgent need we have to cooperate as well as to the uncertainty we feel about our capacity to do so. We now live with extraordinary cultural and ethnic complexities which arouse fear and mistrust. Never before has humanity faced the challenge of creating a sense of community that includes such great diversity. The quality of our business cultures and the very life of the planet and of future generations may depend upon how we respond to King's question.

Can we all get along? It is clear that we don't. One does not have to look solely at racial, ethnic, and religious hostilities to confirm this perception. The national rates of divorce and domestic violence dramatically convey the tensions that abide at the heart of our daily interactions. An honest appraisal of the distance and distrust that separates us from neighbors and co-workers reflects this perception as well. This is a grievous truth of life in corporate America.

How has this circumstance come about? Despite the best intentions of the pilgrims who pledged at Plymouth Rock to live "as members of the same body," the American way emphasizes the rights and privileges of the individual. This great nation was born by freeing individuals to pursue their own forms of happiness and self-expression. Now it is threatened by it's own success. By sacrificing a sense of the common good in society, American business provides fertile ground for narcissism, alienation, isolationism, and fear of anyone who is significantly different.

This continuing emphasis upon individualism conflicts with our critical need for connection and commitment to one another. Our inability to get along leads to cultural and political gridlock, and organizational ineffectiveness. Modern ecological and geopolitical issues are complex, and involve large systems that require sustained collective attention, yet our mistrust of otherness retards our ability to respond collectively. The dilemmas we now face in our organizations and our world ask us to care for the good of the whole as we care for the good of our selves.

How do we achieve this development? When we turn toward traditional concepts of community for guidance we see that community has been associated with long-standing relationships which occur among people who share a geographical location and a common worldview. These communities are distinguished by the common values they hold, by the norms they create to implement those values, and by the shared means they employ to survive and thrive. In the language of sociology these communities would be referred to as "communities of affinity." In organizational development they would be known as "aligned" or "vision driven." They are organized around shared values, demonstrating cooperation and the power of unifying principles.

At the same time, however, these communities of affinity contain seeds of the very dilemma which now threatens our cultural and biological survival. In our multiethnic and multicultural society we are overwhelmed with a diversity and complexity which traditional communities have never had to embrace. If we adhere to traditional approaches we are quickly stymied by the inevitable question: Whose values are the "right" values? Whose principles will determine the organization of society? This question, laden with the struggle for cultural identity and ideological supremacy, fuels much of the conflict now ravaging the planet.

An answer to King's question does not lie in communities based upon similarities. A new basis for community is needed: one that values diversity and confirms the integrity of multiple co-existing realities, and that is based upon a palpable experience of how profoundly connected we all are. This form of community could be described as a shared experience of interconnection, as social communion, or as a collective state of consciousness.

Over the last several years my research in the field of transpersonal psychology has identified large group processes which appear to generate such experiences of a unitive state of consciousness. I have labeled this unitive state of consciousness "communitas," a term borrowed from cultural anthropologist Victor Turner. Fascinated by the collective rituals of indigenous peoples, Turner noted that these rites generated a form of social communion. He called this "communitas" and his observations provided the vision that informed my research. It is my hope that over time we will see some of these ideas filter into our workplaces.

Turner observed that these communal processes created a "ritual space" that existed outside of the normal cultural context. He employed the term "liminality," derived from the Latin word *limen*, meaning threshold, to describe this central aspect of the ritual process. He described liminality as "anti-structural," meaning that in ritual space, cultural structures dissolved, and all forms of identity conferred by cultural status also dissipate. Using our imagination, we could envision a short space in time where the traditional hierarchy collapses and everybody within the company knows each other as whole and equal beings.

Turner also described the "liminal zone" as an empty space. Communitas emerges as equal individuals collectively submit to the ordeal associated with having no status, no role, no mitigating or mediating structure to temper their encounter with the human dilemma. Communitas was described as sacred and holy, and as being suffused with a renewing and generative power. These perceptions led Turner to assert that cultural transformation could be attributed to the impact of communitas upon collectives.

Turner's descriptions of ritual liminality provided useful criteria for identifying contemporary group intensives which might generate experiences of communitas for workgroups. One such group intensive is the Community Building Workshop, developed by M. Scott Peck and The Foundation for Community Encouragement. The workshop is a large group intensive that often involves fifty or more participants. It usually occurs over three full days. It is totally experiential. The sole task of the participants is to create an experience of community: toward this end, they sit in a large circle and interact.

Two trained leaders facilitate the experience; they provide simple guidelines which include: listen deeply, speak when you feel moved to speak, use "I-messages," practice inclusivity, observe how you maintain separation, and share responsibility for the outcome of the workshop. Facilitation includes the use of silence, teaching stories, re-emphasizing the guidelines, and brief feedback to the group as a whole.

According to Peck, the workshop proceeds through four phases: psuedo-community, chaos, emptiness and community. The initial stage of the process, psuedo-community, is marked by congenial, comfortable and polite interactions. These interactions avoid conflict and preserve a superficial sense of harmony.

Chaos emerges when differences come into the open and attempts are made to establish what is appropriate behavior in the group. As different opinions emerge, group members attempt to ignore or change each other's positions. This process leads to tension and distrust. This chaotic phase reveals a struggle for power in the group—the same dynamic which occurs in our larger culture—resulting in fear, hatred, and withdrawal. The chaos phase constellates on a small scale the cultural crisis which is being played out in the streets of our cities and within the halls of our government. In the workshop participants are confronted with the stark realization that, despite their intentions, they themselves are sources of this terrible dilemma.

In Peck's model there are two ways out of the chaotic phase. Both work, but only one leads to community. The group can organize its way out of chaos (and its chance for community) by choosing a task to focus on. (For goal-oriented workgroups this is a particularly difficult trap since problem solving is often a quick escape from struggle in business environments.) Or it can "empty" itself of the expectations, preconceptions, and easy solutions that prevent community from emerging.

Emptiness calls for a form of dying. Group members create a space for community by voluntarily sacrificing their needs to be right, to be in control, and to remain invulnerable. The members surrender their methods for protecting themselves from personal and existential vulnerability. Community emerges as vulnerability increases and as group members surrender their expectations and enter the unknown together.

My research involved surveying and analyzing the reported experiences of over 200 participants in a number of these workshops. Using a statistical method known as factor analysis, the results revealed three primary factors which describe the participant's experience. These factors were labeled: "a sense of community," "the experience of otherness," and "the sense of the human existential dilemma."

The "sense of community" factor reveals that many participants shared what they described as an important and profound experience. This experience included a shift of consciousness to an enlarged sense of self. This shift was accompanied by strong feelings of peace and tranquility. Those who scored high on this factor reported a strong sense of connection, and feelings of compassion and kindness for each other. This experience included a sense of unity, feelings of sacredness, and a sense of timelessness. In essence, participants reported experiencing a collective shift into a unitive state of consciousness.

Remarkably, this shift in consciousness occurred despite a high degree of awareness of the differences, or "experience of otherness," that the group included. The experience was reported to be painful and disturbing; it included feelings of annoyance, resentment, alienation, distrust and conflict with others in the workshop. These same participants also reported awareness that they were judging others, and that their beliefs about these others, or themselves, created distance. This factor highlights the difficulties associated with the encounter with differences, personal and cultural.

The third factor, "the sense of the human existential dilemma," shows that the workshop resolves these difficult feelings, and preserves the diversity of the group, by providing a mutual experience of humankind's underlying existential vulnerability. This indicates recognition of the degree of human uncertainty, of how limited humans are, and of how vulnerable others are. Participants also recognized the desire to avoid feeling the pain and uncertainty that is part of human life. They reported that awareness of this level of shared vulnerability engendered compassionate feelings and an emotional sense of connection.

The findings of this study show that large groups can integrate diversity and survive the difficult tensions that accompany the presence of otherness, that this becomes possible when the group shares an experience of human vulnerability, and that this catalyzes the emergence of a collective state of consciousness. These results bode well for an increasingly diverse workforce. We are assured that this inevitable diversity can be harnessed, creating harmony and community—not chaos.

Study Summary

This quantitative and qualitative study, entitled "An Exploratory Study of the Existential and Transpersonal Dimensions of the Psychological Sense of Community as Found in The Community Building Workshop™," was conducted in the spring of 1991. A ninety-eight item questionnaire was constructed and administered to a pool of 539 workshop graduates living in California. There were a total of 234 respondents.

The survey items included forty-four descriptive statements generated from a synthesis of the phenomenological and affective elements described in the literature of group processes reported to lead to a sense of community. Results were subjected to a principle components factor analysis designed to identify the elements of the participants' experiences offering the greatest explanatory value as descriptors of that experience.

This method extracted a total of six factors, labeled as follows: Sense of Community, Sense of Otherness, Sense of Human Existential Dilemma, Sense of Engagement, Sense of Personal Existential Dilemma, and Sense of a Difficult Experience. Items describing previous experiences, the impact of the workshop, and the demography of the subject population, were also examined for correlation with these factors.

The findings showed that the central experience produced by the workshop was a collective shift of consciousness toward a unitive state. This shift coincided with a collective experience of existential vulnerability catalyzed by the difficulties associated with an experience of otherness. This state was described as including powerful feelings, a strong sense of emotional connection, an enlarged sense of self, an extension of kindness and compassion toward others. It included mystical features described as: feelings of sacredness, an experience of union with a larger whole (including the persons with whom the experience was shared), and the experience of having participated in something that was paradoxical and difficult to communicate in words.

The experience had a positive impact on the respondents' feelings of connection with others and the larger processes of life. The respondents reported that their experience of this collective shift into a unitive state of consciousness had a transformative effect on their trust in others as well as sense of purpose and hope for the future.

These findings have important implications for psychology and for how we view community in business. By establishing that large groups can address the tensions that create and sustain cultural issues, the way is paved for a psychology of interdependence. A managerial philosophy founded on this psychology and its direct experience of the underlying interconnectedness of life would recognize that individuals suffer in organizations that deny interrelatedness. Such suffering provides important feedback about the need for new forms of community and management.

Understanding that large groups such as modern corporations represent a microcosm of the culture at large, this emerging psychology attends to the suffering associated with cultural tensions. It explores and examines the psychological and the cultural dynamics which create racism, ethnic distrust, burnout in our workplace, and our abusive relationship with the environment. It treats individuals and the culture simultaneously.

As a basis for organizational leadership, this perspective is emerging from many sources. A number of independent practitioners are pioneering the development of new models, techniques, and practices which address our ability to get along together. British Psychiatrist Patrick de Mare refers to the beneficial effects these processes generate as "socio-therapy." De Mare reports that groups uncover the underlying dynamics that generate cultural structures by employing "dialogue," a form of collective free association. This method brings to awareness the basic assumptions that shape a group's interactions. It makes explicit the ideological basis for the sub-groups and cultural structures which separate, divide, and create conflict.

Physicist David Bohm, renowned for his theory of a holographic universe, developed the practice of group dialogue over a twenty year span. Viewing dialogue as culturally transformative, he described it as a method for achieving "group mindfulness." With practice, groups achieve a sense of impersonal fellowship and group consciousness. In this state it is possible to examine cultural assumptions and to witness the effects that such collective thoughts produce. Bohm and De Mare both insist that the individual and the society can be simultaneously humanized by the use of group dialogue.

Management and organizational development experts, such as MIT professor Peter Senge, are experimenting with techniques that emphasize systems thinking, dialogue, shared vision, and total participation. They are creating organizations based on systems dynamics models, dialogue, and the experience of interconnectedness. They call these "learning organizations." But increasingly they are being viewed as "learning communities" where collective processes can be practiced that benefit the development of the participating individuals, the organization, and the larger culture. The rapidly changing business climate has made it imperative that organizations adapt quickly and efficiently. The need for such flexibility and responsiveness has led to innovative methods for working with collective processes.

These new practices, employing a larger context to focus upon cultural dynamics, offer a timely response to the concerns of those who have been critical of psychotherapy's effectiveness as an agent for social change. These concerns focus on the "one-to-one" emphasis in therapeutic practice, and its limitations in addressing mass disorders, such as addiction, environmental illness, domestic violence, and the loss of community in our organizations. Healing in the therapeutic context is seen as an "inner" experience. By emphasizing the subjective experience of the client, it reinforces individualism and isolation. This leads to cultural passivity rather than political and social action. James Hillman suggests that self should be redefined so that it becomes more inclusive, that self should be seen as an "interiorization of community."

Critics concerned with the environment are arguing for a therapeutic perspective that views the person and the planet as part of a single continuum. To them, successful treatment must incorporate the needs of life as a whole. Believing that the pain of the ecosystem is being expressed through our private emotional and spiritual anguish, they are concerned that this travail cannot be effectively understood by a psychology which reduces this sensitivity to an individual pathology.

Underlying these concerns we hear the essential recognition that communal models for healing are needed now. This returns us to the question of whether or not we can "get along" in our business organizations. We now live with the uncertainty and urgency embodied in this question. Our best response lies in leaning bravely into this question until, as the poet Rilke points out, we can "live the answer."

The question invites us to struggle together for insight into the psychological dynamics which create the cultural tensions and conflict that threaten us. Engaging with this question can lead to new management practices and abilities for accomplishing our goals together. My research leads me to believe that these abilities can be awakened through an experience of communitas. Subsequent developments have shown that participation in a large group, employing a learning community approach, provides a social context where these capabilities can be further developed.

When individuals realize that their well-being is linked inextricably with the well-being of the whole, and they can see a way to develop the skills that provide them with a functional capacity for interdependence they will very often begin to practice community building as a form of personal mastery.

Turner described the social bond that arose from communitas as a "strong sentiment of humankindness." Practicing community in the workplace means cultivating the conditions which can make an experience of humankindness real. When we practice community as part of our business lives we invest ourselves and our hopes in a mutual effort to insure that we, and the generations to come, will know that we *can* all get along.

Ed Klinge (left) and **Terry Anderson** (right) have for many years worked on improving the effectiveness and developing the potential of multiple organizations and businesses. They have worked with organizations in both the public and private sector, ranging from individual units or sectors to corporations to industries. They have found themselves drawn toward, and working to advance life in, communities throughout their adult lives.

The central aim of their work is the creation of community and business developmental processes that lift the creative potential of people and their socioeconomic vitality in a way that continually revitalizes the community and its core value-adding processes. Their experience in business leads them to believe that a comprehensive thinking technology and disciplined approach is essential to bringing about and sustaining community.

29

Developing a Regenerative Community

Terry Anderson and Ed Klinge

"Money is power," the young man argued. If there is no economic base, he claimed, then money is needed to restore a sense of well-being and identity. "Without money, how can anything change?"

Amid the clamor of argument, a woman, one of the city's elders, slowly stood up. With extreme clarity and doubtless conviction, she said, "Values—like respect, self-esteem, love—are at the center of our community; we will die before we give up our values. For too long now we have gone the other way. Look what's happening to us."

The distinction here is between change and regeneration. While the young man could not see a chance for improvement without the money to "repair" or change things, the elder woman saw the community's own identity, its values, as the base from which all growth, all regeneration, must occur. Like the geographic community, the corporate community must be able to develop and to sustain itself, within the context of its chosen values.

THE ISSUE

Too often in our local communities one experiences a decreasing sense of vitality and optimism and an increasing sense of uncertainty and concern—concern that more and more frequently shows up as fear. Issues of environment, health care, security, crime and increasing violence threaten the very fabric of existence. Many businesses have been engaging in oppressive practices which cause loss of work for many or provide only work that is increasingly dehumanizing for those who are able to continue working. These business and work conditions are undermining the economic base and source of livelihood for our families and urban communities. Nowhere is the condition more visible than in the inner city. Here it is increasingly difficult—if not impossible—for families to thrive and for children to survive, much less become what they have the potential to be.

How do we begin to work on this situation? How do we create solutions which are lasting and are ongoing sources of hope and spirit for all those involved? Can we create urban communities which are value based in their growth and development? Can we create local cultures where people have more control over their own destiny?

Not only is it necessary to create this nature of community which would be an energizing source for society, but it is in fact possible. It requires, however, the coalescence of many disparate entities into common purpose, which in turn must be guided by a fundamental understanding of the workings of a process.

The Process

This essay is a snapshot of such an ongoing process. We will share the guiding thought for our work and then share some of the key experiences and understandings we have acquired while engaging in this process.

For over two years a group of us from within and around the local community have had an ongoing partnership with elders and leaders of an inner-city area (approximately 8,000 people) within a midsize mid-Atlantic city. This district has very serious drug, crime, unemployment and poverty problems with a rising rate of teen-age pregnancies and welfare dependency. It is a part of the city in which the elders and leaders are deeply concerned and committed to creating a new way of evolving—beyond just repairing or correcting current issues or problems. The ongoing courage and conviction of the elders—many of whom are grandparents in their sixties and beyond—have been both fundamental to the approach and a source of spirit and energy for the process.

The group includes business people who are bringing together their experience at leading, managing, and resourcing businesses in major corporations such as Du Pont, Procter and Gamble, FMC, and Scott Paper with their conviction that the ongoing health and competitiveness of their businesses requires healthy communities. They understand that the 20 percent entitlement burden on North American businesses is rapidly decreasing their competitiveness. This is bolstered by their personal commitment towards creating a healthier, more wholesome world for their children and future generations. These people are working in or consulting to these and other corporations while devoting an increasing amount of personal time to this effort.

This process is based on a technology which has been proven successful in developing businesses which are highly competitive, while providing meaningful work for people. These enterprises are significantly more cost effective than other businesses producing similar products and serving the same markets. This technology for managing value-adding processes is primarily about the thinking and behavior that create regenerative businesses—businesses which get better and better through time. At its core is the premise that the quality of thinking that precedes any action ultimately determines people's behavior and the outcome.

REGENERATIVE BUSINESSES = REGENERATIVE CITIES

Essential to the creation of a regenerative enterprise is an understanding of its workings. "Regenerative" implies that the organization has the in-built capacity to evolve itself to higher value platforms from which to operate—that is, the whole system of interacting social, economic, and environmental forces always has the capacity to evolve to a new level of existence with greater potential for its future generations. Figure 1 is a model which depicts the inner workings of such a system.

When this regenerative system is truly working (versus coughing and sputtering along), its values and its value-adding processes which enable it to develop to higher working levels as a whole system are at its heart. For example, through innovation, education, and a focus on wellness, the health and wholeness of individuals in a community will improve each year. This is true for a community of co-workers in a company or a community of neighbors in a district of a town. These are very different from entropic processes which are energy consuming and life

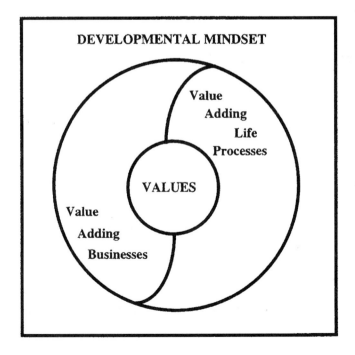

Figure 1. A Regenerative Community

draining—for example, "fighting crime" by building and populating more pris-ons, or, for the corporation, driving short-term financial results to the extent they significantly impair or curtail the health and viability of the business itself.

In the context of a regenerative system there are two value-adding process-es, distinctive but inseparable. One we call "value-adding businesses" and the other "value-adding life processes." The first relates to the material well-being and ongo-ing source of wealth of the local community; the second relates to the cycle and experience of life itself, e.g. from birth, to developing the children, to realizing the potential of adults, to death.

The value-adding businesses in a regenerative community are cared for and developed as assets in the community which sustain and increase the mater-ial well-being of its residents. They are also the primary source of development for all its people—young and old alike. Following the stream of material well-being to its ultimate source, one always finds a value-adding process, that is, the transforming of material into a higher order form, such as the transforming of wood pulp into paper products, or dyes into colorful patterns in clothing. It starts with a raw material and transforms that material into a form (a garment) that has higher value to the customer and to the dressmaker. At the same time, the process for making this garment continually increases in value. This value-adding busi-ness is, in reality, the resource that fills the pond from which all other systems draw. In this sense, everyone in the city or town, is part of the "business family". The health and effectiveness of the value-adding businesses in a community ulti-mately determines its material well-being. These businesses retain their value adding nature by living in harmony with, versus extracting from or degenerating, the socio-ecosystems of which they are a part. By operating this way, they can deliver value to customers, employees, stockholders, society, all the stakeholders and, in fact, deliver more value to each. Therefore, it is essential to future genera-tions to sustain the essential character of these businesses..

As the value-adding business is a source of material well-being, the value-adding life processes are the source of the city's energy and vitality. The business-es and the local community must support, nourish and reciprocally maintain each other for either to have long-term viability. For the community to sustain and evolve its capacity to support and enable healthy businesses, its people need to have access to and experience healthy life processes.

As illustrated in Figure 2, the arrow must go both ways:

Figure 2. Inseparability of How One Lives and Works

Thus, how one lives and how one works are inseparable if their community is to be energized and capable of regenerating itself.

When businesses are separate from the local community, they tend to become more extractive, and communities find themselves trying to "attract jobs" as opposed to trying to grow and develop businesses. The community becomes less self-determined, experiencing an ongoing depletion of its resources, spirit and significance. Ultimately, the people themselves become unable to solve essential problems or to express their uniqueness. The clearest and most widely recognized example of this problem is the welfare cycle entrapment. The challenge is to simultaneously develop a community's value-adding businesses and its value-adding life processes.

A NEW PERSPECTIVE

This dual focus on business and community represents a significant shift of perspective from the current way of community rebuilding. While important work is going on, few recognize that the creation of a self-sustaining, self-determining communities necessitates value-adding businesses. We have to avoid being so caught up in the community's immediate needs that we lose sight of our mission to bring about its regeneration. Our work does not seek remedial actions to stem the current downward slide. It is not about improving the current path but rather about providing the basis for a totally new path—a path grounded in the understanding of what it takes to create a healthy working community. This requires a "developmental mind-set." The sense-based mind looks at what already exists and seeks to fix or improve it, but the developmental mind begins with a vision of what is possible. The two minds employ very different thinking processes.

A way to experience these minds in action would be to walk the streets of an inner city neighborhood. Let your senses freely focus on the different elements around you. Typically, you might notice the disrepair of the sidewalks and streets; there may be trash lying about; a section of run-down retail businesses; or perhaps you would witness a crime. The mind would naturally go to seeking physical remedies: repairing the streets, cleaning up the trash, fixing up the houses, and making it safe to walk about. If you were a politician, you might even make these the central elements in your campaign. If you were a city council member, you might spend much time and effort parceling out resources toward improving one or more of these elements. These remedies have been tried, but they are not effective in regeneration.

Now step back and pause a moment. Reflect on the potential that lies within the people, the resources, including the businesses, and the geography of the community. Can you see healthy businesses providing meaningful work and places of development? Can you envision schools, churches, and other organizations working together to support families and the growth and development of healthy children? Can you see grocery stores, shops, and parks, and how they need to be designed and connected to promote the way of life desired by the community? From this developmental mind-set one starts answering questions that are essential to the visioning process. You ask: What goes where? What effect are we seeking to create? How does everything work together?

The capacity to envision evolves out of the developmental mind, providing direction for regeneration as well as for the city's ongoing maintenance and improvement. It allows the infrastructure to function as a unit rather than a loose collection of discrete, competing elements, so that work is done in ways which continually move the residents toward the desired way of living and working. The developmental mind enables regeneration and evolution to a higher level of existence. Without this perspective, the sense-based mind produces a cosmetic or bandage solution.

A Developmental Partnership

A number of influential and concerned members of the inner city community with whom we are working had concluded that if there were to be a future, in particular for its children, a shift was required from remedial processes to ones more essential in nature. There were a number of concrete ideas about how this work was to be done.

It became clear to us that the intelligence and wisdom to achieve this shift lies in the people of the community, and that what was missing were processes which brought them forth. Our goal in the developmental partnership has been to build upon the community's uniqueness and innate wisdom, and to help them put this wisdom into action. A process we are calling "creative grandparenting," is based on the work by Creative Grandparenting, Inc., a non-profit organization. This is a process that enables the children of the community to experience values that are essential to their well-being and development through creative interactions with caring older adults.

Covenant

As our partnership began, the local residents were clear on these points:
- They were emphatic in their demand that we were not to bring in predetermined fixed approaches—ones that did not reflect their culture and their processes. They had learned that such remedial, cosmetic, sensebased approaches offered short-term improvements and were seductive in their promise of quick and useful fixes. They lacked the capacity to create anything of lasting value. In fact, ultimately, they became less able to create sustainable value.
- Whatever approach we developed together needed to be grounded in the higher values they were trying to live from and hoped their children would have the opportunity to live from. These higher values needed to include trust and honesty, self-respect and respect for others, responsibility, creativity, learning, hard work, spiritual renewal, and a sense of family and community.
- They recognized their need to become something different, to develop the

capacity to take on new roles so that they could direct, develop, and implement their own value-adding processes. They demanded that we help them develop the capacity to do the work—not do it for them.

- The last condition (and the most important for us "outsiders") was the test of our commitment to stay with them throughout the process. Too many times they had followed a person with a "noble idea" only to discover that the person did not have the technology to bring the idea into existence and advance it through time. Their testing of us has been an ongoing process and continues today. Their most common form of challenge is in intense interactions; they test our responsiveness and capability when a process goes awry.

These four conditions then became the basis for a covenant with the local residents. Simply stated: Join with us, stay with us, and share the accountability until we have a process we ourselves can sustain. This covenant deepens in meaning and importance as we go forward, guiding the partnership created between the planners and the community.

Core Values

By applying many of our learnings from developing community spirit in businesses, we discovered several similarities. A community, like a business, must decide what it wants to be. Who are its stakeholders? What do they require? Like business, stakeholder interests will vary, often dramatically. Creating a process for satisfying them can be quite challenging.

One of the processes we established with our inner city groups was a series of open forum sessions. The primary purpose of these Saturday sessions was to define the core values of the community and to deepen our collective understanding of the working of these values in families and the community itself. These sessions were very lively and challenging. It was through these sessions that a commitment to operating from core values was developed. The depth of this commitment was apparent on one memorable Saturday.

We were working to understand the essential activities which surround a value-adding process. We began by sharing the model illustrating the developmental hierarchy (Figure 3).

We indicated that values are at the center of the community and all other activities grow out from these values:

- the value-adding business processes of the community
- the economics those processes generate and what is required to sustain them
- the skill-building required to operate and maintain the effectiveness of the value-adding process
- consortiums which enable continuous development in the fields and professions required to improve the health of businesses
- evolving the business capacity of the whole community.

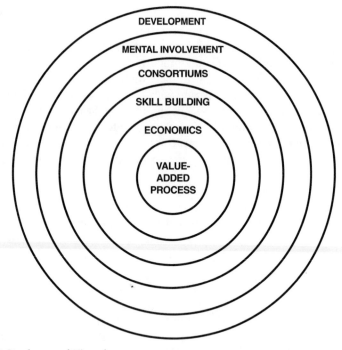

Figure 3. Developmental Hierarchy

It was this model the young man challenged when he said, "Money is power; without money how can anything change?"

In agreeing with the elder woman that values were at the center, the forum participants affirmed the developmental emphasis of their work toward regeneration.

Work in Progress

As we said in the beginning, this is a "snapshot" of a work in progress. Currently we are working with this inner city community to develop an understanding of value-adding businesses, how they work, and what would be appropriate for them. We are examining businesses, such as printing and clothing manufacturing, which would tap into this community's potential and uniqueness and be a source of wealth while also being a source of value to the world.

When we started this work, we believed that both a technology and developmental approach were required to produce a self-sustaining, viable community. Everything we have experienced thus far reinforces this view. The developmental technology,which has provided a framework and thought processes, is proving to be an effective, generative source for our work.

While this is a long-term effort, it has nevertheless yielded many positive results already. You can see the results in the attitude of some of the children and the increased spirit and convictions of the rightness of this path for the elders.

We will know we are making progress when some late evening we talk with a woman strolling through the neighborhood, and she reflects, "This is a community which encourages and supports its people. It is a good place for families to work and live. I *choose* to live here."

SUMMARY

In closing, we'd like to offer some of our recent learnings—from our corporate work beforehand and our present "work in progress" with our inner city colleagues. We believe they are valuable for developing regenerative systems of many sorts.

1. Enable people to identify the values which are most important to their well-being and future development.
2. Form a developmental partnership with people who will lead and be resources to others in advancing the value-adding processes of business and in living from widely held values.
3. Create ongoing open forums where people can challenge and develop each other's thinking.
4. Work to ensure that all value-based activities are directed by the regenerative thinking and the energy of the community itself.
5. Design all processes so they extend the capacity of those who are going to live and work in the community.
6. Develop the capacity of the community members to lead and resource value-adding processes so they can realize a self-sustaining, self-determining community.
7. Above all, remember that only value-adding businesses will retain and advance the potential for future generations.

The work we've described in this essay is the result of the realization that, if we continue on the path we are on, our businesses will continue to lose their competitiveness, our people will continue to lose their spirit and will, and our society will continue to degenerate. Our cities and businesses face the same challenge; both need each other to resolve this pressing issue: What is the world we are creating for future generations?

Ann Roulac
is the National Director of Residential and Community Development Services with Arthur Andersen & Co., L.P. Real Estate Services Group. She has more than twenty years of experience in the real estate and financial services industries and has been involved in more than 2,000 residential communities in the United States, Mexico, Southeast Asia, and Canada as a real estate advisor.

Prior to joining Arthur Andersen & Co., Roulac was president of Ann Roulac & Company, a real estate consulting firm in the San Francisco Bay Area. She also founded and served as president of the Project Loan Division of the Bank of America Mortgage and International Realty Corporation, served as the assistant vice president of the Project Loan Department for First Interstate Mortgage Company, worked as an associate with Questor Associates, and acted as a branch manager with Grubb and Ellis Property Services.

She is a member and past president of the San Francisco Bay Area Mortgage Association. She is a member of the Urban Land Institute, World Business Academy, American Real Estate Society, and National Association of Real Estate Investment Trusts.

30

Tangible and Intangible Structures
Ann Roulac

The environments we create either enhance or block our ability to create the spirit of community—a sense of intimacy, connectedness and partnership. In this context, environment is defined as surroundings that affect our lives, and that includes not only the physical but also the nonphysical aspects of our immediate environment. The rebuilding of inner cities and the planning of new communities will require a holistic understanding of the tangible and the intangible aspects of community development.

All of us, in particular those who live and work in modern structures, are profoundly influenced and affected by the buildings in which we live and work. Their design affects our moods, ideas, creativity, productivity, effectiveness, harmony, or lack of the same. Building design clearly affects whether we come together as a team, group or community, and can dictate whether we work and live together in partnership or in alienation. The structures we design are our legacy for future generations.

> We first design our structures, then they design our lives.
> —Winston Churchill

In other words, we mold our environments and then our environments mold us.

MY FATHER: THE MASTER BUILDER

This essay was inspired by the passing of my father, who was my primary mentor, both in my business and in my personal life. My father was a "master builder" and pioneered a single responsibility concept, which resulted in projects characterized by superior design, faster building cycles, and more cost-effective budgets.

Perhaps what my father did best was observe. He taught me to observe both the tangible aspects of our environment—the terrain, structures, design, and color—and also the intangibles. Through his influence I became a keen observer of my surroundings, seeing how the design of the structures we work and live in affect our lives—culturally, emotionally, psychologically, physically, and economically. This led to my choice of career—advising developers and finance and community development professionals on how intangible and tangible influences are synthesized to obtain a whole systems perspective.

My father used to explain to me that a community developer was like an orchestra leader. The leader needs to understand the capabilities and qualities of each instrument. The successful community developer must consider all parts of the community in the planning and design process. And so it is that I listen for the synergy of the "observation of intangibles" weighted by a correlation with the tangibles.

It is my observation of the tangibles and my correlation of them with the intangibles that enables me to determine the potential feasibility of a community structure and become an effective participant in the community development process. Every site, building, home, and business environment creates a certain energy. Each structure has a message, and these statements result in a structure's acceptance by the market and determine its long-term economic viability as well as its influence on the current culture.

THE COMMUNITY DEVELOPER AS LEADER

My use of the word "community" comes from the Oxford dictionary, which defines it as "a body of people living in one place, district or country." A community developer is an individual or company whose work is to develop new structures or rehabilitate older buildings within a given location. This process requires the partnership of many players who are essential in producing viable community buildings and neighborhoods. Their ability to work together in partnership, dictates the success or failure of the structures, the buildings we live and work in.

The community developer's task is to guide the development process and coordinate the work of land planners, architects, engineers, economic, environmental and financial consultants, and community representatives. Additionally, this process requires obtaining commitments to provide debt and equity financing and a lengthy entitlement process of obtaining the required permits from all city, county, state and federal agencies; this task can take as long as five years to obtain approval for a small apartment complex.

This long and cumbersome process that community developers undertake is not for the timid; it requires a multitude of skills as well as a thorough knowledge of numerous disciplines. The leadership of this process must come from the community developers, those who create the end product and whose role is to implement the private process of real estate development through the public process of entitlement and approvals.

Sadly, most developers have become so frustrated, not only with the length of the process but with the numerous participants they need to please, that they have given up their responsibilities as leaders. Hence, there is a leadership vacuum with no one guiding the process. This leadership vacuum is of course not limited to the community development process, but is also lacking in our corporations, communities and government agencies. In order for us to change, our leadership styles need to allow for more creativity and participation. When this happens we will become more productive, effective and economically viable.

In many cases, community developers need to take back their role as leaders and develop their skills and abilities in creating partnership. In order to create partnership, in an organization or community, the different needs of a community must be acknowledged and orchestrated. This is the only way that we can develop projects that are viable for the long term.

When one party does not consider the objectives and needs of the community, and the design of a structure is dictated only by neighborhood groups or by financial institutions, the result is often a structure designed in an attempt to please everyone. As a result, it is often not a successfully designed building. Granted, leaders within a community need to voice their opinions and concerns about proposed changes to their neighborhoods. But often their suggestions result in so changing the original plan and vision of the developer that the resulting structures do not serve the community for the long term.

In order for community developers to be successful, they need to be community based or have something at stake in the community. When structures are designed and built with no clear vision or concern of serving the target market, the result is the production of buildings that have little or no economic viability. They have little function and do not serve the needs of the intended users of the space.

THE COMMUNITY INVESTMENT PROCESS

Many of our physical structures are uninviting and nonfunctional. Before we can understand why the places we live and work in are displeasing to us we must develop an understanding of how the investment decision that funded their construction predetermined their fate. By uncovering the fundamental error in investment planning—that linear qualitative analysis is insufficient data for sound long-term economic investment and social viability—we open the doorway for a decision-making process that is more appropriate for our times—holistic and integrated decision making.

Investment and development decisions are made today without regard for long-term viability, and the most frequent defense for this faulty investment strategy is the "bottom line." In essence, the "bottom line" argument is a short-sighted justification for removing creativity and intangibles from decisions. Most investment decisions then run against the advice of my father and now me. Observe the tangibles *and* intangibles...weigh the influences and benefits of both...and in so doing preserve the integrity of the intention—to make good decisions. The cultures of our corporations have emphasized quantitative analysis to such an extent that our business decisions are no longer balanced and grounded in any human reality.

The short-term analysis of the 1980s produced tremendous losses in the United States as well as in other countries. It has cost us, as a culture, economic stability. This same short-term analysis continues to dominate the decision-making process and the design of our communities.

This is how the error is perpetuated:

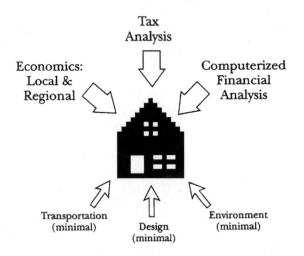

Investment Decisions

Linear Fragmented Approach
Analysis

Figure 1. The Linear Fragmented Approach to Analyzing Investment Decisions

Figure 1 shows the imbalance created by an overemphasis on quantitative analysis. This leads to making investment decisions based upon analyses that are as short as three years.

I see that one of my roles with community development and investment strategists is to make them aware of their decision-making biases and of the way new information and more comprehensive and complex approaches enhance long-term support for all shareholders.

By making explicit the link between the decision framework they apply to a development project and how vital the completed structures will be once completed, I raise awareness of the invisible infrastructure that predetermines the culture and experience of the people who inhabit the dwellings once they are produced. This is indeed an important leverage point for transforming our environments to be more conducive to cultures of community.

A HOLISTIC, SYSTEMS-ORIENTED APPROACH

Community development is experiencing the same major transformation as are our business, political, and social structures. We have already been exposed in the 1990s to new ways of thinking, working and conducting our lives; now we need new patterns for development, both nationally and internationally, that are holistic and sustainable—that incorporate new learnings.

Our traditional approach—fragmented and linear—needs to be replaced by one that is integrated and holistic. Our current polices are inconsistent with long term viability and will not produce sustained well-being in our communities. We need new strategic models that incorporate our cultural and technological shifts as well as a concern for the environment.

Participating in the development of master planned communities or the revitalization of downtown areas provides a multitude of opportunities for citizens of a town or city to come together with a development team and create new structures that enhance the quality of life, improve the economic future of a city, and inspire members of the community. If planned and conceived with vision and from a holistic approach, the new or rehabilitated structures can add a greater sense of community.

For the process of designing communities a whole systems understanding of environments is needed, whether it be the physical structures and layout of a building or the design of the culture within a business. If the relationships among the different structures are synergistic the results will be long term economic viability, increased production and a healthy society.

Figure 2 depicts a model for an integrated and holistic approach to the decision-making process of community investment The various components depicted in the figure must be considered and studied as part of the development process. Starting at the top and listing clockwise, these components are:

- Geomancy and *feng shui* give us intuitive tools to determine the appropriate decision and hence use of space.

Integrated Holistic Approach
Analysis

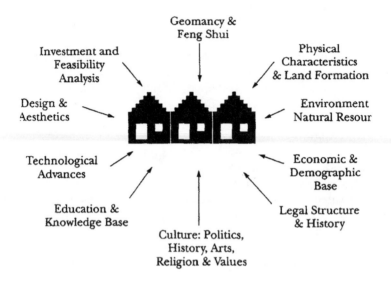

=**Long term/predictable
economic return and production of
quality structures and environments**

Figure 2. The Integrated Holistic Approach to Analyzing Investment Decisions

- Physical characteristics and land formation dictate the appropriate design, density and land use.
- Environment and natural resources indicate whether a development should be considered at all, or what special considerations should be taken in determining the appropriate land use and density.
- Economic and demographic base determines the viability of increasing the existing supply of this particular land use, which must be considered from not only a community perspective, but also a regional, country and world perspective that includes population shifts, ethnic character, household formation, income levels and the subsequent shifts in demand for different structures.

- Legal structure and history also influence the appropriateness, viability and future use of any particular development.
- Culture, which includes politics, history, arts, religion and values, gives us tools to understand the needs of the current residents as well as determine future shifts in those needs.
- Education and knowledge base determines the standards and availability influencing the design and use of space.
- Technological advances spur and predict alternations in the use and demand for space.
- Design and aesthetics are determined by the strength of the economic base, the culture of the region and technological advances.
- Investment and feasibility analysis determine the overall viability of a proposed development only and especially in relation to all the other factors.

We can no longer afford a decision-making process that is linear and fragmented. We can no longer afford to develop structures that do not support our social or economic or community needs. We must expand our development process into a whole-systems approach, by including that which we have previously omitted and that which we have not known or trusted enough to include.

DEVELOPING NEW SKILLS
All human beings have the capacity to see in untangible ways, often defined as our intuition, perception, insight or vision. Most of us tend to value ourselves more for our tangible contributions than for those that are difficult to grasp and see. Another way to describe our intangible senses is through our four intelligences: mental, physical, emotional, and spiritual. Those who heavily rely on their mental intelligence, including citizens of most Western cultures, have less developed physical, emotional, and spiritual intelligences. In my Third World travels I have observed how strongly citizens of other cultures have developed their physical and emotional intelligences, as they are often required as a basis for survival.

When members of a community, whether a neighborhood or organization, have developed intelligences other than their mental ones, it becomes easier to create solutions; we will start to sense where other people are coming from and understand their points of view. When we try to reach solutions only through our limited mental intelligences, we are limiting the potential success and outcome of our decisions.

Feng Shui
In Figure 2, I have put "Geomancy and Feng Shui" at the beginning of the decision-making process. *Feng shui* is an ancient Chinese practice that dates back 3,000 years ago. It spread to Japan and Southeast Asian countries 1,000 years ago. Today it is used in the United States to create harmony, balance, and prosperity. In practice, *feng shui* is something between a science and an art; Westerners may

call it geomancy, or divination by means of signs derived from the earth. The two are not really identical in that feng shui includes astrological and spiritual aspects.

Feng shui experts understand that commercial buildings have a psychological as well as structural function, and that business people need to feel a sense of balance in order to maintain a clear mind and achieve success. *Feng shui* deals with the intangible aspects of the built environment and advocates that buildings should be located and built to harmonize with the surrounding buildings and the natural environment. *Feng shui's* sensitivity to the human and physical environment places an emphasis on the whole with contribution from many of the component parts. *Feng shui* can also assist us in creating the supportive structures that help us experience our workplaces as communities.

One example of *feng shui* use in the 1980s was in the planning and design of a high-rise office building in downtown Oakland, California. The owners and architects consulted a *feng shui* advisor to help them position the building's entrance on the site.

One way of strengthening our non-mental, intuitive skills is by acting as a modern day *feng shui* agent. The ancient practice of *feng shui* masters may take a lifetime of training, yet we can all become apprentice *feng shui* agents. By this process we can become more sensitive to our environments. Although my father never used this practice explicitly, his philosophy is truly congruent with this approach. *Feng shui* translated literally is "wind" and "water"; it evolved from the simple observation that people are affected, for good or ill, by their surroundings and their environment, by the layout and orientation of workplaces and homes. It also concludes that if you change your surroundings you change your life.

The goal of *feng shui* is to change and harmonize the environment to improve fortunes. As Westerners we may not be accustomed to these nuances. When translated as part of the intangible aspect of a holistic decision process, it can be easily incorporated.

Intuition

Developing our intuition and our capacity to be visionaries enables us to see what might be possible. We cannot develop our intuitive skills until we learn to step back and become an observer. In an environment of accelerated change, it becomes even more important to stop and observe. But this is becoming increasingly more difficult. The pressures experienced by business people today are extraordinary. The demands on our time, with our commitments to career, family, friends, personal growth and community, leave very little time for reflection. However, reflection can lead us to the non-obvious.

Self-Reflection

If we slow down sufficiently and take a step back, the next appropriate action might be more evident. Everyone has experienced a sense of knowing, at a gut level, what works and what does not work, whether it is dealing with the structures of interpersonal relationships or the right business decision. Daily I observe people pursuing opportunities that are either not going to happen, or are inappropriate or contradictory to their company's strategic focus. The result is capital and energy being spent needlessly. We tell ourselves, "there is no time for reflection," but we do not count everything we waste by acting before we observe and reflect.

SHIFTING TO A HOLISTIC APPROACH

As current and future leaders, we must be fully developed thinkers with the capacity to grasp long-term implications. We must be aware not only of the economic effects of our decisions but also the future technological changes that will alter our culture. Considerations of our environment and of continually changing ecological priorities are paramount to the pragmatic visionary.

When doing business with different cultures and countries, it is important that we find common needs and goals beyond the barriers of nonverbal behavior, values, and language. We need to pay attention to behavior, to be more sensitive, to be adaptable and cooperative. In North America, cultural diversity will become increasingly important to growth, and we need to be flexible—open to new ideas and able to see multiple perspectives.

We will continue to experience a dramatic restructuring of our economy, organizations, and culture. Our challenge is to train ourselves to be cross-culturally competent and to think and act globally. This will require cognizance of areas beyond economics: law, politics, culture, history. The pragmatic visionary sees more than the bottom line.

How can we benchmark ourselves against what other people have done?

Part Seven: Case Studies and Applications

Do all these ideas work? Or, is all this community-building stuff a giant "head trip"? In this section, seven authors collaborate to show examples of specific applications of some of the previous thinking.

Hope Greenfield reports on work being done at Digital Equipment Corporation while William Clarkson and Lyman Randall recall their incredible achievements turning around Graphic Controls, a New York-based publicly-traded international company.

Jeanne Borei and John Pehrson shine the spotlight on a seldom-discussed byproduct of community building—the "shadow" side—based on their experience with various business and educational organizations, such as the Tel-A-Train Corporation and the Hyde School.

Finally, Dinesh Chandra and Buddy Johnson share one bank's role in discovering its relationship to the community in Broward County, Florida—the case of First Union National.

Hope Greenfield
is vice president, Development and Learning, at Digital Equipment Corporation. She has worldwide responsibility for the development and training of employees, including introducing new approaches and systems to enhance both employee and organizational effectiveness.

In her twenty years' experience in business and education, her work has been focused on enhancing business productivity and human development. She believes that organizational learning is fostered by individual learning and strives to build communities and systems that support people in their development and growth. At Digital, she has worked across all major business areas of the company. In her current job, she plays a key role in ensuring that employees have the right skills for their work as the company realigns its business strategies.

A native of New York City, Greenfield received a B.A. in English from the University of Massachusetts and an Ed.M. in Organization Behavior from Harvard University.

31

Corporate Community

Hope Greenfield

Digital Equipment Corporation, a multinational high tech computer company, is a remarkable place, even after several tough years. It is remarkable for its legion of bright, highly-educated employees who want, and have always wanted, to do the right thing for their customers, their shareholders, and their colleagues.

The "right thing" is not the same today as when the company was founded more than 30 years ago, nor is it likely to be the same a year from now. When Digital first opened its doors in 1957, employees knew what the right thing was. But in recent years that information has changed, forcing the company to recognize its inability to remain competitive and heading it into austere and painful times. Helping employees learn together as a community so they can collectively rediscover the right thing, and continue rediscovering it as they work to return the company to profitability, is the biggest challenge the corporation faces today.

The concept of a corporation nurturing community may seem counterintuitive to some, yet it can be a competitive advantage. How else can an organization ever hope to make genuine consensus-based decisions, achieve widespread organizational competence, adapt quickly and effectively to major changes and shifts in the marketplace, or live comfortably with the ambiguity and chaos it may face?

Still, corporations are not known for supporting community among employees. There is talk of a "corporate culture" or a "corporate identity," but one does not often hear the expression "corporate community."

Issues of size, place, hierarchy, and how authority and leadership are exercised in the corporation profoundly affect any effort to build and maintain community. The story contained in this chapter describes the struggles and triumphs of one organization in Digital and the people in it as they attempted to overcome the obstacles innate in the "corporate community" and become a genuine learning community.

LEARNING THAT LEARNING MUST BE PART OF SUCCESS

In May of 1993, Digital Equipment Corporation formed a new function for employee development and learning. Over the years, the company had spent hundreds of millions of dollars on skills-based, classroom-oriented training. And while successful for a time with state-of-the-art instructional design and technology, it did not remain so.

Over time, numerous Training and Education groups were formed throughout the company—virtually every business unit and major function had one. Although there were efforts to work collaboratively across these groups, the many disparate systems led to an underutilized and overpriced infrastructure, obsolete and inefficient product and service delivery models, few common business practices, and no automated system to track development and learning spending across the company.

Organizational learning was never viewed as a way to achieve competitive advantage at Digital. Skills training had become a tool that managers used only when necessary—a discretionary spending item in the budget. The company had not focused on using development and learning as a lever for profitability or achieving its strategic business goals. It was, however, starting to lose money and market share. As the business changed and the company's strategy with it, Digital's senior executives realized that a radical, company-wide transformation would have to take place if the company was to survive. This would include becoming customer focused and adopting a commodity market approach.

The Worldwide Development and Learning Organization was formed to help the transformation. The explicit goals were: manage spending by integrating the various training programs, increase employee involvement and understanding of customers, and increase management capability. Clearly the corporation needed to move quickly away from the fragmented management strategies that had so completely neglected any whole system thinking. The implicit goals inside the function were to enhance the way people learned—that is, transform the model of what learning is and move from skills-based learning solutions to employee development and collective learning. Included was the desire by the Worldwide Development and Learning leadership to be the first organization to model the behavior of a learning community.

Two major challenges were clear from the outset: define the vision and architecture for the organization and pull together a disenfranchised community of people.

THE HEART OF COMMUNITY AT DIGITAL

Corporations must show compassion and an understanding of how that affects organizational learning and group competence. Although it may be difficult, it is possible for the corporate community to show heart. But it takes more than just the recognition of community. Specifically, the community itself must have regard for each individual's being, honor diversity, have the will to heal itself if unhealthy, and encourage relationships that allow for individual growth. Corporations that have discovered their heart are rising above the rest. They do so by celebrating their employees and by making them feel valued and effective through far-reaching diversity programs, reward and recognition programs, and extensive development and learning opportunities. Although Digital had all of these, efforts were uncoordinated and left employees feeling that the corporate community still lacked heart.

Many employees in Development and Learning felt this way, too. Digital's senior management team had never chartered leadership for them. Instead, a number of senior training and education managers had come and gone with little effect while many employees' colleagues and friends had left the company. Understandably, people were skeptical of anyone's ability to effectively pull the organization together for the long term.

Making decisions based on consensus became vital. Although we all had ideas about doing the work, participating in consensus-based decision making engaged the entire community. We would all need to work together to develop and implement our collective ideas if we were to make the kind of changes we felt were critical.

Focus was also important. We concentrated on specific elements that made a difference for people in the organization, namely providing a vision, using widespread consensus building, and creating a logical and workable organizational structure. We also tried to hold people's ambiguity about the changes Digital was experiencing while remaining consistent and predictable in our own behavior.

We established ten task forces, each with its own leader. We then asked them, on behalf of the company, to look at the work that Development and Learning was carrying out in their assigned area and to offer comments and recommendations for the future. We populated these task forces by inviting not just Development and Learning people, but any Digital employees worldwide who had an interest. Approximately 250 people signed up.

We worked closely with these groups to apply their ideas and learning to create our vision and organizational structure for Development and Learning. To start, we defined a simple vision—that is, in what direction we needed to move. Our beginnings were communicated widely across the company with videotaped presentations and visits to all ten task forces. In addition, we met with people all over the company to share our views and include them in the process. We were bringing the whole system together to articulate its difficulties and weaknesses, to come to a common understanding of the current situation, and to create a vision that would generate creative tension.

We held large group meetings on a regular basis as we progressed. The members of the task forces were invited to these meetings, along with anyone else who wished to attend, either personally or via satellite hook-up. The goal of these meetings was to provide a forum for everyone to work in larger groups beyond their task forces—to share their learning and to move their ideas towards the vision. On several occasions, we had groups of more than a hundred people come together.

Even though they had all been doing development work for many years, it was interesting and new for many people to sit down at the same table with colleagues from other areas of the company. It was an exciting part of the process for everyone—in some ways even more so than the specific contributions they were making.

It was not always a smooth ride. People were skeptical and even cynical. In the large groups, we were asked to "just give them the answer." They assumed we had already figured out what we wanted and these meetings were just to make people feel included. At each meeting, we stated our belief that we needed to be a learning organization and that the best way to achieve this was to model the behavior ourselves. The process itself was structured to be a learning process, so meetings were working sessions with active participation and exchange of ideas. We did not have the answers—we genuinely needed these people to help the organization find them.

In order to create success in the existing hierarchical structure, regular meetings were held with individual members of Digital's senior management team. By focusing not only on our task forces but on upper management's perception of our progress as well, we encouraged overall organizational success by ensuring our work genuinely supported management's strategic business needs. Eventually, a small team incorporated all this information into the final design of the organization. After only four months, our senior management team approved both the design and the architecture for the organization. From there we began to rebuild the Development and Learning organization and refocus the work.

RESPONSIBILITY FOR COMMUNITY

Many of Digital's employees have become confused about who is genuinely responsible for community in the corporation and to what degree. A pitfall of the corporate hierarchy is that it can be too easy to pass the buck—upward or downward. In Digital, the buck often did not stop anywhere.

To address this kind of uncertainty, it was vital to communicate clearly and often, and to ensure that people knew what was expected of them. I expect the people working with and for me to take initiative. With initiative comes autonomy, independence, and responsibility which they are expected to use wisely. It is typical for me to test ideas by suggesting them to groups of people with the notion that they take the initial ideas and experiment with them. In this process it is important to remember that ideas are not tangible things that should be clung to—they are dynamic and fluid, and sometimes do not represent where a team or group may end up. The goal of working this way is to create and sustain a work in progress that the team can improve upon. It brings vitality into the process, and it makes room for unique and creative solutions.

People in the organization also needed to understand what I believed I was responsible for, and what I would hold them responsible for. I found that people often wanted me, as the authority figure, simply to direct them. For example, as this work was evolving, I felt pressure from inside the organization to put together an organizational structure and to come forward with names in boxes, a traditional organization chart. I resisted doing this for six months—well beyond the completion of our design work. Only then did I put together a "working structure," that is, a diagram of how the different parts of the organization should work together. This is not to say that people were not in roles doing vital work during this time. But, by not following an organization chart, they resisted the urge to immediately retreat into their niches. They were forced to stay in the uncomfortable place of uncertainty. It was an ambiguous place for understanding how the work would be done, but it left people more receptive to new ideas and new ways of doing this work. Instead of aligning themselves with a "job" in an organization chart, they focused on the work, and continued to create new ideas about how to get it done. When large-scale transformation is the goal, as was ours, a deliberate comfort with ambiguity and chaos is required. Purposely not creating an organization chart was one way to nurture this skill.

Another way was to increase the level of communication. Communication represents a cornerstone in responsibility. During transition, communication is more important than ever, and when a non-directive leadership style is added to the mix, it becomes imperative. Expectations were not the only things needing to be communicated. Employees needed to know about their progress at every step. Electronic mail and other electronic forums proved powerful tools. We used a public forum in which employees asked questions directly of my staff and me, and we answered them immediately. Employees needed and wanted to hear information from the source, and as leader of the organization, I could provide that. In broad terms, the goal was to model an open and effective communication style so that others would follow the example.

THE PLACE OF COMMUNITY IN DIGITAL

Issues of size and place have been sources of struggle in Digital's wider corporate community. The company has recently restructured, resulting in a more clearly defined, smaller number of businesses, and our product and service offerings are being reorganized as well. We have reduced not only the number of people in the company but also physical space by selling or closing buildings all over the world.

In the Development and Learning community, we have reduced the number of training facilities and the number of courses offered. We have also defined a clear working structure with permeable yet durable boundaries with the functions and businesses in the corporation. In addition, we have created an inner space to recognize harsh realities, including mistakes, ambiguity, and sorrow.

As an example, I mentioned earlier in this chapter the notion of sustaining a work in progress. This implies room for mistakes—that we can all make mistakes and that we can recover from them. Our team had to learn to acknowledge when mistakes were made. Sometimes, the acknowledgment was public, giving people the opportunity to learn from the mistake. Unfortunately, some people thought that a mistake would derail an entire process. Early in the formation of our Development and Learning Leadership Team, I made mistakes in handling aspects of our administrative information. In the end, it was a wonderful opportunity for all of us to learn, as many people expected this mistake to derail our whole process, or at least demonstrate to other managers that I did not know what I was doing.

To the surprise of many, I publicly acknowledged the mistake in a meeting with our managers and invited people to come and see me if they had any concerns. Resolution of the mistake included a mid-course correction that offered a new way of doing a particular piece of work. It proved to be a very useful lesson early on in the process. This situation also exposed the people in the organization who were waiting for me and our efforts to fail, and it allowed me to address those people's intentions head on. It also allowed people to see that, although mistakes are made, they do not have to be fatal. There is a way for us to collectively learn from them and carry on with integrity.

BEING A LEADER IN TOUGH TIMES

My experience prompts me to offer three tenets of leadership:

1. Hold creative tension and chaos.

Holding creative tension and chaos is an important skill for a leader in a disempowered community. Employees want to see their work come to fruition and feel like they can make a positive contribution. That may not seem possible in times of transition. Yet while the system is fluid, dynamic or even confused, the leader can provide grounding—a focus and center that people can depend on to move things forward. It implies, of course, having the courage of one's convictions, exhibiting grace under pressure, and managing unconscious processes. Once I have made a decision, for example, I must have the courage to stick with it and advocate it, even when people think it is wrong. I listen to them, and consider their advice, but, if I believe the decision is right, I must be ready to fight for it. And I will fight for what my team is trying to do, right up to the top of the management chain. But the goal is to be clear about my intentions so that others can follow, even if the environment seems confused and without focus.

2. Do not forget inquiry.

Dialogue is appropriate, and giving people the opportunity to voice their opinions is invaluable. This must be balanced with the understanding that there will always be a difference of opinions in a rich environment where people with varied backgrounds and approaches work together. There comes a time, however, when decisions must be made, and the process of inquiry closed. When that time comes, every leader should be capable and willing to take the necessary action. In leading my organization, I often inform the group in advance of the need to discuss a certain issue. I hear the opinions of the people involved, and I make a decision based on their input. It takes courage to inquire, because once people are drawn into the process, they will expect the decision to reflect in some way the input they gave.

3. Watch for pitfalls.

I believe that people will rally around work even though they may not necessarily rally around the individual who is leading the work. Community is built on integrity and honesty, not popularity. A manager and leader must be willing to risk unpopularity in order to lead effectively and foster that skill within the community itself. Some will look for personal failure in their management, and they are looking for the work to fail. Yet, they are part of the community. Ultimately, the goal is to engage even those people, so that everyone can succeed.

In Conclusion...

Since our organization began work more than a year ago, we have made much progress toward our goals, though it has not always been easy. Keeping people engaged, working to keep the energy going even while transitioning people out of the company, and dealing with resistance at higher levels of management have all been time-consuming concerns. People have had a hard time holding this new vision for themselves and trusting there would really be a change this time. Even doubling my efforts to communicate would have been too little to help make this change a reality for people.

Yet, the ambiguous place we were in, and still are to some degree, has allowed us to put together a first-ever, fully integrated plan for Development and Learning with company-wide initiatives that all of our client organizations understand and support. We now have a set of tools, development processes, and technology approaches that are leading edge and carry a high degree of management support across the company.

Building a learning community does not necessarily buffer a group from larger organizational imperatives that have a tendency to weaken trust and commitment. We will have a 40 percent drop in population in the Development and Learning organization this year due to changes in the company and subsequent reductions of people. But we have tried to stay focused on the positive aspects of these changes. In some ways, the downsizing has helped our efforts to change from a skills-based, classroom-oriented organization, to one that supports more action-oriented learning, learning for specific jobs, major business strategies, and customer focus. It has also encouraged people to look at and share resources and approaches outside our once stovepiped organizations. All this has aided our efforts in providing an integrated yet broader definition of how development happens in the company.

The learning community is slowly building. Our new name—Development and Learning—has been adopted across the company by all groups and is recognized as the function responsible for employee learning. People within the function today feel they can make a difference—not just individually, but also because they can contribute to something larger.

On a corporate-wide scale, we have succeeded in providing a strategic focus for the development and learning work, and saved the company millions of dollars. More specifically, through our efforts to build the learning community, people are able to do the work differently and better able to focus on the good of the company. There is what may best be described as common intentionality among the people—they are learning to hold the vision. They have direction, even during these turbulent times. They are also engaging in advocacy and inquiry, producing effective and creative solutions.

But our work is not done. Digital will change dramatically over the next year, and we will change with it. We will not always be able to continue to work in integrated teams as the company decreases its population and moves to a more divisionalized structure. However, it is our goal to continue to integrate the work with the intentionality behind it. Through our learning community, we will continue to seek out consensus-based decisions, achieve organizational competence, adapt quickly and effectively to major changes, and live comfortably with the ambiguity and chaos we may face.

William Clarkson is former chairman and CEO of Graphic Controls Corporation. He also served as New York State's Executive Deputy Commissioner of Commerce for two years. He has his own management consulting practice, is a member of The Family Business Consultancy, and is an adjunct professor at the State University of New York at Buffalo. He has written many articles on management, focusing on such topics as high involvement, participative management; a presidential selection process for non-profit organizations; and a Peter Drucker retrospective for New Management.

Lyman Randall has been a management practitioner for nearly forty years. He held staff OD and line operating positions at American Airlines and headed Graphic Controls Corporation's largest operating profit-center, which reached $80 million annual sales during his eight–year tenure. He has authored many articles in Harvard Business Review, California Management Review, and publications of the American Management Association. He also is a published poet.

Clarkson and Randall worked together at Graphic Controls from 1974 to 1983. More recently, they have continued their working together as directors on the board of the Foundation for Community Encouragement.

32

Needed:
Leaders to Stick Their Necks Out

William Clarkson & Lyman Randall

In 1970 Graphic Controls, a publicly traded international company head-quartered in Buffalo, New York, was losing money for the first time in its history. The Board of Directors promoted William Clarkson to the presidency with the mandate to "turn the company around." His strategy and actions for accomplishing the Board's mandate were highly unusual for 1970. He decided to use participative management combined with performance objective-setting to rebuild community and profitability. More than 700 jobs were at risk as well as investments from several thousand shareholders. This is the story of that successful turnaround as told by Clarkson and one of his senior executives, Lyman Randall. During the 1974–1983 period the two authors worked closely together helping guide this industrial experiment; for those nine years, company sales and profits grew at an annually compounded rate of 19 percent .

The following pages contain a conversation between Lyman Randall and Will Clarkson, reflecting on their success and learning during the Graphics Controls experiment.

Lyman: Since the positive results of the Graphic Controls' turnaround are now history, the risks you faced as you began your presidency are easily forgotten. Do you still remember what you were thinking and feeling at that time, as you faced so many unknowns?

Will: At the time, the company had been in Buffalo for thirty years. I knew we had good people who were highly motivated to succeed. I also knew we had a good core business which had been profitable in prior years. We once had a vitality which had largely disappeared. Somehow, the spirit had gone out of the organization and its people—including me at times. Losing money for the first time as a public company did not help matters. I sensed that we needed to change the ways we did things if we were to rebuild a vital and productive workplace community.

Lyman: What were some of the things that needed to change if this spirit and vitality were to be found again?

Will: I knew from the moment I became president that I did not have all the answers to the questions which faced us. Prior management behaved as if it believed it knew what was best for the organization. Therefore, the executive group decided most important issues without much input or help from people at lower levels. Despite having had a philosophy of benign paternalism for many years, we had unintentionally become a traditional, top-down, authoritarian-managed company, and this had become part of the problem. Special perks had also been allowed to evolve which reinforced this assumed "specialness" of senior management. I believed we had to let go of this exalted view of our executives—and quickly. So I reframed how I wanted our managers to manage.

Lyman: I know that three of the key elements in that reframing were participation, a decentralized organization structure, and the use of both team and individual performance objectives. Were there other important ingredients?

Will: Yes. We focused on high employee involvement, striving for commitment that comes from participation, team building, self-directed work groups, the survey-feedback-action model, financial and non-financial team incentives, and community-building—all of which I believed would produce better results and create a healthier workplace for our people.

Lyman: All of these new ideas didn't just appear to you in a dream one night. What happened beforehand to make you believe this was a management innovation worth trying?

Will: I knew from twenty years of work experience about the frustration of wanting to do a better job, but feeling prevented from doing so by the constraints of my work environment.

In the 1960s I was introduced to the thinking of McGregor, Likert, Bennis, Maslow, Lewin, Gellerman and Marrow.

I also had some experiential learning in a "human interaction lab" run by the NTL Institute. This gave me a deeper understanding of myself, my impact on others, how to relate to and communicate more effectively with people, and how to apply this knowledge to my relationships at work and at home.

The cumulative impact of these experiences on me was substantial. It led me to the conclusion that the practical application of these theories could make a lot of sense.

As Kurt Lewin said, "There is nothing so practical as a good theory." But when I launched this management adventure (some called it a "misadventure"), I knew I had my neck stuck out more than the proverbial "country mile."

Lyman: You rarely talk about those early risks. Can you elaborate?

Will: First, I wondered if the nine senior managers reporting to me—the Corporate Management Group or CMG—would respond positively and give this new management approach an honest and enthusiastic try? I was deliberately looking the other way on a key element of the new value system, "informed choice." I was pressuring people to take the risk with me; would they be supportive?

Even if my senior managers supported me, I had no guarantee the new approach would work. I did know, however, that all of us working in organizations have at least one characteristic in common: Our potential is greater than our performance. Would a changed and supportive environment enable everyone to reduce these individual gaps by a modest amount with the cumulative impact bringing about a substantial improvement in personal and corporate performance? Would the losses turn into profits as people worked more effectively, both individually and together as teams?

Our financial losses were real and very public. We were in uncharted waters with no map. Would there be enough time to get improved financial results before the financial community and the banks closed in on us?

I was not aware of the biggest risk of all, however. My job was on the line. The Board of Directors (the majority were outside independent directors) didn't know about my decision to lead Graphic Controls with a new, high involvement, participative management style. There was no intent on my part to mislead the directors. However, on a need-to-know basis, I did not see the necessity of conducting a seminar for them on my new management approach. My view was that the board would understand me by what I did rather than by what I preached.

If the financial results had not shown substantial improvement in the first two to three years, I would have been removed. Why? Because the directors believed that "we need a president who manages by tried and true methods we understand, not one who is experimenting with newfangled philosophies!" The directors gradually understood that some different things were happening within the organization, some of which they understood and some that they did not.

Lyman: Considering all of these risks, why in the world did you choose this particular time to test unproven strategies?

Will: A number of pressures were pushing us. There had been a pattern of declining profits, which led to the first loss since the company became public five years earlier. There was much internal tension, dissatisfaction with the status quo, apprehension, suspicion, and mistrust.

The questions I had to answer were important and urgent. What was really going on? I needed to collect valid data about both the internal and external environment. How could the financial losses be stopped? What course needed to be plotted for the future?

The choice was simple; it was an either/or situation. I could either follow the leadership route of conventional wisdom using a hierarchical—authoritarian—managerial style focusing on independence, single-person-power orientation, and ask for commitment by command. Or I could try to be the humanistic manager of the future having a participative, authoritative managerial style focusing on interdependence, individual-and-group knowledge orientation, and ask for commitment via involvement and participation. I chose the latter course for three reasons.

The first was that the organization was in a crisis and I believed that my vision had a better chance of pulling it through. Additionally, there was an experienced and enthusiastic consulting psychologist available to me, whom I trusted and who pledged himself to facilitate helping this experiment be successful.

And, finally, it would be a response to the challenge for every human institution: What is it doing for the making of better men and women?

Lyman: You've referred to various, now familiar phrases, to describe this new approach. But the way you describe the change, it sounds almost radical, at least for the early 1970s. What were the "guts" of what you committed yourself to do? What do you consider the "heart" of your approach?

Will: Like the Ten Commandments, the foundation was our value system. Ours had Five Commandments:

1. *The authority of knowledge.* People's expertise based on their experience was more important than where they happened to be in the old fashioned "command structure".
2. *The sharing of power and decision-making authority, while retaining individual accountability.* As we know from our later community-building experience, this included the principles of inclusivity as well as the key step of emptying ourselves of the old top management belief that power should be retained at the top.
3. *Effective participation and involvement produces commitment.* Once again, the community-building principle of inclusivity was important.
4. *Use of individual and group responsibility*—that is, the whole, via effective collaboration, is greater than the sum of the individual parts. As we later learned from our experience with M. Scott Peck's Foundation for Community Encouragement, a mysterious power and transformed competencies are released in community-building.
5. *Informed choice.* Rarely is our world limited to either/or choices. We were looking for, and got, a broader spectrum of alternatives.

In addition, this clearly stated value system resulted in a different organizational structure. We retained the traditional one-to-one hierarchical reporting relationship but added group structures, like an umbrella, over the one-to-one organization. There were groups of all types, both temporary and permanent task groups, plus senior and middle management groups.

We changed the way we worked and lived together. We wanted to move from the authority of power to the authority of knowledge; from power being concentrated in individual people to the sharing of power and leadership; from people being independent, distrusting, and competitive to being interdependent, trusting, and collaborative. Instead of only one-on-one work relationships, we wanted to include work groups with authentic team building, formed in organic ways. Instead of authoritarian decisions, we aimed at effective involvement and participation so that decisions by consensus could be made, accompanied by high levels of commitment. We believed that people's feelings, behavior, and approaches for accomplishing work were as important as the task to be done. Finally, we wanted to move from people having little or no choice to having informed choices. That's what you found us working on when you joined us in 1974.

Lyman: Do you recall the situation created by the wage/price controls being withdrawn by the Nixon administration in 1974 shortly after I joined the firm? That governmental decision was the seed from which much chaos grew within GC. Many of our people were outspoken about their expectations. They believed they should be "made whole" as soon as the controls were lifted. They clearly felt "entitled" to large pay and benefits increases. We feared we could not meet these expectations and remain a profitable company. We feared our open-shop status might be threatened if people's high expectations were not met. There was no clear answer. It appeared we were in the classic double-bind of "damned if we do...damned if we don't."

Will: So we talked and talked within our management group (the CMG). Many of us expressed our fears and frustrations about not knowing what to do. Differences emerged and were debated vigorously. From this growing chaos, we finally decided to create a Wage-Benefit Task Group comprised of people from all levels and functions of the company.

Lyman: The CMG developed a reasonably clear charter outlining what we expected the Task Group to do. Then we let go of the problem, or at least we tried to. As I recall, our greatest fear was: "What if the Task Group gets out of control? What if they do or recommend something we cannot live with?" But with all the unknowns, we still let go of the traditional role of top management—that is, that we knew the "best answers."

We were guided by many of the principles we now know are essential for community-building—for example, trust, openness, inclusivity, acceptance; tolerance for ambiguity; humility; authenticity. The CMG practiced these among ourselves in dealing with the chaos. We believed that others would be willing to live by these same principles if they saw top management practicing them. Perhaps, without verbalizing it as clearly as we might today, we answered the critical question: "What do you do when you don't know what to do?" Our answer was that in GC we would follow the structure and discipline of these community-building principles as well as the five value cornerstones you mentioned earlier. As was true in the Task Group work, whenever we did this well, outcomes were much more positive than they probably would have been had we followed the traditional hierarchical-authority model.

Will: Yes, I recall that Task Group work. Lots of management people, from the CMG on down, were convinced what we were doing would blow up in our faces. Of course, what they were fearing was loss of control, giving too much power and influence away to others. I confess that a few times I was somewhat nervous myself.

Lyman: That makes two of us. When the Task Group decided to conduct a survey, asking each of our U.S. employees for his or her perceptions about a broad spectrum of working conditions and issues, the chaos increased. The first time we conducted the survey we called it The Wage-Benefit Survey. Ed Lawler and Phil Mirvis from the Institute of Social Research (ISR), University of Michigan, provided us with the necessary outside professional help. I recall one group of manufacturing foremen who came to me pleading their case to stop "The Survey" before it was too late! They feared a whole range of possible negative outcomes such as unionizing efforts and disciplinary problems. Hours of dialogue were required to work through this chaos and the differences which emerged. In the end, however, our CMG's "gut-instinct" to build community by including everyone in finding acceptable solutions proved to be a very effective approach. Two years later, the survey became The Quality of Work Life (QWL) Survey which we administered to all GC employees biannually thereafter until the late 1980s. It opened many doors in the total organization which probably would have remained closed had we followed a more traditional approach to that early crisis.

Will: I'm reminded of another thorny issue which took years to resolve but turned out okay. When you joined GC in early 1974, only the CMG was eligible for our annual bonus, based on the degree to which company profits exceeded the prior year.

Lyman: Yes, I recall. Within the next year or two, however, we extended the bonus to the next management level. Since sales and profits were growing through this period, many of the bonus payments were attractively large. As the CMG discussed extending the bonus to more people, strong differences emerged. Most of these were directly or indirectly linked to the reality that those of us already eligible for bonus would need to reduce the amounts of our own earning opportunities if we included more people in the program. I don't recall any of us naming the underlying issue *greed*, but that's probably an accurate retrospective assessment.

Despite the difficulties, the CMG continued discussing bonus expansion. Slowly the plan was modified to become more inclusive. Finally, by the mid 1980s, every "GCer" working in the United States was eligible for some form of incentive compensation. Although it took ten years of continuous work, our early dream of including everyone was finally achieved. With the benefit of hindsight, my hunch is that involving people in pay decisions which will affect them is one of the severest tests of commitment to community building.

Will, where did we find the time for all those meetings and discussions?

Will: The time issue became a very important one, because managing participatively and building community made demands on us in a number of ways. We asked people for a lot of effort. It was hard work which took all the time we could give it. But there were some aspects that were time-savers.

For example, one of our values was high trust. Along with high trust goes low politicking. The level of politics in this organization was as low as anyone had ever experienced. What a time saver! Also, meeting attendance was restricted to people who had direct responsibility for the subject under discussion or who were authorities of knowledge on that subject. This is very different from the conventional organization where meetings are often attended by people who are just "interested" and people who are there to protect themselves because trust is low.

As Chris Argyris once told us "when trust is high, precision can be low; but when trust is low, precision must be high." There was no need for meticulous recording of everything said or done at meetings. This saved time.

Lyman: I recall many outsiders kept asking us questions like "Can you prove that your excellent financial results are directly related to your management experiment?" Their apparent insistence on "proof" became frustrating at times.

Will: I know exactly what you mean. I felt the same way. Life in the real world of organizations is not as simple as that. Rarely are specific results directly attributable to specific actions. However, I do believe in the Arnie Palmer effect, i.e. that a whole lot of small and specific actions, done right, will have an important end result. And our community building through participative management was one of the actions that contributed to the whole; and the financial part of the whole was a record high net income, annually compounded at 19 percent for nine successive years!

Lyman: While you were addressing the financial results question, I was thinking of other advantages. For example, the minimization of politicking due to the building of trust and openness meant that GC became widely known in Western New York as an excellent place to work. This caused us to receive a large number of employment applications, allowing us to become much more selective in the hiring of new people.

Will: I also recall our commitment to integrate the needs of GC people with the needs of our company as creatively and collaboratively as we could. Our biannual Quality of Work Life surveys helped us to learn how well we were reaching this goal. As a result of doing these audits, I'm reasonably confident that our positive measured outcomes, both financial and non-financial, were the result of our managing participatively and building community.

One of the purposes of our writing this essay is to encourage managers who have not yet experimented with managing participatively and building community in the workplace to stick their necks out and try it.

Lyman: What can a manager do to better prepare himself or herself for this managerial adventure before pushing the launch button?"

Will: Reading articles and books on the subject is good preparation. Although reading can't teach the skills involved, it can help a manager to learn what is needed so that they can later be practiced in a disciplined way. I encourage anyone considering this managerial approach to get some related experiential learning under his or her belt. Although I obtained mine through NTL, community-building workshops conducted by the Foundation for Community Encouragement (FCE) are effective. Another step might be for the manager to work with a trusted outside consultant who has experience in helping organizations move in this direction. This was extremely important to me in launching our participative management approach at GC. But I've left the most important one until last: the manager should identify, as honestly as possible, his or her value system. This is the foundation on which all else is built. What you most deeply believe will always affect what you do. Some of these values must be similar to the principles and values of community discussed earlier. If they are not, the manager should stop before going any further.

Now I have a question for you. How does a manager know if he or she is in a situation which provides a fertile opportunity for managing and building community?

Lyman: I've got a couple of thoughts. First, I believe smaller organizations are more likely both to try and achieve successful community building. One reason relates to worker roles. Many years ago, I read something written by Kenneth Boulding (or one of his associates at the University of Michigan) that compared an organization to a fisherman's net. The knots in the net are the roles and the string connecting each knot with other knots represent the relationships which develop between roles. It's a combination of the knots and string that holds any organization together. In smaller organizations, roles are usually more flexible and people are expected to "wear several hats." Large organizations are usually also older; therefore, roles are more precisely defined and the spaces between the knots in the fisherman's net are more limited. This causes territorial disputes or "turf wars" to erupt. I hasten to add, when I refer to "small organization" I also include a modest sized organizational unit of a larger company such as a manufacturing plant or R & D site many miles distant from corporate headquarters.

My second hunch involves the person who heads the organization, preferably the one who is considering this new management approach. If she or he is role-bound, reluctant to share power with others, or fearful of relaxing controls; usually sees problems as unrelated to herself or himself; and is more interested in protecting things and people instead of encouraging them to move toward what they might become, then the probability is quite low that community-building efforts will be successful. On the other hand, if the person can say openly that he or she doesn't know all of the answers, can cite past actions which demonstrate the application of at least some of the principles of community, can demonstrate a willingness to stick her or his neck out, and show a genuine willingness to create more space and opportunity for people to exercise self-direction and control over their own work, then the odds are favorable that community building can be learned and practiced.

Will: One question remains that we've not yet addressed. Both of us have had several years of intense community-building work since we left GC. As we know, both Scott Peck's writings and the Foundation for Community Encouragement openly stress the important part that *emptying* and the *spirit* play in community building. Emptying is letting go of our attachments, surrendering our ego-based memories and persona. Inviting spirit in to serve as a partner in the process is another key element in achieving community.

During our time working together at GC, neither one of us ever mentioned these concepts even though they were present in our work. How essential are they? How might they help or hinder a person who is launching the management approach we've been discussing?

I am ambivalent, or at least have some serious reservations about speaking to other managers about these two aspects of community building. I know both are essential, but I don't want to frighten anyone away. Let's face it, even today the concepts of emptying and being open to the spirit are used by very few if any businesspeople. We did okay and did not use them. What are your thoughts?

Lyman: In each of us there is a strong attraction toward community. We know at our deepest level that we are not created to live and work alone. We also know that our most valuable and meaningful relationships are those in which we can "let our hair down" or, to put it another way, to take off our mask and reveal ourselves to the other as we really are. I think of this as transforming role-to-role relationships into the much deeper soul-to-soul relationships which characterize community. My experience has been that we cannot will our way into community; however, we can learn the skills that help us to get there. Among the required skills are the abilities to empty ourselves and to invite the spirit to enter relationships via the space we've created through our emptying.

I think anyone who is considering learning these skills is clearly sticking his or her neck out. We need to stick our own necks out in telling people these two concepts and skills are very important if they are to build community. The potential benefits are well worth the risk.

But now let's talk about the future. The year 2000 will soon be here. In the mid 1970s when we were experiencing our early successes, we believed participative management and community building were the "waves of the future." How do we view it now? Was it our "brief and shining hour in Camelot" or something more?

Will: Phil Mirvis recently shared with each of us some encouraging research studies that indicate that our experience was not a "once upon a time" event. According to Phil, the number of U.S. Fortune 1000 companies that have one or more employee involvement or high performing work group projects currently underway has grown from 25 percent in 1986 to 58 percent in 1992. This suggests that in the future we will see even more companies and non-profit organizations being managed by the concepts and principles we've been discussing. What do you think?

Lyman: I am truly excited about the future. I'm with you in believing the trend that Phil Mirvis pointed out will continue. This also means harder work and sticking out our necks even further. Employee participation and involvement currently being reported in the research are only the first or second evolutionary steps toward building deeper levels of community in the workplace. Although employee involvement and self-directed work groups usually yield better results than traditional top-down authoritarian approaches, they involve mostly the head and the hands but very little of the heart and the soul. The focus is still on doing task work better and faster. Granted, when experienced for the first time, they truly are breakthroughs from the past. But eventually this new level of work experience will become the old, the past, from which a newer breakthrough will be required.

I believe the next frontier will involve managers deliberately helping people learn how to become more fully functioning human beings. We occasionally crossed into this new territory when we worked together at GC. We didn't name it anything special, but we knew we had broken through to a deeper level of experience. I now believe these were the occasions when we were able to let go of enough of our past, our personal agendas, our pride, and our fears to enable us to experience a more profound spirit of community in the workplace than any of us ever had experienced before that time. I think we now are learning enough about building deeper community, that we can achieve this more advanced level of "fully functioning human beingness" more often and more intentionally.

Because of its basic nature, community building never stops evolving. It cannot be achieved once and then forgotten. It requires us to stick our necks out continuously and then to learn from the experience.

Perhaps I've been able to capture more succinctly what I'm trying to say about our future in the following poem:

> **Community Builders**
> Doctors?...perhaps;
> Helping older children
> Through pain
> Of being born again.
>
> Pastors?...well maybe;
> Struggling in the quagmire
> Of monotonous days
> To help ourselves
> Find resurrection
> By discovering eternity
> In today's new moment.
>
> Shaman?...secretly, perhaps;
> Learning to be
> Finite gods
> Creating miracles
> Within shadowed mysteries
> Of our lives.

Human-physicists?...that seems to fit;
Exploring the possibilities
For connecting the collective atoms
Of the spirit

Inside and outside ourselves
Into the damndest
Positive chain reaction
Seen 'round these parts
Since Adam and Eve
First bit into their apple.

Jeanne Borei
is executive vice president of Creative Change Technologies, Inc., Chattanooga, Tennessee. She served as director of Human Resources for the Tel-A-Train Corporation, one of the first U.S. private companies to commit themselves to a total community-building process. In 1991, she received the World Business Academy's Willis Harman Award.

John Pehrson
is president of Creative Change Technologies, which is dedicated to helping individuals and organizations live and work with a sense of greater purpose, community, and unlimited potential. He is a recently retired Du Pont manager of a large worldwide business and has served as a director of the New York Open Center, Inc., the largest urban holistic learning center in the world. He is a member of the World Business Academy and a past leader of the New York chapter.

33

Enter: The Shadow

Jeanne Borei & John Pehrson

Again, traveller, you have come a long way led by that star.
But the kingdom of the wish is at the other end of the night.
—Thomas McGrath

Remember the scene out of "The Wizard of Oz" where Dorothy and her friends were standing at the edge of the forest looking across the meadow of poppies toward the magical kingdom of Emerald City? It seemed like such a short distance across the meadow, a brief walk over a field of flowers to the magnificent home of the Wizard who would grant them their deepest wishes. Dorothy had already met Scarecrow, Tin Man and Lion in the forest. They had become friends along the way. Before long, all four of them, along with dog Toto, were skipping merrily down the yellow brick road to Emerald City. They were in sight of their destination. Yet, little did they know that the short jaunt across the poppy field was only the beginning of their journey. When they finally do meet and experience the great and beneficent Wizard, they learn that to realize their ultimate goals—a brain for Scarecrow, a heart for Tin Man, courage for Lion, and back home to Kansas for Dorothy and Toto—they must first confront the wicked witch of the West. The overpowering, central element in the "Wizard of Oz" is the confrontation of Dorothy and her friends with this sinister character.

We have come to see this as a perfect metaphor for confronting a dark element that arises with regularity during community building, an element that seems to occur after the initial attainment of community and one about which little is said. It is something that we were little prepared for in the experiences we have had with organizations who were building authentic communities. It is a deeper stage of community building that we have come to know as the *shadow*— much like holding a photographic negative of the official culture of an organization up to the light and seeing its dark opposite.

Before delving into this mysterious shadow, we will briefly outline the processes by which we became acquainted with building community in the workplace. Between us, we have found that there are several paths to creating an "authentic team." We define such a team as a group of individuals who relate at deep levels of integrity, bringing all of themselves into the relationship as thinking, feeling, spiritual beings to focus on achieving a shared vision and goals.

John's first experience was in 1986 at the Pecos River Ranch, just east of Santa Fe in New Mexico. He was there with twenty other members of a group from a Fortune 50 company, who had come to experience the "Management Leap" program. In John's own words:

> "Management Leap" was a perfect name for the program. I can still remember standing atop a 170 foot high cliff overlooking a small river below. It was a perfect fall day in September. The air was crisp and clear, and carried our voices for a long way. Half of our team was on the cliff looking down at the other half of the team who were across the river about a quarter mile away. They seemed small in the distance but I could still hear them as they cheered me on. I was outfitted in a rock climbing harness that was hooked to a long, long "zip line" that was strung the quarter mile length from the top of the cliff, across the river, to the excited, shouting group of enthusiastic men and women beyond. All I had to do was gather up enough courage to jump. I can still remember the fear I felt standing at the edge of the cliff, the adrenaline rush in jumping spread eagle, and the pure exhilaration of briefly being able to fly high above the river to the group hug waiting at the end of the zip line.
>
> This was the quintessential event at Pecos River Ranch where each person in the group "faced the dragon" that lurked beyond their comfort zone, and overcame their own personal fear. Through physical events like jumping off the cliff, and others that pushed our limits, the group cemented bonds that took each of us into a sacred space. Many of us were able to face our own fears because of the strength and support of the group; each of us helped other group members face theirs. The physical events stripped away pretenses and facades and left us with a deep level of respect and trust that enabled the group to go to deeper levels of sharing. Leaving the physical challenges of the ropes course and many of our interpersonal barriers behind, we spent the rest of our time opening up with each other on emotional levels. As I would come to know later, this is the "emptying" stage that precedes coming into full community. For

many, this was more difficult than jumping from the cliff. And, for many, having the opportunity to share at this level for the first time in a business group was just as exhilarating! At that point, life for me changed forever.

Our first experience together was with the World Business Academy in the Spring of 1991. Almost 30 of us gathered at a rustic site north of Boston. We came from all walks of life and the four corners of the country. None of us knew more than a handful of the other participants when we began. We were led by two facilitators, Ed Groody and Ann Hoewing, both of whom had been trained by Scott Peck's organization, the Foundation for Community Encouragement.

We did not know what to expect. Jeanne found herself caught up in a world of stretching well beyond her comfort zones into deep levels of sharing. For her, it was a life-changing event much like John experienced at Pecos River Ranch. The process took both of us to deeper levels of sharing and vulnerability than either of us had known before in a business group.

This process is one in which a group learns to identify and move through the various stages shown in the diagram below to reach a state of community, as defined by Peck, when:

> a group of two or more people who, regardless of the diversity of their backgrounds (social, spiritual, educational, ethnic, economic, political, etc.) have been able to accept and transcend their differences, enabling them to communicate effectively and openly and work together toward goals identified as being for their common good.

According to James Hillman in his 1993 book *Rag and Bone Shop of the Heart*, Alfred Adler, who originated psychoanalysis along with Freud and Jung, considered community to be the dominant motive of life. He defined *Gemeinshaftsgefühl* as the feeling of intimate belonging to the full spectrum of humanity and considered it to be "as basic as Freud's sexual drive or Jung's urge toward meaning."

The diagram below was created by Groody and Howing to illustrate the stages of community:

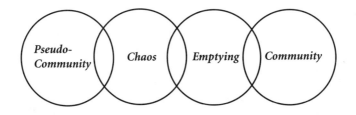

What the New Mexico experience does through physical events, the community-building process does through gentle yet sometimes intense dialogue. Its success involves the willingness of individuals to take risks in sharing themselves authentically and vulnerably with the whole group, who may or may not be ready to hear they have to say. The idea is to move from the "plastic" environment of *Pseudo-Community,* where all members are "the same," where there are "no problems," and everything is kept at a surface level of communication, into the *Chaos* that naturally begins to emerge when individuals in the group begin to recognize differences. This is a time when the "us vs. them" syndrome is most prevalent. In Chaos there is finger pointing and blaming of some outside force for any problems that occur. If the group is allowed to fully experience chaos, it usually will move into the stage of *Emptying,* where letting go of old baggage and the releasing of pretenses and facades takes place. It is through Emptying that *Community* is finally attained, a state in which communication is authentic and persons accept responsibility for themselves and their actions. In Community, diversity becomes the source of strength, individuals find themselves listening to each other perhaps for the first time, and sustaining decisions can be made.

All this sounds simple enough and, though it is stated up front in the workshops that "reaching Community is not guaranteed," our experience is that most groups reach it when individuals and groups are allowed to move *at their own pace* through the preceding stages: Pseudo-Community, Chaos, and Emptying. It was this particular community-building process that Jeanne brought back into her company, which became the first privately owned corporation in the world to commit to the community-building process for all employees.

THE CORPORATE EXPERIENCE

It began with a 3-day workshop for managers that resulted in immediate benefits in the workplace. The employees noticed such differences as the managers being more patient, more willing to listen, and genuinely wanting the opinions and involvement of the employees. The community-building experience was such a profound one that the management committed to taking all of the employees through the process to insure that everyone would be "singing out of the same book" as a corporation. Within the next six months, all employees had in-depth exposure to the process. The culture began to change.

People were hearing each other differently. They made serious attempts at being more inclusive in communicating with each other, particularly in the decision-making process. They also worked at reducing rumors and, one by one, began accepting responsibility for their own actions. All of this was difficult, particularly as they were coming out of a "business as usual" environment where the norm for so many years encouraged the opposite mode of behavior. To monitor their own health and insure that they would not lose the momentum gained through the workshops, they scheduled regular community-building meeting times, based on what they had learned in the workshops.

Jeanne has documented this entire experience in detail in the book *When the Canary Stops Singing*, in her essay entitled "Chaos to Community: One Company's Journey of Transformation." It is worth pursuing for anyone who may be looking for ways to deal with dysfunction inside an organization.

Being a pioneer is not easy! There are no reference points, no one you can call up and ask "How did you handle this?" or "What did you do when faced with that?" Scott Peck made the comment that at this stage of the game "even your mistakes are important." We certainly made our share. Even if someone had effectively warned us, I'm not sure we or anyone could have been properly prepared for what did happen—for the depths and darkness into which we would find ourselves plunging—for the shadow!

ENTER THE SHADOW

It happened subtly at first—a comment here, a comment there, often outside the regular meetings and even more often inside the meetings themselves—the very meetings scheduled to maintain the process and spirit. Then it became more and more obvious that confidences were being broken, truth was being distorted, and rumors were slowly becoming more rampant than ever. "How could this be?" we constantly asked ourselves. "What have we done wrong?" We had taken all employees through a powerful experience of community building to do away with the same issues that started us down this path of deterioration. Just when we thought we had made considerable progress in solving them, issues began to resurface and were now facing us with all the strength, size, and vehemence of large man-eating dragons!

In a nutshell, the community-building meetings that were established after the workshops for the sole purpose of maintaining community were rapidly becoming places in which the opposite seemed to be happening. For example, some individuals were put on the spot as others in the group verbally attacked them and old baggage was released only to reappear under various guises of anger, guilt, and fear. It didn't take long for us to realize that we needed help from outside facilitators in getting us back on track. Groody and Hoewing suggested an ongoing maintenance program involving outside consulting help, but this opinion was not supported by upper management. They reasoned that we could figure out how to handle our own problems with internal resources. As a company, we began to swim around and around in loops of anguish and frustration out of which there seemed to be no escape. As "walls" of isolation began to come down and old "baggage" continued to surface, more and more energy was released. Energy that had supported the walls and the baggage now had no place to go. It was unfocused with no direction. The company began learning to direct this energy into task, but this lesson came slowly and not without much pain and scarring. One left these gatherings with feelings of fear or aloneness, thinking they were a just a waste of time. And as a result of the volatile nature of these meetings, many employees began to withdraw, to go inside themselves for shelter and create an even stronger "shadow" subculture than had existed before community process began. Some repercussions were forced resignations and layoffs. What had gone wrong?

In retrospect, one of the elements we did not do well was implementing the kind of in-depth maintenance program needed to insure the success of the process. The company designated Jeanne as responsible for monitoring the process overall, which was a step in the right direction. But without the financial and upper management support needed to implement the proper maintenance and training, the process found life in a strange sort of "purgatory." Keep in mind, we had no reference points—no other company we could call and ask for help. The consultants were extraordinary during this time, but even their help was limited as a result of our own naiveté and lack of understanding of how and why we needed help from the "outside." A lot has been learned since then!

What was happening was the unleashing of the *shadow*. The community-building process wasn't failing! It was working! It was simply a catalyst that accelerated the surfacing of deeper, hidden issues that would eventually need addressing anyway. The facades and old baggage were being released. In their place, we found ourselves dealing with all the energy, the unbelievably powerful energy, that had gone into supporting the facades and baggage. None of us were prepared for the release of this shadow energy! So, when it was uncovered, it had no focus and no place to go.

Reaching Community

This kind of release is inherent in the process of building authentic teams and is a residual of achieving community. Reaching community requires relating at the feeling level—from a place of authenticity, integrity, and vulnerability. The initial experience lowers interpersonal barriers, clears away psychological surface issues, and helps satisfy a search for meaning that is largely missing from organizational or corporate life. This experience is wonderful—a "sacred space" where people listen better and relate at deeper levels. Personal bonds are strengthened. There is a yearning for greater involvement in the workplace as a reflection of having achieved greater emotional involvement with each other. Lots of energy is available and can be focused toward greater ownership of the business and its practical goals.

Reaching community is the easy part, like Dorothy and her friends arriving at Emerald City and getting their first audience with the Wizard. In fact, we have seen this stage achieved in a variety of different groups within small businesses, Fortune 50 companies, the World Business Academy, and at the Hyde School in Maine between students, faculty, and parents. Maintaining this trust, vulnerability, and cooperation in the workplace, however, is difficult. In each case, there has been the emergence of the *shadow*, the dark side of the process.

The Shadow Unveiled

Jung defines the shadow as both the negative aspects of the personal unconscious and an archetype with its roots in the collective unconscious. Both personal and collective elements are active in the groups we have experienced, where the shadow emerges and becomes the negative side of the desired, official culture, testing the collective values and beliefs of the organization. We believe the emerging of the shadow is a natural stage in the community-building process.

As a group achieves community and works to maintain it, many of the surface issues that normally keep them from relating more authentically are cleared away. Interpersonal barriers are lowered. If you have done any sustained personal work you know that when the psychological surface debris is recognized, dealt with, and cleared away, deeper issues come bubbling to the surface. Our personal experience is that this often happens in a way that tests all of our fundamental beliefs. The same thing happens with groups. As everyone works to go deeper, the negative aspects of both the individual and group unconscious begin to rise to the surface. There are deeper personal issues that must be worked through on a group level. In an uncanny way, the emergence of the shadow tests the core values and beliefs that the group says it stands for. This happens so frequently that after one experience John wrote in his journal, "Take great care in what you choose to believe for you will be tested!"

Empowerment and focus are both important to maintaining community. People are more willing to take responsibility for themselves and want greater involvement in the business. There is greater energy that can be focused toward useful ends. At this point, if people are truly empowered *and* given clear direction, the experience of working together to achieve something useful and significant deepens the feeling of community. More often, however, company culture, systems, and procedures are slow to change. Attempts for greater involvement and focus are frequently frustrated. The new energy can dissipate in disenchantment, cynicism, and a return to the finger-pointing and blaming of chaos.

Coming into community requires a desire to change and the strength to venture beyond personal comfort zones to explore new ways of relating. While change brings the promise of release, it also brings discomfort. Working through the emerging personal and group shadow triggers denial—resistance that tends to force the organization back toward the old status quo. In some sense, the resistance is proportional both to the depth of the shadow and the force employed to move the group forward. The commitment to stay the course and work through this resistance is challenged at this point. Most businesses back away, choosing the road of avoidance in an attempt to go back to "business as usual." Yet just as Dorothy could not return to Kansas without defeating the Wicked Witch, the organization cannot return to "just business" without confronting the shadow.

THE HYDE SCHOOL PROCESS

For organizations and businesses that are unprepared to confront the shadow, this stage is difficult to work through and can be overpowering. Yet, we have experienced a community-building process where this is successfully and consistently achieved—at the Hyde School in Bath, Maine. During the years that they have developed and refined their process, an amazing track record of success has been compiled in preparing students for life after school. While this is not a business enterprise, there are lessons that business can learn from the school's success.

The Hyde School Process builds an authentic community among faculty, teenagers, and parents in such a way as to focus almost solely on the building of *character* in the individual. Joseph Gauld describes this process in his 1993 book, *Character First*. Building character leads to a broad range of achievement in the lives of the students: academics, athletics, performing arts, and leadership. In this process, we have seen the shadow show its face—the ugly and dark areas of the individual persona. Rather than the collective group becoming afraid and over-whelmed by the power evoked by the shadow, it looks the shadow straight in the face and begins to deal with it immediately. This may be done through the group or individual confrontation or self-realization, but, however it happens, the shadow is not allowed to lurk in dark corners and manipulate an individual, much less an entire organization, as it began to do in Jeanne's company.

The Hyde Process is effective in dealing with the shadow in large part because they expect it and are prepared to deal with it. They not only anticipate its emergence, they actively encourage it. They know that each person's unique potential is like a rare jewel that is covered over by layers of systemization, ego, and the darker aspects of the personality. Their process aggressively goes after the unique potential of the group, uncovering and exposing different layers of the shadow along the way. In the "Wizard of Oz," this is accomplished by defeating the Wicked Witch so Dorothy and her friends gain strength and great personal growth. Hyde understands that it is by meeting and overcoming the shadow that we improve ourselves, our relationships, and deepen community.

There are other strong reasons why this process is successful in dealing with the shadow. Each element may be a key for helping to maintain Community. If we can distill some general principles, perhaps business groups can learn from their example.

Hyde creates the context for learning and development through a strong value-based approach. It also creates systems that support the embodiment of these values. Business readers may be familiar with the power of this kind of approach through Max DePree's *Leadership is an Art*. Hyde's motto emphasizes the five central virtues of character which all students are expected to develop:

(1) the *courage* to accept challenges,
(2) the *integrity* to truly be yourself,
(3) *concern* for others,
(4) the *curiosity* to explore life and learning, and
(5) *leadership* in making the school and community work.

These virtues are backed up by five principles that have guided the school's growth and development: destiny, humility, conscience, truth, and brother's keeper (helping others achieve their best). The result of this approach is that students are prepared to enter life as thoughtful, independent and self-assured young adults who have a concern for others and aren't afraid of involvement and risk taking. In short, they have character.

Their success is also due to the strong up-front commitment to the process by parents. The behavior of parents is key to students' consistent growth, much like the behavior of management within a company is crucial to the growth of employees. The net effect is twofold: (1) strong commitment is translated into a willingness to develop the virtues of character and to live by the five principles; and (2) a system of strong maintenance and support for the process is created.

The foundation of the school's philosophy is a strong belief in the unique potential of each individual. Upon this is built a strong learning environment that values the need for students to search for a sense of purpose and destiny that is attained by bringing out the best in themselves. The process takes to heart the Greek philosophy of education expressed in the credos: "Know thyself" and "Become what you are." The objective of the school is to help each student discover their unique potential and express it in the world. This is similar to the concept of "personal mastery," which is one of the five principles that Peter Senge defines as crucial to a learning organization in his book *The Fifth Discipline*. Building community and building a learning organization share many similarities. Whether you start with the fundamental belief in unique potential or in personal mastery, each turns the normal bottom line focus on results upside down. Rather than focusing on the results, which are the *effects*, the focus is shifted to developing the individual as the *source* of those results. At the school, they make growth rather than academic achievement the measure of success, for example. This is based on the understanding that if you uncover the best in the individual, and establish ownership and commitment for shared goals, that positive results will follow.

Unlike many organizations that back away from confronting issues born in the shadow energy, Hyde has pushed through each barrier. It has created, one student at a time, an expectation of success that builds upon itself.

The shadow is not something to be afraid of and is definitely not to be ignored or denied. Getting to community is only the first step of a longer process. Maintaining this level of authenticity, vulnerability, and cooperation ultimately requires confronting and redirecting the shadow energy that initially surfaces. For this to be successful, one must be prepared. It helps to know the steps of an overall program before starting down the path toward community building. Lacking this overview, organizational commitment will falter and the process will stop prematurely. From our experience, the guidelines for a comprehensive process are as follows:

- Focus on the individual. Relationships, teams, organizations, or whole companies only change because individuals change.
- Focus on the environment. The environment sets the context. Community rests on creating an environment free of fear, allowing each individual to work to their unique potential.
- Define unifying values and focus on character. Measure results, but focus on character. If everyone is living to their best, results will follow.
- Gain commitment up front. Then, build in strong maintenance and support. Put together a team to monitor the process with one person in charge. Staying in community takes work. Changing fundamental ways of working together takes time. Both require working through resistance and a desire

to return to "just business."
- Be prepared for the Shadow. Confront deeper issues that surface head-on. The pay-off is in gaining the strength to achieve personal mastery, which builds the overall effectiveness of the group.
- Set a clear direction. Getting to community releases energy which needs a place to go. Without clear direction, the energy dissipates in frustration, disenchantment, and a return to chaos.
- Stay the course and build a track record of successes. Abandoning ship and returning to the old status quo creates cynicism and destroys credibility.

Facing the shadow is an experience that challenges each of us to examine the core of our soul, to see the "stuff" of which we are made. It presents us with the opportunity to move through the quagmire of obstacles we find within us as feelings, belief systems, and old baggage, to a new way of being—to becoming a person of true courage and deep integrity and to build, one person at a time, an authentic community

> What has no shadow has no strength to live.
> — Czeslaw Milosz

Dinesh Chandra is the president of Global Quality Associates, a firm specializing in organizational transformation renewing the strategic planning process and developing the change strategy in an integrated manner—with clients around the globe. He holds a B.S. in Mechanical Engineering, an M.S. in Industrial Engineering, and an M.B.A. in Finance. He has served as Adjunct Faculty for the Graduate School of Nova and Florida International University.

A. G. "Buddy" Johnson, Jr. is a South Carolina native with over 25 years in the banking business. Starting with First Union in Charlotte during the early 1970s, he is now area president for Broward County, Florida. He has been instrumental in bringing Total Quality Management to over 1,000 First Union associates in Broward and has played a significant role in the development of Fort Lauderdale's Quality Council. He is married to Kim and the father of four children.

34

One Bank's Experience

Dinesh Chandra & Buddy Johnson

Traditionally, banks have played a strong role in community development—that is, strengthening the economic foundations of their local neighborhoods and cities. But when it comes to building community within their own workforces, most banks have done very little. For example, although policy manuals may talk enthusiastically about "focus on the family," we have noticed that banks are actually no different from other businesses: they tend to view the family as a source of competition for the employee's time and energy. Although they try to create a collaborative work environment, and even advocate process and consensus, they generally employ a reward system that is based on bottom-line results.

With such a dichotomy, employees always learn what's best for their survival. So rugged individualism remains alive in the higher echelons of corporate America, as does the desire for quick results.

Many firms, including those in the banking industry, have experimented with Total Quality Management, but become impatient when they found that the evolutionary TQM process requires creating a collaborative culture and asking managers to do some soul-searching. Because they feel that this approach takes too long—often three to ten years—they opt for a quicker fix called re-engineering: a fundamental change in processes, imposed from the top down over a year or two, designed to please the customer and produce competitive success.

In re-engineering, employees may be compared to eggs that must be broken in order to prepare the omelet. Although it does seem to produce short-term profit improvement, the process also tends to create great stress, fear, and anxiety in the workforce. In many organizations, we have seen great surges in employee insecurity and family problems as a result of re-engineering. Some of these organizations have had to respond with a damage-control program to rebuild morale. At First Union National Bank in Broward County, Florida, we resolved not to let this damage happen.

In Broward, First Union had grown rapidly as a result of mergers and acquisitions, and the merging of cultures had created a real identity crisis for our company and its employees. Also, we realized we needed both TQM and fundamental process changes (in effect, re-engineering) in order to satisfy our customers' needs while changing our business so rapidly. In order to make our customers happy, our employees needed to be happy as well. We reasoned that if we focused on building a community with empowered individuals, organizational transformation would be a lot easier and quicker.

Our central question was, "How can we maintain sensitivity to employees' needs and simultaneously achieve our business goals?" As a result of focusing on this question, our journey toward quality has been a journey of personal growth, self-discovery, and community building. We were able to create a modified re-engineering approach in which employees developed their own new culture rather than having one forced on them. Although it has been sometimes a frustrating journey, it has also been extremely satisfying.

FINDING LINKS

In community-building workshops outside the bank, we had observed that it is easy for a group of people to come in from different walks of life and, in a short period of time, shed their preconceptions and control needs in order to move toward authentic community. But, within organizations where issues are heated in the oven of distrust, the experience can be very different. Many times, people attend workshops on community-building, return to their organizations, and fail to implement the principles they have learned. So we recognized a need to start building a caring and authentic environment within the bank, an environment in which Total Quality initiatives could take root, grow, and thrive.

First we needed to understand, and communicate to all employees, the linkages between community building and the organizational transformation that was necessary. Otherwise, community building would remain an esoteric concept, viewed as not very useful in a business setting.

The first important linkage we found was the focus on customers. In TQM, we emphasize that we must strive to delight both the external and the internal customer. If we expand this concept, it really means that we must treat everyone who comes into contact with us the same way we would like to be treated: non-judgmentally and with compassion.

The second major linkage is in the involvement of people through team building. Such involvement is necessary for quality as well as for community. In the traditional concept, team size is small, which limits the number of people who can be involved in redesigning the organization. The myth is that the ideal number of people in a team is four to seven, and many trainers even limit their team-building training classes to around twenty people. Organizations that operate under such assumptions have a built-in excuse that it will take too long to involve everyone, and the result is a top-down approach—antithetical to community.

However, through our own experimentation and that of others, we have found that the limit to participation is only a function of the facilitator's imagination and confidence. For example, the Hudson Massachusetts Division of R.R. Donnelley & Sons, as reported in the *Journal for Quality and Participation* (December 1993), followed a "Five Conferences Model" to get all 200 employees involved. Each succeeding conference—Visioning, Customer, Technical, Organizational, and Implementation—included approximately 80 participants, thus creating a new paradigm for the size of a design team.

The third key linkage between quality and community-building has to do with chaos. In community building, chaos (according to the M. Scott Peck model) is a necessary stage in which differences come to the fore. It is part of a natural cycle and fundamental to growth. Similarly, there is great potential for creativity amid the organizational chaos that is created by significant change. It is important to encourage those who can not only live with creative tension but, in fact, welcome conflict as a source of growth. Introducing the concepts of shared vision and stretched goals invariably results in a higher level of creativity, but not without the pain of transition to a higher risk culture. Understanding this, and promoting the value underlying the process, is necessary for transformation.

INITIATIVES FOR QUALITY AND COMMUNITY

Generally, an organization's management retains the prerogative of developing a re-engineered organization and conveying it to others. At First Union Bank, we learned that people must discover their own truth and make choices. The Leadership Team, composed of the Area President and his seven direct reports, initially took responsibility for implementing Total Quality. But because the vision was not jointly created, employees sometimes found it difficult to relate to management's ideas and trust the processes. Only after we began focusing on creating an environment of self-discovery, where people could express themselves and their likes and dislikes, did the transformation begin. For example, when the recommendation to eliminate the copying of certain documents came from the top, employees kept asking, "Why is this necessary?" However, when one of the teams recommended that same idea, it was readily accepted by fellow employees.

About 18 months into the re-engineering process, the Leadership Team decided to send a conscious signal to employees, the corporation, and the customers that we were a team. We did away with hierarchical terms such as "officers" and now refer to each other—employees and managers alike—as "associates."

Successful change is built on employees' positive self-image and a positive image of the organization in which they are involved. So we focused on creating not only customers for life, but associates for life. We sought an environment where the gap between work and family was narrow, where business and pleasure were mixed, where people could feel at home at work. Following are some of our initiatives:

Family Council

Family Council is a volunteer organization made up of associates and their selected family members. Since we believe it is important to recognize that the word "family" means different things to different people, we allowed our associates to determine who they would like involved—spouse, roommate, child, parent, and so on. We now have almost 100 members who meet regularly as a group and on several subcommittees. These subcommittees work on issues related to family events, communication, benefit awareness, and time management. Specifically, some of their accomplishments to date include:

- A family newsletter sent to every associate's home address
- A countywide family picnic
- Kids' day at work, incorporating feedback from children on how we can improve
- Actual involvement by families in county-wide meetings, including surveys on planning the ideal meeting and arranging baby-sitters
- A program to provide Christmas gifts to needy associates

When families began to find a connection to work, the conflict between work time and family time became less meaningful. People stopped asking, "What's in it for me, and why should I give up my personal time?" The Family Council was a primary mechanism for responding to the innate human need for integration of heart, mind, and gut.

Compass

Compass is the team responsible for setting the strategic direction for Broward County's Total Quality effort. Previously a twenty-person steering committee established by corporate headquarters and composed of senior management, this group has been expanded to include representatives from all job functions, elected from each area of the country's operations. When openings occur, each candidate campaigns on his or her own platform for quality, and a general election follows.

While appointed managers often tried to delegate quality, many times steering the direction toward what proved to be comfortable for them, the elected members have brought both personal commitment and different perspectives. Operating with a higher level of involvement, Compass has developed Strategic Quality Objectives. Through a facilitated forum, preceded by empowerment training, associates were encouraged when they challenged and disagreed with the managers. Together they explored the deeper issues that surfaced in the dialogue. This wasn't an easy process, but it was very powerful in developing the authentic communication necessary for shared objectives.

Zappers

Zappers is an all-volunteer group of associates whose job is to communicate the latest in quality to designated areas or departments. This group strives to make quality "fun" through celebrations, recognition, promotional campaigns, and a lighthearted approach. Because they have chosen to be there and have ownership of the process, they feel accountable and provide honest communications to their peers.

At first we suggested ways for them to accomplish tasks, but now we give them the problem and get out of their way. Previously, county-wide meetings were planned and facilitated by management and were limited to officers, who then had to communicate the outcome to others below them. Now, all associates have an opportunity to participate. A recent meeting, planned and organized by the Zappers, was attended by 1,150 people—including family members—and generated a high level of enthusiasm. A live circus performance entertained the group.

Process Y

Process Y (named after McGregor's Theory Y participative management philosophy) is an effort to develop self-directed work teams in a branch banking system. As the company settled down to growing internally rather than through acquisitions, we began to examine the idea of using retail branch outlets as sales centers. The Area President asked the branch managers and Leadership Team, "If we had a totally empowered workforce, why would we need branch managers?"

In four branches, we experimented with freeing up branch managers to become part of our outside sales force. The manager's former responsibility became that of the manager's former boss. Two professional trainers provided sales and work team training. So far, we have observed impressive results. In 120 days, teller turnover decreased from 50–60 percent to zero. Absenteeism went down 75 percent in the same period; people actually want to come to work, even when sick. Survey results show that the customers, as well as the associates, are happier.

Coincidentally, another branch decided to empower itself without much training but with the support and blessing of the branch manager. We found the transformation to be easier in this voluntary branch, reinforcing our belief in the power of individual choice.

An Evolutionary Journey

Our quality journey has been a long-term, evolutionary process, and some people experienced frustration when they found that traditional, short-term measures of success did not always apply. In order to coach people through a transformation such as ours, leaders have to care about people and about building a community—a family. Sometimes that means standing against the short-term result orientation on faith alone.

To move from "professional management" to "shared leadership," our bank first needed to build the bridge of empowerment, liberating all associates who, in turn, could create a community. Our vision is of an organization in which we can all "be leadership." In this vision, we have all learned to care for each other as we would our family, and we rejoice in the success of others. We know that, as with the human body, we must have diversity to work effectively as a whole. Our measure of success is not what we have achieved, it is what we are. Change is all about how we think, how we experience the experience.

We know we are on our way toward realizing this vision when we hear the following comments:

"I found that I am often so preoccupied with things that don't really matter that I lose the essential connection with things that do."

"I was given an environment that allowed me to be successful."

"I feel a sense of belonging and security."

"The words 'how' and 'why' were transformed to 'When do we get started?'"

"It renewed my hope in the power of a gathered community—family, team, company."

We intend to stay on the path until this community is the best it can be.

Conclusion:
Hope for Closing the Gap
Kazimierz Gozdz

Community in organizations is essential for optimal performance and learning capability. Without it, we cannot create aligned organizations that coherently work toward shared goals and objectives. Yet, when we examine the quality of community in large organizations—whether Fortune 500, government, religious, or nonprofit—more often than not we find that there is a gap between the ideal we hold for community and our day-to-day practical efforts to sustain it.

This book is about looking boldly into the gap, while at the same time maintaining the hope and aspiration that true community is possible in most organizations. In this regard, community building is best thought of as a journey toward organizational wholeness.

The successful outcome of such a journey, community as competitive advantage, comes at a price—the price of revising our maps or models of reality: telling the truth to one another about what we know to be real. One of the largest obstacles to community is "untruth," or false images or mental models of reality. When what we say and do matches what we perceive to be real, community has a welcome home. We must acknowledge what is real and have the courage and capability to create actions that move us toward closing the gap in our aspiration for community. Without such capability, the systems, structures, mental models, and organizational and political obstacles that constitute this gap are avoided rather than confronted. Embracing reality as we know can sometimes be a difficult, even painful, process.

This is not to say that individuals within organizations are unwilling to be truthful or incapable of identifying reality. The gap between the ideal and actual conditions of community stems more often from a kind of communal, rather than individual, "unreality." In organizations we need communal practices of reality testing because the models of reality we need to confront are composites drawn from teams, groups, divisions,and even whole organizations. Challenging collective pictures of reality created by organizational cultures is almost impossible for individuals. Learning communities are those which accept the challenge of growing toward organizational wholeness as a collective.

The truth we need to embrace in our organizations transcends yet includes individual perceptions of truth. In The Road Less Traveled, M. Scott Peck describes some attributes of psychospiritual health. Health and wholeness, he says, come from an individual's unending dedication to the truth and a practice of personal mastery he calls discipline. This discipline of psychospiritual growth results in a flexible response system and an ability to meet and transcend life's challenges.

The same principles apply to organizational communities. An absence of psychospiritual health, personal or organizational, is characterized by inflexibility, false maps or models of reality, and an unwillingness to face painful and difficult issues. Organizations often lack a sense of community because there is an air of untruth within their culture. This is a central characteristic of pseudocommunities.

For example, the CEO of one international oil company imposed his will and worldview on the company as it charted its future strategy. Unfortunately, his worldview was flawed, and it went unchallenged by the entire organization. His false map of reality went untested by a communal system of checks and balances which could have circumvented his power for the organization's overall good. The company culture did not allow for communal reality to intrude on his flawed map until financial performance was so bad it could no longer be ignored. Cases like this are commonplace today. Is it happening in some form in your organization?

IN PURSUIT OF REALITY

When John Renesch and I first began to craft a vision for this book, we knew we were plotting a course on a map that would take years to finish. The results that we—a team of editors, writers, and production people, along with our 44 authors—have produced are the culmination of a two-year process. In a quest to constantly improve the detail of our map, we doubled the size of the project. This vision for the book is a statement of what we wished to achieve and a compass that pointed our way:

> To build a sense of authentic community within organizations that is both sustainable and imbued with spirit, we need to articulate a whole systems understanding. We also need a comprehensive technology of community making composed of skills, methodologies, practices, and theory that will inform and guide an organization toward long-term success. The authors of this anthology will create a compelling vision for what successful community

can be, informing the world as to its benefits, potential complexities, and pitfalls within organizational settings.

In all, I think we have fulfilled this vision.

This interdisciplinary collection of essays, represents various—even conflicting—viewpoints about community, pointing to its complexity and plurality. As Peck noted in his introduction, this book does not define community. As a group, our authors were not asked to agree on whether community is "grown," "uncovered," or "built" nor how it should be defined. I simply asked them to share their perspective. Although we may have used definitions for clarity within our individual perspectives, its important not to lose sight of the fact that each definition highlights only a piece of a larger puzzle.

As the larger context for community unfolds with new practices in business, so will broader and richer evolutionary forms of community come into existence. Some of our authors, for example, described a new hybrid form of electronic and face-to-face community.

It was not our purpose to provide simple answers for instantly creating community. Rather, we hoped to show that true community can occur and that tools, mental models, and exemplars exist for our collective map-revising process to extend community to our future. The roots of learning lie not only in the answers within this book but in the questions.

The seven parts of this book serve as a checklist for attending to community building in a systemic way. Each section implies a set of questions that, taken together, lead to a holistic approach. It is my hope that after pondering these stimulating questions, your community can more easily engage in an exercise of collective self-reflection and reality testing.

- Part One asks: How is the global context of a re-emergence of community relevant to this situation?
- Part Two asks: Given my organization's dynamics and culture, how can I best understand key leverage points for change?
- Part Three asks: What skills and practices do we use to create community?
- Part Four asks: What is it within us as people that might stand in the way of our allowing community to happen?
- Part Five asks: How is the use of technology affecting this situation?
- Part Six asks: Since we know from systems dynamics that structure drives behavior, what is the impact of organizational structures on this situation?
- Part Seven asks: How can we benchmark ourselves against what other people have done?

A HOLOGRAPHIC PERSPECTIVE FOR CREATING CHANGE

How can you use the theories, skills, and perspectives presented here to create the highest leverage for transformation in your community?

Leverage in applying individual authors' suggestions requires remembering the whole while at the same time implementing chosen parts. Think of the whole of this book as a hologram. When a holographic plate is broken into parts, any part can be used to reproduce a somewhat weaker yet complete and coherent picture of the original whole. Each chapter acts in some way like a piece of a holographic plate: it is complete in itself, yet reflects back a weaker image of a coherent whole. No single solution will close the gap between desired community and reality unless it acts in harmony with the needs of the whole for change.

Community, in a sense, is rather simple; it is a form of love and discipline manifested in organizational operations. To release this love and discipline, however, we need to uncover community's complexity. This book can serve as a vehicle for focusing on the whole while implementing the parts.

APPLYING SYSTEMS DYNAMICS AS A RESOURCE FOR COMMUNITY BUILDING

A systems view of community can aid you as you begin to apply principles from these chapters to your own sustainable community. Figure 1 shows a generic pattern in system dynamics called a "systems archetype." It is one of a number of analytical tools for tracing how dynamic systems act. This archetype, which is a "Shifting the Burden Archetype," consists of three relationships or feedback loops which can be used to plan a change effort.

I have chosen to include this systems diagram to call your attention to the need for forethought and planning when seeking to support ongoing community. To be truly effective we need to balance the need for short-term systems improvement with long-term fundamental competence building. It is significantly easier to create a short-term sense of community at the cost of the real long-term transformation often required to sustain it. The diagram shows how such choices can backfire over time.

Feedback Loops 1 and 2 are balancing loops—self-correcting processes that create stability for sustaining community. The balance beam symbolizes this behavior. A downhill runaway snowball represents a reinforcing loop—an unintended process that feeds on itself and is running out of control. The timers within the diagram represent delays in time, where cause and effect are not closely linked in time. These time delays are important because intervening in an organizational community will more than likely trigger effects that happen some time down the road, and thus need to be anticipated.

To comprehend the illustration, begin at the center of the diagram with the symptom or presenting problem, which, in this case, is designated by parentheses. Our example shows low productivity as the presenting problem or symptom. When using the diagram in your particular community, you simply select the presenting problem that you feel the archetype represents.

Given that the organization admits the reality of the presenting problem, the low productivity in our example, an organizational leader suggests that "more community" is required to correct it.

The most common convention for creating an enhanced sense of community is represented in Loop 1, in which management reorganizes itself in response to the productivity problem (a simple way to relieve a

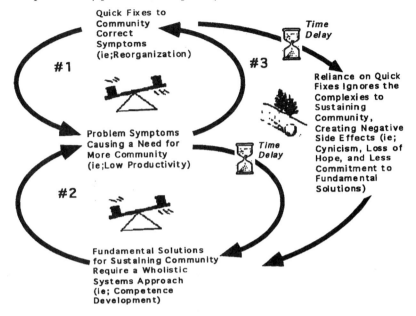

Figure 1: Quick Fixes to Community

temporary crisis). This quick-fix solution does produce a short-term boost in creativity. It also creates a temporary state of crisis, which in turn helps create a temporary state of enhanced community. But when the crisis passes, the low-productivity symptom reappears, the community disappears, and often things are even worse.

Loop 2 represents a more fundamental solution to the productivity problem: the development of competence; for example, building the capability to engineer products using competencies found in multiple strategic business units. Another example might be learning to re-engineer business processes while simultaneously supporting the well-being of the organizational community. These types of fundamental solutions would actually create a more sustainable sense of community if they helped the organization close a gap in competence, but most likely this is only possible over time. These solutions would more than likely require an investment in capital, a new set of mental models for old problems, and changes in infrastructure.

The requisite time delay to implement such changes is accompanied by a sense of anxiety and ambiguity as well as a decline in short-term profitability. Because fundamental solutions require the capability to tolerate discomfort, make definitive decisions, and create an aspiration for some vision, most managers concerned with short-term benefits tend to avoid such solutions even when they are crucial for long-term success.

The runaway Loop 3 in our example is characterized by ever-increasing levels of cynicism, hopelessness, and decreasing commitment to fundamental solutions. By neglecting the larger picture and oversimplifying the intervention, this strategy creates unintended side effects. In this example, management actually fuels an increasing loss of productivity. Relying on Loop 1 quick fixes can create a chronic over-reliance on short-term solutions—which indicates avoidance of responsibility.

Loop 1 represents what we can do if we apply ideas found in individual chapters of this book in isolation. We can make people feel better and quickly decrease the immediate conflicts, eliminating many symptoms. But we lose track of the whole.

When we avoid the pain of the growth and change necessary to address system-level causes over time, we disable the system's ability to respond to fundamental issues of sustaining community. When we overpromise and/or oversimplify sustainable community, we set ourselves up for failed results, shattered hopes, and increased cynicism. This effect snowballs over time, leaving people with less than the energy and commitment that is required to make the fundamental changes required within Loop 2.

Loop 2 is the domain of holistic, systemic, fundamental approaches. A particular solution applied at this level would seek to reflect the seven questions around which this book is structured. A holistic approach to supporting growth and change in community will, by necessity, reflect a composite of these questions—combining long- and short-term thinking. By using this approach to close this gap in our ideal and our real need for community, we address both symptoms and root causes.

HOPE IN A CHANGING WORLD

The world has changed and will continue to do so. You and I are touched by change every day in our organizations. We can either react to change in such a way as to perpetuate separateness, and thus invite despair, or we can work toward establishing a sense of interconnected wholeness. Because there is hope in community, this is the road I have chosen. However, it is not an easy road. Community in organizations requires both creativity and perseverance.

The authors of this collection have laid road markers that point toward ways of creating community in our fragmented world, but they cannot eliminate the bumps along the way. As with all adventures, the journey toward community promises no precise or secure outcome.

But the sweetness of the journey itself, I have found, is more than worth the price. Organizations that close the gap between their ideal for community and their capability to create and sustain it will find themselves not only achieving competitive advantage but also reveling in the joy, freedom, and peace of true community.

Recommended Reading & Resources

Adizes, I., and Borgese, E.M., *Self Management: New Dimensions to Democracy.* Santa Barbara, CA: ABC-Clio, 1975

Agazarian, Y.M. & S. Janoff. "Systems Theory in Small Groups." In H. Kaplan & B. Sadlock (eds.), *Comprehensive Textbook of Group Psychotherapy.* Williams & Wilkins, 1993.

Alban, B. & B. Bunker. "Large Group Interventions." *Journal of Applied Behavioral Science,* Volume 28, Number 4, Newbury Park, CA: Sage, December 1992.

Alinsky, S. *Reveille for Radicals.* New York: Vintage, 1969.

Arnett, R.C. *Communication and Community: Implications of Martin Buber's Dialogue.* Carbondale, IL: Southern Illinois University Press, 1986.

Argyris, Chris. *Reasoning, Learning, and Action.* San Francisco: Jossey-Bass Inc., 1982.

Argyris, Chris. *On Organizational Learning.* Cambridge, MA: Blackwell Publishers, 1992.

Argyris, Chris. *Strategy, Change, and Defensive Routines.* Boston: Pitman, 1985.

Argyris, Chris. *Management and Organization Development.* New York: McGraw-Hill, 1971.

Asch, S. *Social Psychology.* New York: Prentice-Hall, 1952.

Barrentine, Pat (ed.) *When the Canary Stops Singing: Women's Perspectives on Transforming Business.* San Francisco: Berrett-Koehler, 1993.

Bateson, G. *Mind and Nature.* New York: Bantam Books, 1980.

Beck, A.C. & E.D. Hillmar. *Positive Management Practices.* San Francisco: Jossey-Bass, 1986.

Beck, A.C. & E.D. Hillmar. *A Practical Approach to Organizational Development Through MBO.* Reading, MA: Addison-Wesley, 1972.

Beckhard, R. *Organization Development: Strategies and Models.* Reading, MA: Addison-Wesley, 1969.

Bellah, R., R. Madsen, W. Sullivan, A. Swidler & S. Tipler. *Habits of the Heart: Individualism and Commitment in American Life,* New York: Harper & Row, 1985.

Bennis, W.C. *Organization Development: Its Nature, Origins, and Prospects.* Reading, MA: Addison-Wesley, 1969.

Bennis, W.G. & E.H. Schein (eds.) *Leadership and Motivation.* Cambridge, MA: MIT Press, 1966.

Bennis, W.G., C. McGregor & D. McGregor (eds.) *The Professional Manager.* New York: McGraw-Hill, 1967.

Bion, W. *Experience in Groups.* London: Tavistock, 1961.

Block, P. *Stewardship: Choosing Service Over Self-Interest.* San Francisco: Berrett-Koehler, 1993.

Bohm, D. "On Dialogue" (Transcription of a Meeting) Ojai, CA: David Bohm Seminars, 1990.

Bohm, D. *Wholeness and the Implicate Order.* Cambridge, MA: Ark Paperbacks, 1980.

Bohm, D. & M. Edwards. *Changing Consciousness, Exploring the Hidden Source of the Social, Political and Environmental Crisis Facing Our World.* New York: Harper Collins, 1991.

Bohm, D. & M. Edwards. *Proprioception of Thought.* Ojai, CA: David Bohm Seminars, 1989.

Brown, Juanita. "Corporation as Community: A New Image for a New Era." In J. Renesch, (ed.) *New Traditions in Business.* San Francisco: Sterling & Stone, 1991, pp. 123–129.

Buzan, F.E. & E.L. Trist. *Toward a Social Ecology.* New York: Plenum, 1973.

Callenbach, E., F. Capra, L. Goldman, R. Lutz & S. Marburg. *EcoManagement: The Elmwood Guide to Ecological Auditing and Sustainable Business.* San Francisco: Berrett-Koehler, 1993.

Calthorpe, Peter & Van der Ryn Sim. *Sustainable Communities—A New Design Synthesis for Cities, Suburbs and Towns.* San Francisco: Sierra Club Books, 1986.

Campbell, Susan. *Earth Community: Living Experiments in Cultural Transformation.* San Francisco: Evolutionary Press, 1982.

Campbell, Susan. *From Chaos to Confidence: Survival Strategies for the New Workplace.* New York: Simon & Schuster, in press.

Capra, F. "Bringing Forth a World." *Elmwood Quarterly,* Volume 9, Number 3, 1993.

Capra, F. "The Theory of Living Systems." *Elmwood Quarterly,* Volume 9, Numbers 1–2, 1993.

Capra, F. *The Tao of Physics.* New York: Bantam Books, 1976.

Carey, Ken. *Starseed. The Third Millennium: Living in the Posthistoric World.* San Francisco: Harper, 1991.

Carse, James. *Finite and Infinite Games: A Vision of Life as Play and Possibility.* New York: Ballentine Books, 1986.

Cashman, P. & D. Stroll. Proceedings of Conference on Computer-Supported Collaborative Work, 1987.

Catford, Lorna & Michael Ray. *The Path of the Everyday Hero.* Los Angeles: Tarcher, 1991.

Collins, J. C. & J. L. Porras. "Organizational Vision and Visionary Organizations." *California Management Review,* Volume 34, Number 1, 1991.

Collins, J.C. & J. L. Porras. *Built to Last.* New York: HarperBusiness, 1994.

"Corporate Communities: Where Everybody Wins." *The New Leaders,* San Francisco: January/February 1993.

de Mare, P., R. Piper & S. Thompson. *Koinonia: From Hate Through Dialogue to Culture in the Large Group.* London: H. Karnac Books, 1991.

Dixon, N.M. "Organizational Learning: A Review of the Literature with Implications for HRD Professionals." *Human Resource Quarterly,* Spring 1992.

Dyer, W.G. *Team Building: Issues and Alternatives.* Reading, MA: Addison-Wesley, 1977.

Elgin, Duane. *Awakening Earth: Exploring the Evolution of Human Culture and Consciousness.* New York: Morrow,1993.

Emery, M. (ed.) *Participative Design for Participative Democracy.* Centre for Continuing Education, Australian National University, Canberra, Australia, 1993.

Engelbart, D. "Intellectual Implications of Multi-Access Computer Networks." In Douglas C. Englebert (ed.) *The Augmentation Papers,* Fremont, CA: The Bootstrap Institute. 1970.

Engelbart, D. "Coordinated Information Services for a Discipline - or Mission-Oriented Community". In Douglas C. Englebert (ed.) The *Augmentation Papers,* Fremont, CA: The Bootstrap Institute. 1975.

Ewing, D.W., "A Bill of Rights for Employees." *Across the Board,* March 1981.

Freire, P. *Pedagogy of the Oppressed.* New York: Continuum, 1992.

Friedman, Maurice. *The Confrontation of Otherness: In Family, Community and Society.* New York: Pilgrim Press, 1983.

Fritz, Robert. *The Path of Least Resistance.* New York: Fawcett Columbine, 1989.

Gardner, John. *Building Community.* A booklet prepared for the Leadership Studies Program of the Independent Sector, Washington D.C. The booklet is an expansion of the ideas set forth in Chapter 11 of Gardner's book On Leadership. New York: Free Press, 1990.

Gardner, John. *Self-Renewal.* (Revised edition.) New York: Norton, 1981.

Garfield, Charles. *Second to None: How Our Smartest Companies Put People First.* Homewood, IL: Business One Irwin, 1992.

Gatto, John Taylor. "We Need Less School, Not More." *Whole Earth Review,* Winter 1993.

Gauld, Joseph W. *Character First.* San Francisco: ICS Press, 1993.

Goff, David. *Communitas: An Exploratory Study of the Existential and Transpersonal Dimensions of a Psychological Sense of Community as Found in the Community Building Workshop,* unpublished dissertation, The Institute for Transpersonal Psychology, Palo Alto, CA.

Goleman, David, Paul Kaufman & Michael Ray. *The Creative Spirit.* New York: Dutton, 1992.

Gozdz, Kazimierz. "Community Building as a Leadership Discipline." In Michael Ray & Alan Rinzler (eds.) *The New Paradigm in Business: Emerging Strategies for Leadership and Organizational Change.* New York: Tarcher/Perigree.

Greider, W. *Who Will Tell the People: The Betrayal of American Democracy.* New York: Simon & Schuster/Touchstone, 1992.

Gustavsen, B. "Workplace Reform and Democratic Dialogue." *Economic and Industrial Democracy,* Volume 6, 1985.

Hall, Edward T. *The Hidden Dimension.* New York: Anchor Books Doubleday, 1966.

Hample, S. & E. Marshall. *Children's Letters to God,* The New Collection. New York: Workman Publishing, 1991.

Handy, Charles. *The Age of Paradox.* Boston: Harvard Business School Press, 1994.

Harman, Willis. *Global Mind Change.* New York: Warner Books, 1988.

Harman, Willis. "What Is This 'New Paradigm'?" *Meeting Ground,* World Business Academy, Volume 2, Number 6, 1993.

Harman, Willis & John Hormann. *Creative Work.* Indianapolis, IN: Knowledge Systems, Inc., 1990.

Hawley, Jack. *Reawakening the Spirit in Work.* San Francisco: Berrett-Koehler, 1993.

Hillman, James & Michael Ventura. *We're had A Hundred Years of Psychotherapy—And The World Is Getting Worse,* San Francisco: HarperCollins, 1992.

Horton, Myles. *The Long Haul: An Autobiography.* New York: Doubleday, 1990.

Horton, Myles & Paulo Freire. *We Make the Road by Walking: Conversations on Education and Social Change.* Philadelphia: Temple University Press, 1990.

Isaacs, William. "Dialogue: The Power of Collective Thinking." *The Systems Thinker,* April, 1993.

Isaacs, William. "Taking Flight: Dialogue, Collective Thinking and Organizational Learning." *Organizational Dynamics,* Fall 1993.

Jacacci, August. "The Social Architecture of a Learning Culture." *Training and Development,* November, 1989.

Jacobs, Jane. *Cities and the Wealth of Nations. New York*: Random House, 1984.

Johnson-Lenz, Peter & Trudy. "Groupware for a Small Planet." In Peter Lloyd (ed.), *Groupware in the 21st Century.* London: Adamantine Press, 1994.

Johnston, Charles. *Necessary Wisdom: Meeting the Challenge of a New Cultural Maturity.* Seattle, WA: Institute for Creative Development, 1991.

Kanter, Rosabeth Moss. *The Change Masters.* New York: Touchstone/Simon & Schuster, 1984.

Kemmis, Daniel. *Community and the Politics of Place.* Norman, OK: University of Oklahoma Press, 1990.

Kofman, Fred & Peter Senge. "Communities of Commitment: The Heart of Learning Organizations." *Organization Dynamics,* Fall 1993.

Kotter, J. & J. Haskett. As quoted in a review of their book *Corporate Culture and Performance,* appearing in "The Caring Company," The Economist. June 6, 1992.

Kouzes, J. & B. Posner. *The Leadership Challenge.* San Francisco: Jossey-Bass, 1987.

Kuhn, T. S. *The Structure of Scientific Revolutions* (Second ed., Enlarged ed.). Chicago: The University of Chicago Press, 1970.

Kumarappa, J.C. quoted in S. Campbell. *Earth Community: Living Experiments in Cultural Transformation.* San Francisco: Evolutionary Press, 1982.

Land, G., & B. Jarman. *Breakpoint and Beyond: Mastering the Future Today.* New York: Harper Business, 1992.

Laszlo, E. *Evolution, the Grand Synthesis.* Boston: Shambhala Publications, Inc., 1987.

Laszlo, E. *Introduction to Systems Philosophy: Toward a New Paradigm of Contemporary Thought.* New York: Harper Torchbooks, 1972.

Laszlo, E. *The Systems View of the World.* New York: George Braziller, Inc., 1972.

Lave J. & E. Wenger. *Situated Learning: Legitimate Peripheral Participation.* New York: Cambridge University Press, 1991.

Lawler, E.E. *High-Involvement Management.* San Francisco: Jossey-Bass, 1986.

Levey, Joel & Michelle. *Quality of Mind: Tools for Self-Mastery and Enhanced Performance.* Boston: Wisdom Publications, 1991.

Likert, R. *The Human Organization: Its Management and Value.* New York: McGraw-Hill, 1967.

Macy, Joanna. *Mutual Causality In Buddhism And General Systems Theory.* Albany, NY: State University of New York Press, 1991.

Macy, Joanna. *World as Lover, World as Self,* Berkeley, CA: Parallax Press, 1991.

Magaziner, Elemer. "Organizations and People Sink or Swim Together." *The New Leaders Dialogues,* San Francisco, July 1994.

Mander, Jerry. *In the Absence of the Sacred: The Failure of Technology and the Survival of the Indian Nations.* San Francisco: Sierra Club Books, 1991.

Marrow, A.J., D.G. Bowers & S.E. Seashore. *Management by Participation.* New York: Harper & Row, 1967.

Maturana, H. R., & F. J. Varela. *The Tree of Knowledge.* Boston: Shambhala Publications, Inc., 1992.

Maynard, H. B., & S. E. Mehrtens. *The Fourth Wave: Business in the Twenty-First Century.* San Francisco: Berrett-Koehler, 1993.

McGregor, D. *The Human Side of Enterprise.* New York: McGraw-Hill, 1960.

McGregor, D., W.G. Bennis & C. McGregor (eds.) *Leadership and Motivation.* Cambridge, MA: MIT Press, 1966.

McIntosh, P. White *Privilege and Male Privilege: A Personal Account of Comming to See Correspondences Through Work in Women's Studies.* Number 189. Wellesley College, 1988.

Michalski, J. *Community in Release 1.0.* New York: Edventure Holdings, 1993.

Mindell, Arnold. *The Leader as Martial Artist.* San Francisco: Harper, 1992.

Mindell, Arnold. *The Year I, Global Process Work: Community Creation from Global Problems, Tensions and Myths.* London: Arcana, 1989.

Mirvis, P.H., (ed.). *Building the Competitive Workforce.* New York: John Wiley, 1993.

Mollner, T. *The Prophets of the Pyrenees: The Search for the Relationship Age.* Northampton, MA: Trusteeship Institute, Inc., 1991.

Mollner, T. "Interview of Mohammad Yunus, Founder of the Grameen Bank" Northampton, MA: Trusteeship Institute, Inc., 1994.

Morgan, G. *Images of Organization.* Newbury Park, CA: Sage, 1986.

Neuwirth, Marianne. *Occupational Therapy Forum,* May 12, 1991.

Nirenberg, J. *The Living Organization: Transforming Teams into Workplace Communities.* Homewood, IL: Business One Irwin, 1993.

Nhat Hanh, Thich. *The Heart of Understanding.* Berkeley, CA: Parallax Press, 1988.

Oliver, L. *Study Circles: Coming Together for Personal Growth and Social Change.* Cabin John, MD: Seven Locks Press, 1987.

Opper, Susanna & Henry Fersko-Weiss. *Technology for Teams: Enhancing Productivity in Networked Organizations.* New York: Van Nostrand Reinhold, 1991.

Ornstein, Robert & Paul Erlich. *New World New Mind: Moving Toward Conscious Evolution.* New York: Doubleday, 1989.

Orsburn, Jack D. et. al. *Self-Directed Work Teams: The New American Challenge.* Homewood, IL: Business One Irwin, 1990.

Parenti, M., *Power and the Powerless.* New York: St. Martins Press, 1978

Peck, M. Scott. *A World Waiting to Be Born: Rediscovering Civility.* New York: Bantam Books, 1993.

Peck, M. Scott. *Further Along the Road Less Traveled.* New York: Simon & Schuster, 1993.

Peck, M. Scott. *The Different Drum, Community Making and Peace: A Spiritual Journey Toward Self-Acceptance, True Belonging, and New Hope for the World.* New York: Simon and Schuster/Touchstone, 1987.

Peck, M. Scott. *The Road Less Traveled.* New York: Simon & Schuster, Inc., 1978.

Peter, Lloyd (ed.) *Groupware in the 21st Century.* London: Adamantine Press, 1994.

Prigogine, I., & I. Stengers. *Order Out of Chaos.* New York: Bantam Books, 1984.

Ray, M. & A. Rinzler (eds.) *The New Paradigm In Business.* New York: Tarcher/Perigee Books, 1993.

Ray, M. & John Renesch (eds.) *The New Entrepreneurs,* San Francisco, CA: Sterling & Stone Inc., 1994.

Ray, M. "The Emerging New Paradigm in Business." In John Renesch (ed.), *New Traditions in Business: Spirit and Leadership in the 21st Centrury.* San Francisco: Sterling & Stone, Inc., 1991.

Ray, Michael & Rochelle Myers. *Creativity in Business.* New York: Doubleday, 1986.

Renesch, John. "Organizational Transformation and Healing: A Natural Alliance." *The New Leaders,* January/February 1994.

Renesch, John (ed.). *Leadership in a New Era.* San Francisco: Sterling & Stone Inc., 1994.

Renesch, John (ed.). *New Traditions in Business: Spirit & Leadership in the 21st Century.* San Francisco: Benett-Koehler Publishers, 1992.

Rheingold, Howard. *The Virtual Community: Homesteading on the Electronic Frontier.* Reading, MA: Addison-Wesley, 1993.

Rossbach, Sarah. *Feng Shui—The Chinese Art of Placement.* New York: Penguin, 1983.

Roszak, Theodore. *The Voice of the Earth,* New York: Simon & Schuster, 1992.

Rough, Jim. "Choice-Creating: How to Solve Impossible Problems." *Journal for Quality and Participation*, September 1991.

Rough, Jim. "Creative Choices: Breakthroughs in Thinking." *Quality Digest*, December 1992.

Rough, Jim. "A Learning Moment." *The New Leaders*. San Francisco, May/June 1994.

Russell, Peter. *The White Hole in Time: Our Future Evolution and the Meaning of Now.* San Francisco: Harper, 1992.

Schein, E. H. *Organizational Culture and Leadership.* (Second ed.) San Francisco: Jossey-Bass, 1992.

Schindler, Craig & Gary Lapid. *The Great Turning: Personal Peace, Global Victory.* Santa Fe, NM: Bear & Company, 1989.

Schindler-Rainman, Eva & Ronald Lippitt. *Building the Collaborative Community: Mobilizing Citizens for Action.* Irvine: University of California, Irvine, 1980.

Schumacher, E.F. *Good Work.* New York: Harper & Row, 1979.

Senge, Peter M. *The Fifth Discipline: The Art & Practice of the Learning Organization.* New York: Doubleday, 1990.

Senge, Peter M., C. Roberts, R.B. Ross, B. J. Smith & A. Kleiner. *The Fifth Discipline Fieldbook.* New York: Doubleday, 1994.

Short, Ronald. *A Special Kind of Leadership: The Key to Learning Organizations.* Seattle, WA: The Leadership Group, 1991.

Sorokin, P. A. *The Crisis of Our Age.* Chatam, NY: Oneworld Publications Ltd., 1941.

Srivastva, Suresh, David Cooperrider & Associates. *Appreciative Management and Leadership: The Power of Positive Thought and Action in Organizations.* San Francisco: Jossey-Bass, 1990.

Tannen, D. *You Just Don't Understand.* New York: Morrow. 1990.

Tanner Pascale, Richard. *Managing on the Edge.* New York: Touchstone/Simon & Schuster, 1990.

Tarnas, R. *The Passion of the Western Mind.* New York: Ballentine Books, 1991.

Tonnies, F. *Community and Society.* New York, NY: Harper, 1959.

Trist, Eric. *The Evolution of Socio-Technical Systems.* Toronto, Ontario: Ministry of Labor, 1981.

Turner, V. *The Ritual Process: Structure and Anti-Structure.* (Seventh ed.) Ithaca, NY: Cornell University Press, 1974.

Webber, Alan. "What's So New About the New Economy?" *Harvard Business Review,* Jan-Feb 1993.

Weisbord, M.R. *Productive Workplaces: Organizing and Managing for Dignity, Meaning and Community.* San Francisco: Jossey-Bass, 1987.

Weisbord, M.R. *Discovering Common Ground: How Future Search Conferences Bring People Together to Achieve Breakthrough Innovation, Empowerment, Shared Vision, and Collaborative Action.* San Francisco: Berrett-Koehler, 1992.

Weisbord, M.R. & SearchNet Members. *Future Search Conferences: Case Studies and Essays, 1992-1994.* Philadelphia: SearchNet, A Program of Resources for Human Development, 1994.

Wheatley, M. J., *Leadership and the New Science.* San Francisco: Berrett-Koehler, 1992.

Whitney, Rondalyn V. "Mariah, The Birth Angel " © 1990. Originally appeared in *Yankee Magazine.*

Whyte, W.F. & K. King. *Making Mondragon.* Ithaca, NY:ILR Press, 1988.

Wilber, K. *The Holographic Paradigm and Other Paradoxes.* Boston: New Science Library, 1985.

Williams, E. *Participative Management: Concepts, Theory and Implementation.* Atlanta: Georgia State University, 1976.

Zohar, D. & I. Marshall. *The Quantum Society.* New York: Morrow, 1994.

Periodicals

At Work: Stories of Tomorrow's Workplace
(bimonthly newsletter)
Berrett-Koehler Publishers, Inc.
155 Mongomery Street
San Francisco, CA 94104
800/929-2929

Communiqué
(quarterly newsletter)
Foundation for Community
    Encouragement, Inc.
109 Danbury Road, Suite 8
Ridgefield, CT 06877
203/431-9484

Journal for Quality and Participation
(monthly journal)
Association for Quality and Participation
801-B West 8th Street
Cincinnati, OH 45203
513/381-0070

New Leaders Update
(complimentary quarterly newsletter)
New Leaders Press
1668 Lombard Street
San Francisco, CA 94123
800/928-5323

The New Leaders
(bimonthly newsletter)
Sterling & Stone, Inc.
1668 Lombard Street
San Francisco, CA 94123
800/928-5323

The Responsive Community
(quarterly journal)
714 Gelman Library
George Washington University
Washington DC 20052
800/245-7460

World Business Academy Perspectives
(quarterly journal)
Berrett-Koehler Publishers, Inc.
155 Mongomery Street
San Francisco, CA 94104
800/929-2929

Institutes and Centers

Communitarian Network
George Washington University
2130 "H" Street N.W.
Washington DC 20052
202/994-7907

Creative Grandparenting, Inc.
1503 West 13th Street
Wilmington, DE 19806
302/656-2122

**EHAMA Institute for EarthWisdom
Teachings**
31440 Loma Prieta Way
Los Gatos, CA 95030
408/282-4537

**Foundation for Community
    Encouragement**
109 Danbury Road, Suite 8
Ridgefield, CT 06877
203/431-9484

Foundation for Global Community
222 High Street
Palo Alto, CA 94301
415/328-7756

Foundation for Interdependence
470 San Antonio Road, Suite M
Palo Alto, CA 94306
415/856-7853

Independent Sector
1828 "L" Street N.W.
Washington DC 20036
202/223-8100

M.I.T. Organizational Learning Center
30 Memorial Drive
 Building E60 Third Floor
Cambridge, MA 02142
617/253-1549

Trusteeship Institute, Inc.
15 Edwards Square
Northampton, MA 01060
413/584-8191

World Business Academy
P.O. Box 21470
Washington, D.C. 20009
202/822-4022

Index

A

B

W

Y

How to Contact the Authors and Editor

TERRY ANDERSON
832 Meadowville
Kennett Square, PA 19348
215/347-0390

JEANNE BOREI
515 Boulder Place
Signal Mountain, TN 37377
615/266-0113

JUANITA BROWN
Whole Systems Associates
166 Homestead Blvd.
Mill Valley, CA 94941
415/381-3368

SUSAN CAMPBELL
256 Bayview Ave.
Belvedere, CA 94920-2404
415/435-8021

DARLA CHADIMA
The Whole Story...
4055 Branciforte Dr.
Santa Cruz, CA 95065
408/427-3357

DINESH CHANDRA
567 N. University Dr.
Plantation, FL 33324
305/424-1571

WILLIAM CLARKSON
156 Bryant St.
Buffalo, NY 14222
716/885-6917

AMITAI ETZIONI
George Washington
University
2130 "H" St. N.W.
Washington DC 20052
202/994-8190

JIM EWING
Executive Arts Inc.
405 Taylor St.
Port Townsend, WA 98368
360/385-5481

CRAIG FLECK
Green Pastures Estate
38 Ladd's Lane
Epping, NH 03042
603/679-2115

JOHN GARDNER
Graduate School of Business
Stanford University
Stanford, CA 94305
415/725-4198

GLENNA GERARD
290 Pearl St.
Laguna Beach, CA 92651
714/497-9757

DAVID GOFF
Foundation for
Interdependence
470 San Antonio Road,
Suite M
Palo Alto, CA 94306
415/856-7853

KAZIMIERZ GOZDZ
Gozdz and Associates Inc.
21 Yarnell Place
Redwood City, CA
94063415/299-1420

HOPE GREENFIELD
Digital Equipment Corp.
111 Powdermill Rd.,
M/S02-1/E9
Maynard, MA 01754
508/493-1625

GEOFFREY HULIN
The Whole Story...
4055 Branciforte Dr.
Santa Cruz, CA 95065
408/427-3357

DAVID ISAACS
Clearing Communications
166 Homestead Blvd.
Mill Valley, CA 94941
415/383-2671

BETH S. JARMAN
Leadership 2000
3333 N. 44th St. #4
Phoenix, AZ 85018
602/468-9944

BUDDY JOHNSON
200 E. Broward Blvd.,
9th Floor
Fort Lauderdale, FL 33301
305/467-4183

PETER & TRUDY
JOHNSON-LENZ
Awakening Technology
695 Fifth St.
Lake Oswego, OR 97034
503/635-2615

EDWARD KLINGE
17 Burnett Dr.
Wilmington, DE 19810
302/478-4541

GEORGE LAND
Leadership 2000
3333 N. 44th St., Suite 4
Phoenix, AZ 85018
602/468-9944

JOEL & MICHELLE LEVEY
InnerWork Technologies, Inc.
5536 Woodlawn Ave. N.
Seattle, WA 98103
206/632-3551

ELEMER MAGAZINER
Project Linguistics
International
2675 West Highway 89A
Suite 1028
Sedona, AZ 86336
602/282-1804

ROBERT MANG
Evolving Systems
RT. 7 Box 127 TM
Santa Fe, NM 87505
505/984-2254

JERRY MICHALSKI
104 - 5th Ave. 20th Floor
New York, NY 10011
212/924-8800

TERRY MOLLNER
15 Edwards Square
Northampton, MA 01060
413/584-8191

JOHN NIRENBERG
Center for Workplace
Community
1625 Larimer Street,
Suite 1807
Denver, CO 80202
303/436-9511

JORDAN PAUL
250 Spencer Ave.
Sausalito, CA 94965
415/332-6575

M. SCOTT PECK
Foundation for Community
Encouragement
109 Danbury Road, Suite 8
Ridgefield, CT 06877
203/431-9484

JOHN PEHRSON
515 Boulder Place
Signal Mountain, TN 37377
615/886-7657

GEORGE PÓR
Organizational Learning
Systems
374 Sunset Lane
Soquel, CA 95073
408/427-2795
e-mail: gpor@ols.com

LYMAN RANDALL
4306 Freeman Rd.
Orchard Park, NY 14127
716/662-1837

MICHAEL RAY
Graduate School of Business
Stanford University
Stanford, CA 94305-5015
415/723-2762

JIM ROUGH
Jim Rough & Associates
1040 Taylor Street
Port Townsend, WA 98368
360/385-7118

ANN ROULAC
c/o Roulac Group
900 Larkspur Landing Circle, #125
Larkspur, CA 94939
415/925-1895

STEPHANIE RYAN
P.O. Box 832
69 Lincoln St.
Manchester, MA 01944
508/526-9860

PETER SENGE
M.I.T. Organizational
Learning Center
One Amherst, E40-294
Cambridge, MA 02139
617/253-1549

BARBARA SHIPKA
P.O. Box 5005
Minneapolis, MN 55405
612/827-3006

LINDA TEURFS
4265 Marina City Drive #1105
Marina del Ray, CA 90292
310/822-4111

BILL VELTROP
International Center for
Organizational Design
1450 Hidden Valley Road
Soquel, CA 95073
408/462-1992

MARVIN WEISBORD
530 Wynlyn Rd.
Wynnewood, PA 19096
610/896-7035

RONDALYN VARNEY
WHITNEY
1438 Petal Way
San Jose, CA 95129
408/725-2503

ADDITIONAL COPIES OF

Community

Building

Renewing Spirit & Learning in Business

CAN BE PURCHASED FROM THE ORGANIZATIONS LISTED BELOW

ARIZONA
Project Linguistics International, Sedona   602/282-1804, x1028

CALIFORNIA
Whole Systems Associates, Mill Valley   415/381-3368
Susan Campbell, Belvedere   415/435-8021
Foundation for Interdependence, Palo Alto   415/856-7853
Glenna Gerard, Laguna Beach   714/497-9757
Gozdz & Associates, Inc., Redwood City   415/299-1420
Jordan Paul, Sausalito   415/332-6575
Organizational Learning Systems, Soquel   408/427-2795
Michael Ray, Stanford University   415/723-2762
Linda Teurfs, Marina del Rey   310/822-4111
International Center for Organizational Design, Soquel   408/462-1992
Rondalyn Varney Whitney, San Jose   408/725-2503
The Whole Story…, Santa Cruz   408/427-3357

COLORADO
Center for Workplace Community, Denver   303/436-9511

DELAWARE
The Synthesis Group, Inc., Wilmington 302/478-4541

FLORIDA
Buddy Johnson, Fort Lauderdale 305/467-4183

MASSACHUSETTS
Trusteeship Institute, Inc., Northampton 413/584-8191
In Care, Manchester 508/526-9860

MINNESOTA
Barbara Shipka, Minneapolis 612/827-3006

NEW HAMPSHIRE
Craig Fleck, Green Pastures Estate, Epping 603/679-2115

NEW JERSEY
Designed Learning, Plainfield 908/754-5100

NEW MEXICO
Robert Mang, Santa Fe 505/984-2254

NEW YORK
William Clarkson, Buffalo 716/885-6917
Jerry Michalski, New York 212/924-8800
Lyman Randall, Orchard Park 716/662-1837

OREGON
Awakening Technology, Lake Oswego 503/635-2615

TENNESSEE
Creative Change Technologies, Inc., Signal Mountain 615/886-7657

WASHINGTON
Jim Ewing, Port Townsend 360/385-5481
InnerWork Technologies, Seattle 206/632-3551
Jim Rough & Associates, Port Townsend 360/385-7118

FROM THE PUBLISHERS OF *COMMUNITY BUILDING*

THE ONLY BUSINESS NEWSLETTER ON TRANSFORMATIVE LEADERSHIP

- Profiles of exemplars in business
- Articles by visionary business scholars
- News of transformation at work

SUBSCRIBE TODAY & SAVE!!!

☐ 1 year/6 issues, now only $89
☐ 2 years/12 issues, now only $159
(note: foreign subscribers, please add $15/year)

CALL 1-800/928-LEADers for credit card orders
(1-800/928-5323)
FAX 1-415/928-3346
MAIL your order with payment to:

THE NEW LEADERS
1668 Lombard Street
San Francisco, CA 94123